The French Revolution, Volume 2

Hippolyte A. Taine

Table of Contents

The French Revolution, Volume 2

Hippolyte A. Taine

Preface:

In this volume, as in those preceding it and in those to come, there will be found only the history of Public Authorities. Others will write that of diplomacy, of war, of the finances, of the Church; my subject is a limited one. To my great regret, however, this new part fills an entire volume; and the last part, on the revolutionary government, will be as long.

I have again to regret the dissatisfaction I foresee this work will cause to many of my countrymen. My excuse is, that almost all of them, more fortunate than myself, have political principles which serve them in forming their judgments of the past. I had none; if indeed, I had any motive in undertaking this work, it was to seek for political principles. Thus far I have attained to scarcely more than one; and this is so simple that will seem puerile, and that I hardly dare express it. Nevertheless I have adhered to it, and in what the reader is about to peruse my judgments are all derived from that; its truth is the measure of theirs. It consists wholly in this observation: that

HUMAN SOCIETY, ESPECIALLY A MODERN SOCIETY, IS A VAST AND COMPLICATED THING.

Hence the difficulty in knowing and comprehending it. For the same reason it is not easy to handle the subject well. It follows that a cultivated mind is much better able to do this than an uncultivated mind, and a man specially qualified than one who is not. From these two last truths flow many other consequences, which, if the reader deigns to reflect on them, he will have no trouble in defining.

H. A. Taine, Paris 1881.

BOOK FIRST. THE JACOBINS.

CHAPTER I. THE ESTABLISHMENT OF THE NEW POLITICAL ORGAN.

In this disorganized society, in which the passions of the people are the sole real force, authority belongs to the party that understands how to flatter and take advantage of these. As the legal government can neither repress nor gratify them, an illegal government arises which sanctions, excites, and directs these passions. While the former totters and falls to pieces, the latter grows stronger and improves its organization, until, becoming legal in its turn, it takes the other's place.

I.

Principle of the revolutionary party. – Its applications.

As a justification of these popular outbreaks and assaults, we discover at the outset a theory, which is neither improvised, added to, nor superficial, but now firmly fixed in the public mind. It has for a long time been nourished by philosophical discussions. It is a sort of enduring, long–lived root out of which the new constitutional tree has arisen. It is the dogma of popular sovereignty. — Literally interpreted, it means that the government is merely an inferior clerk or servant.[1] We, the people, have established the government; and ever since, as well as before its organization, we are its masters. Between it and us no infinite or long lasting "contract". "None which cannot be done away with by mutual consent or through the unfaithfulness of one of the two parties." Whatever it may be, or provide for, we are nowise bound by it; it depends wholly on us. We remain free to "modify, restrict, and resume as we please the power of which we have made it the depository." Through a primordial and inalienable title deed the commonwealth belongs to us and to us only. If we put this into the hands of the government it is as when kings delegate authority for the time being to a minister He is always tempted to abuse; it is our business to watch him, warn him, check him, curb him, and, if necessary, displace him. We must especially guard ourselves against the craft and maneuvers by which, under the pretext of preserving law and order, he would tie our hands. A law, superior to any he can make, forbids him to interfere with our sovereignty; and he does interfere with it when he undertakes to forestall, obstruct, or impede its exercise. The Assembly, even the Constituent, usurps when it treats the people like a lazybones (roi fainéant), when it subjects them to laws, which they have not ratified, and when it deprives them of action except through their representatives.[2] The people themselves must act directly, must assemble together and deliberate on public affairs. They must control and censure the acts of those they elect; they must influence these with their resolutions, correct their mistakes with their good sense, atone for their weakness by their energy, stand at the helm alongside of them, and even employ force and throw them overboard, so that the ship may be saved, which, in their hands, is drifting on a rock.[3] Such, in fact, is the doctrine of the popular party. This doctrine is carried into effect July 14 and October 5 and 6, 1789. Loustalot, Camille Desmoulins, Fréron, Danton, Marat, Pétion, Robespierre proclaim it untiringly in the political clubs, in the newspapers, and in the assembly. The government, according to them, whether local or central, trespasses everywhere. Why, after having overthrown one despotism, should we install another? We are freed from the yoke of a privileged aristocracy, but we still suffer from "the aristocracy of our representatives."[4] Already at Paris, "the population is nothing, while the municipality is everything". It encroaches on our imprescriptible rights in refusing to let a district revoke at will the five members elected to represent it at the Hôtel-de-Ville, in passing ordinances without obtaining the approval of voters, in preventing citizens from assembling where they please, in interrupting the out-door meetings of the clubs in the Palais Royal where "Patriots are driven away be the patrol." Mayor Bailly, "who keeps liveried servants, who gives himself a salary of 110,000 livres," who distributes captains' commissions, who forces peddlers to wear metallic badges, and who compels newspapers to have signatures to their articles is not only a tyrant, but a crook, thief and "guilty of lése-nation." — Worse are the abuses of the National Assembly. To swear fidelity to the constitution, as this body has just done, to impose its work on us, forcing us to take a similar oath, disregarding our superior rights to veto or ratify their decisions,[5] is to "slight and scorn our sovereignty". By substituting the will of 1200 individuals for that of the people, "our representatives have failed to treat us with respect." This is not the first time, and it is not to be the last. Often do they exceed their mandate, they disarm, mutilate, and gag their legitimate sovereign and they pass decrees against the people in the people's name. Such is their martial law, specially devised for "suppressing the uprising of citizens", that is to say, the only means left to us against conspirators, monopolists, and traitors. Such a decree against publishing any kind of joint placard or petition, is a decree "null and void," and "constitutes a most flagrant attack on the nation's rights."[6] Especially is the electoral law one of these, a law which, requiring a small qualification tax for electors and a larger one for those who are eligible, "consecrates the aristocracy of wealth." The poor, who are excluded by the decree, must regard it as invalid; register themselves as they please and vote without scruple, because natural law has precedence over written law. It would simply be "fair reprisal" if, at the end of the session, the millions of citizens lately deprived of their vote unjustly, should seize the usurping majority by the threat and tell them:

"You cut us off from society in your chamber, because you are the strongest there; we, in our turn, cut you off from the living society, because we are strongest in the street. You have killed us civilly – we kill you physically."

3

Accordingly, from this point of view, all riots are legitimate. Robespierre from the rostrum[7] excuses jacqueries, refuses to call castle–burners brigands, and justifies the insurgents of Soissons, Nancy, Avignon, and the colonies. Desmoulins, alluding to two men hung at Douai, states that it was done by the people and soldiers combined, and declares that: "Henceforth, — I have no hesitation in saying it — they have legitimated the insurrection;" they were guilty, and it was well to hang them.[8] Not only do the party leaders excuse assassinations, but they provoke them. Desmoulins, "attorney–general of the Lantern, insists on each of the 83 departments being threatened with at least one lamppost hanging." (This sobriquet is bestowed on Desmoulins on account of his advocacy of street executions, the victims of revolutionary passions being often hung at the nearest lanterne, or street lamp, at that time in Paris suspended across the street by ropes or chains. – (Tr.)) Meanwhile Marat, in the name of principle, constantly sounds the alarm in his journal:

"When public safety is in peril, the people must take power out of the hands of those whom it is entrusted . . . Put that Austrian woman and her brother–in–law in prison . . . Seize the ministers and their clerks and put them in irons . . . Make sure of the mayor and his lieutenants; keep the general in sight, and arrests his staff. . . The heir to the throne has no rights to a dinner while you want bread. Organize bodies of armed men. March to the National Assembly and demand food at once, supplied to you out of the national stocks. . . Demand that the nation's poor have a future secured to them out of the national contribution. If you are refused join the army, take the land, as well as gold which the rascals who want to force you to come to terms by hunger have buried and share it amongst you. Off with the heads of the ministers and their underlings, for now is the time; that of Lafayette and of every rascal on his staff, and of every unpatriotic battalion officer, including Bailly and those municipal reactionaries – all the traitors in the National Assembly!"

Marat, indeed, still passes for a furious ranter among people of some intelligence. But for all that, this is the sum and substance of his theory: It installs in the political establishment, over the heads of delegated, regular, and legal powers an anonymous, imbecile, and terrific power whose decisions are absolute, whose projects are constantly adopted, and whose intervention is sanguinary. This power is that of the crowd, of a ferocious, suspicious sultan, who, appointing his viziers, keeps his hands free to direct them and his scimitar ready sharpened to cut of their heads.

II. The Jacobins. –

Formation of the Jacobins. – The common human elements of his character. – Conceit and dogmatism are sensitive and rebellious in every community. – How kept down in all well–founded societies. – Their development in the new order of things. –Effect of milieu on imagination and ambitions. – The stimulants of Utopianism, abuses of speech, and derangement of ideas. – Changes in office; interests playing upon and perverted feeling.

That a speculator in his closet should have concocted such a theory is comprehensible; paper will take all that is put upon it, while abstract beings, the hollow simulacra and philosophic puppets he concocts, are adapted to every sort of combination. – That a lunatic in his cell should adopt and preach this theory is also comprehensible; he is beset with phantoms and lives outside the actual world, and, moreover in this ever–agitated democracy he is the eternal informer and instigator of every riot and murder that takes place; he it is who under the name of "the people's friend" becomes the arbiter of lives and the veritable sovereign. — That a people borne down with taxes, wretched and starving, indoctrinated by public speakers and sophists, should have welcomed this theory and acted under it is again comprehensible; necessity knows no law, and where the is oppression, that doctrine is true which serves to throw oppression off.

But that public men, legislators and statesmen, with, at last, ministers and heads of the government, should have made this theory their own;

* that they should have more fondly clung to it as it became more destructive;

* that, daily for three years they should have seen social order crumbling away piecemeal under its blows and not have recognized it as the instrument of such vast ruin;

* that, in the light of the most disastrous experience, instead of regarding it as a curse they should have glorified it as a boon;

* that many of them – an entire party; almost all of the Assembly – should have venerated it as a religious dogma and carried it to extremes with enthusiasm and rigor of faith;

* that, driven by it into a narrow strait, ever getting narrower and narrower, they should have continued to crush each other at every step;

* that, finally, on reaching the visionary temple of their so–called liberty, they should have found themselves in a slaughter–house, and, within its precincts, should have become in turn butcher and brute;

* that, through their maxims of a universal and perfect liberty they should have inaugurated a despotism worthy of Dahomey, a tribunal like that of the Inquisition, and raised human hecatombs like those of ancient Mexico;

* that amidst their prisons and scaffolds they should persist in believing in the righteousness of their cause, in their own humanity, in their virtue, and, on their fall, have regarded themselves as martyrs –

is certainly strange. Such intellectual aberration, such excessive conceit are rarely encountered, and a concurrence of circumstances, the like of which has never been seen in the world but once, was necessary to produce it.[8]

Extravagant conceit and dogmatism, however, are not rare in the human species. These two roots of the Jacobin intellect exist in all countries, underground and indestructible. Everywhere they are kept from sprouting by the established order of things; everywhere are they striving to overturn old historic foundations, which press them down. Now, as in the past, students live in garrets, bohemians in lodgings, physicians without patients and lawyers without clients in lonely offices, so many Brissots, Dantons, Marats, Robespierres, and St. Justs in embryo; only, for lack of air and sunshine, they never come to maturity. At twenty, on entering society, a young man's judgment and pride are extremely sensitive. – – Firstly, let his society be what it will, it is for him a scandal to pure reason:

for it was not organized by a legislative philosopher in accordance with a sound principle, but is the work of one generation after another, according to manifold and changing necessities. It is not a product of logic, but of history, and the new−fledged thinker shrugs his shoulders as he looks up and sees what the ancient tenement is, the foundations of which are arbitrary, its architecture confused, and its many repairs plainly visible. — In the second place, whatever degree of perfection preceding institutions, laws, and customs have reached, these have not received his approval; others, his predecessors, have chosen for him, he is being subjected beforehand to moral, political, and social forms which pleased them. Whether they please him or not is of no consequence. Like a horse trotting along between the poles of a wagon in the harness that happens to have been put on his back, he has to make best of it. — Besides, whatever its organization, as it is essentially a hierarchy, he is nearly always subaltern in it, and must ever remain so, either soldier, corporal or sergeant. Even under the most liberal system, that in which the highest grades are accessible to all, for every five or six men who take the lead or command others, one hundred thousand must follow or be commanded. This makes it vain to tell every conscript that he carriers a marshal's baton in his sack, when, nine hundred and ninety−nine times out of a thousand, he discovers too late, on rummaging his sack, that the baton is not there. − − It is not surprising that he is tempted to kick against social barriers within which, willing or not, he is enrolled, and which predestine him to subordination. It is not surprising that on emerging from traditional influences he should accept a theory, which subjects these arrangements to his judgment and gives him authority over his superiors. And all the more because there is no doctrine more simple and better adapted to his inexperience, it is the only one he can comprehend and manage off−hand. Hence it is that young men on leaving college, especially those who have their way to make in the world, are more or less Jacobin, − it is a disorder of growing up.[9] — In well organized communities this ailment is beneficial, and soon cured. The public establishment being substantial and carefully guarded, malcontents soon discover that they have not enough strength to pull it down, and that on contending with its guardians they gain nothing but blows. After some grumbling, they too enter at one or the other of its doors, find a place for themselves, and enjoy its advantages or become reconciled to their lot. Finally, either through imitation, or habit, or calculation, they willingly form part of that garrison which, in protecting public interests, protects their own private interests as well. Generally, after ten years have gone by, the young man has obtained his rank in the file, where he advances step by step in his own compartment, which he no longer thinks of tearing to pieces, and under the eye of a policeman who he no longer thinks of condemning. He even sometimes thinks that policeman and compartment are useful to him. Should he consider the millions of individuals who are trying to mount the social ladder, each striving to get ahead of the other, it may dawn upon him that the worst of calamities would be a lack of barriers and of guardians.

Here the worm−eaten barriers have cracked all at once, their easy− going, timid, incapable guardians having allowed things to take their course. Society, accordingly, disintegrated and a pell−mell, is turned into a turbulent, shouting crowd, each pushing and being pushed, all alike over−excited and congratulating each other on having finally obtained elbow−room, and all demanding the new barriers shall be as fragile and the new guardians as feeble, as defenseless, and as inert as possible. This is what has been done. As a natural consequence, those who were foremost in the rank have been relegated to the last; many have been struck down in the fray, while in this permanent state of disorder, which goes under the name of lasting order, elegant footwear continue to be stamped upon by hobnailed boots and wooden shoes. − The fanatic and the intemperate egoists can now let themselves go. They are no longer subject to any ancient institutions, nor any armed might which can restrain them. On the contrary, the new constitution, through its theoretical declarations and the practical application of these, invites them to let themselves go. — For, on the one hand, legally, it declares to be based upon pure reason, beginning with a long string of abstract dogmas from which its positive prescriptions are assumed to be rigorously deduced. As a consequence all laws are submitted to the shallow comments of reasoners and quibblers who will both interpret and break them according to the principles.[10] — On the other hand, as a matter of fact, it hands over all government powers to the elections and confers on the clubs the control of the authorities: which is to offer a premium to the presumption of the ambitious who put themselves forward because they think themselves capable, and who defame their rulers purposely to displace them. - Every government department, organization or administrative system is like a hothouse which serves to favor some species of the human plant and wither others. This one is the best one for the propagation and rapid increase of the coffee- house politician, club haranguer, the stump–speaker, the street- rioter, the committee dictator — in short, the revolutionary and the tyrant. In this political hothouse wild dreams and conceit will assume monstrous proportions, and, in a few months, brains that are now only ardent become hotheads.

Let us trace the effect of this excessive, unhealthy temperature on imaginations and ambitions. The old tenement is down; the foundations of the new one are not yet laid; society has to be made over again from top to bottom. All willing men are asked to come and help, and, as one plain principle suffices in drawing a plan, the first comer may succeed. Henceforth political fancies swarm in the district meetings, in the clubs, in the newspapers, in pamphlets, and in every head–long, venturesome brain.

"There is not a merchant's clerk educated by reading the 'Nouvelle Héloise,'[11] not a school teacher that has translated ten pages of Livy, not an artist that has leafed through Rollin, not an aesthete converted into journalists by committing to memory the riddles of the 'Contrat Social,' who does not draft a constitution. . . As nothing is easier than to perfect a daydream, all perturbed minds gather, and become excited, in this ideal realm. They start out with curiosity and end up with enthusiasm. The man in the street rushes to the enterprise in the same manner as a miser to a conjurer promising treasures, and, thus childishly attracted, each hopes to find at once, what has never been seen under even the most liberal governments: perpetual perfection, universal brotherhood, the power of acquiring what one lacks, and a life composed wholly of enjoyment."

One of these pleasures, and a keen one, is to daydream. One soars in space. By means of eight or ten ready–made sentences, found in the six–penny catechisms circulated by thousands in the country and in the suburbs of the towns and cities,[12] a village attorney, a customs clerk, a theater attendant, a sergeant of a soldier's mess, becomes a legislator and philosopher. He criticizes Malouet, Mirabeau, the Ministry, the King, the Assembly, the Church, foreign Cabinets, France, and all Europe. Consequently, on these important subjects, which always seemed forever forbidden to him, he offers resolutions, reads addresses, makes harangues, obtains applause, and congratulates himself on having argued so well and with such big words. To hold fort on questions that are not understood is now an occupation, a matter of pride and profit.

"More is uttered in one day," says an eye–witness,[13] "in one section of Paris than in one year in all the Swiss political assemblies put together. An Englishman would give six weeks of study to what we dispose of in a quarter of an hour."

Everywhere, in the town halls, in popular meetings, in the sectional assemblies, in the wine shops, on the public promenades, on street corners vanity erects a tribune of verbosity.

"Contemplate the incalculable activity of such a machine in a loquacious nation where the passion for being something dominates all other affections, where vanity has more phases than there are starts in the firmament, where reputations already cost no more than the trouble of insisting on their being deserved, where society is divided between mediocrities and their trumpeters who laud them as divinities; where so few people are content with their lot, where the corner grocer is prouder of his epaulette than the Grand Condé of his Marshal's baton, where agitation without object or resources is perpetual, where, from the floor-scrubber to the dramatist, from the academician to the simpleton who gets muddled over the evening newspaper, from the witty courtier down to his philosophic lackey, each one revises Montesquieu with the self-sufficiency of a child which, because it is learning to read, deems itself wise; where self- esteem, in disputation, caviling and sophistication, destroys all sensible conversation; where no one utters a word, but to teach, never imagining that to learn one must keep quiet; where the triumphs of a few lunatics entice every crackbrain from his den; where, with two nonsensical ideas put together out of a book that is not understood, a man assumes to have principles; where swindlers talk about morality, women of easy virtue about civism, and the most infamous of beings about the dignity of the species; where the discharged valet of a grand seignior calls himself Brutus!"

– In reality, he is Brutus in his own eyes. Let the time come and he will be so in earnest, especially against his late master; all he has to do is to give him a thrust with his pike. Until he acts out the part he spouts it, and grows excited over his own tirades; his common sense gives way to the bombastic jargon of the revolution and to declamation, which completes the Utopian performance and eases his brain of its last modicum of ballast.

It is not merely ideas which the new regime has disturbed, but it has also disordered sentiments. "Authority is transferred from the Château of Versailles and the courtier's antechamber, with no intermediary or counterpoise, to the proletariat and its flatterers."[14] The whole of the staff of the old government is brusquely set aside, while a general election has brusquely installed another in is place, offices not being given to capacity, seniority, and experience, but to self-sufficiency, intrigue, and exaggeration. Not only are legal rights reduced to a common level, but natural grades are transposed; the social ladder, overthrown, is set up again bottom upwards; the first effect of the promised regeneration is "to substitute in the administration of public affairs pettifoggers for magistrates, ordinary citizens for cabinet ministers, ex-commoners for ex-nobles, rustics for soldiers, soldiers for captains, captains for generals, curés for bishops, vicars for curés, monks for vicars, brokers for financiers, empiricists for administrators, journalists for political economists, stump-orators for legislators, and the poor for the rich." – Every species of covetousness is stimulated by this spectacle. The profusion of offices and the anticipation of vacancies "has excited the thirst for command, stimulated self-esteem, and inflamed the hopes of the most inept. A rude and grim presumption renders the fool and the ignoramus unconscious of their insignificance. They have deemed themselves capable of anything, because the law granted public functions merely to capacity. There has appeared in front of one and all an ambitious perspective; the soldier thinks only of displacing his captain, the captain of becoming general, the clerk of supplanting the chief of his department, the new-fledged attorney of being admitted to the high court, the curé of being ordained a bishop, the shallow scribbler of seating himself on the legislative bench. Offices and professions vacated by the appointment of so many upstarts afford in their turn a vast field for the ambition of the lower classes." — Thus, step by step, owing to the reversal of social positions, is brought about a general intellectual fever.

"France is transformed into a gaming-table, where, alongside of the discontented citizen offering his stakes, sits, bold, blustering, and with fermenting brain, the pretentious subaltern rattling his dice-box. . . At the sight of a public official rising from nowhere, even the soul of a bootblack will bound with emulation." — He has merely to push himself ahead and elbow his way to secure a ticket "in this immense lottery of popular luck, of preferment without merit, of success without talent, of apotheoses without virtues, of an infinity of places distributed by the people wholesale, and enjoyed by the people in detail." — Political charlatans flock thither from every quarters, those taking the lead who, being most in earnest, believe in the virtue of their nostrum, and need power to impose its recipe on the community; all being saviors, all places belong to them, and especially the highest. They lay siege to these conscientiously and philanthropically ; if necessary, they will take them by assault, hold them through force, and, forcibly or otherwise, administer their cure– all to the human species.

III.

Psychology of the Jacobin. — His intellectual method. — Tyranny of formulae and suppression of facts. — Mental balance disturbed. — Signs of this in the revolutionary language. — Scope and expression of the Jacobin intellect. — In what respect his method is mischievous. — How it is successful. — Illusions produced by it.

Such are our Jacobins, born out of social decomposition like mushrooms out of compost. Let us consider their inner organization, for they have one as formerly the Puritans; we have only to follow their dogma down to its depths, as with a sounding-line, to reach the psychological stratum in which the normal balance of faculty and sentiment is overthrown.

When a statesman, who is not wholly unworthy of that great name, finds an abstract principle in his way, as, for instance, that of popular sovereignty, he accepts it, if he accepts it at all, according to his conception of its practical bearings. He begins, accordingly, by imagining it applied and in operation. From personal recollections and such information as he can obtain, he forms an idea of some village or town, some community of moderate size in the north, in the south, or in the center of the country, for which he has to make laws. He then imagines its inhabitants acting according to his principle, that is to say, voting, mounting guard, levying taxes, and administering their own affairs. Familiar with ten or a dozen groups of this sort, which he regards as examples, he concludes by analogy as to others and the rest on the territory. Evidently it is a difficult and uncertain process; to be exact, or nearly so, requires rare powers of observation and, at each step, a great deal of tact, for a nice calculation has to be made on given quantities imperfectly ascertained and imperfectly noted![15] Any political leader who does this successfully, does it through the ripest experience associated with genius. And even then he keeps his hand on the check-rein in pushing his innovation or reform; he is almost always tentative; he applies his law only in part, gradually and provisionally; he wishes to ascertain its effect; he is always ready to stay its operation, amend it, or modify it, according to the good or ill results of experiment; the state of the human material he has to deal with is never clear to his mind, even when superior, until after many and repeated gropings. — Now the Jacobin pursues just the opposite course. His principle is an axiom of political geometry, which always carries its own proof along with it; for, like the axioms of common geometry, it is formed out of the combination of a few simple ideas, and its evidence imposes itself at once on all minds capable of embracing in one conception the two terms of which it is the aggregate expression. Man in general, the rights of Man, the social contract, liberty, equality, reason, nature, the people, tyrants, are examples of these basic concepts: whether precise or not, they fill the brain of the new sectarian. Often these terms are merely vague and grandiose words, but that makes no difference; as soon as they meet in his brain an axiom springs out of them that can be instantly and absolutely applied on every occasion and to excess. Mankind as it is does not concern him. He does not observe them; he does not require to observe them; with closed eyes he imposes a pattern of his own on the human substance manipulated by him; the idea never enters his head of forming any previous conception of this complex, multiform, swaying material – contemporary peasants, artisans, townspeople, curés and nobles, behind their plows, in their homes, in their shops, in their parsonages, in their mansions, with their inveterate beliefs, persistent inclinations, and powerful wills. Nothing of this enters into or lodges in his mind; all its avenues are stopped by the abstract principle which flourishes there and fills it completely. Should actual experience through the eye or ear plant some unwelcome truth forcibly in his mind, it cannot subsist there; however noisy and relentless it may be, the abstract principle drives it out;[16] if need be it will distort and strangle it, considering it a slanderer since it refutes a principle which is true and undeniable in itself. Obviously, a mind of this kind is not sound; of the two faculties which should pull together harmoniously, one is degenerated and the other overgrown; facts cannot turn the scale against the theory. Charged on one side and empty on the other, the Jacobin mind turns violently over on that side to which it leans, and such is its incurable infirmity.

Consider, indeed, the authentic monuments of Jacobin thought, the "Journal des Amis de la Constitution," the gazettes of Loustalot, Desmoulins, Brissot, Condorcet, Fréron and Marat, Robespierre's, and St. Just's pamphlets and speeches, the debates in the Legislative Assembly and in the Convention, the harangues, addresses and reports of the Girondins and Montagnards, in brief, the forty volumes of extracts compiled by Buchez and Roux. Never has so much been said to so little purpose; all the truth that is uttered is drowned in the monotony and inflation of empty verbiage and vociferous bombast. One experience in this direction is sufficient.[17] The historian who resorts this mass of rubbish for accurate information finds none of any account; in vain will he read kilometers of it: hardly will he there meet one fact, one instructive detail, one document which brings before his eyes a distinct personality, which shows him the real sentiments of a villager or of a gentleman, which vividly portrays the interior of a hôtel–de–ville, of a soldier's barracks, of a municipal chamber, or the character of an insurrection. To define fifteen or twenty types and situations which sum up the history of the period, we have been and shall be obliged to seek them elsewhere – in the correspondence of local administrators, in affidavits on criminal records, in confidential reports of the police,[18] and in the narratives of foreigners,[19] who, prepared for it by a different education, look behind words for things, and see France beyond the "Contrat Social." This teeming France, this grand tragedy which twenty–six millions of players are performing on a stage of 26 000 square leagues, is lost to the Jacobin. His literature, as well as his brain, contain only insubstantial generalizations like those above cited, rolling out in a mere play of ideas, sometimes in concise terms when the writer happens to be a professional reasoner like Condorcet, but most frequently in a tangled, knotty style full of loose and disconnected meshes when the spokesman happens to be an improvised politician or a philosophic tyro like the ordinary deputies of the Assembly and the speakers of the clubs. It is a pedantic scholasticism set forth with fanatical rant. Its entire vocabulary consists of about a hundred words, while all ideas are reduced to one, that of man in himself: human units, all alike equal and independent, contracting together for the first time. This is their concept of society. None could be briefer, for, to arrive at it, man had to be reduced to a minimum. Never were political brains so willfully dried up. For it is the attempt to systematize and to simplify which causes their impoverishment. In that respect they go by the methods of their time and in the track of Jean–Jacques Rousseau: their outlook on life is the classic view, which, already narrow in the late philosophers, has now become even more narrow and hardened. The best representatives of the type are Condorcet,[20] among the Girondins, and Robespierre, among the Montagnards, both mere dogmatists and pure logicians, the latter the most remarkable and with a perfection of intellectual sterility never surpassed. — Unquestionably, as far as the formulation of durable laws is concerned, i.e. adapting the social machinery to personalities, conditions, and circumstances; their mentality is certainly the most impotent and harmful. It is organically short–sighted, and by interposing their principles between it and reality, they shut off the horizon. Beyond their crowd and the club it distinguishes nothing, while in the vagueness and confusion of the distance it erects the hollow idols of its own Utopia. — But when power is to be seized by assault, and a dictatorship arbitrarily exercised, the mechanical inflexibility of such a mind is useful rather than detrimental. It is not embarrassed or slowed down, like that of a statesman, by the obligation to make inquiries, to respect precedents, of looking into statistics, of calculating and tracing beforehand in different directions the near and remote consequences of its work as this affects the interests, habits, and passions of diverse classes. All this is now obsolete and superfluous: the Jacobin knows on the spot the correct form of government and the good laws. For both construction as well as for destruction, his rectilinear method is the quickest and most vigorous. For, if calm reflection is required to get at what suits twenty–six millions of living Frenchmen, a mere glance suffices to understand the desires of the abstract men of their theory. Indeed, according to the theory, men are all shaped to one pattern, nothing being left to them but an elementary will; thus defined, the philosophic robot demands liberty, equality and popular sovereignty, the maintenance of the rights of man and adhesion to the "Contrat Social." That is enough: from now on the will of the people is known, and known beforehand; a consultation among citizens previous to action is not essential; there is no obligation to await their votes. In any events, a ratification by the people is sure; and should this not be forthcoming it is owing to their ignorance, disdain or malice, in which case their response deserves to be considered as null. The best thing to do, consequently, through precaution and to protect the people from what is bad for them, is to dictate to them what is good for them. — Here, the Jacobin might be sincere; for the men in whose behalf he claims rights are not flesh–and–blood Frenchmen, as we see them in the streets and in the fields, but men in general, as they ought to be on leaving the hands of Nature, or after the teachings of Reason. As to the former, there is no need of being scrupulous because they are infatuated with prejudices and their opinions are mere drivel; as for the latter, it is just the opposite: full of respect for the vainglorious images of his own theory, of ghosts produced by his own intellectual device, the Jacobin will always bow down to responses that he himself has provided, for, the beings that he has created are more real in his eyes than living ones and it is their suffrage on which he counts. Accordingly, viewing things in the worst lights, he has nothing against him but the momentary antipathy of a purblind generation. To offset this, he enjoys the approval of humanity, self–obtained; that of a posterity which his acts have regenerated; that of men who, thanks to him, who are again become what they should never have ceased to be. Hence, far from looking upon himself as an usurper or a tyrant, he considers himself the natural mandatory of a veritable people, the authorized executor of the common will. Marching along in the procession formed for him by this imaginary crowd, sustained by millions of metaphysical wills created by himself in his own image, he has their unanimous assent, and, like a chorus of triumphant shouts, he will fill the outward world with the inward echo of his own voice.

IV.

What the theory promises. – How it flatters wounded self–esteem. — The ruling passion of the Jacobin. — Apparent both in style and conduct. — He alone is virtuous in his own estimation, while his adversaries are vile. — They must accordingly be put out of the way. — Perfection of this character. — Common sense and moral sense both perverted.

'When an ideology attracts people, it is less due to its sophistication than to the promises it holds out. It appeals more to their desires than to their intelligence; for, if the heart sometimes may be the dupe of the head, the latter is much more frequently the dupe of the former. We do not accept a system because we deem it a true one, but because the truth we find in it suits us. Political or religious fanaticism, any theological or philosophical channel in which truth flows, always has its source in some ardent longing, some secret passion, some accumulation of intense, painful desire to which a theory affords and outlet. In the Jacobin, as well as in the Puritan, there is a fountain–head of this description. What feeds this source with the Puritan is the anxieties of a disturbed conscience which, forming for itself some idea of perfect justice, becomes rigid and multiplies the commandments it believes that God has promulgated; on being constrained to disobey these it rebels, and, to impose them on others, it becomes tyrannical even to despotism. The first effort of the Puritan, however, wholly internal, is self–control; before becoming political he becomes moral. With the Jacobin, on the contrary, the first precept is not moral, political; it is not his duties which he exaggerates but his rights, while his doctrine, instead of being a prick to his conscience, flatters his pride.[21] However vast and insatiate human pride may be, now it is satisfied, for never before has it had so much to feed upon. — In the program of the sect, do not look for the restricted prerogatives growing out of self–respect which the proud–spirited man claims for himself, such as civil rights accompanied by those liberties that serve as sentinels and guardians of these rights – security for life and property, the stability of the law, the integrity of courts, equality of citizens before the law and under taxation, the abolition of privileges and arbitrary proceedings, the election of representatives and the administration of public funds. Summing it up, the precious guarantees which render each citizen an inviolable sovereign on his limited domain, which protect his person and property against all species of public or private oppression and exaction, which maintain him calm and erect before competitors as well as adversaries, upright and respectful in the presence of magistrates and in the presence of the government.

A Malouet, a Mounier, a Mallet du Pan, partisans of the English Constitution and Parliament, may be content with such trifling gifts, but the Jacobin theory holds them all cheap, and, if need be, will trample them in the dust. Independence and security for the private citizen is not what it promises, not the right to vote every two years, not a moderate exercise of influence, not an indirect, limited and intermittent control of the commonwealth, but political dominion in the full and complete possession of France and the French people. There is no doubt on this point. In Rousseau's own words, the "Contrat Social" prescribes "the complete alienation to the community of each associate and all his rights," every individual surrendering himself wholly, "just as he may actually be, he himself and all his powers of which his possessions form a part," so that the state not only the recognized owner of property, but of minds and bodies as well, may forcibly and legitimately impose on every member of it such education, form of worship, religious faith, opinions and sympathies as it deems best.[22] Now each man, solely because he is a man, is by right a member of this despotic sovereignty. Whatever, accordingly, my condition may be, my incompetence, my ignorance, my insignificance in the career in which I have plodded along, I have full control over the fortunes, lives, and consciences of twenty-six million French people, being accordingly Czar and Pope, according to my share of authority. – – But if I adhere strictly to this doctrine, I am yet more so than my quota warrants. This royal prerogative with which I am endowed is only conferred on those who, like myself, sign the Social Contract in full; others, merely because they reject some clause of it, incur a forfeiture; no one must enjoy the advantages of a pact of which some of the conditions are repudiated. – Even better, as this pact is based on natural right and is obligatory, he who rejects it or withdraws from it, becomes by that act a miscreant, a public wrong-doer and an enemy of the people. There were once crimes of royal lèse-majesty; now there are crimes of popular lèse-majesty. Such crimes are committed when by deed, word, or thought, any portion whatever of the more than royal authority belonging to the people is denied or contested. The dogma through which popular sovereignty is proclaimed thus actually ends in a dictatorship of the few, and a proscription of the many. Outside of the sect you are outside of the laws. We, the five or six thousand Jacobins of Paris, are the legitimate monarch, the infallible Pontiff, and woe betide the refractory and the lukewarm, all government agents, all private persons, the clergy, the nobles, the rich, merchants, traders, the indifferent among all classes, who, steadily opposing or yielding uncertain adhesion, dare to throw doubt on our unquestionable right.

One by one these consequences are to come into light, and it is evident that, let the logical machinery by which they unfold themselves be what it may, no ordinary person, unless of consummate vanity, will fully adopt them. He must have an exalted opinion of himself to consider himself sovereign otherwise than by his vote, to conduct public business with no more misgivings than his private business, to directly and forcibly interfere with this, to set himself up, he and his clique, as guides, censors and rulers of his government, to persuade himself that, with his mediocre education and average intellect, with his few scraps of Latin and such information as is obtained in reading-rooms, coffee-houses, and newspapers, with no other experience than that of a club, or a municipal council, he could discourse wisely and well on the vast, complex questions which superior men, specially devoted to them, hesitate to take up. At first this presumption existed in him only in germ, and, in ordinary times, it would have remained, for lack of nourishment, as dry-rot or creeping mold, But the heart knows not what strange seeds it contains! Any of these, feeble and seemingly inoffensive, needs only air and sunshine to become a noxious excrescence and a colossal plant. Whether third or fourth rate attorney, counselor, surgeon, journalist, curé, artist, or author, the Jacobin is like the shepherd that has just found, in one corner of his hut, a lot of old parchments which entitle him to the throne. What a contrasts between the meanness of his calling and the importance with which the theory invests him! With what rapture he accepts a dogma that raises him so high in his own estimation! Diligently conning the Declaration of Rights, the Constitution, all the official documents that confer on him such glorious prerogatives, charging his imagination with them, he immediately assumes a tone befitting his new position.[23] — Nothing surpasses the haughtiness and arrogance of this tone.

13

It declares itself at the outset in the harangues of the clubs and in the petitions to the Constituent Assembly. Loustalot, Fréron, Danton, Marat, Robespierre, St. Just, always employ dictatorial language, that of the sect, and which finally becomes the jargon of their meanest valets. Courtesy or toleration, anything that denotes regard or respect for others, find no place in their utterances nor in their acts; a swaggering, tyrannical conceit creates for itself a language in its own image, and we see not only the foremost actors, but their minor associates, enthroned on their grandiloquent platform. Each in his own eyes is Roman, savior, hero, and great man.

"I stood in the tribune of the palace," writes Anarcharsis Clootz,[24] "at the head of the foreigners, acting as ambassador of the human species, while the ministers of the tyrants regarded me with a jealous and disconcerted air."

A schoolmaster at Troyes, on the opening of the club in that town, advises the women "to teach their children, as soon as they can utter a word, that they are free and have equal rights with the mightiest potentates of the universe."[25] Pétion's account of the journey in the king's carriage, on the return from Varennes, must be read to see how far self-importance of a pedant and the self-conceit of a lout can be carried.[26] In their memoirs and even down to their epitaphs, Barbaroux, Buzot, Pétion, Roland, and Madame Roland[27] give themselves certificates of virtue and, if we could take their word for it, they would pass for Plutarch's model characters. — This infatuation, from the Girondins to the Montagnards, continues to grow. St. Just, at the age of twenty-four, and merely a private individual, is already consumed with suppressed ambition. Marat says:

"I believe that I have exhausted every combination of the human intellect in relation to morality, philosophy and political science."

Robespierre, from the beginning to the end of the Revolution, is always, in his own eyes, Robespierre the unique, the one pure man, the infallible and the impeccable; no man ever burnt to himself the incense of his own praise so constantly and so directly. – At this level, conceit may drink the theory to the bottom, however revolting the dregs and however fatal its poison even to those defy its nausea for the sake of swallowing it. And, since it is virtue, no one may refuse it without committing a crime. Thus construed, the theory divides Frenchmen into two groups: one consisting of aristocrats, fanatics, egoists, the corrupt, bad citizens in short, and the other patriots, philosophers, and the virtuous, that is to say, those belonging to the sect.[28] Thanks to this reduction, the vast moral and social world with which they deal finds its definition, expression, and representation in a ready-made antithesis. The aim of the government is now clear: the wicked must submit to the good, or, which is briefer, the wicked must be suppressed. To this end let us employ confiscation, imprisonment, exile, drowning and the guillotine and a large scale. All means are justifiable and meritorious against these traitors; now that the Jacobin has canonized his slaughter, he slays through philanthropy. — Thus is the forming of his personality completed like that of a theologian who becomes inquisitor. Extraordinary contrasts are gathered to construct it: – a lunatic that is logical, and a monster that pretends to have a conscience. Under the pressure of his faith and egotism, he has developed two deformities, one of the head and the other of the heart; his common sense is gone, and his moral sense is utterly perverted. In fixing his mind on abstract formulas, he is no longer able to see men as they are. His self-admiration makes him consider his adversaries, and even his rivals, as miscreants deserving of death. On this downhill road nothing stops him, for, in qualifying things inversely to their true meaning, he has violated within himself the precious concepts which brings us back to truth and justice. No light reaches eyes which regard blindness as clear–sightedness; no remorse affects a soul which erects b a r b a r i s m   i n t o   p a t r i o t i s m ,   a n d   w h i c h   s a n c t i o n s   m u r d e r   w i t h   d u t y .

NOTES:

[1] Cf. "The Ancient Régime," p. 242. Citations from the "Contrat Social." – Buchez et Roux, "Histoire Parlementaire," XXVI. 96. Declaration of rights read by Robespierre in the Jacobin club, April 21, 1793, and adopted by the club as its own. "The people is sovereign, the government is its work and its property, and public functionaries are its clerks. The people can displace its mandatories and change its government when it pleases.

[2] Lenin, Stalin, Mao, Pol Pot, and other dictators that like that also organized elections and saw themselves as being the people, speaking and acting on their behalf and therefore entitled to do anything they pleased.(SR).

[3] Rightly so, might Lenin have thought when he first read this text. Later, under his and Stalin's leadership the Party, guided by the first secretary of its central committee, aided by the secret police, should penetrate all affairs slowly extending their power or influence to the entire world through their secret party members, mutually ensuring their promotion into the highest posts, the party will eventually come to govern the world. (SR).

[4] Buchez and Roux, III, 324. . (An article by Loustalot, Sept. 8, 1789). Ibid. 331 Motion of the District of Cordéliers, presided over by Danton. –Ibid 239.. Denunciation of the municipality by Marat. –V., 128, Vi. 24–41 (March, 1790). The majority of the districts demand the permanent authority of the districts, that is to say, of the sovereign political assemblies

[5] Buchez et Roux. IV. 458. Meeting of Feb. 24, 1790, an article by Loustalot. – III 202. Speech by Robespierre, meeting of Oct. 21, 1789. Ibid. 219. Resolution of the district of St. Martin declaring that martial law shall not be enforced. Ibid. 222. Article by Loustalot.

[6] Buchez et Roux, X. 124, an article by Marat. – X. 1–22, speech by Robespierre at the meeting of May 9, 1791.–III. an article by Loustalot. III. 217, speech by Robespierre, meeting of Oct.22, 1789. Ibid. 431, article by Loustalot and Desmoulins, Nov., 1789.—VI. 336, articles by Loustalot and Marat, July, 1790.

[7] Ernest Hamel, "Histoire de Robespierre", passim, (I.436). Robespierre proposed to confer political rights on the blacks. – Buchez et Roux, IX. 264 (March, 1791).

[8] Buchez et Roux, V. 146 (March, 1790) ; VI. 436 (July 26, 1790) ; VIII. 247 (Dec 1790) ; X. 224 (June, 1791).

[9] Gustave Flaubert. "Tout notaire a rêvé des sultanes." (All barristers have dreams of being sultans!) (Madame Bovary"). — "Frédéric trouvait que le bonheur mérité par l'excellence de son âme tardait à

venir." (Frédéric found that the happiness he deserved due to his brilliancy was a long time coming.) ("L'Education sentimentale.)

[10] Such has also been the effect of similar declarations set forth in the Constitutions of the United Nations, the European Community, as well as many individual nations. All that was required for the international Communist movement was then to await the slow promotion of the secret party members directed to seek a career inside the various legal administrations for, one day, to see all superior courts staffed by their men. (SR).

[11] Mallet du Pan, "Correspondance politique." 1796.

[12] "Entretiens du Père Gérard," by Collot d'Herbois. — "Les Etrennes au Peuple," by Barrère.–"La Constitution française pour les habitants des campagnes," etc. – Later "L'Alphabet des Sans–Culottes, le Nouveau Catéchisme républicain, les Commandements de la Patrie et de la République (in verse), etc.

[13] Mercure de France, an article by Mallet du Pan, April 7, 1792. (Summing up of the year 1791.)

[14] Mercure de France, see the numbers of Dec. 30, 1791, and April 7, 1792. (Note the phrase, it is close to Marx statement in 1850 'that the class struggle necessarily leads to the dictatorship of the proletariat.' SR.)

[15] Fox, before deciding on any measure, consulted a Mr. H.——, one of the most uninfluential, and even narrow–minded members of the House of Commons. Some astonishment being expressed at this, he replied that he regarded Mr. H.—— as a perfect type of the faculties and prejudices of a country gentleman, and he used him as a thermometer. Napoleon likewise stated that before framing an important law, he imagined to himself the impression it would make on the mind of a burly peasant.

[16] Just like the strong influence which the current fashionable principles and buzz–words introduced by the media have over today's audiences. (SR).

[17] Alas! This phenomenon should be repeated with the interminable speeches held by Lenin, Stalin, Hitler, Castro, Mao and all the other inheritors of the Jacobin creed. (SR).

[18] Tableaux de la Révolution Française," by Schmidt (especially the reports by Dutard), 3 vols.

[19] "Correspondence of Gouverneur Morris," — "Memoirs of Mallet du Pan," John Moore'

[20] See, in "Progrès de l'esprit humaine," the superiority awarded to the republican constitution of 1793. (Book IX.) "The principles from which the constitution and laws of France have been combined are purer, more exact, and deeper than those which governed the Americans: they have more completely escaped the influence of every sort of prejudice, etc."

[21] Camille Desmoulins, the enfant terrible of the Revolution, confesses this, as well as other truths.

After citing the Revolutions of the sixteenth and seventeenth centuries, "which derived their virtue from and had their roots in conscience, which were sustained by fanaticism and the hopes of another world," he thus concludes: "Our Revolution, purely political, is wholly rooted in egotism, in everybody's amour propre, in the combinations of which is found the common interest." ("Brissot dévoilé," by Camille Desmoulins, January, 1792) — Bouchez et Roux, XIII, 207.)

[22] Rousseau's idea of the omnipotence of the State is also that of Louis XIV and Napoleon... It is curious to see the development of the same idea in the mind of a contemporary bourgeois, like Rétif de la Bretonne, half literary and half one of the people ("Nuits de Paris," XVe nuit, 377, on the September Massacres) "No, I do not pity those fanatical priests; they have done the country too much mischief. Whatever a society, or a majority of it, desires, that is right. He who opposes this, who calls down war and vengeance on the Nation, is a monster. Order is always found in the agreement of the majority. The minority is always guilty, I repeat it, even if it is morally right. Nothing but common sense is needed to see that truth." — Ibid. (On the execution of Louis XVI.), p. 447. "Had the nation the right to condemn and execute him? No thinking person can ask such a question. The nation is everything in itself; its power is that which the whole human kind would have if but one nation, one single government governed the globe. Who would dare then dispute the power of humanity? It is this indisputable power that a nation has, to hang even an innocent man, felt by the ancient Greeks, which led them to exile Aristoteles and put Phocion to death. 'Oh truth, unrecognized by our contemporaries, what evil has arisen through forgetting it!'"

[23] Moniteur, XI. 46. Speech by Isnard in the Assembly, Jan. 5, 1792. "The people are now conscious of their dignity. They know, according to the constitution, that every Frenchman's motto is: 'Live free, the equal of all, and one of the common sovereignty.'"— Guillon de Montléon, I. 445. Speech by Chalier, in the Lyons Central Club, March 21, 1793. "Know that you are kings, and more than kings. Do you not feel sovereignty circulating in your veins?"

[24] Moniteur, V. 136. (Celebration of the Federation, July 14, 1790.)

[25] Albert Babeau, "Histoire de Troyes pendant la Révolution," I. 436 (April 10, 1790).

[26] Mortimer–Ternaux, "Histoire de la Terreur," I. 353. (Pétion's own narrative of this journey.) This pert blockhead cannot even spell: he writes aselle for aisselle, etc. He is convinced that Madame Elizabeth, the king's sister, wants to seduce him, and that she makes advances to him: "If we had been alone, I believe that she would have fallen into my arms, and let the impulses of nature have their way." He makes a display of virtue however, and becomes only the more supercilious as he talks with the king, the young dauphin, and the ladies he is fetching back.

[27] The "Mémoires de Madame Roland" is a masterpiece of that conceit supposed to be so carefully concealed as not to be visible and never off its stilts. "I am beautiful, I am affectionate, I am sensitive, I inspire love, I reciprocate, I remain virtuous, my mind is superior, and my courage indomitable. I am philosopher, statesman, and writer, worthy of the highest success," is constantly in her mind, and always perceptible in her phraseology. Real modesty never shows itself. On the contrary, many indecorous things are said and done by her from bravado, and to set herself above her sex. Cf. the "Memoirs of Mirs. Hutchinson," which present a great contrast. Madame Roland wrote: "I see no part

in society which suits me but that of Providence."— The same presumption shines out in others, with less refined pretensions. The deputy Rouyer addresses the following letter, found among the papers of the iron wardrobe, to the king, "I have compared, examined, and foreseen everything. All I ask to carry out my noble purposes, is that direction of forces, which the law confers on you. I am aware of and brave the danger; weakness defers to this, while genius overcomes it I have turned my attention to all the courts of Europe, and am sure that I can force peace on them." — Robert, an obscure pamphleteer, asks Dumouriez to make him ambassador to Constantinople, while Louvet, the author of "Faublas," declares in his memoirs that liberty perished in 1792, because he was not appointed Minister of Justice.

[28] Moniteur, p. 189. Speech by Collot d'Herbois, on the mitraillades at Lyons. "We too, possess sensibility! The Jacobins have every virtue; they are compassionate, humane, and generous. These virtues, however, are reserved for patriots, who are their brethren, but never for aristocrats." — Meillan, "Mémoires," p. 4. "Robespierre was one day eulogizing a man named Desfieux, well known for his lack of integrity, and whom he finally sacrificed. 'But, I said to him, your man Desfieux is known to be a rascal.' – 'No matter,' he replied, 'he is a good patriot.' – 'But he is a fraudulent bankrupt.'–'He is a good patriot.' — 'But he is a thief.' –'He is a good patriot.' I could not get more than these three words out of him."

CHAPTER II. THE PARTY

I.

Formation of the party. — Its recruits — These are rare in the upper class and amongst the masses. — They are numerous in the low bourgeois class and in the upper stratum of the people. — The position and education which enroll a man in the party.

PERSONALITIES like these are found in all classes of society; no situation or position in life protects one from wild Utopia or frantic ambition. We find among the Jacobins a Barras and a Châteauneuf– Randon, two nobles of the oldest families; Condorcet, a marquis, mathematician, philosopher and member of two renowned academies; Gobel, bishop of Lydda and suffragan to the bishop of Bâle; Hérault de Séchellles, a protégé of the Queen's and attorney–general to the Paris parliament; Lepelletier de St. Fargeau, chief–justice and one of the richest land–owners in France; Charles de Hesse, major–general, born in the royal family; and, last of all, a prince of the blood and fourth personage in the realm, the Duke of Orleans. — But, with the exception of these rare deserters, neither the hereditary aristocracy nor the upper magistracy, nor the highest of the middle class, none of the land–owners who live on their estates, or the leaders of industrial and commercial enterprises, no one belonging to the administration, none of those, in general, who are or deserve to be considered social authorities, furnish the party with recruits. All have too much at stake in the political establishment, shattered as it is, to wish its entire demolition. Their political experience, brief as it is, enables them to see at once that a habitable house is not built by merely tracing a plan of it on paper according the theorems of school geometry. — On the other hand, among the ordinary rural population the ideology finds, unless it can be changed into a legend, no listeners. Share croppers, small holders and farmers looking after their own plots of ground, peasants and craftsmen who work too hard to think and whose minds never range beyond a village horizon, busy only with that which brings in their daily bread, find abstract doctrines unintelligible; should the dogmas of the new catechism arrest their attention the same thing happens as with the old one, they do not understand them; that mental faculty by which an abstraction is reached is not yet formed in them. On being taken to a political club they fall asleep; they open their eyes only when some one announces that tithes and feudal privileges are to be restored; they can be depended on for nothing more than a brawl and a jacquerie; later on, when their grain comes to be taxed or is taken, they prove as unruly under the republic as under the monarchy.

The believers in this theory come from other quarters, from the two extremes of the lower stratum of the middle class and the upper stratum of the low class. Again, in these two contiguous groups, which merge into each other, those must be left out who, absorbed in their daily occupations or professions, have no time or thought to give to public matters, who have reached a fair position in the social hierarchy and are not disposed to run risks, almost all of them well– established, steady–going, mature, married folks who have sown their wild oats and whom experience in life has rendered distrustful of themselves and of theories. Overweening conceit is, most of the time, only average in the average human being, so speculative ideas will with most people only obtain a loose, transient and feeble hold. Moreover, in this society which, for many centuries consists of people accustomed to being ruled, the hereditary spirit is bourgeois that is to say, used to discipline, fond of order, peaceable and even timid. — There remains a minority, a very small one,[1] innovating and restless. This consisted, on the one hand, of people who were discontented with their calling or profession, because they were of secondary or subaltern rank in it.[2] Some were debutantes not fully employed and others aspirants for careers not yet entered upon. Then, on the other hand, there were the men of unstable character and all those who were uprooted by the immense upheaval of things: in the Church, through the suppression of convents and through schism; in the judiciary, in the administration, in the financial departments, in the army, and in various private and public careers, through the reorganization of institutions, through the novelty of fresh resources and occupations, and through the disturbance caused by the changed relationships of patrons and clients. Many who, in ordinary times, would otherwise remain quiet, become in this way nomadic and extravagant in politics. Among the foremost of these are found those who, through a classical education, can take in an abstract proposition and deduce its consequences, but who, for lack of special preparation for it, and confined to the narrow circle of local affairs, are incapable of forming accurate conceptions of a vast, complex social organization, and of the conditions which enable it to subsist. Their talent lies in making a speech, in dashing off an editorial, in composing a pamphlet, and in drawing up reports in more or less pompous and dogmatic style; the genre admitted, a few of them who are gifted become eloquent, but that is all. Among those are the lawyers, notaries, bailiffs and former petty provincial judges and attorneys who furnish the leading actors and two–thirds of the members of the Legislative Assembly and of the Convention: There are surgeons and doctors in small towns, like Bo, Levasseur, and Baudot, second and third–rate literary characters, like Barrère, Louvet, Garat, Manuel, and Ronsin, college professors like Louchet and Romme, schoolmasters like Leonard Bourdon, journalists like Brissot, Desmoulins and Freron, actors like Collot d'Herbois, artists like Sergent, Oratoriens[3] like Fouché, capuchins like Chabot, more or less secularized priests like Lebon, Chasles, Lakanal, and Grégoire, students scarcely out of school like St. Just, Monet of Strasbourg, Rousseline of St. Albin, and Julien of the Drôme — in short, the poorly sown and badly cultivated minds, and on which the theory had only to fall to smother the good grain and thrive like a nettle. Add to these charlatans and others who live by their wits, the visionary and morbid of all sorts, from Fanchet and Klootz to

Châlier or Marat, the whole of that needy, chattering, irresponsible crowd, ever swarming about large cities ventilating its shallow conceits and abortive pretensions. Farther in the background appear those whose scanty education qualifies them to half understand an abstract principle and imperfectly deduce its consequences, but whose roughly–polished instinct atones for the feebleness of a coarse argumentation. Through cupidity, envy and rancor, they divine a rich pasture–ground behind the theory, and Jacobin dogmas become dearer to them, because the imagination sees untold treasures beyond the mists in which they are shrouded. They can listen to a club harangue without falling asleep, applaud its tirades in the rights place, offer a resolution in a public garden, shout in the tribunes, pen affidavits for arrests, compose orders–of–the–day for the national guard, and lend their lungs, arms, and sabers to whoever bids for them. But here their capacity ends. In this group merchants' and notaries' clerks abound, like Hébert and Henriot, Vincent and Chaumette, butchers like Legendre, postmasters like Drouet, boss–joiners like Duplay, school–teachers like that Buchot who becomes a minister, and many others of the same sort, accustomed to jotting down ideas, with vague notions of orthography and who are apt in speech–making,[4] foremen, sub–officers, former begging friars, peddlers, tavern–keepers, retailers, market–porters, and city– journeymen from Gouchon, the orator of the faubourg St. Antoine, down to Simon, the cobbler of the Temple, from Trinchard, the juryman of the Revolutionary Tribunal, down to grocers, tailors, shoemakers, tapster, waiters, barbers, and other shopkeepers or artisans who do their work at home, and who are yet to do the work of the September massacres. Add to these the foul remnants of every popular insurrection and dictatorship, beasts of prey like Jourdain of Avignon, and Fournier the American, women like Théroigne, Rose Lacombe, and the tricoteuses of the Convention who have unsexed themselves, the amnestied bandits and other gallows birds who, for lack of a police, have a wide range, street–rollers and vagabonds, rebels against labor and discipline, the whole of that class in the center of civilization which preserves the instincts of savages, and asserts the sovereignty of the people to glut a natural appetite for license, laziness, and ferocity. — Thus is the party recruited through an enlisting process that gleans its subjects from every station in life, but which reaps them down in great swaths, and gathers them together in the two groups to which dogmatism and presumption naturally belong. Here, education has brought man to the threshold, even to the heart of general ideas; consequently, he feels hampered within the narrow bounds of his profession or occupation, and aspires to something beyond. But as his education has remained superficial or rudimentary, consequently, outside of his narrow circle he feels out of his place. He has a perception or obtains a glimpse of political ideas and, therefore, assumes that he has capacity. But his perception is confided to a formula, and he sees them dimly through a cloud; hence his incapacity, and the reason why his mental lacunae as well as his attainments both contribute to make him a Jacobin.

II.

Spontaneous associations after July 14, 1789. — How these dissolve. – Withdrawal of people of sense and occupation. — Number of those absent at elections. — Birth and multiplication of Jacobin societies. — Their influence over their adherents — Their maneuvers and despotism.

Men thus disposed cannot fail to draw near each other, to understand each other, and combine together; for, in the principle of popular sovereignty, they have a common dogma, and, in the conquest of political supremacy, a common aim. Through a common aim they form a faction, and through a common dogma they constitute a sect, the league between them being more easily effected because they are a faction and sect at the same time.

At first their association is not distinguishable in the multitude of other associations. Political societies spring up on all sides after the taking of the Bastille. Some kind of organization had to be substituted for the deposed or tottering government, in order to provide for urgent public needs, to secure protection against ruffians, to obtain supplies of provisions, and to guard against the probably machinations of the court. Committees installed themselves in the town halls, while volunteers formed bodies of militia: hundreds of local governments, almost independent, arose in the place of the central government, almost destroyed.[5] For six months everybody attended to matters of common interest, each individual getting to be a public personage and bearing his quota of the government load: a heavy load at all times, but heavier in times of anarchy; this, at least, is the opinion of the majority but not of all of them. Consequently, a division arises amongst those who had assumed this load, and two groups are formed, one huge, inert and disintegrating, and the other small, compact and energetic, each taking one of two ways which diverge from each other, and which keep on diverging more and more.

On one hand are the ordinary, sensible people, those who are busy, and who are, to some extent, not over–conscientious, and not over– conceited. The power is in their hands because they find it prostrate, lying abandoned in the street; they hold it provisionally only, for they knew beforehand, or soon discover, that they are not qualified for the post, it being one of those which, to be properly filled, needs some preparation and fitness for it. A man does not become legislator or administrator in one day, any more than he suddenly becomes a physician or surgeon. If an accident obliges me to act in the latter capacity, I yield, but against my will, and I do no more than is necessary to save my patients from hurting themselves, My fear of their dying under the operation is very great, and, as soon as some other person can be found to take my place, I go home.[6] — I should be glad, like everybody else, to have my vote in the selection of this person, and, among the candidates. I should designate, to the best of my ability, one who seemed to me the ablest and most conscientious. Once selected, however, and installed, I should not attempt to dictate to him; his cabinet is private, and I have no right to run there constantly and cross–question him, as if he were a child or under suspicion. It does not become me to tell him what to do; he probably knows more about the case than I do; in any event, to keep a steady hand, he must not be threatened, and, to keep a clear head, he must not be disturbed. Nor must I be disturbed; my office and books, my shop, my customers must be attended to as well. Everybody has to mind his own business, and whoever would attend to his own and another's too, spoils both. — This way of thinking prevails with most healthy minds towards the beginning of the year 1790, all whose heads are not turned by insane ambition and the mania for theorizing, especially after six months of practical experience and knowing the dangers, miscalculation, and vexations to which one is exposed in trying to lead an eager, over–excited population. — Just at this time, December 1789, municipal law becomes established throughout the country; all the mayors and municipal officers are elected almost immediately, and in the following months, all administrators of districts and departments. The interregnum has a length come to an end. Legal authorities now exist, with legitimate and clearly–determined functions. Reasonable, honest people gladly turn power over to those to whom it belongs, and certainly do not dream of resuming it. All associations for temporary purposes are at once disbanded for lack of an object, and if others are formed, it is for the purpose of defending established institutions. This is the object of the Federation, and, for six months, people embrace each other and exchange oaths of fidelity. — After this, July 14, 1790, they retire into private life, and I have no doubt that, from this date, the political ambition of a large plurality of the French people is satisfied, for, although Rousseau's denunciation of the social hierarchy are still cited by them, they, at bottom, desire but little more than the suppression of administrative brutality and state favoritism.[7] All this is obtained, and plenty of other things besides; the august title of sovereign, the respect of the public authorities, honors to all who wield a pen or make a speech, and, better still, actual sovereignty in the appointment to office of all local land national administrators; not only do the people elect their deputies, but every species of functionary of every degree, those of commune, district, and department, officers in the national guard, civil and criminal magistrates, bishops and priests. Again, to ensure the responsibility of the elected to their electors, the term of office fixed by law is a short one,[8] the electoral machine which summons the sovereign to exercise his sovereignty being set agoing about every four months. — This was a good deal, and too much, as the sovereign himself soon discovers. Voting so frequently becomes unendurable; so many prerogatives end in getting to be drudgery. Early in 1790, and after this date, the majority forego the privilege of voting and the number of absentees becomes enormous. At Chartres, in May, 1790,[9] 1,447 out of 1,551 voters do not attend preliminary meetings. At Besançon, in January, 1790, on the election of mayor and municipal officers, 2,141 out of 3,200 registered electors are recorded as absent from the polls, and 2,900 in the following month of November.[10] At Grenoble, in August and November of this year, out of 2,500 registered voters, more than 2,000 are noted as absent.[11] At Limoges, out of about the same number, there are only 150 voters. At Paris, out of 81,400 electors, in August, 1790, 67,200 do not vote, and, three months later, the number of absentees is 71,408.[12]

Thus for every elector that votes, there are four, six, eight, ten, and even sixteen that abstain from voting. — In the election of deputies, the case is the same. At the primary meetings of 1791, in Paris, out of 81,200 registered names more than 74,000 fail to respond. In the Doubs, three out of four voters stay away. In one of the cantons of the Côte d'Or, at the close of the polls, only one-eighth of the electors remain at the counting of the votes, while in the secondary meetings the desertion is not less. At Paris, out of 946 electors chosen only 200 are found to give their suffrage; at Rouen, out of 700 there are but 160, and on the last day of the ballot, only 60. In short, "in all departments," says an orator in the tribune, "scarcely one out of five electors of the second degree discharges his duty."

In this manner the majority hands in its resignation. Through inertia, want of forethought, lassitude, aversion to the electoral hubbub, lack of political preferences, or dislike of all the political candidates, it shirks the task which the constitution imposes on it. Most certainly is has no taste for the painstaking burden of being involved in a league (of human rights). Men who cannot find time once in three months to drop a ballot in the box, will not come three times a week to attend the meetings of a club. Far from meddling with the government, they abdicate, and as they refuse to elect it, they cannot undertake to control it.

It is, on the other hand, just the opposite with the upstarts and dogmatists who regard their royal privileges seriously. They not only vote at the elections, but they mean to keep the authority they delegate in their own hands. In their eyes every official is one of their creatures, and remains accountable to them, for, in point of law, the people may not part with their sovereignty, while, in fact, power has proved so sweet that they are not disposed to part with it.[13] During six months preceding the regular elections, they have come to know, comprehend, and test each other; they have held secret meetings; a mutual understanding is arrived at, and henceforth, as other associations disappear like fleeting bloom, theirs[14] rise vigorously on the abandoned soil. A club is established at Marseilles before the end of 1789; each large town has one within the first six months of 1790, Aix in February, Montpellier in March, Nîmes in April, Lyons in May, and Bordeaux in June.[15] But their greatest increase takes place after the Federation festival. Just when local gatherings merge into that of the whole country, the sectarian Jacobins keep aloof, and form leagues of their own. At Rouen, July 14, 1790, two surgeons, a printer, a chaplain at the prison, a widowed Jewess, and four women or children living in the house, – eight persons in all, pure and not to be confounded with the mass,[16] bind themselves together, and form a distinct association. Their patriotism is of superior quality, and they take a special view of the social compact;[17] in swearing fealty to the constitution they reserve to themselves the Rights of Man, and they mean to maintain not only the reforms already effected, but to complete the Revolution just begun. – During the Federation they have welcomed and indoctrinated their fellows who, on quitting the capital or large cities, become bearers of instructions to the small towns and hamlets; they are told what the object of a club is, and how to form one, and, everywhere, popular associations arise on the same plan, for the same purpose, and bearing the same name. A month later, sixty of these associations are in operation; three months later, one hundred; in March, 1791, two hundred and twenty–nine, and in August, 1791, nearly four hundred.[18] After this date a sudden increase takes place, owing to two simultaneous impulses, which scatter their seeds over the entire territory. — On the one hand, at then end of July, 1791, all moderate men, the friends of law and order, who still hold the clubs in check, all constitutionalists, or Feuillants, withdraw from them and leave them to exaggeration or the triviality of proposing motions; the political tone immediately falls to that of the tavern and guard– house, so that wherever one or the other is found, there is a political club. On the other hand, a convocation of the electoral body is held at the same date for the election of a new National Assembly, and for the renewal of local governments; the prey being in sight, hunting–parties are everywhere formed to capture it. In two months,[19] six hundred new clubs spring up; by the end of September they amount to one thousand, and in June, 1792, to twelve hundred — as many as there are towns and walled boroughs. On the fall of the throne, and at the panic caused by the Prussian invasion, during a period of anarchy which equaled that of July, 1789, there were, according to Roederer, almost as many clubs as there were communes, 26,000, one for every village containing five or six hot–headed, boisterous fellows, or roughs, (tape–durs), with a clerk able to pen a petition.

After November, 1790,[20] "every street in every town and hamlet," says a Journal of large circulation, "must have a club of its own. Let some honest craftsman invite his neighbors to his house, where, with using a shared candle, he may read aloud the decrees of the National Assembly, on which he and his neighbors may comment. Before the meeting closes, in order to enliven the company, which may feel a little disturbed on account of Marat's articles, let him read the patriotic oaths in 'Père Duchesne.'"[21] — The advice is followed. At the meetings in the club are read aloud pamphlets, newspapers, and catechisms dispatched from Paris, the "Gazette Villageoise," the "Journal du Soir," the "Journal de la Montagne," "Père Duchesne," the "Révolutions de Paris," and "Laclos' Gazette." Revolutionary songs are sung, and, if a good speaker happens to be present, a former monk (oratorien), lawyer, or school–master, he pours out his stock of phrases, speaking of the Greeks and Romans, proclaiming the regeneration of the human species. One of them, appealing to the women, wants to see

"the declaration of the Rights of Man suspended on the walls of their bedrooms as their principal ornament, and, should war break out, these virtuous supporters, marching at the head of our armies like new bacchantes with flowing hair, the wand of Bacchus in their hand."

Shouts of applause greet this sentiment. The minds of the listeners, swept away by this gale of declamation, become overheated and ignite through mutual contact; like half–consumed embers that would die out if let alone, they kindle into a blaze when gathered together in a heap. – – Their convictions, at the same time, gain strength. There is nothing like a coterie to make these take root. In politics, as in religion, faith generating the church, the latter, in its turn, nourishes faith. In the club, as in the private religious meeting, each derives authority from the common unanimity, every word and action of the whole tending to prove each in the right. And all the more because a dogma which remains uncontested, ends in seeming incontestable; as the Jacobin lives in a narrow circle, carefully guarded, no contrary opinions find their way to him. The public, in his eyes, seems two hundred persons; their opinion weighs on him without any counterpoise, and, outside of their belief, which is his also, every other belief is absurd and even culpable. Moreover, he discovers through this constant system of preaching, which is nothing but flattery, that he is patriotic, intelligent, virtuous, of which he can have no doubt, because, before being admitted into the club, his civic virtues have been verified and he carries a printed certificate of them in his pocket. – – Accordingly, he is one of an élite corps, a corps which, enjoying a monopoly of patriotism, holds itself aloof, talks loud, and is distinguished from ordinary citizens by its tone and way of conducting things. The club of Pontarlier,[22] from the first, prohibits its members from using the common forms of politeness.

"Members are to abstain from saluting their fellow–citizens by removing the hat, and are to avoid the phrase, 'I have the honor to be,' and others of like import, in addressing persons."

A proper idea of one's importance is indispensable.

"Does not the famous tribune of the Jacobins in Paris inspire traitors and impostors with fear? And do not anti–Revolutionaries return to dust on beholding it?"

All this is true, in the provinces as well as at the capital, for, scarcely is a club organized before it sets to work on the population. In may of the large cities, in Paris, Lyons, Aix and Bordeaux, there are two clubs in partnership,[23] one, more or less respectable and parliamentary, "composed partly of the members of the different branches of the administration and specially devoted to purposes of general utility," and the other, practical and active, made up of bar– room politicians and club–haranguers, who indoctrinate workmen, market–gardeners and the rest of the lower bourgeois class. The latter is a branch of the former, and, in urgent cases, supplies it with rioters.

"We are placed amongst the people," says one of these subaltern clubs, "we read to them the decrees, and, through lectures and counsel, we warn them against the publications and intrigues of the aristocrats. We ferret out and track plotters and their machinations. We welcome and advise all complainants; we enforce their demands, when just; finally, we, in some way, attend to all details."

Thanks to these vulgar auxiliaries, but whose lungs and arms are strong, the party soon becomes dominant; it has force and uses it, and, denying that its adversaries have any rights, it re–establishes all the privileges for its own advantage.[24]

III.

How they view the liberty of the press. – Their political doings.

Let us consider its mode of procedure in one instance and upon a limited field, the freedom of the press.[25] In December, 1790, M. Etienne, an engineer, whom Marat and Fréron had denounced as a spy in their periodicals, brought a suit against them in the police court. The numbers containing the libel were seized, the printers summoned to appear, and M. Etienne claimed a public retraction or 25,000 francs damages with costs. At this the two journalists, considering themselves infallible as well as exempt from arrest, are indignant.

" It is of the utmost importance," writes Marat, "that the informer should not be liable to prosecution as he is accountable only to the public for what he says and does for the public good."

M. Etienne (surnamed Languedoc), therefore, is a traitor: "Monsieur Languedoc, I advise you to keep your mouth shut; if I can have you hung I will." M. Etienne, nevertheless, persists and obtains a first decision in his favor. Fire and flame are at once belched forth by Marat and Fréon:

"Master Thorillon," exclaims Fréron to the commissary of police, "you shall be punished and held up to the people as an example; this infamous decision must be canceled." — "Citizens," writes Marat, "go in a body to the Hôtel–de–Ville and do not allow one of the guards to enter the court–room. " — On the day of the trial, and in the most condescending spirit, but two grenadiers are let in. Even these, however, are too many and shouts from the Jacobin crowd arise "Turn 'em out! We rule here," upon which the two grenadiers withdraw. On the other hand, says Fréron triumphantly, that there were in the court– room "sixty of the victors at the Bastille led by the brave Santerre, who intended to interfere in the trial." – They intervene, indeed, and first against the plaintiff. M. Etienne is attacked at the entrance of the court–room and nearly knocked down He is so maltreated that he is obliged to seek shelter in the guard–room. He is spit upon, and they "move to cut off his ears." His friends receive "hundreds of kicks," while he runs away, and the case is postponed. — It is called up again several times, so no the judges have to be restrained. A certain Mandart in the audience, author of a pamphlet on "Popular Sovereignty," springs to his feet and, addressing Bailly, mayor of Paris, and president of the tribunal, challenges the court. As usual Bailly yields, attempting to cover up his weakness with an honorable pretext: "Although a judge can be challenged only by the parties to a suit, the appeal of one citizen is sufficient for me and I leave the bench." The other judges, who are likewise insulted and menaced, yield also, and, through a sophism which admirably illustrates the times, they discover in the oppression to which the plaintiff is subject a legal device by which they can give a fair color to their denial of justice. M. Etienne having signified to them that neither he nor his counsel could attend in court, because their lives were in danger, the court decides that M. Etienne, "failing to appear in person, or by counsel, is non–suited." — Victorious shouts at once proceed from the two journalists, while their articles on the case disseminated throughout France set a precedence contained in the .ruling. Any Jacobin may after this with impunity denounce, insult, and calumniate whomsoever he pleases, sheltered as he is from the action of courts, and held superior to the law.

Let us see, on the other hand, what liberty they allow their adversaries. A fortnight before this, Mallet du Pan, a writer of great ability, who, in the best periodical of the day, discusses questions week after week free of all personalities, the most independent, straight–forward, and honorable of men, the most eloquent and judicious advocate of public order and true liberty, is waited upon by a deputation from the Palais–Royal,[26] consisting of about a dozen well–dressed individuals, civil enough and not too ill–disposed, but quite satisfied that they have a right to interfere. The conversation which ensues shows to what extent the current political creed had turned peoples' heads.

"One of the party, addressing me, informed me that he and his associates were deputies of the Palais–Royal clubs, and that they had called to notify me that I would do well to change my principles and stop attacking the constitution, otherwise extreme violence would be brought to bear on me. I replied that I recognized no authority but the law and that of the courts; the law is your master and mine, and no respect is shown to the constitution by assailing the freedom of the press."

"The constitution is the common will, resumed the spokesman. The law, is the authority of the strongest. You are subject to the strongest and you ought to submit. We notify you of the will of the nation and that is the law.'"

Mallet du Pan stated to them that he was not in favor of the ancient régime, but that he did approve of royal authority.

"Oh!" exclaimed all together, " we should be sorry not to have a king. We respect the King and maintain his authority. But you are forbidden to oppose the dominant opinion and the liberty which is decreed by the National Assembly."

Mallet du Pan, apparently, knows more about this than they do, for he is a Swiss by birth, and has lived under a republic for twenty years. But this does not concern them. They persist all the same, five or six talking at once, misconstruing the sense the words they use, and each contradicting the other in point of detail, but all agreeing to impose silence on him:

"You should not run counter to the popular will, for in doing this you preach civil war, bring the assembly's decrees into contempt, and irritate the nation."

Evidently, for them, they constitute the nation, or, more or less, they represent it. Through this self–investiture they are at once magistrates, censors, and police, while the scolded journalist is only too glad, in his case, to have them stop at injunctions. — Three days before this he is advised that a body of rioters in his neighborhood "threatened to treat his house like that of M. de Castries," in which everything had been smashed and thrown out the windows. At another time, apropos of the suspensive or absolute veto; "four savage fellows came to his domicile to warn him, showing him their pistols, that if he dared write in behalf of M. Mounier he should answer for it with his life." Thus, from the outset,

"just as the nation begins to enjoy the inestimable right of free thought and free speech, factional tyrants lose no time in depriving citizens of these, proclaiming to all that would maintain the integrity of their consciences: Tremble, die, or believe as we do!"

After this, to impose silence on those who express what is offensive, the crowd, the club, the section, decree and execute, each on its own authority,[27] searches, arrests, assaults, and, at length, assassinations. During the month of June, 1792, "three decrees of arrest and fifteen denunciations, two acts of affixing seals, four civic invasions of his premises, and the confiscation of whatever belonged to him in France" is the experience of Mallet du Pan. He passes four years "without knowing with any certainty on going to bed whether he should get out of it in the morning alive and free." Later on, if he escapes the guillotine and the lantern, it is owing to exile. On the 10th of August, Suleau, a conservative journalist, is massacred in the street. — This shows how the party regards the freedom of the press. Other liberties may be judged of by its encroachments on this domain. Law, in its eyes, is null when it proves an obstacle, and when it affords protection to adversaries; consequently there is no excess which it does not sanction for itself; and no right which it does not refuse to others.

There is no escape from the tyranny of the clubs. "That of Marseilles has forced the city officials to resign;[28] it has summoned the municipal body to appear before it; it has ignored the authority of the department, and has insulted the administrators of the law. Members of the Orleans club have kept the national Supreme Court under supervision, and taken part in its proceedings. Those of the Caen club have insulted the magistrates, and seized and burnt the records of the proceedings commenced against the destroyers of the statue of Louis XIV. At Alby they have forcibly abstracted from the record—office the papers relating to an assassin's trial, and burnt them." The club at Coutance gives the deputies of its district to understand that "no reflections must be cast on the laws of the people." That of Lyons stops an artillery train, under the pretext that the ministry in office does not enjoy the nation's confidence. — Thus does the club everywhere govern, or prepare to govern. On the one hand, at the elections, it sets aside or supports candidates; it alone votes, or, at least, controls the voting. In short, the club is the elective power, and practically, if not legally, enjoys the privileges of a political aristocracy. On the other hand, it assumes to be a spontaneous police—board; it prepares and circulates the lists which designate the ill—disposed, suspected, and lukewarm; it lodges information against nobles whose sons have emigrated; against unsworn priests who still reside in their former parishes, and against nuns, "whose conduct is unconstitutional". It prompts, directs, and rebukes local authorities; it is itself a supplemental, superior, and usurping authority. — All at once, sensible men realize its character, and protest against it.

"A body thus organized," says a petition,[29] "exists solely for arming one citizen against another. . . . Discussions take place there, and denunciations are made under the seal of inviolable secrecy. . . . . Honest citizens, surrendered to the most atrocious calumny, are destroyed without an opportunity of defending themselves. It is a veritable Inquisition. It is the center of seditious publications, a school of cabals and intrigue. If the citizens have to blush at the selection of unworthy candidates, they are all due to this class of associations . . . Composed of the excited and the incendiary, of those who aim to rule the State," the club everywhere tends

"to a mastery of the popular opinion, to thwarting the municipalities, to an intrusion of itself between these and the people," to an usurpation of legal forms and to become a "colossus of despotism."

Vain complaints! The National Assembly, ever in alarm on its own account, shields the popular club and accords it its favor or indulgence. A journal of the party had recommended "the people to form themselves into small platoons." These platoons, one by one, are growing. Each borough now has a local oligarchy, an enlisted and governing band. To create an army out of these scattered bands, simply requires a staff and a central rallying–point. The central point and the staff have both for a long time been ready in Paris, it is the association of the "Friends of the Constitution."

IV.

Their rallying–points. — Origin and composition of the Paris Jacobin club. — It affiliates with provincial clubs. — Its leaders. — The fanatics. — The Intriguers. — Their object. — Their means.

No association in France, indeed, dates farther back, and has an equal prestige. It was born before the Revolution, April 30, 1789.[30] At the assembly of the States–General in Brittany, the deputies from Quimper, Hennebon, and Pontivy saw how important it was to vote in concert, and they had scarcely reached Versailles when, in common with others, they hired a hall, and, along with Mounier, secretary of the States–General of Dauphiny, and other deputies from the provinces, at once organized a union which was destined to last. Up to the 6th of October, none but deputies were comprised in it; after that date, on removing to Paris, in the library of the Jacobins, a convent in the Rue St. Honoré, many well–known eminent men were admitted, such as Condorcet, and then Laharpe, Chénier, Champfort, David, and Talma, among the most prominent, with other authors and artists, the whole amounting to about a thousand notable personages. — No assemblage could be more imposing — two or three hundred deputies are on its benches, while its rules and by–laws seem specially designed to gather a superior body of men. Candidates for admission were proposed by ten members and afterwards voted on by ballot. To be present at one of its meetings required a card of admission. On one occasion, a member of the committee of two, appointed to verify these cards, happens to be the young Duke of Chartres. There is a committee on administration and a president. Discussions took place with parliamentary formalities, and, according to its status, the questions considered there were those under debate in the National Assembly.[31] In the lower hall, at certain hours, workmen received instruction and the constitution was explained to them. Seen from afar, no society seems worthier of directing public opinion; near by, the case is different. In the departments, however, where distance lends enchantment, and where old customs prevail implanted by centralization, it is accepted as a guide because its seat is at the capital. Its statutes, its regulations, its spirit, are all imitated; it becomes the alma mater of other associations and they its adopted daughters. It publishes, accordingly, a list of all clubs conspicuously in its journal, together with their denunciations; it insists on their demands; henceforth, every Jacobin in the remotest borough feels the support and endorsement, not only of his local, club, but again of the great club whose numerous offshoots reached the entire territory and which extends its all–powerful protection to the least of its adherents. In return for this protection, each associated club obeys the word of command given at Paris, and to and from, from the center to the extremities, a constant correspondence maintains the established harmony. A vast political machine is thus set agoing, a machine with thousands of arms, all working at once under one impulsion, and the lever which the motions is in the hands of a few master spirits in the Rue St. Honoré.

No machine could be more effective; never was one seen so well contrived for manufacturing artificial, violent public opinion, for making this appear to be national, spontaneous sentiment, for conferring the rights of the silent majority on a vociferous minority, for forcing the surrender of the government.

"Our tactics were very simple," says Grégoire[32]. "It was understood that one of us should take advantage of the first favorable opportunity to propose some measure in the National Assembly that was sure to be applauded by a small minority and cried down by the majority. But that made no difference. The proposer demanded, which was granted, that the measure should be referred to a committee in which its opponents hoped to see it buried. Then the Paris Jacobins took hold of it. A circular was issued, after which an article on the measure was printed in their journal and discussed in three or four hundred clubs that were leagued together. Three weeks after this the Assembly was flooded with petitions from every quarter, demanding a decree of which the first proposal had been rejected, and which is now passed by a great majority because a discussion of it had ripened public opinion."

In other words, the Assembly must go ahead or it will be driven along, in which process the worst expedients are the best. Those who conduct the club, whether fanatics or intriguers, are fully agreed on this point.

At the head of the former class is Duport, once a counselor in the parliament, who, after 1788, knew how to turn riots to account. The first revolutionary consultations were held in his house. He wants to plough deep, and his devices for burying the ploughshare are such that Sieyès, a radical, if there ever was one, dubbed it a "cavernous policy."[33] Duport, on the 28th of July, 1789, is the organizer of the Committee on Searches, by which all favorably disposed informers or spies form in his hands a supervisory police, which fast becomes a police of provocation. He finds recruits in the lower hall of the Jacobin club, where workmen come to be catechized every morning, while his two lieutenants, the brothers Laurette, have only to draw on the same source for a zealous staff in a choice selection of their instruments. "Ten reliable men receive orders there daily;[34] each of these in turn gives his orders to ten more, belonging to different battalions in Paris. In this way each battalion and section receives the same insurrectionary orders, the same denunciations of the constituted authorities, of the mayor of Paris, of the president of the department, and of the commander of the National Guard," everything taking place secretly. These are dark deeds: the leaders themselves call it 'the Sabbath' and, along with fanatics they enlist ruffians. "They spread the rumor that, on a certain day, there will be a great commotion with assassinations and pillage, preceded by the payment of money distributed from hand to hand by subaltern officers among those that can be relied on, and that these bands are to assemble, as advertised, within a radius of thirty or forty leagues."[35]— — One day, to provoke a riot, "half a dozen men, who have arranged the thing, form a small group, in which one of them holds forth vehemently; at once a crowd of about sixty others gathers around them. Then the six men move on from place to place," to form fresh groups making their apparent excitement pass for popular irritation. — Another day, "about forty fanatics, with powerful lungs, and four or five hundred paid men," scatter themselves around the Tuileries, "yelling furiously," and, gathering under the windows of the Assembly, "move resolutions to assassinate." — "Our ushers," says a deputy to the Assembly, "whom you ordered to suppress this tumult, heard reiterated threats of bringing you the heads of those the crowd wished to proscribe. That very evening, in the Palais–Royal, "I heard a subordinate leader of this factious band boast of having charged your ushers to take this answer back, adding that there was time enough yet for all good citizens to follow his advice." —The watchword of these agitators is, are you true and the response is, a true man. Their pay is twelve francs a day, and when in action they make engagements on the spot at that rate. "From several depositions taken by officers of the National Guard and at the mayoralty," it is ascertained that twelve francs a day were tendered to "honest people to join in with those you may have heard shouting, and some of them actually had the twelve francs put into their hands." — The money comes from the coffers of the Duke of Orleans, and they are freely drawn upon; at his death, with a property amounting to 114,000,000 francs, his debts amount to 74,000,000.[36] Being one of the faction, he contributes to its expenses, and, being the richest man in the kingdom, he contributes proportionately to his wealth. Not because he is a party leader, for he is too effeminate, too nervous; but "his petty council,"[37] and especially one of his private secretaries, Laclos, cherishes great designs for him, their object being to make him lieutenant–general of the kingdom, afterwards regent, and even king,[38] so that they may rule in his name and "share the profits." – – In the mean time they turn his whims to the best account, particularly Laclos, who is a kind of subordinate Macchiavelli, capable of anything, profound, depraved, and long indulging his fondness for monstrous combinations; nobody ever so coolly delighted in indescribable compounds of human wickedness and debauchery. In politics, as in romance, his department is "Les Liaisons Dangereuses." Formerly he maneuvered as an amateur with prostitutes and ruffians in the fashionable world; now he maneuvers in earnest with the prostitutes and ruffians of the sidewalks. On the 5th of October 1789, he is seen, "dressed in a brown coat,"[39] foremost among the women starting for Versailles, while his hand[40] is visible "in the Réveillon affair, also in the burning of barriers and Châteaux," and in the widespread panic which aroused all France against imaginary bandits. His operations, says Malouet, "were all paid for by the Duke of Orleans"; he entered into them "for his own account, and the Jacobins for theirs." — At this time their alliance is plain to everybody. On the 21st of November, 1790, Laclos becomes secretary of the club, chief of the department of correspondence, titular editor of its journal, and the invisible, active, and permanent director of all its enterprises. Whether actual demagogues or prompted by ambition, whether paid agents or earnest revolutionaries, each group works on its own account, both in concert, both in the same direction, and both devoted to the same undertaking, which is the conquest of power by every possible means.

V.

Small number of Jacobins. – Sources of their power. – They form a league. – They have faith. – Their unscrupulousness. – The power of the party vested in the group which best fulfills these conditions.

At first sight their success seems doubtful, for they are in a minority, and a very small one. At Besançon, in November, 1791, the revolutionaries of every shade of opinion and degree, whether Girondists or Montagnards, consist of about 500 or 600 out of 3,000 electors, and, in November, 1792, of not more than the same number out of 6,000 and 7,000.[41] At Paris, in November, 1791, there are 6,700 out of more than 81,000 on the rolls; in October, 1792, there are less than 14,000 out of 160,000.[42] At Troyes, in 1792, there are found only 400 or 500 out of 7,000 electors, and at Strasbourg the same number out of 8,000 electors.[43] Accordingly only about one–tenth of the electoral population are revolutionaries, and if we leave out the Girondists and the semi–conservatives, the number is reduced by one– half. Towards the end of 1792, at Besançon, scarcely more than 300 pure Jacobins are found in a population of from 25,000 to 30,000, while at Paris, out of 700,000 inhabitants only 5,000 are Jacobins. It is certain that in the capital, where the most excitement prevails, and where more of them are found than elsewhere, never, even in a crisis and when vagabonds are paid and bandits recruited, are there more than 10,000.[44] In a large town like Toulouse a representative of the people on missionary service wins over only about 400 persons.[45] Counting fifty or so in each small town, twenty in each large borough, and five or six in each village, we find, on an average, but one Jacobin to fifteen electors and National Guards, while, taking the whole of France, all the Jacobins put together do not amount to 300,000.[46] — This is a small number for the enslavement of six millions of able-bodied men, and for installing in a country of twenty-six millions inhabitants a more absolute despotism than that of an Asiatic sovereign. Force, however, is not measured by numbers; they form a band in the midst of a crowd and, in this disorganized, inert crowd, a band that is determined to push its way like an iron wedge splitting a log.

And against sedition from within as well as conquest from without a nation may only defend itself through the activities of its government, which provides the indispensable instruments of common action. Let it fail or falter and the great majority, undecided about what to do, lukewarm and busy elsewhere, ceases to be a corps and disintegrates into dust. Of the two governments around which the nation might have rallied, the first one, after July 14, 1789, lies prostrate on the ground where it slowly crumbles away. Now its ghost, which returns, is still more odious because it brings with it the same senseless abuses and intolerable burdens, and, in addition to these, a yelping pack of claimants and recriminators. After 1790 it appears on the frontier more arbitrary than ever at the head of a coming invasion of angry émigrés and grasping foreigners. – – The other government, that just constructed by the Constituent Assembly, is so badly put together that the majority cannot use it. It is not adapted to its hand; no political instrument at once so ponderous and so helpless was ever seen. An enormous effort is needed to set it in motion; every citizen is obliged to give it about two days labor per week.[47] Thus laboriously started but half in motion, it poorly meets the various tasks imposed upon it — the collection of taxes, public order in the streets, the circulation of supplies, and security for consciences, lives and property. Toppled over by its own action, another rises out of it, illegal and serviceable, which takes its place and stands. — In a great centralized state whoever possesses the head possesses the body. By virtue of being led, the French have contracted the habit of letting themselves be led.[48] People in the provinces involuntarily turn their eyes to the capital, and, on a crisis occurring, run out to stop the mailman to know what government happens to have fallen, the majority accepts or submits to it. — Because, in the first place, most of the isolated groups which would like to overthrow it dare not engage in the struggle: it seems too strong; through inveterate routine they imagine behind it that great, distant France which, under its impulsion, will crush them with its mass.[49] In the second place, should a few isolated groups undertake to overthrow it, they are not in a condition to keep up the struggle: it is too strong. They are, indeed, not yet organized while it is fully so, owing to the docile set of officials inherited from the government overthrown. Under monarchy or republic the government clerk comes to his office regularly every morning to dispatch the orders transmitted to him.[50] Under monarchy or republic the policeman daily makes his round to arrest those against who he has a warrant. So long as instructions come from above in the hierarchical order of things, they are obeyed. From one end of the territory to the other, therefore, the machine, with its hundred thousand arms, works efficiently in the hands of those who have seized the lever at the central point. Resolution, audacity, rude energy, are all that are needed to make the lever act, and none of these are wanting in the Jacobin. [51]

First, he has faith, and faith at all times "moves mountains.[52] "Take any ordinary party recruit, an attorney, a second–rate lawyer, a shopkeeper, an artisan, and conceive, if you can, the extraordinary effect of this doctrine on a mind so poorly prepared for it, so narrow, so out of proportion with the gigantic conception which has mastered it. Formed for the routine and the limited views of one in his position, he is suddenly carried away by a complete system of philosophy, a theory of nature and of man, a theory of society and of religion, a theory of universal history,[53] conclusions about the past, the present, and the future of humanity, axioms of absolute right, a system of perfect and final truth, the whole concentrated in a few rigid formulae as, for example:

"Religion is superstition, monarchy is usurpation, priests are impostors, aristocrats are vampires, and kings are so many tyrants and monsters."

These ideas flood a mind of his stamp like a vast torrent precipitating itself into a narrow gorge; they upset it, and, no longer under self–direction, they sweep it away. The man is beside himself. A plain bourgeois, a common laborer is not transformed with impunity into an apostle or liberator of the human species. – – For, it is not his country that he would save, but the entire race. Roland, just before the 10th of August, exclaims "with tears in his eyes, should liberty die in France, she is lost the rest of the world forever! The hopes of philosophers will perish! The whole earth will succumb to the cruelest tyranny!"[54] — Grégoire, on the meeting of the Convention, obtained a decree abolishing royalty, and seemed overcome with the thought of the immense benefit he had conferred on the human race.

"I must confess," said he, "that for days I could neither eat nor sleep for excess of joy!"

One day a Jacobin in the tribune declared: "We shall be a nation of gods!" — Fancies like these bring on lunacy, or, at all events, they create disease. "Some men are in a fever all day long," said a companion of St. Just; "I had it for twelve years . . ."[55] Later on, "when advanced in life and trying to analyze their experiences, they cannot comprehend it."[56] Another tells that, in his case, on a "crisis occurring, there was only a hair's breadth between reason and madness." — "When St. Just and myself," says Baudot, "discharged the batteries at Wissenbourg, we were most liberally thanked for it. Well, there was no merit in that; we knew perfectly well that the shot could not do us any harm." – – Man, in this exalted state, is unconscious of obstacles, and, according to circumstances, rise above or falls below himself, freely spilling his own blood as well as the blood of others, heroic as a soldier and atrocious as a civilian; he is not to be resisted in either direction for his strength increases a hundredfold through his fury, and, on his tearing wildly through the streets, people get out of his way as on the approach of a mad bull.

If they do not jump aside of their own accord, he will run at them, for he is unscrupulous as well as furious. — In every political struggle certain kinds of actions are prohibited; at all events, if the majority is sensible and wishes to act fairly, it repudiates them for itself. It will not violate any particular law, for, if one law is broken, this tends to the breaking of others. It is opposed to overthrowing an established government because every interregnum is a return to barbarism. It is opposed to the element of popular insurrection because, in such a resort, public power is surrendered to the irrationality of brutal passion. It is opposed to a conversion of the government into a machine for confiscation and murder because it deems the natural function of government to be the protection of life and property. — The majority, accordingly, in confronting the Jacobin, who allows himself all this,[57] is like a unarmed man facing one who is fully armed.[58] The Jacobin, on principle, holds the law in contempt, for the only law, which he accepts is arbitrary mob rule. He has no hesitation in proceeding against the government because, in his eyes, the government is a clerk which the people always has the right to remove. He welcomes insurrection because, through it, the people recover their sovereignty with no limitations. — Moreover, as with casuists, "the end justifies the means."[59] "Let the colonies perish," exclaims a Jacobin in the Constituent Assembly, "rather than sacrifice a principle." "Should the day come," says St. Just, "when I become convinced that it is impossible to endow the French with mild, vigorous, and rational ways, inflexible against tyranny and injustice, that day I will stab myself." Meanwhile he guillotines the others. "We will make France a graveyard," exclaimed Carrier, "rather than not regenerating it our own way!"[60] They are ready to risk the ship in order to seize the helm. From the first, they organize street riots and jacqueries in the rural districts, they let loose on society prostitutes and ruffians, vile and savage beasts. Throughout the struggle they take advantage of the coarsest and most destructive passions, of the blindness, credulity, and rage of an infatuated crowd, of dearth, of fear of bandits, of rumors of conspiracy, and of threats of invasion. At last, having seized power through a general upheaval, they hold on to it through terror and executions. — Straining will to the utmost, with no curb to check it, steadfastly believing in its own right and with utter contempt for the rights of others, with fanatical energy and the expedients of scoundrels, a minority may, in employing such forces, easily master and subdue a majority. So true is that, with faction itself, that victory is always on the side of the group with the strongest faith and the least scruples. Four times between 1789 and 1794, political gamblers take their seats at a table where the stake is supreme power, and four times in succession the "Impartiaux," the "Feuillants," the "Girondins," and the "Dantonists," form the majority and lose the game. Four times in succession the majority has no desire to break customary rules, or, at the very least, to infringe on any rule universally accepted, to wholly disregard the teachings of experience, the letter of the law, the precepts of humanity, or the suggestions of pity. — The minority, on the contrary, is determined beforehand to win at any price; its views and opinion are correct, and if rules are opposed to that, so much the worse for the rules. At the decisive moment, it claps a pistol to its adversary's head, overturns the table, and collects the stakes.

NOTES:

[1] See the figures further on.

[2] Mallet du Pan, II. 491. Danton, in 1793, said one day to one of his former brethren an advocate to the Council. : "The old régime made a great mistake. It brought me up on a scholarship in Plessis College. I was brought up with nobles, who were my comrades, and with whom I lived on familiar terms. On completing my studies, I had nothing; I was poor and tried to get a place. The Paris bar was very expensive, and it required extensive efforts to be accepted. I could not get into the army, having neither rank nor patronage. There was no opening for me in the Church. I could purchase no employment, for I hadn't a cent. My old companions turned their backs on me. I remained without a situation, and only after many long years did I succeed in buying the post of advocate in the Royal Council. The Revolution came, when I, and all like me, threw themselves into it. The ancient régime forced us to do so, by providing a good education for us, without providing an opening for our talents." This applies to Robespierre, C. Desmoulins, Brissot, Vergniaud, and others.

[3] Religious order founded in Rome in 1654 by saint Philippe Neri and who dedicated their efforts to preaching and the education of children. (SR)

[4] Dauban, "La Demagogie à Paris en 1793," and "Paris in 1794." Read General Henriot's orders of the day in these two works. Comparton, "Histoire du Tribunal Révolutionaire de Paris," a letter by Trinchard, I. 306 (which is here given in the original, on account of the ortography): "Si tu nest pas toute seulle et que le compagnion soit a travailler tu peus ma chaire amie ventir voir juger 24 mesieurs tous si devent président ou conselier au parlement de Paris et de Toulouse. Je t'ainvite a prendre quelque chose aven de venir parcheque nous naurons pas fini de 3 hurres. Je t'embrase ma chaire amie et épouge."– Ibid. II. 350, examination of André Chenier. – Wallon, "Hist. Du Trib. Rév.", I, 316. Letter by Simon. "Je te coitte le bonjour mois est mon est pousse."

[5] Cf. "The Revolution," page 60.

[6] Cf. On this point the admissions of the honest Bailly ("Mémoires," passim)

[7] Rétif de la Bretonne: "Nuits de Paris," 11éme nuit, p. 36. "I lived in Paris twenty–five years as free as air. All could enjoy as much freedom as myself in two ways – by living uprightly, and by not writing pamphlets against the ministry. All else was permitted, my freedom never being interfered with. It is only since the Revolution that a scoundrel could succeed in having me arrested twice."

[8] Cf. "The Revolution," vol. I. p.264.

[9] Moniteur, IV. 495. (Letter from Chartres, May 27, 1790.)

[10] Sauzay, I.147, 195 218, 711.

[11] Mercure de France, numbers of August 7, 14, 26, and Dec. 18, 1790.

[12] Ibid. number of November 26, 1790. Pétion is elected mayor of Paris by 6,728 out of 10,632 voters. "Only 7,000 voters are found at the election of the electors who elect deputies to the legislature. Primary and municipal meetings are deserted in the same proportion." – –Moniteur, X. 529 (Number of Dec. 4, 1791). Manuel is elected Attorney of the Commune by 3,770 out of 5,311 voters. — Ibid. XI. 378. At the election of municipal officers for Paris, Feb.10 and 11, 1792, only 3,787 voters present themselves; Dussault, who obtains the most votes, has 2,588; Sergent receives 1,648. — Buchez et Roux, XI. 238 (session of Aug.12, 1791). Speech by Chapelier; "Archives Nationales," F.6 (carton), 21. Primary meeting of June 13, 1791, canton of Bèze (Cote d'Or). Out of 460 active citizens, 157 are present, and, on the final ballot, 58. —Ibid., F7, 3235, (January, 1792). Lozerre: "1,000 citizens, at most, out of 25,000, voted in the primary meetings. At. Saint–Chèly, capital of the district, a few armed ruffians succeed in forming the primary meeting and in substituting their own election for that of eight parishes, whose frightened citizens who withdrew from it. . . At Langogne, chief town of the canton and district, out of more than 400 active citizens, 22 or 23 at most — just what one would suppose them to be when their presence drove away the rest — alone formed the meeting."

[13] This power, with its gratifications, is thus shown, Beugnot, I. 140, 147. "On the publication of the decrees of August 4, the committee of surveillance of Montigny, reinforced by all the patriots of the country, came down like a torrent on the barony of Choiseul, and exterminated all the hares and partridges. . . They fished out the ponds . At Mandres we find, in the best room of the inn, a dozen peasants gathered around a table decked with tumblers and bottles, amongst which we noticed an inkstand, pens, and something resembling a register. — 'I don't know what they are about,' said the landlady, 'but there they are, from morning till night, drinking, swearing, and storming away at everybody, and they say that they are a committee.'"

[14] Albert Babeau, I. 206, 242. — The first meeting of the revolutionary committee of Troyes in the cemetery of St. Jules, August, 1789. This committee becomes the only authority in the town, after the assassination of the mayor, M. Huez (Sept 10, 1790).

[15] "The French Revolution," Vol.I. pp. 235, 242, 251. – Buchez et Roux, VI, 179. – Guillon de Montléon, "Histoire de la Ville de Lyon pendant la Revolution," I. 87. — Guadet, "Les Girondins."

[16] Michelet, "Histoire de la Révolution," II.47.

[17] The rules of the Paris club state that members must "labor to establish and strengthen the Constitution, according to the spirit of the club."

[18] Mercure de France, Aug.11, 1790. — "Journal de la Société des Amis la Constitution," Nov.21, 1790. — Ibid., March, 1791. – Ibid., March, 1791. – Ibid., Aug.14, 1791 (speech by Rœderer) — Buchez et Roux, XI. 481.

[19] Michelet, II. 407. — Moniteur, XII 347 (May 11, 1792), article by Marie–Joseph Chénier, according to whom 800 Jacobin clubs exist at this date. — Ibid., XII. 753 (speech by M. Delfaux session of June 25, 1792). –Rœderer, preface to his translation of Hobbes.

[20] "Les Révolutions de Paris," by Prudhomme, number 173.

[21] Constant, "Histoire d'un Club Jacobin en province, "passim (Fontainbleau Club, founded May 5, 1791). — Albert Babeau, I.434 and following pages (foundation of the Troyes Club, Oct 1790). — Sauzay, I 206 and following pages (foundation of the Besançon Club Aug. 28, 1790). — Ibid., 214 (foundation of the Pontarlier Club, March, 1791)

[22] Sauzay, I. 214 (April 2, 1791)

[23] "Journal des Amis de la Constitution," I. 534 (Letter of the "Café National" Club of Bordeaux, Jan.29, 1791). Guillon de Monthléon, I. 88.–"The French Revolution," vol. I. 128, 242.

[24] Here we have a complete system of propaganda and organizational tactics identical to those used by the NAZIS, the Marxist–Leninists and other 'children' of the original communist–Jacobins. (SR.)

[25] Eugène Hatin, "Histoire politique et littéraire de la presse," IV. 210 (with Marat's text in "L'Ami

"l'Ami du peuple," and Fréron's in "l'Orateur du peuple").

[26] Mercure de France, Nov. 27, 1790.

[27] Mercure de France, Sept. 3, 1791 (article by Mallet du Pan). "On the strength of a denunciation, the authors of which I knew, the Luxembourg section on the 21st of June, the day of the king's departure, sent commissaries and a military detachment to my domicile. There was no judicial verdict, no legal order, either of police–court, or justice of the peace, no examination whatever preceding this mission. . . The employees of the section overhauled my papers, books and letters, transcribing some of the latter, and carried away copies and the originals, putting seals on the rest, which were left in charge of two fusiliers."

[28] Mercure de France, Aug. 27, 1791 (report by Duport–Dutertre, Minister of Justice). — Ibid., Cf. numbers of Sept. 8, 1790, and March 12, 1791.

[29] Sauzay, I.208. (Petition of the officers of the National Guard of Besançon, and observations of the municipal body, Sept. 15, 1790. — Petition of 500 national guards, Dec. 15, 1790). — Observations of the district directory, which directory, having authorized the club, avows that "three–quarters" of the national guard and a portion of other citizens "are quite hostile to it." — Similar petitions at Dax, Chalons–sur–Saône, etc., against the local club.

[30] "Lettres" (manuscript) of M. Roullé, deputy from Pontivy, to his constituents (May 1, 1789).

[31] A rule of the association says: "The object of the association is to discuss questions beforehand which are to be decided by the National Assembly, . . . and to correspond with associations of the same character which may be formed in the kingdom."

[32] Grégoires, "Mémoires," I. 387.

[33] Malouet, II. 248. "I saw counselor Duport, who was a fanatic, and not a bad man, with two or three others like him, exclaim: 'Terror! Terror! What a pity that it has become necessary!

[34] Lafayette, "Mémoires" (in relation to Messieurs de Lameth and their friends). — According to a squib of the day: "What Duport thinks, Barnave says and Lameth does" — This trio was named the Triumvirate. Mirabeau, a government man, and a man to whom brutal disorder was repugnant, called it the Triumgueusat. (A trinity of shabby fellows)

[35] Moniteur, V.212, 583. (Report and speech of Dupont de Nemours, sessions of July 31 and September 7, 1790.) — Vagabonds and ruffians begin to play their parts in Paris on the 27th of April, 1789 (the Réveillon affair). — Already on the 30th of July, 1789, Rivarol wrote: "Woe to whoever stirs up the dregs of a nation! The century Enlightenment has not touched the populace!" — In the preface of his future dictionary, he refers to his articles of this period: "There may be seen the precautions I took to prevent Europe from attributing to the French nation the horrors committed by the crowd of ruffians which the Revolution and the gold of a great personage had attracted to the capital." — "Letter of a deputy to his constituents," published by Duprez, Paris, in the beginning of

1790 (cited by M. de Ségur, in the Revue de France, September 1, 1880). It relates to the maneuvers for forcing a vote in favor of confiscating clerical property. "Throughout All–Saints' day (November 1, 1789), drums were beaten to call together the band known here as the Coadjutors of the Revolution. On the morning of November 2, when the deputies went to the Assembly, they found the cathedral square and all the avenues to the archbishop's palace, where the sessions were held, filled with an innumerable crowd of people. This army was composed of from 20,000 to 25,000 men, of which the greater number had no shoes or stockings; woollen caps and rags formed their uniform and they had clubs instead of guns. They overwhelmed the ecclesiastical deputies with insults, as they passed on their way, and shouted that they would massacre without mercy all who would not vote for stripping the clergy. . . Near 300 deputies who were opposed to the motion did not dare attend the Assembly. . . The rush of ruffians in the vicinity of the hall, their comments and threats, excited fears of this atrocious project being carried out. All who did not feel courageous enough to sacrifice themselves, avoided going to the Assembly." (The decree was adopted by 378 votes against 346.)

[36] Cf. "The Ancient Régime," p. 51.

[37] Malouet, 1.247, 248. — "Correspondence (manuscript) of M. de Staël," Swedish Ambassador, with his court, copied from the archives at Stockholm by M. Léouzon–le–Duc. Letter from M. Staël of April 21, 1791: "M. Laclos, secret agent of this wretched prince, (is a) clever and subtle intriguer." April 24: "His agents are more to be feared than himself. Through his bad conduct, he is more of a nuisance than a benefit to his party.

[38] Especially after the king's flight to Varennes, and at the time of the affair in the Champ de Mars. The petition of the Jacobins was drawn up by Laclos and Brissot.

[39] Investigations at the Chatelet, testimony of Count d'Absac de Ternay.

[40] Malouet I. 247, 248. This evidence is conclusive. "Apart from what I saw myself," says Malouet, "M. de Montmorin and M. Delessart communicated to me all the police reports of 1789 and 1790."

[41] Sauzay, II.79 (municipal election, Nov.15, 1791). — III. 221 (mayoralty election, November, 1792). The half–way moderates had 237 votes, and the sans–culottes, 310.

[42] Mercure de France, Nov. 26, 1791 (Pétion was elected mayor, Nov.17, by 6,728 votes out of 10,682 voters). — Mortimer–Ternaux, V. 95. (Oct 4, 1792, Pétion was elected mayor by 13,746 votes out of 14,137 voters. He declines. – Oct. 21, d'Ormessan, a moderate, who declines to stand, has nevertheless, 4,910 votes. His competitor, Lhuillier, a pure Jacobin, obtains only 4,896.)

[43] Albert Babeau, II. 15. (The 32,000 inhabitants of Troyes indicate about 7,000 electors. In December, 1792, Jacquet is elected mayor by 400 votes out of 555 voters. A striking coincidence is found in there being 400 members of the Troyes club at this time.) — Carnot, Mémoires," I. 181. "Dr. Bollmann, who passed through Strasbourg in 1792, relates that out of 8,000 qualified citizens, only 400 voters presented themselves.

[44] Mortimer–Ternaux, VI. 21. In February, 1793, Pache is elected mayor of Paris by 11,881 votes.

– Journal de Paris, number 185. Henriot, July 2, 1793, is elected commander–in–chief of the Paris national guard, by 9,084, against 6,095 votes given for his competitor, Raffet. The national guard comprises at this time110,000 registered members, besides 10,000 gendarmes and federates. Many of Henriot's partisans, again, voted twice. (Cf. on the elections and the number of Jacobins at Paris, chapters XI. and XII. of this volume.)

[45] Michelet, VI. 95. "Almost all (the missionary representatives) were supported by only, the smallest minority. Baudot, for instance, at Toulouse, in 1793, had but 400 men for him."

[46] For example, "Archives Nationales," Fl 6, carton 3. Petition of the inhabitants of Arnay–le–Duc to the king (April, 1792), very insulting, employing the most familiar language; about fifty signatures. — Sauzay, III. ch. XXXV. and XXXIV. (details of local elections). – Ibid., VII. 687 (letter of Grégoire, Dec. 24, 1796). — Malouet, II. 531 (letter by Malouet, July 22, 1779). Malouet and Grégoire agree on the number 300,000. Marie–Joseph Chénier (Moniteur, XII, 695, 20 avril 1792) carries it up to 400,000.

[47] Cf. "The French Revolution," Vol. I. book II. Ch. III.

[48] Cf. "The Ancient Régime," p.352.

[49] "Memoires de Madame de Sapinaud," p. 18. Reply of M. de Sapinaud to the peasants of La Vendée, who wished him to act as their general: "My friends, it is the earthen pot against the iron pot. What could we do? One department against eighty–two – we should be smashed!"

[50] Malouet, II. 241. "I knew a clerk in one of the bureaus, who, during these sad days "September, 1792), never missed going. as usual, to copy and add up his registers. Ministerial correspondence with the armies and the provinces followed its regular course in regular forms. The Paris police looked after supplies and kept its eye on sharpers, while blood ran in the streets." — Cf. on this mechanical need and inveterate habit of receiving orders from the central authority, Mallet du Pan, "Mémoires," 490: "Dumouriez' soldiers said to him: 'F—, papa general, get the Convention to order us to march on Paris and you'll see how we will make mince–meat of those b— in the Assembly!'"

[51] With want great interest did any aspiring radical politicians read these lines, whether the German socialist from Hitler learned so much or Lenin during his long stay in Paris around 1906. Taine maybe thought that he was arming decent men to better understand and defend the republic against a new Jacobin onslaught while, in fact, he provided them with an accurate recipe for repeating the revolution. (SR).

[52] At. Matthew, 17:20. (SR.)

[53] Buchez et Roux, XXVIII 55. Letter by Brun–Lafond, a grenadier in the national guard, July 14, 1793, to a friend in the provinces, in justification of the 31st of May. The whole of this letter requires to be read. In it are found the ordinary ideas of a Jacobin in relation to history: "Can we ignore, that it is ever the people of Paris which, through its murmurings and righteous insurrections against the oppressive system of many of our kings, has forced them to entertain milder sentiments regarding the

relief of the French people, and principally of the tiller of the soil? . . Without the energy of Paris, Paris and France would now be inhabited solely by slaves, while this beautiful soil would present an aspect as wild and deserted as that of the Turkish empire or that of Germany," which has led us "to confer still greater lustre on this Revolution, by re–establishing on earth the ancient Athenian and other Grecian republics in all their purity. Distinctions among the early people of the earth did not exist; early family ties bound people together who had no ancient founders or origin; they had no other laws in their republics but those which, so to say, inspired them with those sentiments of fraternity experienced by them in the cradle of primitive populations."

[54] Barbaroux, "Mémoires" (Ed. Dauban), 336. — Grégoire, "Mémoires," I. 410.

[55] "La Révolution Française," by Quinet (extracts from the unpublished "Mémoires" of Baudot), II. 209, 211, 421, 620. — Guillon de Montléon I. 445 (speech by Chalier, in the Lyons Central Club, March 23, 1793). "They say that the sans–culottes will go on spilling their blood. This is only the talk of aristocrats. Can a sans–culotte be reached in that quarter? Is he not invulnerable, like the gods whom he replaces on this earth?" — Speech by David, in the Convention, on Barra and Viala: "Under so fine a government woman will bring forth without pain." — Mercier "Le Nouveau Paris," I. 13. "I heard (an orator) exclaim in one of the sections, to which I bear witness: 'Yes, I would take my own head by the hair, cut it off, and, presenting it to the despot, I would say to him: Tyrant, behold the act of a free man!'"

[56] Now, one hundred years later, I consider the tens of thousands of western intellectuals, who, in their old age, seem unable to understand their longtime fascination with Lenin, Stalin and Mao, I cannot help to think that history might be holding similar future surprises in store for us. (SR).

[57] And my lifetime, our Jacobins the communists, have including in their register the distortion, the lie and slander as a regular tool of their trade. (SR).

[58] Lafayette, "Mémoires," I.467 (on the Jacobins of August 10, 1792). "This sect, the destruction of which was desired by nineteen– twentieths of France."— Durand–Maillan, 49. The aversion to the Jacobins after June 20, 1792, was general. "The communes of France, everywhere wearied and dissatisfied with popular clubs, would gladly have got rid of them, that they might no longer be under their control."

[59] The words of Leclerc, a deputy of the Lyons committee in the Jacobin Club at Paris May 12, 1793. "Popular machiavelianism must be established . . . Everything impure must disappear off the French soil. . . I shall doubtless be regarded as a brigand, but there is one way to get ahead of calumny, and that is to exterminate the calumniators."

[60] Buchez et Roux, XXXIV. 204 (testimony of François Lameyrie). "Collection of authentic documents for the History of the Revolution at Strasbourg," II. 210 (speech by Baudot, Frimaire 19, year II., in the Jacobin club at Strasbourg). "Egoists, the heedless, the enemies of liberty, the enemies of all nature should not be regarded as her children. Are not all who oppose the public good, or who do not share it, in the same case? Let us, then, utterly destroy them. . . Were they a million, would not one sacrifice the twenty–fourth part of one's self to get rid of a gangrene which might infect the rest

of the body?.." For these reasons, the orator thinks that every man who is not wholly devoted to the Republic must be put to death. He states that the Republic should at one blow cause the instant disappearance of every friend to kings and feudalism.—Beaulieu, "Essai," V. 200. M. d'Antonelle thought, "like most of the revolutionary clubs, that, to constitute a republic, an approximate equality of property should be established; and to do this, a third of the population should be suppressed." — " This was the general idea among the fanatics of the Revolution. " — Larevellière-Lépaux, "Mémoires," I.150 "Jean Bon St. André . . . suggested that for the solid foundation of the Republic in France, the population should be reduced one-half." He is violently interrupted by Larevellière-Lépeaux, but continues and insists on this. – Guffroy, deputy of the Pas-de-Calais, proposed in his journal a still larger amputation; he wanted to reduce France to five millions of inhabitants.

BOOK SECOND. THE FIRST STAGE OF THE CONQUEST.

CHAPTER I. THE JACOBINS COME INTO IN POWER. – THE ELECTIONS OF 1791. – PROPORTION OF PLACES GAINED BY THEM.

In June, 1791, and during the five following months, the class of active citizens[1] are convoked to elect their representatives, which, as we know, according to the law, are of every kind and degree. In the first place, there are 40,000 members of electoral colleges of the second degree and 745 deputies. Next, there are one-half of the administrators of 83 departments, one-half of the administrators of 544 districts, one-half of the administrators of 41,000 communes, and finally, in each municipality, the mayor and syndic-attorney. Then in each department they have to elect the president of the criminal court and the prosecuting-attorney, and, throughout France, officers of the National Guard; in short, almost the entire body of the agents and depositories of legal authority. The garrison of the public citadel is to be renewed, which is the second and even the third time since 1789. — At each time the Jacobins have crept into the place, in small bands, but this time they enter in large bodies. Pétion becomes mayor of Paris, Manual, syndic-attorney, and Danton the deputy of Manuel. Robespierre is elected prosecuting-attorney in criminal cases. The very first week,[2] 136 new deputies enter their names on the club's register. In the Assembly the party numbers about 250 members. On passing all the posts of the fortress in review, we may estimate the besiegers as occupying one-third of them, and perhaps more. Their siege for two years has been carried on with unerring instinct, the extraordinary spectacle presenting itself of an entire nation legally overcome by a troop of insurgents.[3]

I.

Their siege operations. — Means used by them to discourage the majority of electors and conservative candidates. — Frequency of elections. – Obligation to take the oath.

First of all, they clear the ground, and through the decrees forced out of the Constituent Assembly, they keep most of the majority away from the polls. — On the one hand, under the pretext of better ensuring popular sovereignty, the elections are so multiplied, and held so near together, as to demand of each active citizen one–sixth of his time; such an exaction is very great for hard–working people who have a trade or any occupation,[4] which is the case with the great mass; at all events, with the useful and sane portion of the population. Accordingly, as we have seen, it stays away from the polls, leaving the field open to idlers or fanatics.[5] — On the other hand, by virtue of the constitution, the civic oath, which includes the ecclesiastical oath, is imposed on all electors, for, if any one takes the former and reserves the latter, his vote is thrown out: in November, in the Doubs, the municipal elections of thirty– three communes are invalidated solely on this pretext.[6] Not only forty thousand ecclesiastics are thus rendered unsworn (insermentés), but again, all scrupulous Catholics lose the right of suffrage, these being by far the most numerous in Artois, Doubs and the Jura, in the Lower and Upper Rhine district,[7] in the two Sévres and la Vendée, in the Lower Loire, Morbihan, Finisterre and Côtes du Nord, in Lozère and Ardèche, without mentioning the southern departments.[8] Thus, aided by the law which they have rendered impracticable, the Jacobins, on the one hand, are rid of all sensible voters in advance, counting by millions; and, on the other, aided by a law which they have rendered intolerant, they are rid of the Catholic vote which counts by hundreds of thousands. On entering the electoral lists, consequently, thanks to this double exclusion, they find themselves confronted by only the smallest number of electors.

II.

Annoyances and dangers of public elections. – The constituents excluded from the Legislative body.

Operations must now be commenced against these, and a first expedient consists in depriving them of their candidates. The obligation of taking the oath has already partly provided for this, in Lozère all the officials send in their resignations rather than take the oath;[9] here are men who will not be candidates at the coming elections, for nobody covets a place which he was forced to abandon; in general, the suppression of all party candidatures is effected in no other way than by making the post of a magistrate distasteful. — The Jacobins have successfully adhered to this principle by promoting and taking the lead in innumerable riots against the King, the officials and the clerks, against nobles, ecclesiastics, corn–dealers and land–owners, against every species of public authority whatever its origin. Everywhere the authorities are constrained to tolerate or excuse murders, pillage and arson, or, at the very least, insurrections and disobedience. For two years a mayor runs the risk of being hung on proclaiming martial law; a captain is not sure of his men on marching to protect a tax levy; a judge on the bench is threatened if he condemns the marauders who devastate the national forests. The magistrate, whose duty it is to see that the law is respected, is constantly obliged to strain the law, or allow it to be strained; if refractory, a summary blow dealt by the local Jacobins forces his legal authority to yield to their illegal dictate, so that he has to resign himself to being either their accomplice or their puppet. Such a rôle is intolerable to a man of feeling or conscience. Hence, in 1790 and 1791, nearly all the prominent and reputable men who, in 1789, had seats in the Hôtels–de–villes, or held command in the National Guard, all country–gentlemen, chevaliers of St. Louis, old parliamentarians, the upper bourgeoisie and large landed–proprietors, retire into private life and renounce public functions which are no longer tenable. Instead of offering themselves to public suffrage they avoid it, and the party of order, far from electing the magistracy, no longer even finds candidates for it.

Through an excess of precaution, its natural leaders have been legally disqualified, the principal offices, especially those of deputy and minister, being interdicted beforehand to the influential men in whom we find the little common sense gained by the French people during the past two years.—In the month of June, 1779, even after the irreconcilables had parted company with the "Right," there still remained in the Assembly about 700 members who, adhering to the constitution but determined to repress disorder, would have formed a sensible legislature had they been re-elected. All of these, except a very small group of revolutionaries, had learned something by experience, and, in the last days of their session, two serious events, the king's flight and the riot in the Champ de Mars, had made them acquainted with the defects of their machinery. With this executive instrument in their hands for three months, they see that it is racked, that things are tottering, and that they themselves are being run over by fanatics and the crowd. They accordingly attempt to put on a drag, and several even think of retracing their steps.[10] They cut loose from the Jacobins; of the three or four hundred deputies on the club list in the Rue St. Honoré[11] but seven remain; the rest form at the Feuillants a distinct opposition club, and at their head are the first founders, Duport, the two Lameths, Barnave, the authors of the constitution, all the fathers of the new régime.[12] In the last decree of the Constituent Assembly they loudly condemn the usurpations of popular associations, and not only interdict to these all meddling in administrative or political matters, but likewise any collective petition or deputation.[13] — Here may the friends of order find candidates whose chances are good, for, during two years and more, each in his own district is the most conspicuous, the best accredited, and the most influential man there; he stands well with his electors on account of the popularity of the constitution he has made, and it is very probable that his name would rally to it a majority of votes.—The Jacobins, however, have foreseen this danger: Four months earlier,[14] with the aid of the Court, which never missed an opportunity to ruin itself and everything else,[15] they made the most of the grudges of the conservatives and the wearyness of the Assembly. Tired and disgusted, in a fit of mistaken selflessness, the Assembly, through enthusiasm and taken by surprise, passes an act declaring all its members ineligible for election to the next Assembly dismissing in advance the leaders of the gentlemen's party.

III.

The friends of order deprived of the right of free assemblage. — Violent treatment of their clubs in Paris and the provinces. — Legal prevention of conservative associations.

If the latter (the honest men of the Right), in spite of so many drawbacks, attempt a struggle, they are arrested at the very first step. For, to enter upon an electoral campaign, requires preliminary meetings for conference and to understand each other, while the faculty of forming an association, which the law grants them as a right, is actually withheld from them by their adversaries. As a beginning, the Jacobins hooted at and "stone" the members of the "Right"[16] holding their meetings in the Salon français of the Rue Royale, and, according to the prevailing rule, the police tribunal, "considering that this assemblage is a cause of disturbance, that it produces gatherings in the street, that only violent means can be employed to protect it," orders its dissolution.[17] — Towards the month of August, 1790, a second club is organized, and, this time, composed of the wisest and most liberal men. Malouet and Count Clermont-Tonnerre are at the head of it. It takes the name of "Friends of a Monarchical Constitution," and is desirous of restoring public order by maintaining the reforms which have been reached. All formalities on its part have been complied with. There are already about 800 members in Paris. Subscriptions flow into its treasury. The provinces send in numerous adhesions, and, what is worse than all, bread is distributed by them at a reduced price, by which the people, probably, will be conciliated. Here is a center of opinion and influence, analogous to that of the Jacobin club, which the Jacobins cannot tolerate.[18] M. de Clermont–Tonnerre having leased the summer Vauxhall, a captain in the National Guard notifies the proprietor of it that if he rents it, the patriots of the Palais–Royal will march to it in a body, and close it; fearing that the building will be damaged, he cancels the lease, while the municipality, which fears skirmishes, orders a suspension of the meetings. The club makes a complaint and follows it up, while the letter of the law is so plain that an official authorization of the club is finally granted. Thereupon the Jacobin newspapers and stump–speakers let loose their fury against a future rival that threatens to dispute their empire. On the 23rd of January, 1791, Barnave, in the National Assembly, employing metaphorical language apt to be used as a death–shout, accuses the members of the new club "of giving the people bread that carries poison with it." Four days after this, M. Clermont–Tonnerre's dwelling is assailed by an armed throng. Malouet, on leaving it, is almost dragged from his carriage, and the crowd around him cry out, "There goes the bastard who denounced the people! "– At length, its founders, who, out of consideration for the municipality, have waited two months, hire another hall in the Rue des Petites–Ecuries, and on the 28th of March begin their sessions. "On reaching it," writes one of them, "we found a mob composed of drunkards, screaming boys, ragged women, soldiers exciting them on, and especially those frightful hounds, armed with stout, knotty cudgels, two feet long, which are excellent skull–crackers."[19] The thing was made up beforehand. At first there were only three or four hundred of them, and, ten minutes after, five or six hundred; in a quarter of an hour, there are perhaps four thousand flocking in from all sides; in short, the usual make–up of an insurrection. "The people of the quarter certified that they did not recognize one of the faces." Jokes, insults, cuffs, clubbings, and saber–cuts, — the members of the club "who agreed to come unarmed" being dispersed, while several are knocked down, dragged by the hair, and a dozen or fifteen more are wounded. To justify the attack, white cockades are shown, which, it is pretended, were found in their pockets. Mayor Bailly arrives only when it is all over, and, as a measure of "public order," the municipal authorities have the club of Constitutional Monarchists closed for good.

Owing to these outrages by the faction, with the connivance of the authorities, other similar clubs are suppressed in the same way. There are a good many of them, and in the principal towns —"Friends of Peace," "Friends of the Country," "Friends of the King, of Peace, and of Religion," "Defenders of Religion, Persons, and Property". Magistrates and officers, the most cultivated and polished people, are generally members; in short, the élite of the place. Formerly, meetings took place for conversation and debate, and, being long– established, the club naturally passes over from literature to politics. — The watch–word against all these provincial clubs is given from the Rue St. Honoré.[20] "They are centers of conspiracy, and must be looked after" forthwith, and be at once trodden out. — At one time, as at Cahors,[21] a squad of the National Guard, on its return from an expedition against the neighboring gentry, and to finish its task breaks in on the club, "throws its furniture out of the windows and demolishes the house." — At another time, as at Perpignan, the excited mob surrounds the club, dancing a fandango, and yell out, to the lantern! The club–house is sacked, while eighty of its members, covered with bruises, are shut up in the citadel for their safety.[22] — At another time, as at Aix, the Jacobin club insults its adversaries on their own premises and provokes a scuffle, whereupon the municipality causes the doors of the assailed club to be walled up and issues warrants of arrest against its members. — Always punishment awaits them for whatever violence they have to submit to. Their mere existence seems an offense. At Grenoble, they scarcely assemble before they are dispersed. The fact is, they are suspected of "incivism;" their intentions may not be right; in any event, they cause a division of the place into two camps, and that is enough. In the department of Gard, their clubs are all broken up, by order of the department, because "they are centers of malevolence." At Bordeaux, the municipality, considering that "alarming reports are current of priests and privileged persons returning to town," prohibits all reunions, except that of the Jacobin club. — Thus, "under a system of liberty of the most exalted kind, in the presence of the famous Declaration of the Rights of Man which legitimates whatever is not unlawful," and which postulates equality as the principle of the French constitution, whoever is not a Jacobin is excluded from common rights. An intolerant club sets itself up as a holy church, and proscribes others which have not received from it "orthodox baptism, civic inspiration, and the aptitude of languages." To her alone belongs the right of assemblage, and the right of making proselytes. Conservative, thoughtful men in all towns throughout the kingdom are forbidden to form electoral committees, to possess a tribune, a fund, subscribers and adherents, to cast the weight of their names and common strength into the scale of public opinion, to gather around their permanent nucleus the scattered multitude of sensible people, who would like to escape from the Revolution without falling back into the ancient régime. Let them whisper amongst themselves in corners, and they may still be tolerated, but woe to them if they would leave their lonely retreat to act in concert, to canvass voters, and support a candidate. Up to the day of voting they must remain in the presence of their combined, active, and obstreperous adversaries, scattered, inert, and mute.

IV. Turmoil of the elections of 1790. — Elections in 1791. — Effect of the King's flight.— Domiciliary visits. — Montagne during the electoral period.

Will they at least be able to vote freely on that day? They are not sure of it, and, judging by occurrences during the past year, it is doubtful. — In April, 1790, at Bois d'Aisy, in Burgundy, M. de Bois d'Aisy, a deputy, who had returned from Paris to deposit his vote,[23] was publicly menaced. He was informed that nobles and priests must take no part m the elections, while many were heard to say, in his hearing, that in order to prevent this it would be better to hang him. Not far off; at Ste. Colombe, M. de Viteaux was driven out of the electoral assembly, and then put to death after three hours of torture. The same thing occurred at Semur; two gentlemen were knocked down with clubs and stones, another saved himself with difficulty, and a curé died after being stabbed six times. — A warning for priests and for gentlemen: they had better not vote, and the same good advice may be given to dealers in grain, to land–owners, and every other suspected person. For this is the day on which the people recover their sovereignty; the violent believe that they have the right to do exactly what suits them, nothing being more natural than to exclude candidates in advance who are distrusted, or electors who do not vote as they ought to. — At Villeneuve–St.–Georges, near Paris,[24] a barrister, a man of austere and energetic character, is about to be elected judge by the district electors; the proletariat, however, mistrust a judge likely to condemn marauders, and forty or fifty vagabonds collect together under the windows and cry out: "We don't want him elected." The curé of Crosne, president of the electoral assembly, informs them in vain that the assembled electors represent 90 communes, nearly 100,000 inhabitants, and that "40 persons should not prevail against 100,000. Shouts redouble and the electors renounce their candidate.– At Pau, patriots among the militia[25] forcibly release one of their imprisoned leaders, circulate a list for proscriptions, attack a poll–teller with their fists and afterwards with sabers, until the proscribed hide themselves away; on the following day "nobody is disposed to attend the electoral assembly." – – Things are much worse in 1791. In the month of June, just at the time of the opening of the primary meetings, the king has fled to Varennes, the Revolution seems compromised, civil war and a foreign war loom up on the horizon like two ghosts; the National Guard had everywhere taken up arms, and the Jacobins were making the most of the universal panic for their own advantage. To dispute their votes is no longer the question; it is not well to be visible: among so many turbulent gatherings a popular execution is soon over. The best thing now for royalists, constitutionalists, conservatives and moderates of every kind, for the friends of law and of order, is to stay at home — too happy if they may be allowed to remain there, to which the armed rabble agrees; on the condition of frequently paying them visits.

Consider their situation during the whole of the electoral period, in a calm district, and judge of the rest of France by this corner of it. At Mortagne,[26] a small town of 6,000 souls, the laudable spirit of 1789 still existed up to the journey to Varennes. Among the forty or fifty noble families were a good many liberals. Here, as elsewhere among the gentry, the clergy and the middle class, the philosophic education of the eighteenth century had revived the old provincial spirit of initiative, and the entire upper class had zealously and gratuitously undertaken the public duties which it alone could perform well. District presidents, mayors, and municipal officers, were all chosen from among ecclesiastics and the nobles; the three principal officers of the National Guard were chevaliers of St. Louis, while other grades were filled by the leading people of the community. Thus had the free elections placed authority in the hands of the socially superior, the new order of things resting on the legitimate hierarchy of conditions, educations, and capacities. – But for six months the club, formed out of "a dozen hot-headed, turbulent fellows, under the presidency and in the hands of a certain Rattier, formerly a cook," worked upon the population and the rural districts. Immediately on the receipt of the news of the King's flight, the Jacobins "give out that nobles and priests had supplied him with money for his departure, to bring about a counter-revolution." One family had given such an amount, and another so much; there was no doubt about it; the precise figures are given, and given for each family according to its known resources.— Forthwith, "the principal clubbists, associated with the dubious part of the National Guard," spread through the streets in squads: the houses of the nobles and of other suspected persons are invaded. All the arms, "guns, pistols, swords, hunting-knives, and sword-canes," are carried off. Every hole and corner is ransacked; they make the inmates open, or they force open, secretaries and clothes-presses in search of ammunition, the search extending "even to the ladies' toilette-tables". By way of precaution "they break sticks of pomatum in two, presuming that musket-balls are concealed in them, and they take away hair-powder under the pretext that it is either colored or masked gunpowder." Then, without disbanding, the troop betakes itself to the environs and into the country, where it operates with the same promptness in the chateaux, so that "in one day all honest citizens, those with the most property and furniture to protect, are left without arms at the mercy of the first robber that comes along." All reputed aristocrats are disarmed. As such are considered those who "disapprove of the enthusiasm of the day, or who do not attend the club, or who harbor any unsworn ecclesiastic," and, first of all, "the officers of the National Guard who are nobles, beginning with the commander and his entire staff." — The latter allow their swords to be taken without resistance, and with a forbearance and patriotic spirit of which their brethren everywhere furnish an example "they are obliging enough to remain at their posts so as not to disorganize the army, hoping that this frenzy will soon come to an end," contenting themselves with making their complaint to the department. — But in vain the department orders their arms to be restored to them. The clubbists refuse to give them up so long as the king refuses to accept the Constitution; meanwhile they do not hesitate to say that "at the very first gun on the frontier, they will cut the throats of all the nobles and unsworn priests." — After the royal oath to the Constitution is taken, the department again insists, but no attention is paid to it. On the contrary, the National Guard, dragging cannons along with them, purposely station themselves before the mansions of the unarmed gentry; the ladies of their families are followed in the streets by urchins who sing ÇA IRA[27] in their faces, and, in the final refrain, they mention them by name and promise them the lantern; "not one of them could invite a dozen of his friends to supper without incurring the risk of an uproar." — On the strength of this, the old chiefs of the National Guard resign, and the Jacobins turn the opportunity to account. In contempt of the law the whole body of officers is renewed, and, as peaceable folks dare not deposit their votes, the new staff "is composed of maniacs, taken for the most part, from the lowest class." With this purged militia the club expels nuns, drives off unsworn priests, organizes expeditions in the neighborhood, and goes so far as to purify suspected municipalities.[28] — So many acts of violence committed in town and country, render town and country uninhabitable, and for the élite of the propriety owners, or for well-bred persons, there is no longer any asylum but Paris. After the first disarmament seven or eight families take refuge there, and a dozen or fifteen more join them after a threat of having their throats cut; after the religious persecution, unsworn ecclesiastics, the rest of the nobles, and countless other townspeople, "even with little means," betake themselves there in a mass. There, at least, one is lost in the crowd; one is protected by an incognito against the outrages of the commonalty; one can live there as a private individual. In the provinces even civil rights do not exist; how could any one there exercise political rights? "All honest citizens are kept away from the primary meetings by threats or maltreatment . . . The electoral battlefield is left for those who pay forty-five sous of taxes, more than one-half of them being registered on the poor list." – Thus the elections are decided beforehand! The former cook is the one who authorizes or creates candidatures, and on the election of the department deputies at the county town, the electors elected are, like himself, true Jacobins.[29]

V.

Intimidation and withdrawal of the Conservatives. — Popular outbreaks in Burgundy, Lyonnais, Provence, and the large cities. — Electoral proceedings of the Jacobins; examples at Aix, Dax, and Montpellier. — Agitators go unpunishes — Denunciations by name. — Manoeuvres with the peasantry. — General tactics of the Jacobins.

Such is the pressure under which voting takes place in France during the summer and fall of 1791. Domiciliary visits[30] and disarmament everywhere force nobles and ecclesiastics, landed proprietors and people of culture, to abandon their homes, to seek refuge in the large towns and to emigrate,[31] or, at least, confine themselves strictly to private life, to abstain from all propaganda, from every candidature, and from all voting. It would be madness to be seen in so many cantons where searches end in a riot; in Burgundy and the Lyonnais, where castles are sacked, where aged gentlemen are mauled and left for dead, where M. de Guillin has just been assassinated and cut to pieces; at Marseilles, where conservative party leaders are imprisoned, where a regiment of Swiss guards under arms scarcely suffices to enforce the verdict of the court which sets them at liberty, where, if any indiscreet person opposes Jacobin resolutions his mouth is closed by being notified that he will be buried alive; at Toulon, where the Jacobins shoot down all conservatives and the regular troops, where M. de Beaucaire, captain in the navy, is killed by a shot in the back, where the club, supported by the needy, by sailors, by navvies, and "vagabond peddlers," maintains a dictatorship by right of conquest; at Brest, at Tulle, at Cahors, where at this very moment gentlemen and officers are massacred in the street. It is not surprising that honest people turn away from the ballot–box as from a center of cut–throats. — Nevertheless, let them come if they like; it will be easy to get rid of them. At Aix, the assessor whose duty it is to read the electors' names is informed that "the names should be called out by an unsullied mouth, that, being an aristocrat and fanatical, he could neither speak nor vote," and, without further ceremony, they put him out of the room.[32] The process is an admirable one for converting a minority into a majority and yet here is another, still more effective. — At Dax, the Feuillants, taking the title of "Friends of the French Constitution," have split up with the Jacobins,[33] and, moreover, they insist on excluding from the National Guard "foreigners without property or position," the passive citizens who are admitted into it in spite of the law, who usurp the right of voting and who "daily affront tranquil inhabitants." Consequently, on election day, in the church where the primary meeting is held, two of the Feuillants, Laurède, formerly collector of the vingtièmes,, and Brunache, a glazier, propose to exclude an intruder, a servant on wages. The Jacobins at once rush forward. Laurède is pressed back on the holy–water basin and wounded on the head; on trying to escape he is seized by the hair, thrown down, pierced in the arm with a bayonet, put in prison, and Brunache along with him. Eight days afterwards, at the second meeting none are present but Jacobins; naturally, "they are all elected". They form the new municipality, which, notwithstanding the orders of the department, not only refuses to liberate the two prisoners, but throws them into a dungeon. — At Montpellier, the delay in the operation is greater, but it is only the more complete. The votes are deposited, the ballot–boxes closed and sealed up and the conservatives obtain a majority. Thereupon the Jacobin club, with the Society of the "iron–clubs," calling itself the Executive power, betake themselves in force to the sectional meetings, burn one of the ballots, use firearms and kill two men. To restore order the municipality stations each company of the National Guard at its captain's door, The moderates among them naturally obey orders, but the violent party do not. They overrun the town, numbering about 2,000 inhabitants, enter the houses, kill three men in the street or in their domiciles, and force the administrative body to suspend its electoral assemblies. In addition to this they require the disarmament "of the aristocrats," and this not being done soon enough, they kill an artisan who is walking in the street with his mother, cut off his head, bear it aloft in triumph, and suspend it in front of his dwelling. The authorities are now convinced and accordingly decree a disarmament, and the victors parade the streets in a body. In exuberance or as a precaution, they fire, as they pass along, at the windows of suspected houses and happen to kill an additional man and woman. During the three following days six hundred families emigrate, while the authorities report that everything is going on well, and that order is restored. "The elections," they say, "are now proceeding in the quietest manner since the ill–intentioned voluntarily keeping away from them, a large number having left the town. "[34] A void is created around the ballot–box and this is called the unanimity of voters. — The effect of such assassinations is great and only a few are required; especially when they go unpunished, which is always the case. Henceforth all that the Jacobins have to do is to threaten; people no longer resist them for they know that it costs too much to face them down. They do not care to attend electoral meetings where they meet insult and danger; they acknowledge defeat at the start. Have not the Jacobins irresistible arguments, without taking blows into account? At Paris,[35] Marat in three successive numbers of his paper has just denounced by name "the rascals and thieves" who canvass for electoral nominations, not the nobles and priests but ordinary citizens, lawyers, architects, physicians, jewellers, stationers, printers, upholsterers and other artisans, each name being given in full with the professions, addresses and one of the following qualifications, "hypocrite (tartufe), immoral, dishonest, bankrupt, informer, usurer, cheat," not to mention others that I cannot write down. It must be noted that this slanderous list may become a proscriptive list, and that in every town and village in France similar lists are constantly drawn up and circulated by the local dub, which enables us to judge whether the struggle between it and its adversaries is a fair one.–As to rural electors, it has suitable means for persuading them, especially in the innumerable cantons ravaged or threatened by the jacqueries, (country– riots) or, for example, in Corrèze, where "the whole department is smattered with insurrections and devastation's, and where nobody talks of anything but of hanging the officers who serve papers."[36] Through–out the electoral operations the sittings of the dub are permanent; "its electors are incessantly summoned to its meetings; " at each of these "the main question is the destruction of fish–ponds and rentals, their principal speakers summing it all up by saying that none ought to be paid." The majority of electors, composed of rustics, are found to be sensitive to speeches like this; all its candidates are obliged to express themselves against fishponds and rentals; its deputies and the public prosecuting attorney are nominated on this profession of faith; in other words, to be elected, the Jacobins promise to greedy tenants the incomes and property of their owners. — We already see in the proceedings by which they secure one–third of the offices in 1791 the germ of the methods by which they will secure the whole of them in 1792; in this first electoral campaign their acts indicate not merely their maxims and policy but, again, the condition, education, spirit and character of the men whom they place in power locally as well as at the capital.

NOTES:

[1] Law of May 28, 29, 1791 (according to official statements, the total of active citizens amounted to 4,288,360). — Laws of July 23, Sept. 12, Sept. 29, 1791. — Buchez et Roux, XII. 310.

[2] Bucher Ct Roux, XII. 33. — Mortimer–Ternaux, "Histoire de la Terreur," II. 205, 348. — Sauzay, II. ch. XVIII — Albert Babeau, I. ch. XX.

[3] Lenin repeated this performance in 1917 and Stalin attempted to do the same in the rest of the World. (SR)..

[4] The following letter, by Camille Desmoulins (April 3, 1792), shows at once the time consumed by public affairs, the sort of attraction they had, and the kind of men which they diverted from their business. "I have gone back to my old profession of the law, to which I give nearly all the time which my municipal or electoral functions, and the Jacobins (club), allow me — that is to say, very little. It is very disagreeable to me to come down to pleading bourgeois cases after having managed interests of such importance, and the affairs of the government, in the face of all Europe."

[5] I cannot help but think of the willful proliferation of idle functionaries, pensioners and other receivers of public funds which today vote for the party which represents their interests. (SR.)

[6] Sauzay, II. 83–89 and 123. A resolution of the inhabitants of Chalèze, who, headed by their municipal officers, declare themselves unanimously "non–conformists," and demand "the right of using a temple for the exercise of their religious opinions, belonging to them and built with their contributions" On the strength of this, the municipal officers of Chalèze are soundly rated by the

district administration, which thus states what principles are: "Liberty, indefinite for the private individual, must be restricted for the public man whose opinions must conform to the law: otherwise, . . he must renounce all public functions."

[7] Archives Nationales," F7, 3,253 (letter of the department directory, April 7, 1792). "On the 25th of January, in our report to the National Assembly, we stated the almost general opposition which the execution of the laws relating to the clergy has found in this department . . . nine–tenths, at least, of the Catholics refusing to recognize the sworn priests. The teachers, influenced by their old curés or vicars, are willing to take the civic oath, but they refuse to recognize their legitimate pastors and attend their services. We are, therefore, obliged to remove them, and to look out for others to replace them. The citizens of a large number of the communes, persisting in trusting these, will lend no assistance whatever to the election of the new ones; the result is, that we are obliged, in selecting these people, to refer the matter to persons whom we scarcely know, and who are scarcely better known to the directories of the district. As they are elected against the will of the citizens, they do not gain their confidence, and draw their salaries from the commune treasury, without any advantage to public instruction,"

[8] Mercure de France, Sep. 3, 1791. "The right of attending primary meetings is that of every citizen who pays a tax of three livres; owing to the violence to which opinions are subject, more than one–half of the French are compelled to stay away from these reunions, which are abandoned to persons who have the least interest in maintaining public order and in securing stable laws, with the least property, and who pay the fewest taxes."

[9] "The French Revolution," Vol. I. p. 182 and following pages.

[10] "Correspondence of M. de Staël" (manuscript), Swedish ambassador, with his court, Sept 4, 1791. "The change in the way of thinking of the democrats is extraordinary; they now seem convinced that it is impossible to make the Constitution work. Barnave, to my own knowledge, has declared that the influence of assemblies in the future should be limited to a council of notables, and that all power should be in the government"

[11] Ibid. Letter of July 17, 1791. "All the members of the Assembly, with the exception of three or four, have passed a resolution to separate from the Jacobins; they number about 3oo." — The seven deputies who remain at the Jacobin Club, are Robespierre, Pétion, Grégoire, Buzot, Coroller, and Abbé Royer.

[12] "Les Feuillants" Was a political club consisting of constitutional monarchists who held their meetings in the former Feuillants monastery in Paris from 1791 to 1792. (SR).

[13] Decree of Sept 29, 30, 1791, with report and instructions of the Committee on the Constitution.

[14] Decree of May 17, 1791. — Malouet, XII. 161. 'There was nothing left to us but to make one great mistake, which we did not fail to do."

[15] A few months after this, on the election of a mayor for Paris, the court voted against Lafayette,

and for Pétion

[16] M. de Montlosier, "Mémoires," II. 309. "As far as concerns myself, truth compels me to say, that I was stuck on the head by three carrots and two cabbages only." — Archives of the prefecture of police (decisions of the police court, May 15, 1790). Moniteur, V. 427. "The prompt attendance of the members at the hour of meeting, in spite of the hooting and murmurings of the crowd, seemed to convince the people that this was yet another conspiracy against liberty."

[17] This is what is, today in 1998, taking place whenever any political faction, disliked by the Socialists, try to arrange a meeting. (SR).

[18] Malout, II. 50. – Mercure de France, Jan. 7, Feb. 5, and April 9, 1791 (letter of a member of the Monarchical Club

[19] Ferrières, II. 222. "The Jacobin Club sent five or six hundred trusty men, armed with clubs," besides "about a hundred national guards, and some of the Palais–Royal prostitutes."

[20] Journal des Amis de la Constitution." Letter of the Café National! Club at Bordeaux, Jan. 20, 1791. — Letters of the "Friends of the Constitution," at Brives and Cambray, Jan. 19, 1791.

[21] "The French Revolution," I. pp. 243, 324.

[22] Mercure de France, Dec.18, 1790, Jan. 17, June 8, and July 14, 1791. — Moniteur, VI. 697. — "Archives Nationales," F7, 3,193. Letter from the Directory of the department of Aveyron, April 20, 1792. Narrative of events after the end of 1790. — May 22, 1791, the club of "The Friends of Order and Peace" is burned by the Jacobins, the fire lasting all night and a part of the next day. (Official report of the Directory of Milhau, May 22, 1791).

[23] "The French Revolution," I. 256, 307.

[24] Mercure de France, Dec. 14, 1790 (letter from Villeneuve–St.– Georges, Nov.29).

[25] "Archives Nationales," II. 1,453. Correspondence of M. Bercheny. Letter from Pau, Feb. 7, 1790. "No one has any idea of the actual state of things, in this once delightful town. People are cutting each other's throats. Four duels have taken place within 48 hours, and ten or a dozen good citizens have been obliged to hide themselves for three days past"

[26] "Archives Nationales," F7, 3,249. Memorial on the actual condition of the town and district of Mortagne, department of Orne (November, 1791).

[27] Revolutionary song with the refrain: "Les aristocrates, à la lanterne, tous les aristocrates on les pendra" (all the aristocrats will hang). (SR)

[28] On the 15th of August, 1791, the mother–superior of the Hôtel– Dieu hospital is forcibly carried off and placed in a tavern, half a league from the town, while the rest of the nuns are driven out and

replaced by eight young girls from the town. Among other motives that require notice is the hostility of two pharmacists belonging to the club; in the Hotel–Dieu the nuns, keeping a pharmacy from which they sold drugs at cost and thereby brought themselves into competition with the two pharmacists.

[29] Cf. "Archives Nationales," DXXIX. 13. Letter of the municipal officers and notables of Champceuil to the administrators of Seine–et– Oise, concerning elections, June 17, 1791. — Similar letters, from various other parishes, among them that of Charcon, June 16: "They have the honor to inform you that, at the time of the preceding primary meetings, they were exposed to the greatest danger; that the curé of Charcon, their pastor, was repeatedly stabbed with a bayonet, the marks of which he will carry to his grave. The mayor, and several other inhabitants of Charcon, escaped the same peril with difficulty." – Ibid., letters from the administrators of Hautes–Alpes to the National Assembly (September, 1791), on the disturbances in the electoral assembly of Gap, August 29, 1791.

[30] Police searches of private homes. (SR).

[31] "The French Revolution," pp. 159, 160, 310, 323, 324. – Lauvergne, "Histoire du département du Var," (August 23).

[32] '"Archives Nationales," F7, 3,198, deposition of Vérand–Icard, an elector at Arles, Sep. 8, 1791. – Ibid., F7, 3,195. Letter of the administrators of the Tarascon district, Dec. 8, 1791. Two parties confront each other at the municipal elections of Barbantane, one headed by the Abbé Chabaud, brother of one of the Avignon brigands, composed of three or four townsmen, and of "the most impoverished in the country," and the other, three times as numerous, comprising all the land–owners, the substantial métayers and artisans, and all "who are most interested in a good administration" The question is, whether the Abbé Chabaud is to be mayor. The elections took place Dec.5th, 1791. Here is the official report of the acting mayor: mayor: "We, Pierre Fontaine, mayor, addressed the rioters, to induce them to keep the peace. At this very moment, the said Claude Gontier, alias Baoque, struck us with his fist on the left eye, which bruised us considerably, and on account of which we are almost blind, and, conjointly with others, jumped upon us, threw us down, and dragged us by the hair, continuing to strike us, from in front of the church door, till we came in front of the door a, the town hall."

[33] Ibid., F7, 3,229. Letters of M. de Laurède, June 18, 1791; from the directory of the department, June 8, July 31, and Sept. 22, 1791; from the municipality, July 15, 1791. The municipality "leaves the release of the prisoners in suspense," for six months, because, it says, the people is disposed to "insurrectionise against their discharge." – Letter of many of the national guard, stating that the factions form only a part of it.

[34] Mercure de France, Dec. 10, 1791, letter from Montpellier, dated Nov. 17, 1791. — " Archives Nationales," F7, 3,223. Extracts from letters, on the incidents of Oct. 9 and 12, 1791. Petition by Messrs. Théri and Devon, Nov. 17, 1791. Letter addressed them to the Minister, Oct. 25. Letters of M. Dupin, syndical attorney of the department, to the Minister, Nov.14 and 15, and Dec. 26, 1791 (with official reports). — Among those assassinated on the 14th and 15th of November, we find a jeweler, an attorney, a carpenter, and a dyer. "This painful Scene," writes the syndic attorney, "has

restored quiet to the town."

[35] Buchez et Roux, X. 223 (l'Ami du Peuple, June 17, 19, 21, 1791)

[36] "'Archives Nationales,' F7, 3204. letter by M. Melon de Tradou, royal commissary at Tulle, Sept. 8, 1791

CHAPTER II. THE LEGISLATIVE ASSEMBLY

I. Composition of the Legislative Assembly. — Social rank of the Deputies. Their inexperience, incompetence, and prejudices.

If it be true that a nation should be represented by its superior men, France was strangely represented during the Revolution. From one Assembly to another we see the level steadily declining; especially is the fall very great from the Constituent to the Legislative Assembly. The actors entitled to perform withdraw just as they begin to understand their parts; and yet more, they have excluded themselves from the theatre, while the stage is surrendered to their substitutes.

"The preceding Assembly," writes an ambassador,[1] "contained men of great talent, large fortune, and honorable name, a combination which had an imposing effect on the people, although violently opposed to personal distinctions. The actual Assembly is but little more than a council of lawyers, got together from every town and village in France."

In actual fact, out of 745 deputies, indeed, "400 lawyers belong, for the most part, to the dregs of the profession"; there are about twenty constitutional priests, "as many poets and literary men of but little reputation, almost all without any fortune," the greater number being less than thirty years old, sixty being less than twenty–six,[2] nearly all of them trained in the clubs and the popular assemblies". There is not one noble or prelate belonging to the ancient régime, no great landed proprietor,[3] no head of a service, no eminent specialist in diplomacy, in finance, in the administrative or military arts. But three general officers are found there, and these are of the lower rank,[4] one of them having held his appointment but three months, and the other two being wholly unknown. — At the head of the diplomatic committee stands Brissot, itinerant journalist, lately traveling about in England and the United States. He is supposed to be competent in the affairs of both worlds; in reality he is one of those presuming, threadbare, talkative fellows, who, living in a garret, lecture foreign cabinets and reconstruct all Europe. Things, to them, seem to be as easily worked out as words and sentences: one day,[5] to entice the English into an alliance with France, Brissot proposes to place two towns, Dunkirk and Calais, in their hands as security; another day, he proposes "to make a descent on Spain, and, at the same time, to send a fleet to conquer Mexico." — The leading member on the committee on finances is Cambon, a merchant from Montpellier, a good accountant, who, at a later period, is to simplify accounting and regulate the Grand Livre of the public debt, which means public bankruptcy. Mean–while, he hastens this on with all his might by encouraging the Assembly to undertake the ruinous and terrible war that is to last for twenty–three years; according to him, "there is more money than is needed for it."[6] In actual fact, the guarantee of assignats is used up and the taxes do not come in. They live only on the paper money they issue. The assignats lose forty per centum, and the ascertained deficit for 1792 is four hundred millions.[7] But this revolutionary financier relies upon the confiscations which he instigates in France, and which are to be set agoing in Belgium; here lies all his invention, a systematic robbery on a grand scale within and without the kingdom.

As to the legislators and manufacturers of constitutions, we have Condorcet, a cold—blooded fanatic and systematic leveler, satisfied that a mathematical method suits the social sciences fed on abstractions, blinded by formulœ, and the most chimerical of perverted intellects. Never was a man versed in books more ignorant of mankind; never did a lover of scientific precision better succeed in changing the character of facts. It was he who, two days before the 20th of June, amidst the most brutal public excitement, admired "the calmness" and rationality of the multitude; "considering the way people interpret events, it might be supposed that they had given some hours of each day to the study of analysis." It is he who, two days after the 20th of June, extolled the red cap in which the head of Louis XVI. had been muffled. "That crown is as good as any other. Marcus Aurelius would not have despised it."[8] — Such is the discernment and practical judgment of the leaders; from these one can form an opinion of the flock. It consists of novices arriving from the provinces and bringing with them the principles and prejudices of the newspaper. So remote from the center, having no knowledge of general affairs or of their unity, they are two years behind their brethren of the Constituent Assembly. They are described in the following manner by Malouet,[9]

"Most of them, without having decided against a monarchy, had decided against the court, the aristocracy, and the clergy, ever imagining conspiracies and believing that defense consisted solely in attack. There were still many men of talent among them, but with no experience; they even lacked that which we had obtained. Our patriot deputies, in great part, were aware of their errors; the novices were not, they were ready to begin all over again."

Moreover, they have their own political bent, for nearly all of them are upstarts of the new régime. We find in their ranks 264 department administrators, 109 district administrators, 125 justices and prosecuting—attorneys, 68 mayors and town officers, besides about twenty officers of the National Guard, constitutional bishops and curés. The whole amounting to 566 of the elected functionaries, who, for the past twenty months, have carried on the government under the direction of their electors. We have seen how this was done and under what conditions, with what compliances and with what complicity, with what deference to clamorous opinion, with what docility in the presence of rioters, with what submission to the orders of the mob, with what a deluge of sentimental phrases and commonplace abstractions. Sent to Paris as deputies, through the choice or toleration of the clubs, they bear along with them their politics and their rhetoric. The result is an assemblage of narrow, perverted, hasty, inflated and feeble minds; at each daily session, twenty word— mills turn to no purpose, the greatest of public powers at once becoming a manufactory of nonsense, a school of extravagancies, and a theatre for declamation.

II.

Degree and quality of their intelligence and Culture.

Is it possible that serious men could have listened to such weird nonsense until the bitter end?

"I am a tiller of the soil,"[10] says one deputy, "I now dare speak of the antique nobility of my plow.

A yoke of oxen once constituted the pure, incorruptible legal worthies before whom my good ancestors executed their contracts, the authenticity of which, far better recorded on the soil than on flimsy parchment, is protected from any species of revolution whatever."

Is it conceivable that the reporter of a law, that is about to exile or imprison forty thousand priests, should employ in an argument such silly bombast as the following?[11]

"I have seen in the rural districts the hymeneal torch diffusing only pale and somber rays, or, transformed into the flambeaux of furies, the hideous skeleton of superstition seated even on the nuptial couch, placed between nature and the wedded, and arresting, etc. . . . Oh Rome, art thou satisfied? Art thou then like Saturn, to whom fresh holocausts were daily imperative? . . . Depart, ye creators of discord! The soil of liberty is weary of bearing you. Would ye breathe the atmosphere of the Aventine mount? The national ship is already prepared for you. I hear on the shore the impatient cries of the crew; I see the breezes of liberty swelling its sails. Like Telemachus, ye will go forth on the waters to seek your father; but never will you have to dread the Sicilian rocks, nor the seductions of a Eucharis."

Courtesies of pedants, rhetorical personifications, and the invective of maniacs is the prevailing tone. The same defect characterizes the best speeches, namely, an overexcited brain, a passion for high–sounding terms, the constant use of stilts and an incapacity for seeing things as they are and of so describing them. Men of talent, Isnard, Guadet, Vergniaud himself, are carried away by hollow sonorous phrases like a ship with too much canvas for its ballast. Their minds are stimulated by souvenirs of their school lessons, the modern world revealing itself to them only through their Latin reminiscences. — François de Nantes is exasperated at the pope "who holds in servitude the posterity of Cato and of Scœvola." — Isnard proposes to follow the example of the Roman senate which, to allay discord at home, got up an outside war: between old Rome and France of 1792, indeed, there is a striking resemblance. — Roux insists that the Emperor (of Austria) should give satisfaction before the 1st of March; "in a case like this the Roman people would have fixed the term of delay; why shouldn't the French people fix one? . . ." "The circle of Popilius" should be drawn around those petty, hesitating German princes. When money is needed to establish camps around Paris and the large towns, Lasource proposes to dispose of the national forests and is amazed at any objection to the measure. "Cœsar's soldiers," he exclaims, "believing that an ancient forest in Gaul was sacred, dared not lay the axe to it; are we to share their superstitious respect?"[12] —— Add to this collegiate lore the philosophic dregs deposited in all minds by the great sophist then in vogue. Larivière reads in the tribune[13] that page of the "Contrat Social," where Rousseau declares that the sovereign may banish members "of an unsocial religion," and punish with death "one who, having publicly recognized the dogmas of civil religion, acts as if he did not believe in them." On which, another hissing parrot, M. Filassier, exclaims, "I put J. J. Rousseau's proposition into the form of a motion and demand a vote on it." — In like manner it is proposed to grant very young girls the right of marrying in spite of their parents by stating, according to the "Nouvelle Héloise"

"that a girl thirteen or fourteen years old begins to sigh for the union which nature dictates. She struggles between passion and duty, so that, if she triumphs, she becomes a martyr, something that is rare in nature. It may happen that a young person prefers the serene shame of defeat to a wearisome eight year long struggle."

Divorce is inaugurated to "preserve in matrimony that happy peace of mind which renders the sentiments livelier."[14] Henceforth this will no longer be a chain but "the acquittance of an agreeable debt which every citizen owes to his country. . . Divorce is the protecting spirit of marriage."[15]

On a background of classic pedantry, with only vague and narrow notions of ordinary instruction, lacking exact and substantial information, flow obscenities and enlarged commonplaces enveloped in a mythological gauze, spouting in long tirades as maxims from the revolutionary manual. Such is the superficial culture and verbal argumentation from which vulgar and dangerous ingredients the intelligence of the new legislators is formed.[16]

III.

Aspects of their sessions. — Scenes and display at the club. — Co- operation of spectators.

From this we can imagine what their sessions were. "More in-coherent and especially more passionate than those of the Constituent Assembly"[17] they present the same but intensified characteristics. The argument is weaker, the invective more violent, and the dogmatism more intemperate. Inflexibility degenerates into insolence, prejudice into fanaticism, and near-sightedness into blindness. Disorder becomes a tumult and constant din an uproar. Suppose, says an eye- witness,

"a classroom with hundreds of pupils quarreling and every instant on the point of seizing each other by the hair. Their dress neglected, their attitudes angry, with sudden transitions from shouting to hooting . . is a sight hard to imagine and to which nothing can be compared."

It lacks nothing for making it a club of the lowest species. Here, in advance, we contemplate the ways of the future revolutionary inquisition. They welcome burlesque denunciations; enter into petty police investigations; weigh the tittle-tattle of porters and the gossip of servant-girls; devote an all-night session to the secrets of a drunkard.[18] They enter on their official report and without any disapproval, the petition of M. Huré, "living at Pont-sur-Yonne, who, over his own signature, offers one hundred francs and his arm to become a killer of tyrants." Repeated and multiplied hurrahs and applause with the felicitations of the president is the sanction of scandalous or ridiculous private misconduct seeking to display itself under the cover of public authority. Anacharsis Clootz, "a Mascarille officially stamped," who proposes a general war and who hawks about maps of Europe cut up in advance into departments beginning with Savoy, Belgium and Holland "and thus onward to the Polar Sea," is thanked and given a seat on the benches of the Assembly.[19] Compliments are made to the Vicar of Sainte-Marguerite and his wife is given a seat in the Assembly and who, introducing "his new family," thunders against clerical celibacy.[20] Crowds of men and women are permitted to traverse the hall letting out political cries. Every sort of indecent, childish and seditious parade is admitted to the bar of the house.[21] To-day it consists of "citoyennes of Paris," desirous of being drilled in military exercises and of having for their commandants "former French guardsmen;" to-morrow children come and express their patriotism with "touching simplicity," regretting that "their trembling feet do not permit them to march, no, fly against the tyrants;" next to these come convicts of the Château – Vieux escorted by a noisy crowd; at another time the artillerymen of Paris, a thousand in number, with drums beating; delegates from the provinces, the faubourgs and the clubs come constantly, with their furious harangues, and imperious remonstrances, their exactions, their threats and their summonses. — In the intervals between the louder racket a continuous hubbub is heard in the clatter of the tribunes.[22] At each session "the representatives are chaffed by the spectators; the nation in the gallery is judge of the nation on the floor;" it interferes in the debates, silences the speakers, insults the president and orders the reporter of a bill to quit the tribune. One interruption, or a simple murmur, is not all; there are twenty, thirty, fifty in an hour, clamoring, stamping, yells and personal abuse. After countless useless entreaties, after repeated calls to order, "received with hooting," after a dozen "regulations that are made, revised, countermanded and posted up" as if better to prove the impotence of the law, of the authorities and of the Assembly itself, the usurpations of these intruders keep on increasing. They have shouted for ten months "Down with the civil list! Down with the ministerials! Down with those curs! Silence, slaves!' On the 26th of July, Brissot himself is to appear lukewarm and be struck on the face with two plums. "Three or four hundred individuals without either property, title, or means of subsistence . . . have become the auxiliaries, petitioners and umpires of the legislature," their paid violence completely destroying whatever is still left of the Assembly's reason.[23]

IV.

The Parties.– The "Right." – "Center." – The "Left." – Opinions and sentiments of the Girondins. – Their Allies of the extreme "left."

In an assembly thus composed and surrounded, it is easy to foresee on which side the balance will turn. — Through the meshes of the electoral net which the Jacobins have spread over the whole country, about one hundred well–meaning individuals of the common run, tolerably sensible and sufficiently resolute, Mathieu Dumas, Dumolard, Becquet, Gorguereau, Vaublanc, Beugnot, Girardin, Ramond, Jaucourt, were able to pass and form the party of the "Right."[24] They resist to as great an extent as possible, and seem to have obtained a majority. — For, of the four hundred deputies who have their seats in the center, one hundred and sixty–four are inscribed on the rolls with them at the Feuillants club, while the rest, under the title of "Independents," pretend to be of no party.[25] Besides, the whole of these four hundred, through monarchical traditions, respect the King; timid and sensible, violence is repugnant to them. They distrust the Jacobins, dread what is unknown, desire to be loyal to the Constitution and to live in peace. Nevertheless, the pompous dogmas of the revolutionary catechism still have their prestige with them; they cannot comprehend how the Constitution which they like produces the anarchy which they detest; they are "foolish enough to bemoan the effects while swearing to maintain their causes; totally deficient in spirit, in union and in boldness," they float backwards and forwards between contradictory desires, while their predisposition to order merely awaits the steady impulsion of a vigorous will to turn it in the opposite direction. — On such docile material the "Left" can work effectively. It comprises, indeed, but one hundred and thirty–six registered Jacobins and about a hundred others who, in almost all cases, vote with the party;[26] rigidity of opinion, however, more than compensates for lack of numbers. In the front row are Guadet, Brissot, Gensonné, Veygniaud, Ducos, and Condorcet, the future chiefs of the Girondists, all of them lawyers or writers captivated by deductive politics, absolute in their convictions and proud of their faith. According to them principles are true and must be applied without reservation;[27] whoever would stop half–way is wanting in courage or intelligence. As for themselves their minds are made up to push through. With the self–confidence of youth and of theorists they draw their own conclusions and hug themselves with their strong belief in them. "These gentlemen," says a keen observer,[28]

"professed great disdain for their predecessors, the Constituents, treating them as short–sighted and prejudiced people incapable of profiting by circumstances."

"To the observations of wisdom, and disinterested wisdom,[29] they replied with a scornful smile, indicative of the aridity proceeding from self–conceit. One exhausted himself in reminding them of events and in deducing causes from these; one passed in turn from theory to experience and from experience to theory to show them their identity and, when they condescended to reply it was to deny the best authenticated facts and contest the plainest observations by opposing to these a few trite maxims although eloquently expressed. Each regarded the other as if they alone were worthy of being heard, each encouraging the other with the idea that all resistance to their way of looking at things was pusillanimity."

In their own eyes they alone are capable and they alone are patriotic. Because they have read Rousseau and Mably, because their tongue is untied and their pen flowing, because they know how to handle the formulæ of books and reason out an abstract proposition, they fancy that they are statesmen.[30] Because they have read Plutarch and "Le Jeune Anacharsis," because they aim to construct a perfect society out of metaphysical conceptions, because they are in a ferment about the coming millennium, they imagine themselves so many exalted spirits. They have no doubt whatever on these two points even after everything has fallen in through their blunders, even after their obliging hands are sullied by the foul grasp of robbers whom they were the first to instigate, and by that of executioners of which they are partners in complicity.[31] To this extent is self–conceit the worst of sophists. Convinced of their superior enlightenment and of the purity of their sentiments, they put forth the theory that the government should be in their hands. Consequently they lay hold of it in the Legislative body in ways that are going to turn against them in the Convention. They accept for allies the worst demagogues of the extreme "Left," Chabot, Couthon, Merlin, Bazière, Thuriot, Lecointre, and outside of it, Danton, Robespierre, Marat himself, all the levelers and destroyers whom they think of use to them, but of whom they themselves are the instruments. The motions they make must pass at any cost and, to ensure this, they let loose against their adversaries the low, yelping mob which others, still more factious, will to–morrow let loose on them.

V.

Their means of action. — Dispersion of the Feuillants' club.— Pressure of the tribunes on the Assembly. — Street mobs.

Thus, for the second time, the pretended freedom fighters seek power by boldly employing force. — They begin by suppressing the meetings of the Feuillants club.[32] The customary riot is instigated against these, whereupon ensue tumult, violent outcries and scuffles; mayor Pétion complains of his position "between opinion and law," and lets things take their course; finally, the Feuillants are obliged to evacuate their place of meeting. – – Inside the Assembly they are abandoned to the insolence of the galleries. In vain do they get exasperated and protest. Ducastel, referring to the decree of the Constituent Assembly, which forbids any manifestation of approbation or disapprobation, is greeted with murmurs. He insists on the decree being read at the opening of each session, and "the murmurs begin again."[33] "Is it not scandalous," says Vaublanc, "that the nation's representatives speaking from the tribune are subject to hootings like those bestowed upon an actor on the stage!" whereupon the galleries give him three rounds more. "Will posterity believe," says Quatremère, "that acts concerning the honor, the lives, and the fortunes of citizens should be subject, like games in the arena, to the applause and hisses of the spectators!" "Come to the point!" shout the galleries. "If ever," resumes Quatremère, "the most important of judicial acts (an act of capital indictment) can be exposed to this scandalous prostitution of applause and menaces . . . " "The murmurs break out afresh." — Every time that a sanguinary or incendiary measure is to be carried, the most furious and prolonged clamor stops the utterance of its opponents: "Down with the speaker! Send the reporter of that bill to prison! Down! Down! Sometimes only about twenty of the deputies will applaud or hoot with the galleries, and sometimes it is the entire Assembly which is insulted. Fists are thrust in the president's face. All that now remains is "to call down the galleries on the floor to pass decrees," which proposition is ironically made by one of the "Right."[34]

Great, however, as this usurpation may be, the minority, in order to suppress the majority, accommodate themselves to it, the Jacobins in the chamber making common cause with the Jacobins in the galleries. The disturbers should not be put out; "it would be excluding from our deliberations," says Grangeneuve, "that which belongs essentially to the people." On one of the deputies demanding measures to enforce silence, "Torné demands that the proposition be referred to the Portugal inquisition." Choudieu "declares that it can only emanate from deputies who forget that respect which is due to the people, their sovereign judge."[35] "The action of the galleries," says Lecointe–Puyraiveaux, "is an outburst of patriotism." Finally, this same Choudieu, twisting and turning all rights about with incomparable audacity, wishes to confer legislative privileges on the audience, and demands a decree against the deputies who, guilty of popular lèse– majesté, presume to complain of those who insult them. — Another piece of oppressive machinery, still more energetic, operates outside on the approaches to the Assembly. Like their predecessors of the Constituent Assembly, the members of the "Right" "cannot leave the building without encountering the threats and imprecations of enraged crowds. Cries of 'to the lantern!' greet the ears of Dumolard, Vaublanc, Raucourd, and Lacretelle as often as those of the Abbé Maury and Montlosier."[36] After having hurled abuse at the president, Mathieu Dumas, they insult his wife who has been recognized in a reserved gallery.[37] In the Tuileries, crowds are always standing there listening to the brawlers who denounce suspected deputies by name, and woe to any among them who takes that path on his way to the chamber! A broadside of insults greets him as he passes along. If the deputy happens to be a farmer, they exclaim: "Look at that queer old aristocrat — an old peasant dog that used to watch cows!" One day Hua, on going up the steps of the Tuileries terrace, is seized by the hair by an old vixen who bids him "Bow your head to your sovereigns, the people, you bastard of a deputy!" On the 20th of June one of the patriots, who is crossing the Assembly room, whispers in his ear, "You scamp of a deputy, you'll never die but by my hand!" Another time, having defended the juge–de–paix Larivière, there awaits him at the door, in the middle of the night, "a set of blackguards, who crowd around him and thrust their fists and cudgels in his face;" happily, his friends Dumas and Daverhoult, two military officers, foreseeing the danger, present their pistols and set him free "although with some difficulty." — As the 10th of August draws near there is more open aggression. Vaublanc, for having defended Lafayette, just misses being cut to pieces three times on leaving the Assembly; sixty of the deputies are treated in the same fashion, being struck, covered with mud, and threatened with death if they dare go back.[38] — With such allies a minority is very strong. Thanks to its two agencies of constraint it will detach the votes it needs from the majority and, either through terror or craft, secure the passage of all the decrees it needs.

VI.

Parliamentary maneuvers. — Abuses of urgency. — Vote on the principle. — Call by name. –Intimidation of the "Center." — Opponents inactive. — The majority finally disposed of.

Sometimes it succeeds surreptitiously by rushing them through. As "there is no order of the day circulated beforehand, and, in any event, none which anybody is obliged to adhere to,"[39] the Assembly is captured by surprise. "The first knave amongst the 'Left,' (which expression, says Hua, I do not strike out, because there were many among those gentlemen), brought up a ready–made resolution, prepared the evening before by a clique. We were not prepared for it and demanded that it should be referred to a committee. Instead of doing this, however, the resolution was declared urgent, and, whether we would or not, discussion had to take place forthwith."[40] — "There were other tactics equally perfidious, which Thuriot, especially, made use of. This great rascal got up and proposed, not the draft of a law, but what he called a principle; for instance, a decree should be passed confiscating the property of the émigrés, . . or that unsworn priests should be subject to special surveillance.[41] . . . In reply, he was told that his principle was the core of a law, the very law itself; so let it be debated by referring it to a committee to make a report on it. — Not at all — the matter is urgent; a committee might fix the articles as it pleases; they are worthless if the principle is not common sense." Through this expeditious method discussion is stifled. The Jacobins purposely prevent the Assembly from giving the matter any consideration. They count on its bewilderment. In the name of reason, they discard reason as far as they can, and hasten a vote because their decrees do not stand up to analysis. — At other times, and especially on grand occasions, they compel a vote. In general, votes are given by the members either sitting down or standing up, and, for the four hundred deputies of the "Center," subject to the scolding of the exasperated galleries, it is a tolerably hard trial. "Part of them do not arise, or they rise with the 'Left'."[42] If the "Right" happens to have a majority, "this is contested in bad faith and a call of the house is demanded." Now, "the calls of the house, through an intolerable abuse, are always published; the Jacobins declaring that it is well for the people to know their friends from their enemies." The meaning of this is that this list of the opposition will soon serve as a list of the outlaws, on which the timid are not disposed to inscribe themselves. The result is an immediate defection in the heavy battalions of the "Centre"; "this is a positive fact," says Hua, "of which we were all witnesses; we always lost a hundred votes on the call of the house." — Towards the end they give up, and protest no more, except by staying away: on the 14th of June, when the abolishment of the whole system of feudal credit was being dealt with, only the extreme left was attending; the rest of the "Assembly hall was nearly empty"; out of 497 deputies in attendance, 200 had left the session.[43] Encouraged for a moment by the appearance of some possible protection, they twice exonerate General Lafayette, behind whom they see an army,[44] and brave the despots of the Assembly, the clubs, and the streets. But, for lack of a military chief and base, the visible majority is twice obliged to yield, to keep silent, and fly or retreat under the dictatorship of the victorious faction, which has strained and forced the legislative machine until it has become disjointed and broken down.[45]

NOTES:

[1]"Correspondence (manuscript) of Baron de Staël," with his Court in Sweden. Oct. 6, 1791.

[2] "Souvenirs", by PASQUIER (Etienne–Dennis, duc), chancelier de France. in VI volumes, Librarie Plon, Paris 1893. – Dumouriez, "Mémoires," III. ch. V: "The Jacobin party, having branches all over the country, used its provincial clubs to control the elections. Every crackbrain, every seditious scribbler, all the agitators were elected . . . very few enlightened or prudent men, and still fewer of the nobles, were chosen."— Moniteur, XII. 199 (meeting of April 23, 1792). Speech M. Lecointe-Puyravaux. "We need not dissimulate; indeed, we are proud to say, that this legislature is composed of persons who are not rich."

[3] Mathieu Dumas, "Mémoires," I. 521. "The excitement in the electoral assemblages was very great; the aristocrats and large land– owners abstained from coming there." — Correspondance de Mirabeau et du Comte de la Mark, III. 246, Oct.10, 1791. "Nineteen twentieths of this legislature have no other transportation (turn–out) than galoshes and umbrellas. It has been estimated, that all these deputies put together do not possess 300,000 livres solid income. The majority of the members of this Assembly have received no education whatever."

[4] They rank as Maréchaux de camp, a grade corresponding to that of brigadier–general. They are Dupuy–Montbrun (deceased in March, 1792), Descrots–d'Estrée, a weak and worn old man whom his children forced into the Legislative Assembly, and, lastly, Mathieu Dumas, a conservative, and the only prominent one.

[5] "Correspondance du Baron de Staël," Jan.19, 1792. — Gouverneur Morris (II.162, Feb. 4, 1792) writes to Washington that M. de Warville, on the diplomatic committee, proposed to cede Dunkirk and Calais to England, as a pledge of fidelity by France, in any engagement which she might enter into. You can judge, by this, of the wisdom and virtue of the faction to which he belongs — Buchez et Roux, XXX 89 (defense of Brissot, Jan. 5, 1793) "Brissot, like all noisy, reckless, ambitious men, started in full blast with the strangest paradoxes. In 1780. in his 'Recherches philosophiques sur le droit de propriété,' he wrote as follows: 'If 40 crowns suffice to maintain existence, the possession of 200,000 crowns is plainly unjust and a robbery . . . Exclusive ownership is a veritable crime against nature . . . The punishment of robbery in our institutions is an act of virtue which nature herself commands.'"

[6] Moniteur, speech by Cambon, sittings of Feb. 2 and April 20, 1792.

[7] Ibid., (sitting of April 3). Speech by M. Cailliasson. The property belonging to the nation, sold and to be sold, is valued at 2,195 millions, while the assignats already issued amount to 2,100 millions. — Cf. Mercure de France, Dec. 17, 1791, p.201; Jan.28, 1792, p. 215; May 19, 1792, p. 205. — Dumouriez, "Mémoires," III. 296, and 339, 340, 344, 346. – "Cambon, a raving lunatic, without education, humane principle, or integrity (public) a meddler, an ignoramus, and very giddy. He tells me that one resource remained to him, which is, to seize all the coin in Belgium, all the plate belonging to the churches, and all the cash deposits . . . that, on ruining the Belgians, on reducing them to the same state of suffering as the French, they would necessarily share their fate with them; that they would then be admitted members of the Republic, with the prospect of always making headway, through the same line of policy; that the decree of Dec. 15, 1792, admirably favored this

and, because it tended to a complete disorganization, and that the luckiest thing that could happen to France was to disorganize all its neighbors and reduce them to the same state of anarchy." (This conversation between Cambon and Dumouriez occurs in the middle of January, 1793.) – Moniteur, XIV. 758 (sitting of Dec. 15, 1792). Report by Cambon.

[8] Chronique de Paris, Sept. 4, 1792. "It is a sad and terrible situation which forces a people, naturally amiable and generous, to take such vengeance! " – Cf. the very acute article, by St. Beuve, on Condorcet, in "Causeries du Lundi," — Hua (a colleague of Condorcet, in the Legislative Assembly), "Mémoires," 89. "Condorcet, in his journal, regularly falsified things, with an audacity which is unparelleled. The opinions of the 'Right' were so mutilated and travestied the next day in his journal, that we, who had uttered them, could scarcely recognise them. On complaining of this to him and on charging him with perfidy, the philosopher only smiled."

[9] Malouet, II. 215. — Dumouriez, III. ch. V. "They were elected to represent the nation to defend, they say, its interests against a perfidious court."

[10] Moniteur, X. 223 (session of Oct. 26, 1791). Speech by M. François Duval. — Grandiloquence is the order of the day at the very first meeting. On the 1st of October, 1791, twelve old men, marching in procession, go out to fetch the constitutional act. "M. Camus, keeper of the records, with a composed air and downcast eyes, enters with measured steps," bearing in both hands the sacred document which he holds against his breast, while the deputies stand up and bare their heads. "People of France," says an orator, "citizens of Paris, all generous Frenchmen, and you, our fellow citizens — virtuous, intelligent women, bringing your gentle influence into the sanctuary of the law — behold the guarantee of peace which the legislature presents to you!" — We seem to be witnessing the last act of an opera.

[11] Ibid., XII. 230 (sessions of April 26 and May 5). Report and speech by François de Nantes. The whole speech, a comic treasure from the beginning to the end, ought to have been quoted: "Tell me, pontiff of Rome, what your sentiments will be when you welcome your worthy and faithful co−operators? . . I behold your sacred hands, ready to launch those pontifical thunderbolts, which, etc. . . Let the brazier of Scœvola be brought in, and, with our outstretched palms above the burning coals, we will show that there is no species of torture, no torment which can excite a frown on the brow of him whom the love of country exalts above humanity!" — Suppose that, just at this moment, a lighted candle had been placed under his hand!

[12] Moniteur, XI. 179 (session of Jan. 20, 1792). – Ibid., 216 (session of Jan. 24). – XII. 426 (May 9).

[13] Ibid., XII. 479 (session of May 24). – XIII. 71 (session of July 7, speech by Lasource). – Cf. XIV. 301 (session of July 31) a quotation from Voltaire brought in for the suppression of the convents.

[14] Moniteur. Speech by Aubert Dubayer, session of Aug. 30.

[15] Speech by Chaumette, procureur of the commune, to the newly married. (Mortimer−Ternaux,

IV. 408).

[16] The class to which they belonged has been portrayed, to the life, by M. Roye–Collard (Sainte–Beuve, "Nouveaux Lundis," IV. 263): "A young lawyer at Paris, at first received in a few houses on the Ile St. Louis, he soon withdrew from this inferior world of attorneys and pettyfoggers, whose tone oppressed him. The very thought of the impression this gallant and intensely vulgar mediocrity made upon him, still inspired disgust. He much preferred to talk with longshoremen, if need be, than with these scented limbs of the law."

[17] Etienne Dumont, "Mémoires," 40. — Mercure de France, Nov. 19, 1791; Feb. 11 and March 3, 1792. (articles by Mallet du Pan).

[18] Moniteur, Dec. 17 (examination at the bar of the house of Rauch, a pretended labor contractor, whom they are obliged to send off acquitted). Rauch tells them: "I have no money, and cannot find a place where I can sleep at less than 6 sous, because I pee in the bed." — Moniteur, XII. 574. (session of June 4), report by Chabot: "A peddler from Mortagne, says that a domestic coming from Coblentz told him that there was a troop about to carry off the king and poison him, so as to throw the odium of it on the National Assembly." Bernassais de Poitiers writes: "A brave citizen told me last evening: 'I have been to see a servant–girl, living with a noble. She assured me that her master was going to–night to Paris, to join the 30,000, who, in about a month, meant to cut the throats of the National Assembly and set fire to every corner of Paris!'" – "M. Gerard, a saddler at Amiens, writes to us that Louis XVI is to be aided in his flight by 5,000 relays, and that afterwards they are going to fire red–hot bullets on the National Assembly."

[19] Mercure de France, Nov. 5, 1791 (session of Oct. 25). — Ibid., Dec. 23.–Moniteur, XII. 192 (session of April 21, 1792). — XII. 447 (address to the French, by Clootz): "God brought order out of primitive chaos; the French will bring order out of feudal chaos. God is mighty, and manifested his will; we are mighty, and we will manifest our will. . . The more extensive the seat of war the sooner, and more fortunately, will the suit of plebeians against the nobles be decided. . . We require enemies, . . Savoy, Tuscany, and quickly, quickly!"

[20] Cf. Moniteur, XI. 192 (sitting of Jan. 22, 1792). "M. Burnet, chaplain of the national guard, presents himself at the bar of the house with an English woman, named Lydia Kirkham, and three small children, one of which is in her arms. M. Burnet announces that she is his wife and that the child in her arms is the fruit of their affection. After referring to the force of natural sentiments which he could not resist, the petitioner thus continues: 'One day, I met one of those sacred questioners. Unfortunate man, said he, of what are you guilty? Of this child, sir; and I have married this woman, who is a Protestant, and her religion has nothing to do with mine. . . Death or my wife! Such is the cry that nature now and always will, inspire me with." – The petitioner receives the honors of the Assembly. – (Ibid., XII 369).

[21] The grotesque is often that of a farce. "M. Piorry, in the name of poor; but virtuous citizens, tenders two pairs of buckles, with this motto: 'They have served to hold the shoe–straps on my feet; they will serve to reduce under them, with the imprint and character of truth, all tyrants leagued against the constitution' (Moniteur, XII. 457, session of May 21)" – Ibid., XIII. 249 (session of July

25). "A young citoyenne offers to combat, in person, against the enemies of her country;" and the president, with a gallant air, replies: "Made rather to soothe, than to combat tyrants, your offer, etc."

[22] Moniteur, XL 576 (session of March 6); XII. 237, 314, 368 (sessions of April 27, May 5 and 14).

[23] Mercure de France. Sept. 19,1791, Feb.11, and March 3, 1792. — Buchez et Roux, XVI 185 (session of July 26, 1792).

[24] "Mémoires de Mallet du Pan," 1433 (tableau of the three parties, with special information).

[25] Buchez et Roux, XII. 348 (letter by the deputy Chéron, president of the Feuillants Club). The deputies of the Legislative Assembly, registered at the Feuillants Club, number 264 besides a large number of deputies in the Constituent Assembly. — According to Mallet du Pan the so-called Independents number 250.

[26] These figures are verified by decisive ballottings (Mortimer– Ternauz, II. 205, 348.)

[27] Moniteur, XII. 393 (session of May 15, speech by Isnard): "The Constituent Assembly only half dared do what it had the power to do. It has left in the field of liberty, even around the very roots of the young constitutional tree, the old roots of despotism and of the aristocracy . . . It has bound us to the trunk of the constitutional tree, like powerless victims given up to the rage of their enemies." – – Etienne Dumont saw truly the educational defects peculiar to the party. He says, apropos of Madame Roland: "I found in her too much of that distrustful despotism which belongs to ignorance of the world . . . What her intellectual development lacked was a greater knowledge of the world and intercourse with men of superior judgment to her own. Roland himself had little intellectual breadth, while all those who frequented her house never rose above the prejudices of the vulgar."

[28] "Souvenirs", by PASQUIER (Etienne–Dennis, duc), chancelier de France. in VI volumes, Librarie Plon, Paris 1893.

[29] Madame de Stael, "Considerations sur la Révolution Française, IIIrd part, ch. III.–Madame de Staël conversed with them and judges them according to the shrewd perceptions of a woman of the world.

[30] Louvet, "Mémoires" 32. "I belonged to the bold philosophers who, before the end of 1791, lamented the fate of a great nation, compelled to stop half–way in the career of freedom," and, on page 38 — "A minister of justice was needed. The four ministers (Roland, Servane, etc.) "cast their eyes on me. . . Duranthon was preferred to me. This was the first mistake of the republican party. It paid dear for it. That mistake cost my country a good deal of blood and many tears." Later on, he thinks that he has the qualifications for ambassador to Constantinople.

[31] Buzot, "Mémoires" (Ed. Dauban), pp.31, 39. "Born with a proud and independent spirit which never bowed at any one's command, how could I accept the idea of a man being held sacred? With my heart and head possessed by the great beings of the ancient republics, who are the greatest honor to the human species, I practiced their maxims from my earliest years, and nourished myself on a

study of their virtues. . . The pretended necessity of a monarchy . . . could not amalgamate, in my mind, with the grand and noble conceptions formed by me, of the dignity of the human species. Hope deceived me, it is true, but my error was too glorious to allow me to repent of it." – Self– admiration is likewise the mental substratum of Madame Roland, Roland, Pétion, Barbaroux, Louvet, etc., (see their writings). Mallet du Pan well says: "On reading the memoirs of Madame Roland, one detects the actress, rehearsing for the stage. " — Roland is an administrative puppet and would–be orator, whose wife pulls the strings. There is an odd, dull streak in him, peculiarly his own. For example, in 1787 (Guillon de Montléon, "Histoire de la ville de Lyon, pendant la Révolution," 1.58), he proposes to utilize the dead, by converting them into oil and phosphoric acid. In 1788, he proposes to the Villefranche Academy to inquire "whether it would not be to the public advantage to institute tribunals for trying the dead?" in imitation of the Egyptians. In his report of Jan. 5, 1792, he gives a plan for establishing public festivals, "in imitation of the Spartans," and takes for a motto, Non omnis moriar (Baron de Girardot, "Roland and Madame Roland". I. 83, 185)

[32] Political club uniting moderate and constitutional monarchists. They got their nickname because they held their meetings in the old convent formerly used by the feullants, a branch of Cistercians who, led by LaBarrière, broke away in 1577. The Feuillant Club was dissolved in 1791. (SR).

[33] Moniteur, XI. 61 (session of Jan 7, 1792). – Ibid., 204 (Jan. 25); 281 (Feb. 1); 310 (Feb. 4); 318 (Feb. 6); 343 (Feb. 9); 487 (Feb. 26). – XII. 22 (April 2). Reports of all the sessions must be read to appreciate the force of the pressure. See, especially, the sessions of April 9 and 16, May 15 and 29, June 8, 9, 15, and 25, July 1, 2, 5, 9, 11, 17, 18, and 21, and, after this date, all the sessions. – Lacretelle, "Dix Ans d'Epreuves," p. 78–81. "The Legislative Assembly served under the Jacobin Club while keeping up a counterfeit air of independence. The progress which fear had made in the French character was very great, at a time when everything was pitched in the haughtiest key. . . The majority, as far as intentions go, was for the conservatives; the actual majority was for the republicans."

[34] Moniteur, XIII. 212, session of July 22.

[35] Moniteur, XII. 22, session of April 2. – Mortimer–Ternaux, II. 95. – Moniteur, XIII. 222, session of July 22.

[36] Lacretelle, "Dix Ans d'Epreuves," 80.

[37] Mathieu Dumas, "Mémoires," II. 88 (Feb. 23). – Hua, "Mémoires" d'un Avocat au Parliament de Paris," 106, 121, 134, 154. Moniteur, XIII. 212 (session of July 21), speech by M. —— "The avenues to this building are daily beset with a horde of people who insult the representatives of the nation."

[38] De Vaublanc, "Mémoires," 344. – Moniteur, XIII. 368 (letters and speeches of deputies, session of Aug. 9).

[39] Hua, 115. — Ibid., 90. 3 out of 4 deputies of Seine–et–Oise were Jacobins. "We met once a week to talk over the affairs of the department. We were obliged to drive out the vagabonds who, even at the table, talked of nothing but killing."

[40] Moniteur, XII. 702. For example, on the 19th of June, 1792, on a motion unexpectedly proposed by Condorcet, that the departments be authorized to burn all titles (to nobility) in the various depots. — Adopted at once, and unanimously.

[41] Later Stalin and his successors should invest the United Nations and other international organizations to indirectly propose and ensure the acceptance of a new convention of human rights, children's rights, the rights of refugees etc. In many cases these became the base of national legislation which is now giving trouble to many of the Western democracies. (SR).

[42] Hua, 114.

[43] Moniteur, XII. 664. – Mercure de France, June 23, 1792.

[44] Hua, 141. — Mathieu Dumas, II. 399: "It is remarkable that Lafond de Ladébat, one of our trustiest friends, was elected president on the 23rd of July, 1792. This shows that the majority of the Assembly was still sound; but it was only brought about by a secret vote in the choice of candidates. The same men who obeyed their consciences, through a sentiment of justice and of propriety, could not face the danger which surrounded them in the threats of the factions when they were called upon to vote by rising or sitting."

[45] This description and others of the same period have undoubtedly been studied carefully by thousands of socialists and political hopefuls who, in any case, made use of similar tactics to take over thousands of governing committees, institutions and organizations. (SR).

CHAPTER III. POLITICS OF THE ASSEMBLY

I.

Policy of the Assembly. – State of France at the end of 1791. – Powerlessness of the Law.

If the deputies who, on the 1st of October, 1791, so solemnly and enthusiastically swore to the Constitution, had been willing to open their eyes, they would have seen this Constitution constantly violated, both in its letter and spirit, over the entire territory. As usual, and through the vanity of authorship, M. Thouret, the last president of the Constituent Assembly, had, in his final report, hidden disagreeable truth underneath pompous and delusive phrases; but it was only necessary to look over the monthly record to see whether, as guaranteed by him, "the decrees were faithfully executed in all parts of the empire." — " Where is this faithful execution to be found?" inquires Mallet du Pan.[1] "Is it at Toulon, in the midst of the dead and wounded, shot in the very face of the amazed municipality and Directory? Is it at Marseilles, where two private individuals are knocked down and massacred as aristocrats," under the pretext "that they sold to children poisoned sugar–plums with which to begin a counter–revolution?" Is it at Arles, "against which 4,000 men from Marseilles, dispatched by the club, are at this moment marching?" Is it at Bayeux, "where the sieur Fauchet against whom a warrant for arrest is out, besides being under the ban of political disability, has just been elected deputy to the Legislative Assembly?" Is it at Blois, "where the commandant, doomed to death for having tried to execute these decrees, is forced to send away a loyal regiment and submit to licentious troops?" Is it at Nîmes, "where the Dauphiny regiment, on leaving the town by the Minister's orders, is ordered by the people" and the club "to disobey the Minister and remain?" Is it in those regiments whose officers, with pistols at their breasts, are obliged to leave and give place to amateurs? Is it at Toulouse, "where, at the end of August, the administrative authorities order all unsworn priests to leave the town in three days, and withdraw to a distance of four leagues?" Is it in the outskirts of Toulouse, "where, on the 28th of August, a municipal officer is hung at a street–lamp after an affray with guns?" Is it at Paris, where, on the 25th of September, the Irish college, vainly protected by an international treaty, has just been assailed by the mob; where Catholics, listening to the orthodox mass, are driven out and dragged to the authorized mass in the vicinity; where one woman is torn from the confessional, and another flogged with all their might?[2]

These troubles, it is said, are transient; on the Constitution being proclaimed, order will return of itself. Very well, the Constitution is voted, accepted by the King, proclaimed, and entrusted to the Legislative Assembly. Let the Legislative Assembly consider what is done in the first few weeks. In the eight departments that surround Paris, there are riots on every market–day; farms are invaded and the cultivators of the soil are ransomed by bands of vagabonds; the mayor of Melun is riddled with balls and dragged out from the hands of the mob streaming with blood.[3] At Belfort, a riot for the purpose of retaining a convoy of coin, and the commissioner of the Upper–Rhine in danger of death; at Bouxvillers, owners of property attacked by poor National Guards, and by the soldiers of Salm–Salm, houses broken into and cellars pillaged; at Mirecourt, a flock of women beating drums, and, for three days, holding the Hôtel–de–Ville in a state of siege. – – One day Rochefort is in a state of insurrection, and the workmen of the harbor compel the municipality to unfurl the red flag.[4] On the following day, it is Lille, the people of which, "unwilling to exchange its money and assignats for paper–rags, called billets de confiance, gather into mobs and threaten, while a whole garrison is necessary to prevent an explosion." On the 16th of October, it is Avignon in the power of bandits, with the abominable butchery of the Glacière. On the 5th of November, at Caen, there are eighty–two gentlemen, townsmen and artisans, knocked down and dragged to prison, for having offered their services to the municipality as special constables. On the 14th of November, at Montpellier, the roughs triumph; eight men and women are killed in the streets or in their houses, and all conservatives are disarmed or put to flight. By the end of October, it is a gigantic column of smoke and flame shooting upward suddenly from week to week and spreading everywhere, growing, on the other side of the Atlantic, into civil war in St. Domingo, where wild beasts are let loose against their keepers; 50,000 blacks take the field, and, at the outset, 1,000 whites are assassinated, 15,000 Negroes slain, 200 sugar–mills destroyed and damage done to the amount of 600,000,000; "a colony of itself alone worth ten provinces, is almost annihilated."[5] At Paris, Condorcet is busy writing in his journal that "this news is not reliable, there being no object in it but to create a French empire beyond the seas for the King, where there will be masters and slaves." A corporal of the Paris National Guard, on his own authority, orders the King to remain indoors, fearing that he may escape, and forbids a sentinel to let him go out after nine o'clock in the evening;[6] at the Tuileries, stump–speakers in the open air denounce aristocrats and priests; at the Palais–Royal, there is a pandemonium of public lust and incendiary speeches.[7] There are centers of riot in all quarters, "as many robberies as there are quarter–hours, and no robbers punished; no police; overcrowded courts; more delinquents than there are prisons to hold them; nearly all the private mansions closed; the annual consumption in the faubourg St. Germain alone diminished by 250 millions; 20,000 thieves, with branded backs, idling away time in houses of bad repute, at the theaters, in the Palais–Royal, at the National Assembly, and in the coffee–houses; thousands of beggars infesting the streets, crossways, and public squares. Everywhere an image of the deepest poverty which is not calling for one's pity as it is accompanied with insolence. Swarms of tattered vendors are offering all sorts of paper–money, issued by anybody that chose to put it in circulation, cut up into bits, sold, given, and coming back in rags, fouler than the miserable creatures who deal in it."[8] Out of 700,000 inhabitants there are 100,000 of the poor, of which 60,000 have flocked in from the departments;[9] among them are 30,000 needy artisans from the national workshops, discharged and sent home in the preceding month of June, but who, returning three months later, are again swallowed up in the great sink of vagabondage, hurling their floating mass against the crazy edifice of public authority and furnishing the forces of sedition. — At Paris, and in the provinces, disobedience exists throughout the hierarchy. Directories countermand ministerial orders. Here, municipalities brave the commands of their Directory; there, communities order around their mayor with a drawn sword. Elsewhere, soldiers and sailors put their officers under arrest. The accused insult the judge on the bench and force him to cancel his verdict; mobs tax or plunder wheat in the market; National Guards prevent its distribution, or seize it in the storehouses. There is no security for property, lives, or consciences. The majority of Frenchmen are deprived of their right to worship in their own faith, and of voting at the elections. There is no safety, day or night, for the élite of the nation, for ecclesiastics and the gentry, for army and navy officers, for rich merchants and large landed proprietors; no protection in the courts, no income from public funds; denunciations abound, expulsions, banishments to the interior, attacks on private houses; there is no right of free assemblage, even to enforce the law under the orders of legal authorities.[10] Opposed to this, and in contrast with it, is the privilege and immunity of a sect formed into a political corporation, "which extends its filiations over the whole kingdom, and even abroad; which has its own treasury, its committees, and its by–laws; which rules the government, which judges justice,"[11] and which, from the capital to the hamlet, usurps or directs the administration. Liberty, equality, and the majesty of the law exist nowhere, except in words. Of the three thousand decrees given birth to by the Constituent Assembly, the most lauded, those the best set off by a philosophic baptism, form a mass of stillborn abortions of which France is the burying–ground. That which really subsists underneath the false appearances of right, proclaimed and sworn to over and over again, is, on the one hand, an oppression of the upper and cultivated classes, from which all the rights of man are withdrawn, and, on the other hand, the tyranny of the fanatical and brutal rabble which assumes to itself all the rights of sovereignty.

II.

The Assembly hostile to the oppressed and favoring oppressors. — Decrees against the nobles and clergy. — Amnesty for deserters, convicts, and bandits. — Anarchical and leveling maxims.

In vain do the honest men of the Assembly protest against this scandal and this overthrow. The Assembly, guided and forced by the Jacobins, will only amend the law to damn the oppressed and to authorize their oppressors. — Without making any distinction between armed assemblages at Coblentz, which it had a right to punish, and refugees, three times as numerous, old men, women and children, so many indifferent and inoffensive people, not merely nobles but plebeians,[12] who left the soil only to escape popular outrages, it confiscates the property of all emigrants and orders this to be sold.[13] Through the new restriction of the passport, those who remain are tied to their domiciles, their freedom of movement, even in the interior, being subject to the decision of each Jacobin municipality.[14] It completes their ruin by depriving them without indemnity of all income from their real estate, of all the seignorial rights which the Constituent Assembly had declared to be legitimate.[15] It abolishes, as far as it can, their history and their past, by burning in the public depots their genealogical titles.[16] — To all unsworn ecclesiastics, two-thirds of the French clergy, it withholds bread, the small pension allowed them for food, which is the ransom of their confiscated possessions;[17] it declares them "suspected of revolt against the law and of bad intentions against the country;" it subjects them to special surveillance; it authorizes their expulsion without trial by local rulers in case of disturbances; it decrees that in such cases they shall be banished.[18] It suppresses "all secular congregations of men and women ecclesiastic or laic, even those wholly devoted to hospital service will take away from 600,000 children the means of learning to read and write."[19] It lays injunctions on their dress; it places episcopal palaces in the market for sale, also the buildings still occupied by monks and nuns.[20] It welcomes with rounds of applause a married priest who introduces his wife to the Assembly. — Not only is the Assembly destructive but it is insulting; the authors of each decree passed by it add to its thunderbolt the rattling hail of their own abuse and slander.

"Children," says a deputy, "have the poison of aristocracy and fanaticism injected into them by the congregations."[21]

"Purge the rural districts of the vermin which is devouring them!" – "Everybody knows," says Isnard, "that the priest is as cowardly as he is vindictive. . . Let these pestiferous fellows be sent back to Roman and Italian lazarettos . . What religion is that which, in its nature, is unsocial and rebellious in principle?"

Whether unsworn, whether immigrants actually or in feeling, "large proprietors, rich merchants, false conservatives,"[22] are all outspoken conspirators or concealed enemies. All public disasters are imputed to them. "The cause of the troubles," says Brissot,[23] "which lay waste the colonies, is the infernal vanity of the whites who have three times violated an engagement which they have three times sworn to maintain." Scarcity of work and short crops are accounted for through their cunning malevolence.

"A large number of rich men, "says François de Nantes,[24] "allow their property to run down and their fields to lie fallow, so as to enjoy seeing the suffering of the people."

France is divided into two parties, on the one hand, the aristocracy to which is attributed every vice, and, on the other hand, the people on whom is conferred every virtue.[25]

"The defense of liberty," says Lamarque,[26] "is basely abandoned every day by the rich and by the former nobility, who put on the mask of patriotism only to cheat us. It is not in this class, but only in that of citizens who are disdainfully called the people, that we find pure beings, those ardent souls really worthy of liberty." — One step more and everything will be permitted to the virtuous against the wicked; if misfortune befalls the aristocrats so much the worse for them. Those officers who are stoned, M. de la Jaille and others, "wouldn't they do better not to deserve being sacrificed to popular fury?"[27] Isnard exclaims in the tribune, "it is the long-continued immunity enjoyed by criminals which has rendered the people executioners. Yes, an angry people, like an angry God, is only too often the terrible supplement of silent laws."[28] — In other words crimes are justified and assassinations still provoked against those who have been assassinated for the past two years.

By a forced conclusion, if the victims are criminals, their executioners are honest, and the Assembly, which rigorously proceeds against the former, reserves all its indulgence for the latter. It reinstates the numerous deserters who abandoned their flags previous to the 1st of January, 1789;[29] it allows them three sous per league mileage, and brings them back to their homes or to their regiments to become, along with their brethren whose desertion is more recent, either leaders or recruits for the mob. It releases from the galleys the forty Swiss guards of Chateauroux whom their own cantons desired to have kept there; it permits these "'martyrs to Liberty " to promenade the streets of Paris in a triumphal car;[30] it admits them to the bar of the house, and, taking a formal vote on it, extends to them the honors of the session.[31] Finally, as if it were their special business to let loose on the public the most ferocious and foulest of the rabble, it amnesties Jourdan, Mainvielle, Duprat, and Raphel, fugitive convicts, jail-birds, the condottieri of all lands assuming the title of "the brave brigands of Avignon," and who, for eighteen months, have pillaged and plundered the Comtat[32]; it stops the trial, almost over, of the Glacière butchers; it tolerates the return of these as victors,[33] and their installation by their own act in the places of the fugitive magistrates, allowing Avignon to be treated as a conquered city, and, henceforth, to become their prey and their booty. This is a willful restoration of the vermin to the social body, and, in this feverish body, nothing is overlooked that will increase the fever. The most anarchical and deleterious maxims emanate, like miasma, from the Assembly benches. The reduction of things to an absolute level is adopted as a principle; "equality of rights," says Lamarque,[34] "is to be maintained only by tending steadily to an equality of fortunes;" this theory is practically applied on all sides since the proletariat is pillaging all who own property. — "Let the communal possessions be partitioned among the citizens of the surrounding villages," says François de Nantes, "in an inverse ratio to their fortunes, and let him who has the least inheritance take the largest share in the divisions."[35] Conceive the effect of this motion read at evening to peasants who are at this very moment claiming their lord's forest for their commune. M. Corneille prohibits any tax to be levied for the public treasury on the wages of manual labor, because nature, and not society, gives us the "right to live."[36] On the other hand, he confers on the public treasury the right of taking the whole of an income, because it is society, and not nature, which institutes public funds; hence, according to him, the poor majority must be relieved of all taxation, and all taxes must fall on the rich minority. The system is well-timed and the argument apt for convincing indigent or straitened tax-payers, namely, the refractory majority, that its taxes are just, and that it should not refuse to be taxed. –

"Under the reign of liberty," says President Daverhoult,[37] "the people have the right to insist not merely on subsistence, but again on plenty and happiness."[38]

Accordingly, being in a state of poverty they have been betrayed. — "Elevated to the height achieved by the French people," says another president, "it looks down upon the tempests under its feet."[39] The tempest is at hand and bursts over its head. War, like a black cloud, rises above the horizon, overspreads the sky, thunders and wraps France filled with explosive materials in a circle of lightening, and it is the Assembly which, through the greatest of its mistakes, draws down the bolt on the nation's head.

III.

War. – –Disposition of foreign powers. – – The King's dislikes. — Provocation of the Girondins. — Dates and causes of the rupture.

It might have been turned aside with a little prudence. Two principal grievances were alleged, one by France and the other by the Empire. — On the one hand, and very justly, France complained of the gathering of émigré's, which the Emperor and Electors tolerated against it on the frontier. In the first place, however, a few thousand gentlemen, without troops or stores, and nearly without money,[40] were hardly to be feared, and, besides this, long before the decisive hour came these troops were dispersed, at once by the Emperor in his own dominions, and, fifteen days afterwards, by the Elector of Trèves in his electorate.[41] — On the other hand, according to treaties, the German princes, who owned estates in Alsace, made claims for the feudal rights abolished on their French possessions and the Diet forbade them to accept the offered indemnity. But, as far as the Diet is concerned, nothing was easier nor more customary than to let negotiations drag along, there being no risk or inconvenience attending the suit as, during the delay, the claimants remained empty- handed. — If, now, behind the ostensible motives, the real intentions are sought for, it is certain that, up to January, 1792, the intentions of Austria were pacific. The grants made to the Comte d'Artois, in the Declaration of Pilnitz, were merely a court- sprinkling of holy-water, the semblance of an illusory promise and subject to a European concert of action, that is to say, annulled beforehand by an indefinite postponement, while this pretended league of sovereigns is at once "placed by the politicians in the class of august comedies.[42]" Far from taking up arms against "New France" in the name of old France, the emperor Leopold and his prime minister Kaunitz, were delighted to see the constitution completed and accepted by the King; it "got them out of an embarrassing position,"[43] and Prussia as well. In the running of governments, political advantage is the great incentive and both powers needed all their forces in another direction, in Poland. One for retarding, and the other for accelerating the division of this country, and both, when the partition took place, to get enough for themselves and prevent Russia from getting too much. — The sovereigns of Prussia and Austria, accordingly, did not have any idea of saving Louis XVI, nor of conducting the émigrés back, nor of conquering French provinces. If anything was to be expected from them on account of personal ill-will, there was no fear of their armed intervention. — In France it is not the King who urges a rupture; he knows too well that the hazards of war will place him and his dependents in mortal danger. Secretly as well as publicly, in writing to the émigrés, his wishes are to bring them back or to restrain them. In his private correspondence he asks of the European powers not physical but moral aid, the external support of a congress which will permit moderate men, the partisans of order, all owners of property, to raise their heads and rally around the throne and the laws against anarchy. In his ministerial correspondence every precaution is taken not to touch off or let someone touch off an explosion. At the critical moment of the discussion[44] he entreats the deputies, through M. Delessart, his Minister of Foreign Affairs, to weigh their words and especially not to send a demand containing a "dead line." He resists, as far as his passive nature allows him, to the very last. On being forced to declare war he requires beforehand the signed advice of all his ministers. He does not utter the fatal words, until he, "with tears in his eyes" and in the most dire straits, is dragged on by an Assembly qualifying all caution as treason and which has just dispatched M. Delessart to appear, under a capital charge, before the supreme court at Orléans.

It is the Assembly then which launches the disabled ship on the roaring abysses of an unknown sea, without a rudder and leaking at every seam. It alone slips the cable which held it in port and which the foreign powers neither dared nor desired to sever. Here, again, the Girondists are the leaders and hold the axe; since the last of October they have grasped it and struck repeated blows.[45] — As an exception, the extreme Jacobins, Couthon, Collot d'Herbois, Danton, Robespierre, do not side with them. Robespierre, who at first proposed to confine the Emperor "within the circle of Popilius,"[46] fears the placing of too great a power in the King's hands, and, growing mistrustful, preaches distrust. — But the great mass of the party, led by clamorous public opinion, impels on the timid marching in front. Of the many things of which knowledge is necessary to conduct successfully such a complex and delicate affair, they know nothing. They are ignorant about cabinets, courts, populations, treaties, precedents, timely forms and requisite style. Their guide and counselor in foreign relations is Brissot whose pre-eminence is based on their ignorance and who, exalted into a statesman, becomes for a few months the most conspicuous figure in Europe.[47] To whatever extent a European calamity may be attributed to any one man, this one is to be attributed to him. It is this wretch, born in a pastry-cook's shop, brought up in an attorney's office, formerly a police agent at 150 francs per month, once in league with scandal-mongers and black- mailers,[48] a penny-a-liner, busybody, and meddler, who, with the half-information of a nomad, scraps of newspaper ideas and reading-room lore,[49] added to his scribblings as a writer and his club declamation, directs the destinies of France and starts a war in Europe which is to destroy six millions of lives. In the attic where his wife is washing his shirts, he enjoys rebuking rulers and, on the 20th of October, in the tribune,[50] he begins by insulting thirty foreign sovereigns. Such keen, intense enjoyment is the stuff on which the new fanaticism daily feeds itself. Madame Roland herself delights, with evident complacency, in it, something which can be seen in the two famous letters in which, with a supercilious tone, she first instructs the King and next the Pope.[51] Brissot, at bottom, regards himself as a Louis XIV, and expressly invites the Jacobins to imitate the haughty ways of the Great Monarch.[52] — To the tactlessness of the intruder, and the touchiness of the parvenu, we can add the rigidity of the sectarian. The Jacobins, in the name of abstract rights, deny historic rights; they impose from above, and by force, that truth of which they are the apostles, and allow themselves every provocation which they prohibit to others.

"Let us tell Europe," cries Isnard,[53] "that ten millions of Frenchmen, armed with the sword, with the pen, with reason, with eloquence, might, if provoked, change the face of the world and make tyrants tremble on their thrones of clay."

"Wherever a throne exists," says Hérault de Séchelles, "there is an enemy."[54]

"An honest peace between tyranny and liberty," says Brissot, "is impossible. Our Constitution is an eternal anathema to absolute monarchs . . . It places them on trial, it pronounces judgment on them; it seems to say to each: to-morrow thou have ceased to be or shalt be king only through the people. . . War is now a national benefit, and not to have war is the only calamity to be dreaded." [55]

" Tell the king," says Gensonné, "that the war is a must, that public opinion demands it, that the safety of the empire makes it a law."[56]

"The state we are in," concludes Vergniaud, "is a veritable state of destruction that may lead us to disgrace and death. So then to arms! to arms! Citizens, freemen, defend your liberty, confirm the hopes of that of the human race. . . Lose not the advantage of your position. Attack now that there is every sign of complete success. . . The spirits of past generations seem to me crowding into this temple to conjure you, in the name of the evils which slavery had compelled them to endure, to protect the future generations whose destinies are in your hands! Let this prayer be granted! Be for the future a new Providence! Ally yourselves with eternal justice!"[57]

Among the Marseilles speakers there is no longer any room for serious discussion. Brissot, in reply to the claim made by the Emperor on behalf of the princes' property in Alsatia, replies that "the sovereignty of the people is not bound by the treaties of tyrants."[58] As to the gatherings of the émigrés, the Emperor having yielded on this point, he will yield on the others.[59] Let him formally renounce all combinations against France.

"I want war on the 10th of February," says Brissot, "unless we have received his renunciation."

No explanations; it is satisfaction we want; "to require satisfaction is to put the Emperor at our mercy."[60] The Assembly, so eager to start the quarrel, usurps the King's right to take the first step and formally declares war, fixing the date.[61] — The die is now cast.

"They want war," says the Emperor, "and they shall have it."

Austria immediately forms an alliance with Prussia, threatened, like herself, with revolutionary propaganda.[62] By sounding the alarm belles the Jacobins, masters of the Assembly, have succeeded in bringing about that "monstrous alliance," and, from day to day, this alarm sounds the louder. One year more, thanks to this policy, and France will have all Europe for an enemy and as its only friend, the Regency of Algiers, whose internal system of government is about the same as her own.

IV.

Secret motives of the leaders. — Their control compromised by peace. — Discontent of the rich and cultivated class. — Formation and increase of the party of order. — The King and this party reconciled.

Behind their carmagnoles[63] we can detect a design which they will avow later on.

"We were always obstructed by the Constitution," Brissot is to say, "and nothing but war could destroy the Constitution."[64]

Diplomatic wrongs, consequently, of which they make parade, are simply pretexts; if they urge war it is for the purpose of overthrowing the legal order of things which annoys them; their real object is the conquests of power, a second internal revolution, the application of their system and a final state of equality.— Concealed behind them is the most politic and absolute of theorists, a man "whose great art is the attainment of his ends without showing himself, the preparation of others for far−sighted views of which they have no suspicion, and that of speaking but little in public and acting in secret."[65] This man is Sieyès, "the leader of everything without seeming to lead anything."[66] As infatuated as Rousseau with his own speculations, but as unscrupulous and as clear–sighted as Macchiavelli in the selection of practical means, he was, is, and will be, in decisive moments, the consulting counsel of radical democracy.

"His pride tolerates no superiority. He causes nobility to be abolished because he is not a noble; because he does not possess all he will destroy all. His fundamental doctrine for the consolidation of the Revolution is, that it is indispensable to change religion and to change the dynasty."

Now, had peace been maintained all this was impossible; moreover the ascendance of the party was compromised. Entire classes that had adhered to the party when it launched insurrection against the privileged, broke loose from it now that insurrection was directed against them; among thoughtful men and among those with property, most were disgusted with anarchy, and likewise disgusted with the abettors of it. Many administrators, magistrates and functionaries recently elected, loudly complained of their authority being subject to the mob. Many cultivators, manufacturers and merchants have become silently exasperated at the fruits of their labor and economy being surrendered at discretion to robbers and the indigent. It was hard for the flour–dealers of Etampes not to dare send away their wheat, to be obliged to supply customers at night, to tremble in their own houses, and to know that if they went out–doors they risked their lives.[67] It was hard for wholesale grocers in Paris to see their warehouses invaded, their windows smashed, their bags of coffee and boxes of sugar valued at a low price, parceled out and carried away by old hags or taken gratis by scamps who ran off and sold them at the other end of the street.[68] It was hard in all places for the families of the old bourgeoisie, for the formerly prominent men in each town and village, for the eminent in each art, profession or trade, for reputable and well–to–do people, in short, for the majority of men who had a good roof over their heads and a good coat on their backs, to undergo the illegal domination of a crowd led by a few hundred or dozens of stump–speakers and firebrands. — Already, in the beginning of 1792, this dissatisfaction was so great as to be denounced in the tribune and in the press. Isnard[69] railed against "that multitude of large property–holders, those opulent merchants, those haughty, wealthy personages who, advantageously placed in the social amphitheater, are unwilling to have their seats changed." The bourgeoisie," wrote Pétion,[70] "that numerous class free of any anxiety, is separating itself from the people; it considers itself above them, . . . they are the sole object of its distrust. It is everywhere haunted by the one idea that the revolution is a war between those who have and those who have not." — It abstains, indeed, from the elections, it keeps away from patriotic clubs, it demands the restoration of order and the reign of law; it rallies to itself "the multitude of conservative, timid people, for whom tranquility is the prime necessity," and especially, which is still more serious, it charges the disturbances upon their veritable authors. With suppressed indignation and a mass of undisputed evidence, André Chénier, a man of feeling, starts up in the midst of the silent crowd and openly tears off the mask from the Jacobins.[71] He brings into full light the daily sophism by which a mob, "some hundreds of idlers gathered in a garden or at a theater, are impudently called the people." He portrays those "three or four thousand usurpers of national sovereignty whom their orators and writers daily intoxicate with grosser incense than any adulation offered to the worst of despots;" those assemblies where "an infinitely small number of French appears large, because they are united and yell;" that Paris club from which honest, industrious, intelligent people had withdrawn one by one to give place to intriguers in debt, to persons of tarnished reputations, to the hypocrites of patriotism, to the lovers of uproar, to abortive talents, to corrupted intellects, to outcasts of every kind and degree who, unable to manage their own business, indemnify themselves by managing that of the public. He shows how, around the central factory and its twelve hundred branches of insurrection, the twelve hundred affiliated clubs, which, "holding each other's hands, form a sort of electric chain around all France" and giving it a shock at every touch from the center; their confederation, installed and enthroned, is not only as a State within the State, but rather as a sovereign State in a vassal State; summoning their administrative bodies to their bar, judicial verdicts set aside through their intervention, private individuals searched, assessed and condemned through their verdicts. All this constitutes a steady, systematic defense of insubordination and revolt; as, "under the name of hoarding and monopoly, commerce and industry are described as misdemeanors;" property is unsettled and every rich man rendered suspicious, "talent and integrity silenced." In short, a public conspiracy made against society in the very name of society, "while the sacred symbol of liberty is made use of as a seal" to exempt a few tyrants from punishment. Such a protest said aloud what most Frenchmen muttered to themselves, and from month to month, graver excesses exited greater censure.

"Anarchy exists[72] to a degree scarcely to be paralleled, wrote the ambassador of the United States. The horror and apprehension, which the licentious associations have universally inspired, are such that there is reason to believe that the great mass of the French population would consider even despotism a blessing, if accompanied with that security to persons and property, experienced even under the worst governments in Europe."

Another observer, not less competent,[73] says:

"it is plain to my eyes that when Louis XVI. finally succumbed, he had more partisans in France than the year previous, at the time of his flight to Varennes."

The truth of this, indeed, was frequently verified at the end of 1791 and beginning of 1792, by various investigations.[74] "Eighteen thousand officers of every grade, elected by the constitutionalists, seventy–one department administrations out of eighty–two, most of the tribunals,[75] all traders and manufacturers, every chief and a large portion of the National Guard of Paris," in short, the élite of the nation, and among citizens generally, the great majority who lived from day to day were for him, and for the "Right" of the Assembly against the "Left". If internal trouble had not been complicated by external difficulties, there would have been a change in opinion, and this the King expected. In accepting the Constitution, he thought that its defects would be revealed in practical operation and that they would lead to a reform. In the mean time he scrupulously observed the Constitution, and, through interest as well as conscience, kept his oath to the letter. "The most faithful execution of the Constitution," he said to one of his ministers, "is the surest way to make the nation see the changes that ought to be made in it."[76] — In other words, he counted on experience, and it is very probable that if there had been nothing to interfere with experience, his calculations would have finally chosen between the defenders of order and the instigators of disorder. It would have decided for the magistrates against the clubs, for the police against rioters, for the king against the mob. In one or two years more it would have learned that a restoration of the executive power was indispensable for securing the execution of the laws; that the chief of police, with his hands tied, could not do his duty; that it was undoubtedly wise to give him his orders, but that if he was to be of any use against knaves and fools, his hands should first be set free.

V.

Effects of the war on the common people.— Its alarms and fury. — The second revolutionary outburst and its characteristics. — Alliance of the Girondists with the mob. — The red cap and pikes. — Universal substitution of government by force for government by law.

Just the contrary with war; the aspect of things changes, and the alternative is the other way. It is no longer a choice between order and disorder, but between the new and the old regime, for, behind foreign opponents on the frontier, there stand the émigrés. The commotion is terrible, especially amongst the lower classes which mainly bore the whole weight of the old establishment; among the millions who live by the sweat of their brow, artisans, small farmers, métayers, day–laborers and soldiers, also the smugglers of salt and other articles, poachers, vagabonds, beggars and half–beggars, who, taxed, plundered, and harshly treated for centuries, have to endure, from father to son, poverty, oppression and disdain. They know through their own experience the difference between their late and their present condition. They have only to fall back on personal knowledge to revive in their imaginations the enormous royal, ecclesiastical, and seignorial taxes, the direct tax of eighty–one per cent., the bailiffs in charge, the seizures and the husbandry service, the inquisition of excise men, of inspectors of the salt tax, wine tax (rats de cave) and game–keepers, the ravages of wild birds and of pigeons, the extortions of the collector and his clerk, the delay and partiality in obtaining justice, the rashness and brutality of the police, the kicks and cuffs of the constabulary, the poor wretches gathered like heaps of dirt and filth, the promiscuousness, the over– crowding, the filth and the starvation of the prisons.[77] They have simply to open their eyes to see their immense deliverance; all direct or indirect taxes for the past two years legally abolished or practically suppressed, beer at two pennies a pot, wine at six, pigeons in their meat–safes, game on their turn–spits, the wood of the national forests in their lofts, the gendarmerie timid, the police absent, in many places the crops all theirs, the owner not daring to claim his share, the judge avoiding condemning them, the constable refusing to serve papers on them, privileges restored in their favor, the public authorities cringing to the crowds and yielding to their exactions, remaining quiet or unarmed in the face of their misdeeds, their outrages excused or tolerated, their superior good sense and deep feeling lauded in thousands of speeches, the jacket and the blouse considered as symbols of patriotism, and supremacy in the State claimed for the sans–culottes[78] in the name their merits and their virtues. — And now the overthrow of all this is announced to them, a league against them of foreign kings, the emigrants in arms, an invasion imminent, the Croats and Pandours in the field, hordes of mercenaries and barbarians crowding down on them again to put them in chains. — From the workshop to the cottage there rolls along a formidable outburst of anger, accompanied with national songs, denouncing the plots of tyrants and summoning the people to arms.[79] This is the second wave of the Revolution, fast swelling and roaring, less general than the first, since it bears along with it but little more than the lower class, but higher and much more destructive.

Not only, indeed, is the mass now launched forth coarse and crude, but a new sentiment animates it, the force of which is incalculable, that of plebeian pride, that of the poor man, the subject, who, suddenly erect after ages of debasement, relishes, far beyond his hopes and unstintedly, the delights of equality, independence, and dominion. "Fifteen millions white Negroes," says Mallet du Pan,[80] worse fed, more miserable than those of St. Domingo, like them rebelled and freed from all authority by their revolt, accustomed like them, through thirty months of license, to ruling over all that is left of their former masters, proud like them of the restoration of their caste and exulting in their horny hands. One may imagine their transports of rage on hearing the trumpet–blast which awakens them, showing them on the horizon the returning planters, bringing with them new whips and heavier manacles? — Nothing is more distrustful than such a sentiment in such breasts — quickly alarmed, ready to strike, ready for any act of violence, blindly credulous, headlong and easily impelled, not merely against real enemies on the outside, but at first against imaginary enemies on the inside,[81] but also against the King, the ministers, the gentry, priests, parliamentarians, orthodox Catholics; against

all administrators and magistrates imprudent enough to have appealed to the law;

all manufacturers, merchants, and owners of property who condemn disorder;

the wealthy whose egotism keeps them at home;

all those who are well–off, well–bred and well–dressed.

They are all under suspicion because they have lost by the new regime, or because they have not adopted its ways. — Such is the colossal brute which the Girondins introduce into the political arena.[82] For six months they shake red flags before its eyes, goad it on, work it up into a rage and drive it forward by decrees and proclamations,

* against their adversaries and against its keepers,

* against the nobles and the clergy,

* against aristocrats inside France in complicity with those of Coblentz,

* against "the Austrian committee" the accomplice of Austria,

* against the King, whose caution they transform into treachery,

* against the whole government to which they impute the anarchy they excite, and the war of which they themselves are the instigators.[83]

Thus over–excited and topsy–turvy, the proletariat require only arms and a rallying–point. The Girondins furnish both. Through a striking coincidence, one which shows that the plan was concerted,[84] they start three political engines at the same time. Just at the moment when, through their deliberate saber–rattling, they made war inevitable, they invented popular insignia and armed the poor. At the end of January, 1792, almost during one week, they announced their ultimatum to Austria using a fixed deadline, they adopted the red woolen cap and began the manufacture of pikes. — It is evident that pikes are of no use in the open field against cannon and a regular army; accordingly the are intended for use in the interior and in towns. Let the national–guard who can pay for his uniform, and the active citizen whose three francs of direct tax gives him a privilege, own their guns; the stevedore, the market–porter, the lodger, the passive citizen, whose poverty excludes them from voting must have their pikes, and, in these insurrectionary times, a ballot is not worth a good pike wielded by brawny arms. — The magistrate in his robes may issue any summons he pleases, but it will be rammed down his throat, and, lest he should be in doubt of this he is made to know it beforehand. "The Revolution began with pikes and pikes will finish it."[85] "Ah," say the regulars of the Tuileries gardens, "if the good patriots of the Champs de Mars only had had pikes like these the blue-coats (Lafayette's guards) would not have had such a good hand!" – "They are to be used everywhere, wherever there are enemies of the people, to the Château, if any can be found there!" They will override the veto and make sure that the National Assembly will approve the good laws. To this purpose, the Faubourg St. Antoine volunteers its pikes, and, to mark the use made of them, it complains that "efforts are made to substitute an aristocracy of wealth for the omnipotence of inherited rank." It demands "severe measures against the rascally hypocrites who, with the Constitution in their hands, slaughter the people." It declares that "kings, ministers and a civil list will pass away, but that the rights of man, national sovereignty and pikes will not pass away," and, by order of the president, the National Assembly thanks the petitioners, "for the advice their zeal prompts them to give.

The leaders of the Assembly and the people armed with pikes unite against the rich, against Constitutionalists, against the government, and henceforth, the Jacobin extremists march side by side with the Girondins, both reconciled for the attack but reserved their right to disagree until after the victory.

"The object of the Girondists[86] is not a republic in name, but an actual republic through a reduction of the civil lists to five millions, through the curtailment of most of the royal prerogatives, through a change of dynasty of which the new head would be a sort of honorary president of the republic to which they would assign an executive council appointed by the Assembly, that is to say, by themselves." As to the Jacobin extremists we find no principle with them but "that of a rigorous, absolute application of the Rights of Man. With the aid of such a charter they aim at changing the laws and public officers every six months, at extending their leveling process to every constituted authority, to all legal pre-eminence and to property. The only regime they long for is the democracy of a contentious rabble. . . The vilest instruments, professional agitators, brigands, fanatics, every sort of wretch, the hardened and armed poverty-stricken, who, in wild disorder" march to the attack of property and to "universal pillage" in short, barbarians of town and country "who form their ordinary army and never leave it inactive one single day." – Under their universal, concerted and growing usurpation the substance of power melts wholly away in the hand of the legal authorities; little by little, these are reduced to vain counterfeits, while from one end of France, to the other, long before the final collapse, the party, in the provinces as well as at Paris, substitutes, under the cry of public danger, a government of might for the government of law.

NOTES:

[1] Mercure de France, September 24, 1791. — Cf. Report of M. Alquier (session of Sept. 23).

[2] Mercure de France, Oct. 15, 1792 (the treaty with England was dated Sep. 26, 1786). — Ibid., Letter of M. Walsh, superior of the Irish college, to the municipality of Paris. Those who use the

whips, come out of a neighboring grog–shop. The commissary of police, who arrives with the National Guard, "addresses the people, and promises them satisfaction," requiring M. Walsh to dismiss all who are in the chapel, without waiting for the end of the mass. — M. Walsh refers to the law and to treaties. — The commissary replies that he knows nothing about treaties, while the commandant of the national guard says to those who laving the chapel, "In the name of human justice, I order you to follow me to the church of Saint–Etienne, or I shall abandon you to the people."

[3] "The French Revolution," Vol. I. pp.261, 263. — "Archives Nationales," F7, 3185 and 3186 (numerous documents on the rural disturbances in Aisne). – Mercure de France, Nov. 5 and 26, Dec. 10, 1791. – Moniteur, X. 426 (Nov.22, 1791).

[4] Moniteur, X. 449, Nov. 23, 1791. (Official report of the crew of the Ambuscade, dated Sep. 30). The captain, M. d'Orléans, stationed at the Windward Islands, is obliged to return to Rochefort and is detained there on board his ship: "Considering the uncertainty of his mission, and the fear of being ordered to use the same hostilities against brethren for which he is already denounced in every club in the kingdom, the crew has forced the captain to return to France."

[5] Mercure de France, Dec. 17, address of the colonists to the king.

[6] Moniteur, XIII. 200. Report of Sautereau, July 20, on the affair of Corporal Lebreton. (Nov. 11, 1791).

[7] Saint Huruge is first tenor. Justine (Sado–machosistic book by de Sade) makes her appearance in the Palais–Royal about the middle of 1791. They exhibit two pretended savages there, who, before a paying audience, revive the customs of Tahiti. (" Souvenirs of chancelier Pasquier. Ed. Plon, 1893))

[8] Mercure de France, Nov. 5, 1791. – Buchez et Roux, XII. 338. Report by Pétion, mayor, Dec. 9, 1791. "Every branch of the police is in a state of complete neglect. The streets are dirty, and full of rubbish; robbery, and crimes of every kind, are increasing to a frightful degree." "Correspondance de M. de Staël" (manuscript), Jan. 22, 1792. "As the police is almost worthless, freedom from punishment, added to poverty, brings on disorder."

[9] Moniteur, XI. 517 (session of Feb. 29, 1792). Speeches by de Lacépède and de Mulot.

[10] Lacretelle, "Dix ans d'Epreuves." "I know no more dismal and discouraging aspect than the interval between the departure of the National Assembly, on the 10th August consummated by that of September 2."

[11] Mercure de France, Sept. 3, 1791, article by Mallet du Pan.

[12] Moniteur, XI. 317 (session of Feb. 6, 1792). Speech by M. Cahier, a minister. Many of the emigrants belong to the class formerly called the Third–Estate. No reason for emigrating, on their part, can be supposed but that of religious anxieties."

[13] Decree of Nov. 9, 1791. The first decree seems to be aimed only at the armed gatherings on the frontier. We see, however, by the debates, that it affects all emigrants. The decrees of Feb. 9 and March 30, 1792, bear upon all, without exception. — "Correspondance de Mirabeau et du Comte de la Marck," III. 264 (letter by M. Pellenc, Nov. 12, 1791) The decree (against the emigrants) was prepared in committee; it was expected that the emigrants would return, but there was fear of them. It was feared that the nobles, associated with the unsworn priests in the rural districts, might add strength to a troublesome resistance. The decree, as it was passed, seemed to be the most suitable for keeping the emigrants beyond the frontiers."

[14] Decree of Feb. 1, 1792. — Moniteur, XI. 412 (session of Feb. 17). Speech by Goupilleau. "Since the decree of the National Assembly on passports, emigrations have redoubled." People evidently escaped from France as from a prison.

[15] Decrees of June 18 and August 25.

[16] Decree of June 19. — Moniteur, XIII. 331. "In execution of the law . . . there will be burnt, on Tuesday, August 7, on the Place Vendôme, at 2 o'clock: 1st, 600, more or less, of files of papers, forming the last of genealogical collections, titles and proofs of nobility; 2nd, about 200 files, forming part of a work composed of 263 volumes, on the Order of the Holy Ghost."

[17] Decree of Nov. 29, 1791. (This decree is not in Duvergier's collection~) — Moniteur, XII. 59, 247 (sessions of April 5 and 28, 1792).

[18] At the Jacobin Club, Legendre proposes a much a more expeditious measure for getting rid of the priests. "At Brest, he says, boats are found which are called Marie–Salopes, so constructed that, on being loaded with dirt, they go out of the harbor themselves. Let us have a similar arrangement for priests; but, instead of sending them out of the harbor, let us send them out to sea, and, if necessary, let them go down." ("Journal de Amis de la Constitution," number 194, May 15, 1792.)

[19] Moniteur, XII. 560 (decree of June 3).

[20] Decrees of July 19 and Aug. 4, completed by those of Aug. 16 and 19.

[21] Moniteur, XII. 59, 61 (session of April 3); X. 374 (session of Nov. 13; XII 230 (session of April 26). — The last sentence quoted was uttered by François de Nantes.

[22] Moniteur, XI. 43. (session of Jan. 5, speech by Isnard).

[23] Moniteur, XI. 356 (session of Feb. 10).

[24] Moniteur, XI. 230 (session of April 26).

[25] When I was a child the socialists etc. had substituted aristocracy with capitalists and today, in France, when the capitalists have largely disappeared, a great many evils are caused by the 'patronat'. (SR).

[26] Moniteur (session of June 22).

[27] The words of Brissot (Patriote Français), number 887. — Letter addressed Jan. 5 to the club of Brest, by Messrs. Cavalier and Malassis, deputies to the National Assembly: "As to the matter of the sieur Lajaille, even though we would have taken an interest in him, that decorated aristocrat only deserved what he got. . . We shall not remain idle until all these traitors, these perjurers, whom we have spared so long, shall be exterminated" (Mercure de France, Feb. 4). — This Jaille affair is one of the most instructive, and the best supported by documents (Mercure de France, Dec.10 and 17). — "Archives Nationales," F7, 3215, official report of the district administrators, and of the municipal officers of Brest, Nov. 27, 1791. — Letter by M. de Marigny, commissary in the navy, at Brest, Nov. 28. — Letters by M. de la Jaille, etc. — M. de la Jaille, sent to Brest to take command of the Dugay–Trouin, arrives there Nov.27. While at dinner, twenty persons enter the room, and announce to him, "in the name of many others," that his presence in Brest is causing trouble, that he must leave, and that "he will not be allowed to take command of a vessel." He replies, that he will leave the town, as soon as he has finished his dinner. Another deputation follows, more numerous than the first one, and insists on his leaving at once; and they act as his escort. He submits, is conducted to the city gates, and there the escort leaves him. A mob attacks him, and "his body is covered with contusions. He is rescued, with great difficulty, by six brave fellows, of whom one is a pork–dealer, sent to bleed him on the spot. "This insurrection is due to an extra meeting of 'The Friends of the constitution,' held the evening before in the theater, to which the public were invited." M. de la Jaille, it must be stated, is not a proud aristocrat, but a sensible man, in the style of Florian's and Berquin's heroes. But just pounded to a jelly, he writes to the president of the "Friends of the Constitution," that, "could he have flown into the bosom of the club, he would have gladly done so, to convey to it his grateful feelings. He had accepted his command only at the solicitation of the Americans in Paris, and of the six commissioners recently arrived from St. Domingo." — Mercure de France, April 14, article by Mallet du Pan "I have asked in vain for the vengeance of the law against the assassins of M. de la Jaille. The names of the authors of this assault in full daylight, to which thousands can bear witness, are known to everybody in Brest. Proceedings have been ordered and begun, but the execution of the orders is suspended. More potent than the law, the motionnaires, protectors of assassins, frighten or paralyze its ministrants."

[28] Mercure de France, Nov. 12 (session of Oct. 31st, 1792).

[29] Decree of Feb. 8, and others like it, on the details, as, for instance, that of Feb. 7.

[30] April 9, at the Jacobin Club, Vergniaud, the president, welcomes and compliments the convicts of Chateau–vieux.

[31] Mortimer–Ternaux, book I, vol. I. (especially the session of April 15).

[32] Comtat (or comtat Venaisssin) ancient region in France under papal authority from 1274 to 1791.(SR)

[33] Moniteur, XII. 335. – Decree of March 20 (the triumphal entry of Jourdan and his associates belongs to the next month).

[34] Moniteur, XII. 730 (session of June 23).

[35] Moniteur, XII. 230 (session of April 12).

[36] Moniteur. XI. 6, (session of March 6).

[37] Moniteur, XI. 123, (session of Jan. 14)

[38] 150 years later these rights were written into the International Declaration of Human Rights in Paris in 1948. (SR).

[39] Mercure de France, Dec. 23 (session of Dec. 23), p.98.

[40] Moniteur, X. 178 (session of Oct. 20, 1791). Information supplied by the deputies of the Upper and Lower Rhine departments. — M. Koch says: "An army of émigrés never existed, unless it be a petty gathering, which took place at Ettenheim, a few leagues from Strasbourg. . . (This troop) encamped in tents, but only because it lacked barracks and houses." — M. ——, deputy of the lower Rhine, says: "This army at Ettenheim is composed of about five or six hundred poorly–clad, half–paid men, deserters of all nations, sleeping in tents, for lack of other shelter, and armed with clubs, for lack of fire–arms and deserting every day, because money is getting scarce. The second army, at Worms, under the command of a Condé, is composed of three hundred gentlemen, and as many valets and grooms. I have to add, that the letters which reach me from Strasbourg, containing extracts of inside information from Frankfort, Munich, Regensburg, and Vienna, announce the most pacific intentions on the part of the different courts, since receiving the notification of the king's submission." The number of armed emigrants increases, but always remain very small (Moniteur, X. 678, letter of M. Delatouche, an eyewitness, Dec. 10). "I suppose that the number of emigrants scattered around on the territories of the grand–duke of Baden, the bishop of Spires, the electorates, etc., amounts to scarcely 4,000 men."

[41] Moniteur, X. 418 (session of Nov. 15, 1791). Report by the minister Delessart. In August, the emperor issued orders against enlistments, and to send out of the country all Frenchmen under suspicion; also, in October, to send away the French who formed too numerous a body at Ath and at Tournay (Now in Belgium). — Buchez et Roux, XII. 395, demands of the king, Dec. 14, — Ibid., XIII. 15, 16, 19, 52, complete satisfaction given by the Elector of Trèves, Jan. 1, 1792, communicated to the Assembly Jan. 6; publication of the elector's orders in the electorate, Jan. 3. The French envoy reports that they are fully executed, which news with the documents, are communicated to the Assembly, on the 8th, 16, and 19th of January. — " Correspondance de Mirabeau et M. de la Marck," III.287. Letter of M. de Mercy–Argenteau, Jan. 9, 1792. "The emperor has promised aid to the elector, under the express stipulation that he should begin by yielding to the demands of the French, as otherwise no assistance would be given to him in case of attack."

[42] Mallet du Pan, "Mémoires," I. 254 (February, 1792). — " Correspondance de Mirabeau et du M. de la Marck," III. 232 (note of M. de Bacourt). On the very day and at the moment of signing the treaty at Pilnitz, at eleven o'clock in the evening, the Emperor Leopold wrote to his prime minister, M. de Kaunitz, "that the convention which he had just signed does not really bind him to anything;

that it only contains insignificant declarations, extorted by the Count d'Artois." He ends by assuring him that "neither himself nor his government is in any way bound by this instrument."

[43] Words of M. de Kaunitz, Sept. 4, 1791 ("Recueil," by Vivenot, I. 242).

[44] Moniteur, XI. 142 (session of Jan. 17). – Speech by M. Delessart. – Decree of accusation against him March 10. – Declaration of war, April 20. – On the real intentions of the King, cf. Malouet, "Malouet, "Mémoires" II. 199–209; Lafayette, "Mémoires," I. 441 (note 3); Bertrand de Molleville, "Mémoires," VI. 22; Governor Morris, II. 242, letter of Oct. 23, 1792.

[45] Moniteur, X. 172 (session of Oct. 20, 1791). Speech by Brissot. – – Lafayette, I. 441. "It is the Girondists who, at this time, wanted a war at any price" – Malouet, II. 209. "As Brissot has since boasted, it was the republican party which wanted war, and which provoked it by insulting all the powers."

[46] Buchez et Roux, XII. 402 (session of the Jacobin Club, Nov. 28, 1791).

[47] Gustave III., King of Sweden, assassinated by Ankerstrom, says: "I should like to know what Brissot will say."

[48] On Brissot's antecedents, cf. Edmond Biré, "La Légende des Girondins." Personally, Brissot was honest, and remained poor. But he had passed through a good deal of filth, and bore the marks of it. He had lent himself to the diffusion of an obscene book, "Le Diable dans un bénitier," and, in 1783, having received 13,355 francs to found a Lyceum in London, not only did not found it, but was unable to return the money.

[49] Moniteur, XI. 147. Speech by Brissot, Jan. 17. Examples from whom he borrows authority, Charles XII., Louis XIV., Admiral Blake, Frederic II., etc.

[50] Moniteur. X. 174. "This Venetian government, which is nothing but a farce . . . Those petty German princes, whose insolence in the last century despotism crushed out. . . Geneva, that atom of a republic. . .That bishop of Liège, whose yoke bows down a people that ought to be free . . . I disdain to speak of other princes. . . That King of Sweden, who has only twenty–five millions income, and who spends two–thirds of it in poor pay for an army of generals and a small number of discontented soldiers. . . As to that princess (Catherine II.), whose dislike of the French constitution is well known, and who is about as good looking as Elizabeth, she cannot expect greater success than Elizabeth in the Dutch revolution." (Brissot, in this last passage, tries to appear at once witty and well read.)

[51] Letter of Roland to the king, June 10, 1792, and letter of the executive council to the pope, Nov. 25, 1792. Letter of Madame Roland to Brissot, Jan. 7, 1791. "Briefly, adieu. Cato's wife need not gratify herself by complimenting Brutus."

[52] Buchez et Roux, XII. 410 (meeting of the Jacobin club, Dec. 10, 1791). "A Louis XIV. declares war against Spain, because his ambassador had been insulted by the Spanish ambassador. And we, who are free, might hesitate for an instant!"

[53] Moniteur, X, 503 (session of Nov.29). The Assembly orders this speech to be printed and distributed in the departments.

[54] Moniteur , X. 762 (session of Dec. 28).

[55] Moniteur, XI. 147, 149 (session of Jan.17); X. 759 (session of Dec. 28). — Already, on the 10th of December, he had declared at the Jacobin club: "A people that has conquered its freedom, after ten centuries of slavery, needs war. War is essential to it for its consolidation." (Buchez et Roux, XII. 410). — On the 17th of January, in the tribune, he again repeats: "I have only one fear, and that is, that we may not have war."

[56] Moniteur, XI. 119 (session of Jan.13). Speech by Gensonné, in the name of the diplomatic committee, of which he is the reporter.

[57] Moniteur, XI. 158 (session of Jan. 18). The Assembly orders the printing of this speech.

[58] Moniteur, XI. 760 (session of Dec. 28).

[59] Moniteur, XI. 149 (session of Jan. 17). Speech by Brissot.

[60] Moniteur, XI. 178 (session of Jan.20). Fauchet proposes the following decree: "All partial treaties actually existent are declared void. The National Assembly substitutes in their place alliances with the English, the Anglo–American, the Swiss, Polish, and Dutch nations, as long as they will be free . . When other nations want our alliance, they have only to conquer their freedom to have it. Meanwhile, this will not prevent us from having relations with them, as with good natured savages . . . Let us occupy the towns in the neighborhood which bring our adversaries too near us . . . Mayence, Coblentz, and Worms are sufficient" – Ibid.,, p.215 (session of Jan.25). One of the members, supporting himself with the authority of Gélon, King of Syracuse, proposes an additional article: "We declare that we will not lay down our arms until we shall have established the freedom of all peoples." These stupidities show the mental condition of the Jacobin party.

[61] The decree is passed Jan. 25. The alliance between Prussia and Austria takes place Feb. 7 (De Bourgoing, "Histoire diplomatique de l'Europe pendant la Révolution Française," I. 457).

[62] Albert Sorel, "La Mission du Comte de Ségur à Berlin" (published in the Temps, Oct. 15, 1878). Dispatch of M. de Ségur to M. Delessart, Feb. 24, 1792. Count Schulemburg repeated to me that they had no desire whatever to meddle with our constitution. But, said he with singular animation, we must guard against gangrene. Prussia is, perhaps, the country which should fear it least; nevertheless, however remote a gangrened member may be, it is better to it off than risk one's life. How can you expect to secure tranquility, when thousands of writers every day . . . mayors, office–holders, insult kings, and publish that the Christian religion has always supported despotism, and that we shall be free only by destroying it, and that all princes must be exterminated because they are all tyrants?"

[63] A popular jig of these revolutionary times, danced in the streets and on the public squares. –TR.

[64] Buchez et Roux, XXV. 203 (session of April 3, 1793). Speech by Brissot. –Ibid., XX. 127. "A tous les Républicains de France, par Brissot," Oct. 24, 1792. "In declaring war, I had in view the abolition of royalty." He refers, in this connection, to his speech of Dec. 30, 1791, where he says, "I fear only one thing, and that is, that we shall not be betrayed. We need treachery, for strong doses of poison still exist in the heart of France, and heavy explosions are necessary to clear it out."

[65] Mallet du Pan, "Mémoires," I. 260 (April, 1792), and I. 439 (July, 1792).

[66] Any revolutionary leader, from Lenin, through Stalin to Andropov may confirm the advantage of acting in secret. (SR).

[67] "The French Revolution," I. 262 and following pages.

[68] Buchez et Roux, XIII. 92–99 (January, 1792); (February). — Coral, "Lettres inédites," 33. (One of these days, out of curiosity, he walked along as far as the Rue des Lombards.) "Witness of such crying injustice, and indignant at not being able to seize any of the thieves that were running along the street, loaded with sugar and coffee to sell again, I suddenly felt a feverish chill over all my body." (The letter is not dated. The editors conjectures that the year was 1791. I rather think that it was 1792.)

[69] Moniteur, XI. 45 and 46 (session of Jan. 5). The whole of Isnard's speech should be read.

[70] Buchez et Roux, XIII. 177. Letter by Pétion, Feb. 10.

[71] Buchez et Roux, XIII. 252. Letter of André Chénier, in the Journal de Paris, Feb. 26. – Schmidt, "Tableaux de la Révolution Franaise," I. 76. Reply of the Directory of the Department of the Seine to a circular by Roland, June 12, 1792. The contrast between the two classes is here clearly defined. "We have not resorted to those assemblages of men, most of them foreigners, for the opinion of the people, among the enemies of labor and repose standing by themselves and having no part in common interests, already inclined to vice through idleness, and who prefer the risks of disorder to the honorable resources of indigence. This class of men, always large in large cities, is that whose noisy harangues fill the streets, Squares, and public gardens of the capital, that which excites seditious gatherings, that which constantly fosters anarchy and contempt for the laws — that, in fine, whose clamor, far from reflecting public Opinion, indicates the extreme effort made to prevent the expression of public opinion. . . We have studied the opinion of the people of Paris among those useful and laborious men warmly attached to the State at all points of their existence through every object of their affection, among owners of property, tillers of the soil, tradesmen and workers . . . An inviolable attachment . . . to the constitution, and mainly to national Sovereignty, to political equality and constitutional monarchy, which are its most important characteristics and their almost unanimous sentiment."

[72] Governor Morris, letter of June 20, 1792.

[73] "Souvenirs", by Pasquier (Etienne–Dennis, duc), chancelier de France. in VI volumes, Librarie Plon, Paris 1893. Vol. I. page 84.

[74] Malouet, II. 203. Every report that came in from the provinces announced (to the King and Queen) a perceptible amelioration of public opinion, which was becoming more and more perverted. That which reached them was uninfluenced, whilst the opinions of clubs, taverns, and street–corners gained enormous power, the time being at hand when there was to be no other power." The figures given above are by Mallet du Pan, "Mémoires," II. 120.

[75] Moniteur, XII. 776 (session of June 28). Speech by M. Lamarque, in a district court: "The incivism of the district courts in general is well known."

[76] Bertand de Molleville, "Mémoires," VI. 22. — After having received the above instructions from the King, Bertrand calls on the Queen, who makes the same remark: "Do you not think that fidelity to one's oath is the only plan to pursue?" "Yes, Madame, certainly." "Very well; rest assured that we shall not waver. Come, M. Bertrand, take courage; I hope that with firmness, patience, and what comes of that, all is not yet lost."

[77] M. de Lavalette, "Mémoires," I. 100. — Lavalette, in the beginning of September, 1792, enlists as a volunteer and sets out, along with two friends, carrying his knapsack on his back, dressed in a short and wearing a forage cap. The following shows the sentiments of the peasantry: In a village of makers of wooden shoes, near Vermanton (in the vicinity of Autun), "two days before our arrival a bishop and two vicars, who were escaping in a carriage, were stopped by them. They rummaged the vehicle and found some hundreds of francs, and, to avoid returning these, they thought it best to massacre their unfortunate owners. This sort of occupation seeming more lucrative to these good people than the other one, they were on the look–out for all wayfarers." The three volunteers are stopped by a little hump– backed official and conducted to the municipality, a sort of market, where their passports are read and their knapsacks are about to be examined. "We were lost, when d'Aubonnes, who was very tall jumped on the table. . . and began with a volley of imprecations and market slang which took his hearers by surprise. Soon raising his style, he launched out in patriotic terms, liberty, sovereignty of the people, with such vehemence and in so loud a voice, as to suddenly effect a great change and bring down thunders of applause. But the crazy fellow did not stop there. Ordering Leclerc de la Ronde imperiously to mount on the table, he addressed the assemblage: "You shall see whether we are not Paris republicans. Now, sir, say your republican catechism – 'What is God? what are the People? and what is a King?' His friend, with an air of contrition and in a nasal tone of voice, twisting himself about like a harlequin, replies: 'God is matter, the People are the poor, and the King is a lion, a tiger, an elephant who tears to pieces, devours, and crushes the people down.'" — "They could no longer restrain themselves. The shouts, cries, and enthusiasm were unbounded. They embraced the actors, hugged them, and bore them away. Each strove to carry us home with him, and we had to drink all round"

[78] The reader will meet the French expression sans–culottes again and again in Taine's or any other book about the French revolution. The nobles wore a kind of breeches terminating under the knee while tight long stockings, fastened to the trousers, exposed their calves. The male leg was as important an adornment for the nobles as it was to be for the women in the 20th Century. The poor, on the other hand, wore crude long trousers, mostly without a crease, often without socks or shoes, barefoot in the summer and wooden shoed in the winter. (SR).

[79] The song of "Veillons au salut de l'empire" belongs to the end of 1791. The "Marseillaise" was composed in April, 1792.

[80] Mercure de France, Nov. 23, 1791.

[81] Philippe de Ségur, "Mémoires," I. (at Fresnes, a village situated about seven leagues from Paris, a few days after Sep. 2, 1792). "A band of these demagogues pursued a large farmer of this place, suspected of royalism and denounced as a monopoliser because he was rich. These madmen had seized him, and, without any other form of trial, were about to put an end to him, when my father ran up to them. He addressed them, and so successfully as to change their rage into a no less exaggerated enthusiasm for humanity. Animated by their new transports, they obliged the poor farmer, still pale and trembling, and whom they were just going to hang on its branches, to drink and dance along with them around the tree of liberty."

[82] Lacretelle, "Dix ans d'Epreuves," 78. "The Girondists wanted to fashion a Roman people out of the dregs of Romulus, and, what is worse, out of the brigands of the 5th of October."

[83] These pages must have made a strong impression upon Lenin when he read them in the National Library in Paris around 1907. (SR).

[84] Lafayette, I. 442. "The Girondists sought in the war an opportunity for attacking with advantage, the constitutionalists of 1791 and their institutions." — Brissot (Address to my constituents). "We sought in the war an opportunity to set traps for the king, to expose his bad faith and his relationship with the emigrant princes." – Moniteur, (session of April 3, 1793). Speech by Brissot: "'I had told the Jacobins what my opinion was, and had proved to them that war was the sole means of unveiling the perfidy of Louis XVI. The event has justified my opinion." — Buchez et Roux, VIII. 60, 216, 217. The decree of the Legislative Assembly is dated Jan. 25, the first money voted by a club for the making of pikes is on Jan. 31, and the first article by Brissot, on the red cap, is on Feb. 6.

[85] Buchez et Roux, XIII. 217 (proposal of a woman, member of the club of l'Evêché, Jan. 31, 1792). — Articles in the Gazette Universelle, Feb.11, and in the Patriote Français, Feb. 13. – Moniteur, XI. 576 (session of March 6). – Buchez et Roux, XV. (session of June 10). Petition of 8,000 national guards in Paris: "This faction which stirs up popular vengeance . . . which seeks to put the caps of labor in conflict with the military casques, the pike with the gun, the rustic's dress with the uniform."

[86] Mallet du Pan, "Mémoires," II 429 (note of July, 1792). – Mercure de France, March 10, 1792, article by Mallet du Pan.

CHAPTER IV. THE DEPARTMENTS.

I.

Provence in 1792. — Early supremacy of the Jacobins in Marseilles. — Composition of the party. — The club and the municipality. — Expulsion of the "Earnest" regiment.

Should you like to see the revolutionary tree when, for the first time, it came fully into leaf, it is in the department of the Bouches– du–Rhône you have to look. Nowhere else had it been so precocious, nowhere were local circumstances and native temperament so well adapted to enhance its growth. — " A blistering sky, an excessive climate, an arid soil, rocks, . . . savage rivers, torrential or dry or overburdened," blinding dust, nerves upset by steady northern blasts or by the intermittent gusts of the sirocco. A sensual race choleric and impetuous, with no intellectual or moral ballast, in which the mixture of Celt and Latin has destroyed the humane suavity of the Celt and the serious earnestness of the Roman; "complete, tough, powerful, and restless men,"[1] and yet gay, spontaneous, eloquent, dupes of their own bombast, suddenly carried away by a flow of words and superficial enthusiasm. Their principal city numbering 120,000 souls, in which commercial and maritime risks foster innovating and adventurous spirits; in which the sight of suddenly– acquired fortunes expended on sensual enjoyments constantly undermines all stability of Character; in which politics, like speculation, is a lottery offering its prizes to audacity; besides all this, a free port and a rendezvous for lawless nomads, disreputable people, without steady trade,[2] scoundrels, and blackguards, who, like uprooted, decaying seaweed, drift from coast to coast around the entire circle of the Mediterranean sea; a veritable sink filled with the dregs of twenty corrupt and semi–barbarous civilizations, where the scum of crime cast forth from the prisons of Genoa, Piedmont, Sicily, indeed, of all Italy, of Spain, of the Archipelago, and of Barbary,3 accumulates and ferments.2 No wonder that, in such a time the reign of the mob should be established there sooner than elsewhere.[3] — After many an explosion, this reign is inaugurated August 17, 1790, by the removal of M. Lieutaud, a sort of bourgeois, moderate Lafayette, who commands the National Guard. Around him rally a majority of the population, all men "honest or not, who have anything to lose."[4] After he is driven out, then proscribed, then imprisoned, they resign themselves, and Marseilles belongs to the low class, to 40,000 destitute and rogues led by the club.

The better to ensure their empire, the municipality, one month after the expulsion of M. Lieutaud, declared every citizen "active" who had any trade or profession[5]; the consequence is that vagabonds attend the meetings of the sections in contempt of constitutional law. The consequence, was that property–owners and commercial men withdrew, which was wise on their part, for the usual demagogic machinery is set in motion without delay. "Each section–assembly is composed of a dozen factious spirits, members of the club, who drive out honest people by displaying cudgels and bayonets. The deliberations are prepared beforehand at the club, in concert with the municipality, and woe to him who refuses to adopt them at the meeting! They go so far as to threaten citizens who wish to make any remarks with instant burial in the cellars under the churches."[6] The argument proved irresistible: "the majority of honest people are so frightened and so timid" that not one of them dare attend these meetings, unless protected by public force. "More than 80,000 inhabitants do not sleep peacefully," while all the political rights are vested in "five or six hundred individuals," legally disqualified. Behind them marches the armed rabble, "the horde of brigands without a country,"[7] always ready for plundering, murder, and hanging. In front of them march the local authorities, who, elected through their influence, carry on the administration under their guidance. Patrons and clients, members of the club and its satellites, they form a league which plays the part of a sovereign State, scarcely recognizing, even in words, the authority of the central government.[8] The decree by which the National Assembly gives full power to the Commissioners to re– establish order is denounced as plébécide; these conscientious and cautious moderators are qualified as "dictators"; they are denounced in circular letters to all the municipalities of the department, and to all Jacobin clubs throughout the kingdom;[9] the club is somewhat disposed to go to Aix to cut off their heads and send them in a trunk to the president of the National Assembly, with a threat that the same penalty awaits himself and all the deputies if they do not revoke their recent decrees. A few days after this, four sections draw up an act before a notary, stating the measures they had taken towards sending an army of 6,000 men from Marseilles to Aix, to get rid of the three intruders. The commissioners dare not enter Marseilles, where "gibbets are ready for them, and a price set on their heads." It is as much as they can do to rescue from the faction M. Lieutaud and his friends, who, accused of lése–nation, confined without a shadow of proof, treated like mad dogs, put in chains,[10] shut up in privies and holes, and obliged to drink their own urine for lack of water, impelled by despair to the brink of suicide, barely escape murder a dozen times in the courtroom and in prison.[11] Against the decree of the National Assembly ordering their release, the municipality makes reclamations, contrives delays, resists, and finally stirs up its usual instruments. Just as the prisoners are about to be released a crowd of "armed persons without uniform or officer," constantly increased "by vagabonds and foreigners," gathers on the heights overlooking the Palais de Justice, and makes ready to fire on M. Lieutaud. Summoned to proclaim martial law, the municipality refuses, declaring that "the general detestation of the accused is too manifest"; it demands the return of the Swiss regiment to its barracks, and that the prisoners remain where they are; the only thing which it grants them is a secret permission to escape, as if they were guilty; they, accordingly, steal away clandestinely and in disguise.[12] — The Swiss regiment, however, which prevents the magistrates from violating the law, must pay for its insolence, and, as it is incorruptible, they decide to drive it out of the town. For four months the municipality multiplies against it every kind of annoyance,[13] and, on the 16th of October, 1791, the Jacobins provoke a row in the theater against its officers. The same night, outside the theater, four of these are attacked by armed bands; the post to which they retreat is nearly taken by assault; they are led to a prison for safety, and there they still remain five days afterwards, "although their innocence is admitted." Meanwhile, to ensure "public tranquility," the municipality has required the commander of the post to immediately replace the Swiss Guard with National Guards on all the military posts; the latter yields to force, while the useless regiment, insulted and threatened, has nothing to do but to pack off.[14] This being done, the new municipality, still more Jacobin than the old one,[15] separates Marseilles from France, erects the city into a marauding republican government, gets up expeditions, levies contributions, forms alliances, and undertakes an armed conquest of the department.

II. The expedition to Aix.

The town of Marseilles send an expedition to Aix. — The regiment is disarmed. — The Directory driven out. — Pressure on the new Directory.

The first thing is to lay its hand on the district capital, Aix, where the Swiss regiment is stationed in garrison and where the superior authorities are installed. This operation is the more necessary inasmuch as the Directory of the department loudly commends the loyalty of the Swiss Guard and takes occasion to remind the Marseilles municipality of the respect due to the law. Such remonstrance is an insult, and the municipality, in a haughty tone, calls upon the Directory to avow or disavow its letter; "if you did not write it, it is a foul report which it is our duty to examine into, and if you did, it is a declaration of war made by you against Marseilles."[16] The Directory, in polite terms and with great circumspection, affirms both its right and its utterance, and remarks that "the prorata list of taxes of Marseilles for 1791 is not yet reported;" that the municipality is much more concerned with saving the State than with paying its contribution and, in short, it maintains its censure. — If it will not bend it must break, and on the 4th of February, 1792, the municipality sends Barbaroux, its secretary, to Paris, that he may mitigate the outrages they are preparing. During the night of the 25– 26, the drums beat the general alarm, and three or four thousand men gather and march to Aix with six pieces of cannon. As a precaution they pretend to have no leaders, no captains or lieutenants or even corporals; to quote them, all are equal, all volunteers, each being summoned by the other; in this fashion, as all are responsible, no one is.[17] They reach Aix at eleven o'clock in the forenoon, find a gate open through the connivance of those in league with them among the populace of the town and its suburbs, and summon the municipality to surrender the sentinels. In the mean time their emissaries have announced in the neighboring villages that the town was menaced by the Swiss regiment; consequently four hundred men from Aubagne arrive in haste, while from hour to hour the National Guards from the surrounding villages likewise rush in. The streets are full of armed men; shouts arise and the tumult increases; the municipal body, in the universal panic, loses its wits. This body is afraid of a nocturnal fight "between troops of the line, citizens, National Guards and armed strangers, no one being able to recognize one another or know who is an enemy." It sends back a detachment of three hundred and fifty Swiss Guards, which the Directory had ordered to its support, and consigns the regiment to its quarters. — At this the Directory takes to flight. Military sentinels of all kinds are disarmed while the Marseilles throng, turning its advantages to account, announces to the municipality at two o'clock in the morning that, "allow it or not " it is going to attack the barracks immediately; in fact, cannon are planted, a few shots are fired, a sentinel killed, and the hemmed−in regiment is compelled to evacuate the town, the men without their guns and the officers without their swords. Their arms are stolen, the people seize the suspected, the street−lamp is hauled down and the noose is made ready. Cayol, the flower−girl, is hung. The municipality, with great difficulty, saves one man who is already lifted by the rope two feet from the ground, and obtains for three others "a temporary refuge" in prison.

Henceforth there is no authority at the department headquarters, or rather it has changed hands. Another Directory, more pliable, is installed in the place of the fugitive Directory. Of the thirty−six administrators who form the Council only twelve are present at the election. Of the nine elected only six consent to sit, while often only three are found at its sessions, which three, to recruit their colleagues, are obliged to pay them.[18] Hence, notwithstanding their position is the best in the department, they are worse treated and more unfortunate than their servants outside. The delegates of the club, with the municipal officers of Marseilles seated alongside of them, oblige them either to keep silent, or to utter what they dictate to them.[19] "Our arms are tied," writes one of them, "we are wholly under the yoke" of these intruders. "We have twice in succession seen more than three hundred men, many of them with guns and pistols, enter the hall and threaten us with death if we refused them what they asked. We have seen infuriate motionnaires, nearly all belonging to Avignon, mount the desks of the Directory, harangue their comrades and excite them to rioting and crime. "You must decide between life or death," they exclaimed to us, "you have only a quarter of an hour to choose." "National guards have offered their sabers through the windows, left open on account of the extreme heat, to those around us and made signs to them to cut our throats." — Thus fashioned, reduced and drilled, the Directory is simply an instrument in the hands of the Marseilles demagogues. Camoïn, Bertin and Rebecqui, the worst agitators and usurpers, rule there without control. Rebecqui and Bertin, appointed delegates in connection with matters in Arles, have themselves empowered to call for defensive troops; they immediately demand them for attack, to which the Directory vainly remonstrates; they declare to it that "not being under its inspection, it has no authority over them; being independent of it, they have no orders to receive from it nor to render to it any account of their conduct." So much the worse for the Directory on attempting to revoke their powers. Bertin informs its vice–president that, if it dares do this he will cut off his head. They reply to the Minister's observations with the utmost insolence.[20] They glory in the boldness of the stroke and prepare another, their march on Aix being only the first halt in the long–meditated campaign which involves the possession of Arles.

III.

The Constitutionalists of Arles. — The Marseilles expedition against Arles. — Excesses committed by them in the town and its vicinity. — Invasion of "Apt," the club and its volunteers.

No city, indeed, is more odious to them. — For two years, led or pushed on by its mayor, M. d'Antonelle, it has marched along with them or been dragged along in their wake. D'Antonelle, an ultra– revolutionary, repeatedly visited and personally encouraged the bandits of Avignon. To supply them with cannon and ammunition he stripped the Tour St. Louis of its artillery, at the risk of abandoning the mouths of the Rhone to the Barbary pirates.[21] In concert with his allies of the Comtat, the Marseilles club, and his henchmen from the neighboring boroughs, he rules in Arles "by terror." Three hundred men recruited in the vicinity of the Mint, artisans or sailors with strong arms and rough hands, serve him as satellites. On the 6th of June 1791, they drive away, on their own authority, the unsworn priests, who had taken refuge in the town.[22] — At this, however, the "property–owners and decent people," much more numerous and for a long time highly indignant, raise their heads; twelve hundred of them assemble in the church of Saint–Honorat, swore to maintain the constitution and public order,"[23] and then moved to the (Jacobin) club, where, in their quality of national guards and active citizens and in conformity with its by–laws, they were admitted en masse. At the same time, acting in concert with the municipality, they reorganize the National Guard and form new companies, the effect of which is to put an end to the Mint gang, thus depriving the faction of all its strength. Thenceforth, without violence or illegal acts, the majority of the club, as well as of the National Guard, consists of constitutional monarchists, the elections of November, 1791, giving to the partisans of order nearly all the administrative offices of the commune and of the district. M. Loys, a physician and a man of energy, is elected mayor in the place of M. d'Antonelle; he is known as able to suppress a riot, "holding martial law in one hand, and his saber in the other." — This is too much; so Marseilles feel compelled to bring Arles under control "to atone for the disgrace of having founded it."[24] In this land of ancient cities political hostility is embittered with old municipal grudges, similar to those of Thebes against Platœe, of Rome against Veii, of Florence against Pisa. The Guelphs of Marseilles brooded over the one idea of crushing the Ghibellins of Arles. — Already, in the electoral assembly of November, 1791, M. d'Antonelle, the president, had invited the communes of the department to take up arms against this anti–jacobin city.[25] Six hundred Marseilles volunteers set out on the instant, install themselves at Salon, seize the syndic–attorney of the hostile district, and refuse to give him up, this being an advance–guard of 4,000 men promised by the forty or fifty clubs of the party.[26] To arrest their operations requires the orders of the three commissioners, resolutions passed by the Directory still intact, royal proclamations, a decree of the Constituent Assembly, the firmness of the still loyal troops and the firmer stand taken by the

Arlesians who, putting down an insurrection of the Mint band, had repaired their ramparts, cut away their bridges and mounted guard with their guns loaded.[27] But it is only a postponement. Now that the commissioners have gone, and the king's authority a phantom, now that the last loyal regiment is disarmed, the terrified Directory recast and obeying like a servant, with the Legislative Assembly allowing everywhere the oppression of the Constitutionalists by the Jacobins, a fresh Jacobin expedition may be started against the Constitutionalists with impunity. Accordingly, on the 23rd of March, 1792, the Marseilles army of 4,500 men sets out on its march with nineteen pieces of cannon.

In vain the commissioners of the neighboring departments, sent by the Minister, represent to them that Arles submits, that she has laid down her arms, and that the town is now garrisoned with troops of the line; — the Marseilles army requires the withdrawal of this garrison. — In vain the garrison departs. Rebecqui and his acolytes reply that "nothing will divert them from their enterprise; they cannot defer to anybody's decision but their own in relation to any precaution tending to ensure the safety of the southern departments." — In vain the Minister renews his injunctions and counter-orders. The Directory replies with a flagrant falsehood, stating that it is ignorant of the affair and refuses to give the government any assistance. — In vain M. de Wittgenstein, commander-in-chief in the south, offers his services to the Directory to repel the invaders. The Directory forbids him to take his troops into the territory of the department.[28] — Meanwhile, on the 29th of March, the Marseilles army effects a breach with its cannon in the walls of defenseless Arles; its fortifications are demolished and a tax of 1,400,000 francs is levied on the owners of property. In contempt of the National Assembly's decree the Mint bandits, the longshoremen, the whole of the lowest class again take up their arms and lord it over the disarmed population. Although "the King's commissioner and most of the judges have fled, jury examinations are instituted against absentees," the juries consisting of the members of the Mint band.[29] The conquerors imprison, smite and slaughter as they please. Countless peaceable individuals are struck down and mauled, dragged to prison and many of them are mortally wounded. An old soldier, eighty years of age, retired to his country home three months earlier, dies after twenty days' confinement in a dungeon, from a blow received in the stomach by a rifle butt; women are flogged. "All citizens that with an interest in law and order," nearly five thousand families, have emigrated; their houses in town and in the country are pillaged, while in the surrounding boroughs, along the road leading from Arles to Marseilles, the villains forming the hard core of the Marseilles army, rove about and gorge themselves as in a vanquished country.[30]

They eat and drink voraciously, force the closets, carry off linen and food, steal horses and valuables, smash the furniture, tear up books, and burn papers.[31] All this is only the appropriate punishment of the aristocrats. Moreover, it is no more than right that patriots should be indemnified for their toil, and a few blows too many are not out of place in securing the rule of the right party. — For example, on the false report of order being disturbed at Château-Renard, Bertin and Rebecqui send off a detachment of men, while the municipal body in uniform, followed by the National Guard, with music and flags, comes forth to meet and salute it. Without uttering a word of warning, the Marseilles troop falls upon the cortège, strikes down the flags, disarms the National Guard, tears the epaulettes off the officers' shoulders, drags the mayor to the ground by his scarf, pursues the counselors, sword in hand, puts the mayor and syndic-attorney in arrest, and, during the night, sacks four dwellings, the whole under the direction of three Jacobins of the place under indictment for recent crimes or misdemeanors. Henceforth at Château-Renard they will look twice before subjecting patriots to indictment.[32] — At Vélaux "the country house of the late seignior is sacked, and everything is carried away, even to the tiles and window–glass." A troop of two hundred men "overrun the village, levy contributions, and put all citizens who are well–off under bonds for considerable sums." Camoïn, the Marseille chief, one of the new department administrators, who is in the neighborhood, lays his hand on everything that is fit to be taken, and, a few days after this, 30,000 francs are found in his carpet–bag.–Taught by the example others follow and the commotion spreads. In every borough or petty town the club profits by these acts to satiate its ambition its greed, and its hatred. That of Apt appeals to its neighbors, whereupon 1,500 National Guards of Gordes, St. Saturnin, Gouls and Lacoste, with a thousand women and children armed with clubs and scythes, arrive one morning before the town. On being asked by whose orders they come in this fashion, they reply, "by the orders which their patriotism has given them." — "The fanatics," or partisans of the sworn priests, "are the cause of their journey": they therefore "want lodgings at the expense of the fanatics only." The three day's occupation results for the latter and for the town in a cost of 20,000 livres.[33] They begin by breaking everything in the church of the Récollets, and wall up its doors. They then expel unsworn ecclesiastics from the town, and disarm their partisans. The club of Apt, which is the sole authority, remains in session three days: "the municipal bodies in the vicinity appear before it, apologize for themselves, protest their civism, and ask as a favor that no detachment be sent to their places. Individuals are sent for to be interrogated"; several are proscribed, among whom are administrators, members of the court, and the syndic–attorney. A number of citizens have fled; — the town is purged, while the same purging is pursued in numbers of places in and out of the district.[34] It is, indeed, attractive business. It empties the purses of the ill–disposed, and fills the stomachs of patriots; it is agreeable to be well entertained, and especially at the expense of one's adversaries; the Jacobin is quite content to save the country through a round of feastings. Moreover, he has the satisfaction of playing king among his neighbors, and not only do they feed him for doing them this service, but, again, they pay him for it.[35] – All this is enlivening, and the expedition, which is a "sabbath," ends in a carnival. Of the two Marseilles divisions, one, led back to Aix, sets down to "a grand patriotic feast," and then dances fandangoes, of which "the principal one is led off by the mayor and commandant";[36] the other makes its entry into Avignon the same day, with still greater pomp and jollity.

IV.

The Jacobins of Avignon.— How they obtain recruits. – –Their robberies in the Comtat. — The Avignon municipality in flight or in prison. — Murder of Lécuyer and the Glacière massacre. — Entry of the murderers, supported by their Marseilles allies. — Jacobin dictatorship in Vaucluse and the Buches–du–Rhône.

Nowhere else in France was there another nest of brigands like it: not that a great misery might have produced a more savage uprising; on the contrary, the Comtat, before the Revolution, was a land of plenty. There was no taxation by the Pope; the taxes were very light, and were expended on the spot. "For one or two pennies, one here could have meat, bread, and wine."[37] But, under the mild and corrupt administration of the Italian legates, the country had become "the safe asylum of all the rogues in France, Italy, and Genoa, who by means of a trifling sum paid to the Pope's agents, obtained protection and immunity." Smugglers and receivers of stolen goods abounded here in order to break through the lines of the French customs. "Bands of robbers and assassins were formed, which the vigorous measures of the parliaments of Aix and Grenoble could not wholly extirpate. Idlers, libertines, professional gamblers,"[38] kept–cicisbeos, schemers, parasites, and adventurers, mingle with men with branded shoulders, the veterans "of vice and crime, "the scapegraces of the Toulon and Marseilles galleys." Ferocity here is hidden in debauchery, like a serpent hidden in its own slime, here all that is required is some chance event and this bad place will be transformed into a death trap.

The Jacobin leaders, Tournal, Rovère, the two Duprats, the two Mainvielles, and Lécuyer, readily obtain recruits in this sink. – They begin, aided by the rabble of the town and of its suburbs, peasants enemies of the octroi, vagabonds opposed to order of any kind, porters and watermen armed with scythes, turnspits and clubs, by exciting seven or eight riots. Then they drive off the legate, force the Councils to resign, hang the chiefs of the National Guard and of the conservative party,[39] and take possession of the municipal offices. —After this their band increases to the dimensions of an army, which, with license for its countersign and pillage for its pay, is the same as that of Tilly and Wallenstein, "a veritable roving Sodom, at which the ancient city would have stood aghast." Out of 3,000 men, only 200 belong in Avignon; the rest are composed of French deserters, smugglers, fugitives from justice, vagrant foreigners, marauders and criminals, who, scenting a prey, come from afar, and even from Paris;[40] along with them march the women belonging to them, still more base and bloodthirsty. In order to make it perfectly plain that with them murder and robbery are the order of the day, they massacred their first general, Patrix, guilty of having released a prisoner, and elected in his place an old highway tramp named Jourdan, condemned to death by the court at Valence, but who had escaped on the eve of his execution, and who bore the nickname of Coupe–tête, because he is said to have cut off the heads at Versailles of two of the King's guards.[41] — Under such a commander the troop increases until it forms a body of five or six thousand men, which stops people in the streets and forcibly enrolls them; they are called Mandrins, which is severe for Mandrin,[42] because their war is not merely on public persons and property, as his was, but on the possessions, the proprieties, and the lives of private individuals. One detachment alone, at one time, extorts in Cavaillon 25,000 francs, in Baume 12,000, in Aubignon 15,000, in Pioline 4,800, while Caumont is taxed 2,000 francs a week. At Sarrians, where the mayor gives them the keys, they pillage houses from top to bottom, carry off their plunder in carts, set fire, violate and slay with all the refinements of torture of so many Hurons. An old lady of eighty, and a paralytic, is shot at arms length, and left weltering in her blood in the midst of the flames. A child five years of age is cut in two, its mother decapitated, and its sister mutilated; they cut off the ears of the curé, set them on his brow like a cockade, and then cut his throat, along with that of a pig, and tear out the two hearts and dance around them.[43] After this, for fifty days around Carpentras, to which they lay siege in vain, the unprovoked, cruel instincts of the chauffeurs manifested at a later date, the ancient cannibalistic desires which sometimes reappear in convicts, and the perverted and over–strained sensuality found in maniacs, have full play.

On beholding the monster it has nourished, Avignon, in alarm, utters cries of distress.[44] But the brute, which feels its strength, turns against its former abettors, shows its teeth, and exacts its daily food. Ruined or not, Avignon must furnish its quota. "In the electoral assembly, Mainvielle the younger, elected elector, although he is only twenty–two, draws two pistols from his belt and struts around with a threatening air."[45] Duprat, the president, the better to master his colleagues, proposes to them to leave Avignon and go to Sorgues, which they refuse to do; upon this he orders cannon to be brought, promises to pay those who will accompany him, drags along the timid, and denounces the rest before an upper national court, of which he himself has designated the members. Twenty of the electors thus denounced are condemned and proscribed; Duprat threatens to enter by force and have them executed on the spot, and, under his leadership, the army of Mandrins advances against Avignon. — Its progress is arrested, and, for two months, restrained by the two mediating commissioners for France; they reduce its numbers, and it is on the point of being disbanded, when the brute again boldly seizes its prey, about to make its escape. On the 21st of August, Jourdan, with his herd of miscreants, obtains possession of the palace. The municipal body is driven out, the mayor escapes in disguise, Tissot, the secretary, is cut down, four municipal officers and forty other persons are thrown into prison, while a number of houses belonging to the fugitives and to priests are pillaged, and thus supply the bandits with their first financial returns.[46] — Then begins the great fiscal operation which is going to fill their pockets. Five front men, chosen by Duprat and his associates, compose, with Lécuyer as secretary, a provisional municipal body, which, taxing the town 300,000 francs and suppressing the convents, offers the spoils of the churches for sale. The bells are taken down, and the hammers of the workmen engaged in breaking them to pieces are heard all day long. A strong–box full of plate, diamonds, and gold crosses, left with the director of the Mont–de–Piété, on deposit, is taken and carried off to the commune; a report is spread that the valuables pawned by the poor had been stolen by the municipality, and that those "robbers had already sent away eighteen trunks full of them." Upon this the women, exasperated at the bare walls of the churches, together with the laborers in want of work or bread, all the common class, become furious, assemble of their own accord in the church of the Cordeliers, summon Lécuyer to appear before them, drag him from the pulpit and massacre him.[47]

This time there seems to be an end of the brigand party, for the entire town, the populace and the better class, are against them, while the peasants in the country shoot them down wherever they come across them. — Terror, however, supplies the place of numbers, and, with the 350 hired killers bravos still left to them, the extreme Jacobins undertake to overcome a city of 30,000 souls. Mainvielle the elder, dragging along two cannon, arrives with a patrol, fires at random into the already semi–abandoned church, and kills two men. Duprat assembles about thirty of the towns–people, imprisoned by him on the 31st of August, and, in addition to these, about forty artisans belonging to the Catholic brotherhoods, porters, bakers, coopers, and day–laborers, two peasants, a beggar, a few women seized haphazard and on vague denunciations, one of them, "because she spoke ill of Madame Mainvielle." Jourdan supplies the executioners; the apothecary Mende, brother–in–law of Duprat, plies them with liquor, while a clerk of Tournal, the newsman, bids them "kill all, so that there shall be no witnesses left." Whereupon, at the reiterated orders of Mainvielle, Tournal, Duprat, and Jourdan, with a complications of hilarious lewdness,[48] the massacre develops itself on the 16th of October and following days, during sixty–six hours, the victims being a couple of priests, three children, an old man of eighty, thirteen women, two of whom are pregnant, in all, sixty–one persons, with their throats slit or knocked out and then cast one on top of each other into the Glacière hole, a mother on the body of her infant, a son on the body of his father, all finished off with rocks, the hole being filled up with stones and covered over with quicklime on account of the smell.[49] In the meantime about a hundred more, killed in the streets, are pitched into the Sorgues canal; five hundred families make their escape. The ousted bandits return in a body, while the assassins who are at the head of them, enthroned by murder, organize for the benefit of their new band a legal system of brigandage, against which nobody defends himself.[50]

These are the friends of the Jacobins of Arles and Marseilles, the respectable men whom M. d'Antonelle has come to address in the cathedral at Avignon.[51] These are the pure patriots, who, with their hands in the till and their feet in gore, caught in the act by a French army, the mask torn off through a scrupulous investigation, universally condemned by the emancipated electors, also by the deliberate verdict of the new mediating commissioners,[52] are included in the amnesty proclaimed by the Legislative Assembly a month before their last crime. – But the sovereigns of the Bouches−du−Rhône do not regard the release of their friends and allies as a pardon: something more than pardon and forgetfulness must be awarded to the murderers of the Glacière. On the 29th of April, 1792, Rebecqui and Bertin, the vanquishers of Arles, enter Avignon[53] along with a cortége, at the head of which are from thirty to forty of the principal murderers whom the Legislative Assembly itself had ordered to be recommitted to prison, Duprat, Mainvielle, Toumal, Mende, then Jourdan in the uniform of a commanding general crowned with laurel and seated on a white horse, and, lastly, the dames Duprat, Mainvielle and Tournal, in dashing style, standing on a sort of triumphal chariot; during the procession the cry is heard, "The Glacière will be full this time! " — On their approach the public functionaries fly; twelve hundred persons abandon the town. Forthwith each terrorist, under the protection of the Marseilles bayonets, resumes his office, like a man at the head of his household. Raphel, the former judge, along with his clerk, both with warrants of arrest against them, publicly officiate, while the relatives of the poor victims slain on the 16th of October, and the witnesses that appeared on the trial, are threatened in the streets; one of them is killed, and Jourdan, king of the department for an entire year, begins over again on a grand scale, at the head of the National Guard, and afterwards of the police body, the same performance which, on a small scale, he pursued under the ancient régime, when, with a dozen "armed and mounted" brigands, he traversed the highways, forced open lonely houses at night, and, in one château alone, stole 24,000 francs.

V.

The other departments. — Uniform process of the Jacobin conquest. — Preconceived formation of a Jacobin State.

The Jacobin conquest takes place like this: already in during April, 1792, through acts of violence almost equal to those we have just described, it spreads over more than twenty departments and, to a smaller degree, over the other sixty.[54] The composition of the parties is the same everywhere. On one side are the irresponsible of all conditions,

"squanderers who, having consumed their own inheritance, cannot tolerate that of another, men without property to whom disorder is a door open to wealth and public office, the envious, the ungrateful whose obligations to their benefactors the revolution cancels, the hot−headed, all those enthusiastic innovators who preach reason with a dagger in their hand, the poor, the brutal and the wretched of the lower class who, possessed by one leading anarchical idea, one example of immunity, with the law dumb and the sword in the scabbard, are stimulated to dare all things

On the other side are the steady−going, peaceable class, minding their own business, upper and lower middle class in mind and spirit,

"weakened by being used to security and wealth, surprised at any unforeseen disturbance and trying

95

to find their way, isolated from each other by diversity of interests, opposing only tact and caution to persevering audacity in defiance of legitimate means, unable either to make up their mind or to remain inactive, perplexed over sacrifices just at the time when the enemy is going to render it impossible to make any in the future, in a word, bringing weakness and egoism to bear against the liberated passions, great poverty and hardened immorality."[55]

The issue of the conflict is everywhere the same. In each town or canton an aggressive squad of unscrupulous fanatics and resolute adventurers imposes its rule over a sheep−like majority which, accustomed to the regularity of an old civilization, dares neither disturb order for the sake of putting and end to disorder, or get together a mob to put down another mob. Everywhere the Jacobin principle is the same.

"Your system," says one of the department Directories to them,[56] "is to act imperturbably on all occasions, even after a constitution is established, and the limitations to power are fixed, as if the empire would always be in a state of insurrection, as if you were granted a dictatorship essential for the city's salvation, as if you were given such full power in the name of public safety."

Everywhere are Jacobin tactics the same. At the outset they assume to have a monopoly of patriotism and, through the brutal destruction of other associations, they are the only visible organ of public opinion. Their voice, accordingly, seems to be the voice of the people; their control is established on that of the legal authorities; they have taken the lead through persistent and irresistible misdeeds; their crimes are consecrated by exemption from punishment.

"Among officials and agents, good or bad, constituted or not constituted, that alone governs which is inviolable. Now the club, for a long time, has been too much accustomed to domineering, to annoying, to persecuting, to wreaking vengeance, for any local administration to regard it in any other light than as inviolable."[57]

They accordingly govern and their indirect influence is promptly transformed into direct authority. — Voting alone, or almost alone, in the primary meetings, which are deserted or under constraint, the Jacobins easily choose the municipal body and the officers of the National Guard.[58] After this, through the mayor, who is their tool or their accomplice, they have the legal right to launch or arrest the entire armed force and they avail themselves of it. — Two obstacles still stand in their way. One the one hand, however conciliatory or timid the Directory of the district or department may be, elected as it is by electors of the second degree, it usually contains a fair proportion of well−informed men, comfortably off, interested in keeping order, and less inclined than the municipality to put up with gross violations of the law. Consequently the Jacobins denounce it to the National Assembly as an unpatriotic and anti−revolutionary center of "bourgeois aristocracy." Sometimes, as at Brest,[59] they shamefully disobey orders which are perfectly legal and proper, often repeated and strictly formal; afterward, still more shamefully, they demand of the Minister if, "placed in the cruel alternative of giving offense to the hierarchy of powers, or of leaving the commonwealth in danger, they ought to hesitate." Sometimes, as at Arras, they impose themselves illegally on the Directory in session and browbeat it so insolently as to make it a point of honor with the latter to solicit its own suspension.[60] Sometimes, as a Figeac, they summon an administrator to their bar, keep him standing three−quarters of an hour, seize his papers and oblige him, for fear of something worse, to leave the town.[61] Sometimes, as at Auch, they invade the Directory's chambers, seize the administrators by the throat, pound them with their fists and clubs, drag the president by the hair, and, after a good deal of trouble, grant him his life.[62] — On the other hand, the gendarmerie and the troops brought for the suppression of riots, are always in the way of those who stir up the rioters. Consequently, they expel, corrupt and, especially purify the gendarmerie together with the troops. At Cahors they drive out a sergeant of the gendarmerie, "alleging that he keeps company with none but aristocrats."[63] At Toulouse, without mentioning the lieutenant– colonel, whose life they threaten by anonymous letters and oblige to leave the town, they transfer the whole corps to another district under the pretense that "its principles are adverse to the Constitution."[64] At Auch, and at Rennes, through the insubordination which they provoke among the men, they exhort resignations from their officers. At Perpignan, by means of a riot which they foment, they seize, beat and drag to prison, the commandant and staff whom they accuse "of wanting to bombard the town with five pounds of powder."[65]– Meanwhile, through the jacquerie, which they let loose from the Dordogne to Aveyron, from Cantal to the Pyrenees and the Var, under the pretense of punishing the relatives of émigrés and the abettors of unsworn priests, they create an army of their own made up of robbers and the destitute who, in anticipation of the exploits of the coming revolutionary army, freely kill, burn, pillage, hold to ransom and prey at large on the defenseless flock of proprietors of every class and degree.[66]

In this operation each club has its neighbors for allies, offering to them or receiving from them offers of men and money. That of Caen tenders its assistance to the Bayeux association for expelling unsworn priests, and to help the patriots of the place "to rid themselves of the tyranny of their administrators."[67] That of Besançon declares the three administrative bodies of Strasbourg "unworthy of the confidence with which they have been honored," and openly enters into a league with all the clubs of the Upper and Lower Rhine, to set free a Jacobin arrested as a fomenter of insurrections.[68] Those of the Puy–de–Dôme and neighboring departments depute to and establish at Clermont a central club of direction and propaganda.[69] Those of the Bouches–du–Rhône treat with the commissioners of the departments of Drôme, Gard, and Hérault, to watch the Spanish frontier, and send delegates of their own to see the state of the fortifications of Figuières.[70] — There is no recourse to the criminal tribunals. In forty departments, these are not yet installed, in the forty–three others, they are cowed, silent, or lack money and men to enforce their decisions.[71]

Such is the foundation of the Jacobin State, a confederation of twelve hundred oligarchies, which maneuver their proletariat clients in obedience to the word of command dispatched from Paris. It is a complete, organized, active State, with its central government, its active force, its official journal, its regular correspondence, its declared policy, its established authority, and its representative and local agents; the latter are actual administrators alongside of administrations which are abolished, or athwart administrations which are brought under subjection. — In vain do the latest ministers, good clerks and honest men, try to fulfill their duties; their injunctions and remonstrances are only so much waste paper.[72] They resign in despair, declaring that,

"in this overthrow of all order, . . . in the present weakness of the public forces, and in the degradation of the constituted authorities, . . . it is impossible for them to maintain the life and energy of the vast body, the members of which are paralyzed." –

When the roots of a tree are laid bare, it is easy to cut it down; now that the Jacobins have severed them, a push on the trunk suffices to bring the tree to the ground.

NOTES:

[1] De Loménie, "Les Mirabeaus," I. 11. (Letter of the Marquis de Mirabeau).

[2] " Archives Nationales," F7, 7171, No. 7915. Report on the situation in Marseilles, by Miollis, commissioner of the Directory in the department, year V. Nivôse 15. "A good many strangers from France and Italy are attracted there by the lust of gain, a love of pleasure, the want of work, a desire to escape from the effects of ill conduct . . . Individuals of both sexes and of every age, with no ties of country or kindred, with no profession, no opinions, pressed by daily necessities that are multiplied by debauched habit, seeking to indulge these without too much effort, the means for this being formerly found in the many manual operations of commerce, gone astray during the Revolution and, subsequently, scared of the dominant party, accustomed unfortunately at that time to receiving pay for taking part in political strife, and now reduced to living on almost gratuitous distributions of food, to dealing in small wares, to the menial occupations which chance rarely presents — in short, to swindling. Such is what the observer finds in that portion of the population of Marseilles most in sight; eager to profit by whatever occurs, easily won over, active through its necessities, flocking everywhere, and appearing very numerous . . . The patriot Escalon had twenty rations a day; Féri, the journalist, had six; etc. . . Civil officers and district commissioners still belong, for the most part, to that class of men which the Revolution had accustomed to live without work, to making those who shared their principles the beneficiaries of the nation's favors, and finally, to receiving contributions from gambling halls and brothels. These commissioners give notice to their protégés, even the crooks, when warrants against them are to be enforced."

[3] Blanc–Gilly, "Réveil d'alarme d'un député de Marseilles" (cited in the Memoirs" of Barbaroux, 40, 41). Blanc–Gilly must have been acquainted with these characters, inasmuch as he made use of them in the August riot, 1789, and for which he was indicted. – Cf. Fabre "Histoire de Marseilles," II. 422.

[4] "Archives Nationales," F7, 3197. Correspondence of Messrs. Debourge, Gay, and Lafitte, commissioners sent to Provence to restore order in accordance with an act of the National Assembly. Letter of May 10, 1791. Letter of May 10. 1791, and passim.

[5] Mayor Martin, says Juste, was a sort of Pétion, weak and vain. — Barbaroux, clerk of the municipality, is the principal opponent of M. Lieutaud. – The municipal decree referred to is dated Sept. 10, 1790.

[6] "Archives Nationales," F7, 3197. Letters of three commissioners, April 13, 17, 18, and May 10, 1791.

[7] Blanc–Gilly, "Réveil d'Alarme." Ibid., "Every time that the national guard marched outside the city walls, the horde of homeless brigands never failed to close up in their rear and carry devastation

wherever they went."

[8] "Archives Nationales," F7, 3197. Correspondence of the three commissioners, letter of May 10,1791. "The municipality of Marseilles obeys only the decrees it pleases, and for eighteen months has not paid a cent into the city treasury.–Proclamation of April 13. – Letters of April 13 and 18.

[9] "Archives Nationales," letter of the municipal officers of Marseilles to the minister, June 11, 1791. — They demand the recall of the three commissioners, one of their arguments being as follows: "In China, every mandarin against whom public opinion is excited is dismissed from his place; he is regarded as an ignorant instructor, who is incapable of gaining the love of children for their parent."

[10] "Archives Nationales," letter of the commissioners, May 25, 1791. "It is evident, on recording the proceedings at Aix and Marseilles, that only the accusers and the judges were guilty." — Petition of the prisoners, Feb. 1. "The municipality, in despair of our innocence and not knowing how to justify its conduct, is trying to buy up witnesses. They say openly that it is better to sacrifice one innocent man than disgrace a whole body. Such ale the speeches of the sieur Rebecqui, leading man, and of Madame Elliou, wife of a municipal officer, in the house of the sieur Rousset."

[11] Letter of M. Lieutaud to the commissioners, May 11 and 18, 1791. "If I have not fallen under the assassin's dagger I owe my preservation to your strict orders and to the good behavior of the national guard and the regular troops . . . At the hearing of the case today, the prosecutor on the part of the commune ventured to threaten the court with popular opinion and its avenging fury. . . The people, stirred up against us, and brought there, shouted, 'Let us seize Lieutaud and take him there by force and if he will not go up the steps, we will cut his head off!' The hall leading to the courtroom and the stairways were filled with barefooted vagabonds."— Letter of Cabrol, commander of the national guard, and of the municipal officers to the commissioners, May 21. That picket–guard of fifty men on the great square, is it not rather the cause of a riot than the means of preventing one? A requisition to send four national guards inside the prison, to remain there day and night, is it not insulting citizen soldiers, whose function it is to see that the laws are maintained, and not to do jail duty?"

[12] Letter of M. d'Olivier, lieutenant–colonel of the Ernest regiment, May 28. — Extracts from the papers of the secretary to the municipality, May 28 (Barbaroux is the clerk). – Letter of the commissions, May 29

[13] Letter of the commissioners, June 29.

[14] Letter of M. Laroque–Dourdan, naval commander at Marseilles, Oct. 18, 1791. (in relation to the departure of the Swiss regiment).

[15] The elections are held on the 13th of November, 1791. Martin, the former mayor, showed timidity, and Mouraille was elected in his place.

[16] "Archives Nationales." F 7 3197. Letter (printed) of the Directory to the Minister of War, Jan. 4, 1792. — Letter of the municipality of Marseilles to the Directory, Jan. 4, and the Directory's reply. – Barbaroux, "Mémoires," 19. — Here we see the part played by Barbaroux at Marseilles. Guadet

played a similar part at Bordeaux. This early political period is essential for a comprehension of the Girondists.

[17] "Archives Nationales." F7, 3195. Official report of the municipality of Aix (on the events of Feb. 26). March 1st. — Letter of M. Villardy, president of the directory, dated Avignon, March 10. (He barely escaped assassination at Aix.) — Ibid., F7,3196. Report of the district administrators of Arles, Feb. 28 (according to private letters from Aix and Marseilles). – Barbaroux, "Mémoires" (collection of Berville and Barrière), 106. (Narrative of M. Watteville, major in the Ernest regiment. Ibid., 108 (Report from M. de Barbentane, commanding general). These two documents show the liberalism, want of vigor, and the usual indecision of the superior authorities, especially the military authorities – Mercure de France, March 24, 1792 (letters from Aix).

[18] "Archives Nationales," F7, 3196. Dispatches of the new Directory to the Minister, March 24 and April 4, 1792. "Since the departure of the Directory, our administrative assembly is composed of only six members, notwithstanding our repeated summons to every member of the Council. . . Only three members of the Council consent to act with us; the reason is a lack of pecuniary means." The new Directory, consequently, passes a resolution to indemnify members of the Council. This, indeed, is contrary to a royal proclamation of Jan. 15; but "this proclamation was wrested from the King, on account of his firm faith. You must be aware that, in a free nation, the influence of a citizen on his government must not be estimated by his fortune; such a principle is false, and destructive of equality of rights. We trust that the King will consent to revoke his proclamation."

[19] Ib., Letters of Borelly, vice-president of the Directory, to the Minister, April 10, 17, and 30, 1792. — Letter from another administrator, March 10. "They absolutely want us to march against Arles, and to force us to give the order. – Ibid., F7, 3195. Letters from Aix, March 12 and 16, addressed to M. Verdet.

[20] "Archives Nationales," F7, 3195. Letter of the administrators of the department Council to the Minister, March 10, "The Council of the administration is surprised, sir, at the false impressions given you of the city of Marseilles; it should be regarded as the patriotic buckler of the department . . . If the people of Paris did not wait for orders to destroy the Bastille and begin the Revolution, can you wonder that in this fiery climate the impatience of good citizens should make them anticipate legal orders, and that they cannot comply with the slow forms of justice when their personal safety and the safety of the country is in peril?"

[21] "Archives Nationales." F7, 3197. Dispatches of the three commissioners, passim, and especially those of May 11, June 10 and 19, 1791 (on affairs in Arles). "The property-owners were a long time subject to oppression. A few of the factions maintained a reign of terror over honest folks, who trembled in secret."

22 Ibid., Dispatch of the commissioners, June 19: "One of the Mint gang causes notes to be publicly distributed (addressed to the unsworn) in these words: 'If you don't "piss-off" you will have to deal with the gang from the Mint.'"

[23] "Archives Nationales." F7, 3198. Narration (printed) of what occurred at Arles, June 9 and 10,

1791. — Dispatch of M. Ripert, royal commissioner, Aug. 5, 1791. — F 7, 3197. Dispatch of the three commissioners, June 19. "Since then, many of the farm laborers have taken the same oath. It is this class of citizens which most eagerly desires a return to order. " — Other dispatches to the same effect, Oct. 24 and 29, and Dec. 14, 1791. — Cf. "The French Revolution," I. 301, 302.

[24] "Archives Nationales." F7, 3196. Dispatch of the members of the Directory of Arles and the municipal officers to the Minister, March 3, 1792 (with a printed diatribe of the Marseilles municipality)

[25] Ibid.,F7, 3198. Dispatches of the procureur– syndic of the department to the Minister, Aix, Sept. 14, 15, 20, and 23, 1791. The electoral assembly declared itself permanent, the constitutional authorities being fettered and unrecognized. — Dispatch of the members of the military bureau and correspondence with the Minister, Arles, Sept.17, 1791.

[26] Ibid., Dispatch of the commandant of the Marseilles detachment to the Directory of the department, Sept. 22, 1791: "I feel that our proceedings are not exactly legal, but I thought it prudent to acquiesce in the general desire of the battalion."

[27] "Archives Nationales." Official report of the municipal officers of Arles on the insurrection of the Mint band, Sept. 2, 1791. — Dispatch of Ripert, royal commissioner, Oct. 2 and 8. — Letter of M. d'Antonelle, to the Friends of the Constitution, Sept.22. "I cannot believe in the counter–orders with which we are threatened. Such a decision in the present crisis would be too inhuman and dangerous. Our co–workers, who have had the courage to devote themselves to the new law, would be deprived of their bread and shelter. . . The king's proclamation has all the appearance of having been hastily prepared. and every sign of having been secured unawares."

[28] De Dampmartin (an eye–witness), II. 60–70. — " Archives Nationales," F7, 3196. — Dispatch of the two delegated commissioners to the Minister, Nimes, March 25, 1792. – Letter of M. Wittgenstein to the Directory of the Bouche–du– Rhône, April 4, 1792. — Reply and act passed by the Directory, April 5. — Report of Bertin and Rebecqui to the administrators of the department, April 3. — Moniteur, XII. 379. Report of the Minister of the Interior to the National Assembly, April 4.

[29] Moniteur, XII. 408 (session of May 16). Petition of M. Fossin, deputy from Arles. — "Archives Nationales," F7, 3196. Petition of the Arlesians to the Minister, June 28. — Despatches of M. Lombard, provisional royal commissioner, Arles, July 6 and 10. "Neither persons nor property have been respected for three months by those who wear the mask of patriotism."

[30] "Archives Nationales," F7, 3196. Letter of M. Borelly, vice– president of the Directory, to the Minister, Aix, April 30, 1792. "The course pursued by the sieur: Bertin and Rébecqui is the cause of all the disorders committed in these unhappy districts. . . Their sole object is to levy contributions, as they did at Aries, to enrich themselves and render the Comtat–Venaisson desolate."

[31] "Archives Nationales," F7, 3196. Deposition of one of the keepers of the sieur Coye, a proprietor at Mouriez–les–Baux, April 4. — Petition of Peyre, notary at Maussane, April 7. — Statement by

Manson, a resident of Mouriez–les–Baux, March 27. — Petition of Andrieu, March 30. – Letter of the municipality of Maussane, April 4: "They watch for a favorable opportunity to devastate property and especially country villas."

[32] "Archives Nationales," Claim of the national guard presented to the district administrators of Tarascon by the national guard of Château–Renard, April 6. — Petition of Juliat d'Eyguières, district administrator of Tarascon, April 2 (in relation to a requisition of 30,000 francs by Camoïn on the commune of Eyguières). — Letter of M. Borelly, April 30. "Bertin and Rébecqui have openly protected the infamous Camoïn, and have set him free. " – Moniteur, XII. 408. Petition of M. Fossin, deputy from Arles.

[33] "Archives Nationales," F7, 3195. Dispatch of M. Mérard, royal commissioner at the district court of Apt, Apt, March 15, 1792 (with official report of the Apt municipality and debates of the district, March 13). — Letter of M. Guillebert, syndic–attorney of the district March 5.. (He has fled.) — Dispatches of the district Directory, March 23 and 28. "It must not be supposed for a moment that either the court or the juge–de–paix will take the least notice of this circumstance. One step in this direction would, in a week, bring 10,000 men on our hands."

[34] "Archives Nationales," F7, 3195. Letter of the district Directory of Apt, March 28. "On the 26th of March 600 armed men, belonging to the communes of Apt, Viens, Rustrel, etc. betook themselves to St.–Martin–de–Castillon and, under the pretense of restoring order, taxed the inhabitants, lodging and feeding themselves at their charge" — The expeditions extend even to the neighboring departments, one of them March 23, going to Sault, near Forcalquier, in the Upper–Alps.

[35] Ib., F7, 3195. On the demand of a number of petitioning soldiers who went to Aries on the 22d of March, 1792, the department administration passes an act (September, 1793) granting them each forty–five francs indemnity. There are 1,916 of them, which makes 86,200 francs "assessed on the goods and property of individuals for the authors, abettors, and those guilty of the disturbances occasioned by the party of Chiffonists in the commune of Arles." The municipality of Aries designates fifty–one individuals, who pay the 86,200 livres, plus 2,785 francs exchange, and 300 francs for the cost of sojourn and delays. — Petition of the ransomed, Nov.21, 1792.

[36] Ib., F7, 3165. Official report of the Directory on the events which occurred in Aix, April 27, 28, and 29, 1792.

[37] Michelet, "Histoire de la Révolution Française," III.56 (according to the narratives of aged peasants). — Mercure de France, April 30, 1791 (letter from an inhabitant of the Comtat). — All public dues put together (octrois and interest on the debt) did not go beyond 800,000 francs for 126,684 inhabitants. On the contrary, united with France, it would pay 3,793,000 francs. — André, "Histoire de la Révolution Avignonaise," I. 61. — The Comtat possessed representative institutions, an armed general assembly, composed of three bishops, the elected representative of the nobility, and thirteen consuls of the leading towns. — Mercure de France, Oct. 15, 1791 (letter from an inhabitant of the Comtat). — There were no bodies of militia in the Comtat; the privileges of nobles were of little account. Nobody had the exclusive right to hunt or fish, while people without property could own guns and hunt anywhere.

[38] "Archives Nationales," F7, 3272. Letter of M. Pelet de la Lozère, prefect of Vaucluse; to the Minister, year VIII. Germinal 30. – Ibid., DXXIV. 3. Letter of M. Mulot, one of the mediating commissioners, to the Minister, Oct. 10, 1791. "What a country you have sent me to! It is the land of duplicity. Italianism has struck its roots deep here, and I fear that they are very hardy."

[39] The details of these occurrences may be found in André and in Soulier, "Histoire de la Révolution Avignonaise." The murder of their seven principal opponents, gentlemen, priests and artisans, took place June 11, 1790. — "Archives Nationales," DXXIV. 3. The starting–point of the riots is the hostility of the Jansenist Camus, deputy to the Constituent Assembly. Several letters, the first from April, 1790, may be found in this file, addressed to him from the leading Jacobins of Avignon, Mainvielle, Raphel, Richard, and the rest, and among others the following (3uly, 1790): "Do not abandon your work, we entreat you. You, sir, were the first to inspire us with a desire to be free and to demand our right to unite with a generous nation, from which we have been severed by fraud."— As to the political means and enticements, these are always the same. Cf., for instance, this letter of a protégé, in Avignon, of Camus, addressed to him July 13, 1791: "I have just obtained from the commune the use of a room inside the Palace, where I can carry on my tavern business . . My fortune is based on your kindness . . . what a distance between you and myself!"

[40] "Archives Nationales," DXXIV. 3. Report on the events of Oct.10, 1791. — Ibid., F7, 3197. Letter of the three commissioners to the municipality of Avignon, April 21, and to the Minister, May 14, 1791. "The deputies of Orange certify that there were at least 500 French deserters in the Avignon army. " — In the same reports, May 21 and June 8: "It is not to be admitted that enrolled brigands should establish in a small territory, surrounded by France on all sides, the most dangerous school of brigandage that ever disgraced or preyed upon this human species. " — Letter of M. Villardy, president of the Directory of the Bouches–du–Rhône May 21. "More than two millions of the national property is exposed to pillage and total destruction by the new Mandrins who devastate this unfortunate country. " — Letter of Méglé, recruiting sergeant of the La Mark regiment, arrested along with two of his comrades. "The corps of Mandrins which arrested us set us at liberty. . . We were arrested because we refused to join them, and on our refusal we were daily threatened with the gallows."

[41] Mortimer–Ternaux, I. 379 (note on Jourdan, by Faure, deputy). — Barbaroux, "Mémoires"(Ed. Dauban), 392. "After the death of Patrix a general had to be elected. Nobody wanted the place in an army that had just shown so great a lack of discipline. Jourdan arose and declared that as far as he was concerned, he was ready to accept the position. No reply was made. He nominated himself, and asked the soldiers if they wanted him for general. A drunkard is likely to please other drunkards; they applauded him, and he was thus proclaimed."

[42] After a famous brigand in Dauphiny, named Mandrin.–TR. [Mandrin, (Louis) (Saint Étienne–de– Saint-Geoirs, Isère, 1724 – Valence, 1755). French smuggler who, after 1750, was active over an enormous territory with the support of the population; hunted down by the army, caught, condemned to death to be broken alive on the wheel. See also Taine's explanation in Ancient Régime page 356 app. (SR).]

[43] Cf. André, passim, and Soulier, passim. – Mercure de France, June 4, 1791. — "Archives

Nationales," F7, 3197. Letter of Madame de Gabrielli, March 14, 1791. (Her house is pillaged Jan. 10, and she and her maid escape by the roof.) — Report of the municipal officers of Tarascon, May 22. "The troop which has entered the district pillages everything it can lay its hands on." — Letter of the syndic–attorney of Orange, May 22. "Last Wednesday, a little girl ten years of age, on her way from Châteauneuf to Courtheson, was violated by one on of them, and the poor child is almost dead. " — Dispatch of the three commissioners to the Minister, May 21. "It is now fully proved by men who are perfectly reliable that the pretended patriots, said to have acted so gloriously at Sarrians, are cannibals equally execrated both at Avignon and Carpentras."

[44] "Archives Nationales," letter of the Directory of the Bouches–du– Rhône, May 21, 1791. — Deliberations of the Avignon municipality, associated with the notables and the military committee, May 15: "The enormous expense attending the pay and food for the detachments . . .forced contributions. . . What is most revolting is that those who are charged with the duty arbitrarily tax the inhabitants, according as they arc deemed bad or good patriots. . . The municipality, the military committee, and the club of the Friends of the Constitution dared to make a protest; the proscription against them is their reward for their attachment to the French constitution.

[45] Letter of M. Boulet, formerly physician in the French military hospitals and member of the electoral assembly, May 21.

[46] "Archives Nationales," DXXIv. 16–23, No.3. Narrative of what took place yesterday, August 21, in the town of Avignon. — Letters by the mayor, Richard, and two others, Aug. 21. — Letter to the president of the National Assembly, Aug.22 (with five signatures, in the name of 200 families that had taken refuge in the Ile de la Bartelasse).

[47] "Archives Nationales," DXXIV. 3. — Letter of M. Laverne, for M. Canonge, keeper of the Mont–de–Piété. (The electoral assembly of Vaucluse and the juge–de–paix had forbidden him to give this box into any other hands.) — Letters of M. Mulot, mediating commissioner, Gentilly les Sorgues, Oct. 14, 15, 16, 1791. — Letter of M. Laverne, mayor, and the municipal officers, Avignon, Jan. 6, 1792. — Statement of events occurring at Avignon, Oct. 16, 17, and 18 (without a signature, but written at once on the spot). — Official rapport of the provisional administrators of Avignon, Oct. 16. — Certified copy of the notice found posted in Avignon in different places this day, Oct. 16 (probably written by one of the women of the lower class and showing what the popular feeling was). — A letter written to M. Mulot, Oct. 13' already contains this phrase: "Finally, even if they delay stopping their robberies and pillage, misery and the miserable will still remain " — Testimony of Joseph Sauton, a chasseur in the paid guard of Avignon, Oct. 17 (an eye–witness of what passed at the Cordeliers).

[48] André. II.62. Deposition of la Ratapiole. — Death of the girl Ayme and of Mesdames Niel et Crouzet. — De Dampmartin, II. 2.

[49] "Archives Nationales," DXXIV, 3. Report on the events of Oct. 16: "Two sworn priests were killed, which proves that a counter– revolution had nothing to do with it, . . Six of the municipal officers were assassinated. They had been elected according to the terms of the decree; they were the fruit of the popular will at the outbreak of the Revolution; they were accordingly patriots." — Buchez

et Roux, XII. 420.— Official report of the Commune of Avignon, on the events of Oct. 16.

[50] "Archives Nationales," DXXIV. 3. Dispatch of the civil Commissioners deputized by France (Messrs. Beauregard, Lecesne, and Champion) to the Minister Jan. 8, 1792. (A long and admirable letter, in which the difference between the two parties is exhibited, supported by facts, in refutation of the calumnies of Duprat. The oppressed party is composed not of royalists, but of Constitutionalists.)

[51] "Archives Nationales," F7, 3177. Dispatches of the three commissioners, April 27, May 4, 18, and 21.

[52] Three hundred and thirty-five witnesses testified during the trial. — De Dampmartin, I.266. Entry of the French army into Avignon, Nov. 16, 1791: "All who were rich, except a very small number, had taken flight or perished. The best houses were all empty or closed." – – Elections for a new municipality were held Nov.26, 1791. Out of 2,287 active citizens Mayor Levieux de Laverne obtains 2,227 votes, while the municipal officer lowest on the list 1,800. All are Constitutionalists and conservatives.

[53] "Archives Nationales," F7, 3196. Official report of Augier and Fabre, administrators of the Bouches-du-Rhône, Avignon, May 11, 1792. — Moniteur, XII. 313. Report of the Minister of Justice, May 5. — XII. 324. Petition of forty inhabitants of Avignon, May 7. — XII 334. Official report of Pinet, commissioner of the Drôme, sent to Avignon. — XII. 354 Report of M. Chassaignac and other papers, May 10.— XI. 741 Letter of the civil commissioners, also of the Avignon municipality, March 23.

[54] "The French Revolution," vol. I . pp. 344–352, on the sixth jacquerie, everywhere managed by the Jacobins. Two or three traits show its spirit and course of action. ("Archives Nationales," F7, 3202. Letter of the Directory of the district of Aurillac, March 27, 1792, with official reports.) "On the 20th of March, about forty brigands, calling themselves patriots and friends of the constitution, force honest and worthy but very poor citizens in nine or ten of the houses of Capelle-Viscamp to give them money, generally five francs each person, and sometimes ten, twenty, and forty francs." Others tear down or pillage the châteaux of Rouesque, Rode, Marcolès, and Vitrac and drag the municipal officers along with them. "We, the mayor and municipal officers of the parish of Vitrac, held a meeting yesterday, March 22, following the example of our neighboring parishes on the occasion of the demolition of the châteaux. We marched at the head of our national guard and that of Salvetat to the said châteaux. We began by hoisting the national flag and to demolish . . . The national guard of Boisset, eating and drinking without stint, entered the château and behaved in the most brutal manner; for whatever they found in their way, whether clocks, mirrors, doors, closets, and finally documents, all were made way with. They even sent off forty of the men to a patriotic village in the vicinity. They forced the inmates of every house to give them money, and those who refused were threatened with death." Besides this the national guard of Boisset carried off the furniture of the château. — There is something burlesque in the conflicts of the municipalities with the Jacobin expeditions (letter of the municipal officers of Cottines to the Directory of St. Louis, March 26). "We are very glad to inform you that there is a crowd in our parish, amongst which are many belonging to neighboring parishes; and that they have visited the house of sieur Tossy and a sum of money of which we do not know the amount is demanded, and that they will not leave without that sum so that

they cam have something to live on, these people being assembled solely to maintain the constitution and give greater éclat to the law."

[55] Mercure de France, numbers for Jan. 1 and 14, 1792 (articles by Mallet du Pan). – " Archives Nationales," F7, 3185, 3186. Letter of the president of the district of Laon (Aisne) to the Minister, Feb. 8, 1792: "With respect to the nobles and priests, any mention of them as trying to sow discord among us indicates a desire to spread fear. All they ask is tranquility and the regular payment of their pensions." — De Dampmartin, II. 63 (on the evacuation of Arles, April, 1792). On the illegal approach of the Marseilles army, M. de Dampmartin, military commander, orders the Arlesians to rise in a body. Nobody comes forward. Wives hide away their husbands' guns in the night. Only one hundred volunteers are found to act with the regular troops.

[56] "Archives Nationales," F7, 3224. Speech of M. Saint–Amans, vice–president of the Directory of Lot–et–Garonne, to the mayor of Tonneins, April 20 and the letter of the syndic–attorney–general to M. Roland, minister, April 22: "According to the principles of the mayor of Tonneins, all resistance to him is aristocratic, his doctrine being that all property–owners are aristocrats. You can readily perceive, sir, that he is not one of them." — Dubois, formerly a Benedictine and now a Protestant minister. — Act of the Directory against the municipality of Tonneins, April 13. The latter appeals to the Legislative Assembly. The mayor and one of the municipal counselors appear in its name (May 19) at the bar of the Assembly.

[57] "Archives Nationales," F7, 3198. Letter of M. Debourges, one of the three commissioners sent by the National Assembly and the king, Nov. 2, 1791 (apropos of the Marseilles club). "This club has quite recently obtained from the Directory of the department, on the most contemptible allegation, an order requiring of M. de Coincy, lieutenant–general at Toulon, to send the admirable Ernest regiment out of Marseilles, and M. de Coincy has yielded."

[58] For instance (Guillon de Montléon, "Mémoires pour servir à l'histoire de Lyon," I. 109), the general in command of the national guard of this large town in 1792 is Juillard, a poor silk–weaver of the faubourg of the Grande Côte, a former soldier.

[59] "Archives Nationales," F7, 3215, affair of Plabennec (very curious, showing the tyrannical spirit of the Jacobins and the good disposition at bottom of the Catholic peasantry) — The commune of Brest dispatches against that of Plabennec 400 men, with two cannon and commissioners chosen by the club. — Many documents, among them: Petition of 150 active citizens of Brest, May 16, 1791. Deliberations of the council–general and commune of Brest, May 17. Letter of the Directory of the district, May 17 (very eloquent). Deliberations of the municipality of Plabennec, May 20. Letter of the municipality of Brest to the minister, May 21. Deliberations of the department Directory, June 13.

[60] Mortimer–Ternaux, II. 376 (session of the Directory of the Pas– du–Calais, July 4, 1792). The petition, signed by 127 inhabitants of Arras, is presented to the Directory by Robespierre the younger and Geoffroy. The administrators are treated as impostors, conspirators, etc., while the president, listening to these refinements, says to his colleagues: "Gentlemen, let us sit down; we can attend to insults sitting as well as standing."

[61] "Archives Nationales," F7, 3223. Letter of M. Valéry, syndic– attorney of the department, April 4, 1792.

[62] "Archives Nationales," F7, 3220. Extract from the deliberations of the department Directory and letter to the king, Jan.28, 1792. — Letter of M. Lafiteau, president of the Directory, Jan. 30. (The mob is composed of from five to six hundred persons. The president is wounded on the forehead by a sword–cut and obliged to leave the town.) Feb. 20, following this, a deputy of the department denounces the Directory as unpatriotic.

[63] "Archives Nationales," F7, 3223. Letter of M. de Riolle, colonel of the gendarmerie, Jan. 19, 1792. — "One hundred members of the club Friends of Liberty" come and request the brigadier's discharge. On the following day, after a meeting of the same club, "four hundred persons move to the barracks to send off or exterminate the brigadier."

[64] "Archives Nationales," F7, 3219. Letter of M. Sainfal, Toulouse, March 4, 1792. — Letter of the department Directory, March 14.

[65] "Archives Nationales," F7, 3229. Letter of M. de Narbonne, minister, to his colleague M. Cahier, Feb. 3, 1792. — "The municipality of Auch has persuaded the under–officers and soldiers of the 1st battalion that their chiefs were making preparation to withdraw." — The same with the municipality and club of the Navarreins. "All the officers except three have been obliged to leave and send in their resignations." – F7, 3225. The same to the same, March 8. — The municipality of Rennes orders the arrest of Col. de Savignac, and four other officers. Mercure de France, Feb. 18, 1792. De Dampmartin, I. 230; II. 70 (affairs of Landau, Lauterbourg, and Avignon).

[66] "'The French Revolution," I. 344 and following pages. Many other facts could be added to those cited in this volume. – "Archives Nationales," F7, 3219. Letter of M. Neil, administrator of Haute–Garonne, Feb. 27, 1792. "The constitutional priests and the club of the canton of Montestruc suggested to the inhabitants that all the abettors of unsworn priests and of aristocrats should be put to ransom and laid under contribution." – Cf. 7, 3193, (Aveyron), F7, 3271 (Tarn), etc.

[67] "Archives Nationales," F7, 3200. Letter of the syndic–attorney of Bayeux, May 14, 1792, and letter of the Bayeux Directory, May 21. "The dubs should be schools of patriotism; they have become the terror of it. If this scandalous struggle against the law and legitimate authority does not soon cease liberty, a constitution, and safeguards for the French people will no longer exist"

[68] "Archives Nationales," F7, 3253. Letter, of the Directory of the Bas–Rhin, April 26, 1792, and of Dietrich, Mayor of Strasbourg, May 8. (The Strasbourg club had publicly invited the citizens to take up arms, "to vigorously pursue priests and administrators.") — Letter of the Besançon club to M. Dietrich, May 3. "If the constitution depended on the patriotism or the perfidy of a few magistrates in one department, like that of the Bas–Rhin, for instance, we might pay you some attention, and all the freemen of the empire would then stoop to crush you. " — Therefore the Jacobin clubs of the Upper and Lower Rhine send three deputies to the Paris club.

[69] Moniteur, XII. 558, May 19, 1792. "Letter addressed through patriotic journalists to all clubs of

the Friends of the Constitution by the patriotic central society, formed at Clermont–Ferrand." (there is the same centralization between Lyons and Bordeaux.)

[70] " Archives Nationales," F7, 3198. Report of Commissioners Bertin and Rebecqui, April 3, 1792. — Cf. Dumouriez, book II. ch. V. The club at Nantes wants to send commissioners to inspect the foundries of the Ile d'Indrette.

[71] Moniteur, X. 420. Report of M. Cahier, Minister of the Interior, Feb. 18, 1792. "In all the departments freedom of worship has been more or less violated. . . Those who hold power are cited before the tribunals of the people as their enemies." — On the radical and increasing powerlessness of the King and his ministers, Cf. Moniteur, XI. 11 (Dec. 31, 1791). — Letter of the Minister of Finances. — XII. 200 (April 23, 1792), report of the Minister of the Interior. — XIII. 53 (July 4, 1792), letter of the Minister of Justice.

[72] Mortimer–Ternaux, II. 369. Letter of the Directory of the Basses– Pyrénées, June 25, 1792. — "Archives Nationales," F7, 3200. Letter of the Directory of Calvados to the Minister of the Interior, Aug. 3. "We are not agents of the king or his ministers." – Moniteur, XIII. 103. Declaration of M. de Joly, minister, in the name of his colleagues (session of July 10, 1792).

CHAPTER V. PARIS.

I.

Pressure of the Assembly on the King. — His veto rendered void or eluded. — His ministers insulted and driven away. — The usurpations of his Girondist ministry. — He removes them. – Riots being prepared.

PREVIOUS to this the tree was so shaken as to be already tottering at its base. — Reduced as the King's prerogative is, the Jacobins still continue to contest it, depriving him of even its shadow. At the opening session they refuse to him the titles of Sire and Majesty; to them he is not, in the sense of the constitution, a hereditary representative of the French people, but "a high functionary," that is to say, a mere employee, fortunate enough to sit in an equally good chair alongside of the president of the Assembly, whom they style "president of the nation."[1] The Assembly, in their eyes, is sole sovereign, "while the other powers," says Condorcet, "can act legitimately only when specially authorized by a positive law;[2] the Assembly may do anything that is not formally prohibited to it by the law," 'in other words, interpret the constitution, then change it, take it to pieces, and do away with it. Consequently, in defiance of the constitution, it takes upon itself the initiation of war, and, on rare occasions, on the King using his veto, it sets this aside, or allows it to be set aside.[3] In vain he rejects, as he has a legal right to do, the decrees which sanction the persecution of unsworn ecclesiastics, which confiscate the property of the émigrés, and which establish a camp around Paris. At the suggestion of the Jacobin deputies,[4] the unsworn ecclesiastics are interned, expelled, or imprisoned by the municipalities and Directories; the estates and mansions of the émigrés and of their relatives are abandoned without resistance to the jacqueries; the camp around Paris is replaced by the summoning of the Federates to Paris. In short, the monarch's sanction is eluded or dispensed with. — As to his ministers, "they are merely clerks of the Legislative Body decked with a royal leash."[5] In full session they are maltreated, reviled, grossly insulted, not merely as lackeys of bad character, but as known criminals. They are interrogated at the bar of the house, forbidden to leave Paris before their accounts are examined; their papers are overhauled; their most guarded expressions and most meritorious acts are held to be criminal; denunciations against them are provoked; their subordinates are incited to rebel against them;[6] committees to watch them and calumniate them are appointed; the perspective of a scaffold is placed before them in every relation, acts or threats of accusation being passed against them, as well as against their agents, on the shallowest pretexts, accompanied with such miserable quibbling,[7] and such an evident falsification of facts and texts that the Assembly, forced by the evidence, twice reverses its hasty decision, and declares those innocent whom it had condemned the evening before.[8] Nothing is of any avail, neither their strict fulfillment of the law, their submission to the committees of the Assembly, nor their humble attitude before the Assembly itself; "they are careful now to treat it politely and avoid the galleys."[9] — But this does not suffice. They must become Jacobins; otherwise the high court of Orleans will be for them as for M. Delessart, the ante−room to the prison and the guillotine. "Terror and dismay," says Vergniaud, pointing with his finger to the Tuileries, "have often issued in the name of despotism in ancient times from that famous palace; let them to−day go back to it in the name of law."[10]

Even with a Jacobin Minister, terror and dismay are permanent. Roland, Clavières, and Servan not only do not shield the King, but they give him up, and, under their patronage and with their connivance, he is more victimized, more harassed, and more vilified than ever before. Their partisans in the Assembly take turns in slandering him, while Isnard proposes against him a most insolent address.[11] Shouts of death are uttered in front of his palace. An abbé or soldier is unmercifully beaten and dragged into the Tuileries basin. One of the gunners of the Guard reviles the queen like a fish woman, and exclaims to her, "How glad I should be to clap your head on the end of my bayonet!"[12] They supposed that the King is brought to heel under this double pressure of the Legislative Body and the street; they rely on his accustomed docility, or at least, on his proven lethargy; they think that they have converted him into what Condorcet once demanded, a signature machine.[13] Consequently, without notifying him, just as if the throne were vacant, Servan, on his own authority, proposes to the Assembly the camp outside Paris.[14] Roland, for his part, reads to him at a full meeting of the council an arrogant, pedagogical remonstrance, scrutinizing his sentiments, informing him of his duties, calling upon him to accept the new "religion," to sanction the decree against unsworn ecclesiastics, that is to say, to condemn to beggary, imprisonment, and transportation[15] 70,000 priests and nuns guilty of orthodoxy, and authorize the camp around Paris, which means, to put his throne, his person, and his family at the mercy of 20,000 madmen, chosen by the clubs and other assemblages expressly to do him harm;[16] in short, to discard at once his conscience and his common sense. — Strange enough, the royal will this time remains staunch; not only does the King refuse, but he dismisses his ministers. So much the worse for him, for sign he must, cost what it will; if he insists on remaining athwart their path, they will march over him. — Not because he is dangerous, and thinks of abandoning his legal immobility. Up to the 10th of August, through a dread of action, and not to kindle a civil war, he rejects all plans leading to an open rupture. Up to the very last day he resigns himself even when his personal safety and that of his family is at stake, to constitutional law and public common sense. Before dismissing Roland and Servan, he desires to furnish some striking proof of his pacific intentions by sanctioning the dissolution of his guard and disarming himself not only for attack but for defense; henceforth he sits at home and awaits the insurrection with which he is daily menaced; he resigns himself to everything, except drawing his sword; his attitude is that of a Christian in the amphitheatre.[17] — The proposition of a camp outside Paris, however, draws out a protest from 8,000 Paris National Guards. Lafayette denounces to the Assembly the usurpations of the Jacobins; the faction sees that its reign is threatened by this reawakening and union of the friends of order. A blow must be struck. This has been in preparation for a month past, and to renew the days of October 5th and 6th, the materials are not lacking.

II.

The floating and poor population of Paris. — Disposition of the workers.— Effect of poverty and want of work. — Effect of Jacobin preaching. — The revolutionary army. – Quality of its recruits — Its first review. — Its actual effective force.

Paris always has its interloping, floating population. A hundred thousand of the needy, one–third of these from the departments, "beggars by race," those whom Rétif de la Bretonne had already seen pass his door, Rue de Bièvre, on the 13th of July, 1789, on their way to join their fellows on the suburb of St. Antoine,[18] along with them "those frightful raftsmen," pilots and dock–hands, born and brought up in the forests of the Nièvre and the Yonne, veritable savages accustomed to wielding the pick and the ax, behaving like cannibals when the opportunity offers,[19] and who will be found foremost in the ranks when the September days come. Alongside these stride their female companions "barge–women who, embittered by toil, live for the moment only," and who, three months earlier, pillaged the grocer–shops.[20] All this "is a frightful crowd which, every time it stirs, seems to declare that the last day of the rich and well–to–do has come; tomorrow it is our turn, to–morrow we shall sleep on eiderdown." — Still more alarming is the attitude of the steady workmen, especially in the suburbs. And first of all, if bread is not as expensive as on the 5th of October, the misery is worse. The production of articles of luxury has been at a standstill for three years, and the unemployed artisan has consumed his small savings. Since the ruin of St. Domingo and the pillaging of grocers' shops colonial products are dear; the carpenter, the mason, the locksmith, the market–porter, no longer has his early cup of coffee,[21] while they grumble every morning at the thought of their patriotism being rewarded by an increase of deprivation.

But more than all this they are now Jacobins, and after nearly three years of preaching, the dogma of popular sovereignty has taken deep root in their empty brains. "In these groups," writes a police commissioner, "the Constitution is held to be useless and the people alone are the law. The citizens of Paris on the public square think themselves the people, populus, what we call the universality of citizens."[22] — It is of no use to tell them that, alongside of Paris, there is a France. Danton has shown them that the capital " is composed of citizens belonging one way or another to the eighty–three departments; that is has a better chance than any other place to appreciate ministerial conduct; that it is the first sentinel of the nation," which makes them confident of being right.[23] — It is of no use to tell them that there are better–informed and more competent authorities than themselves. Robespierre assures them that "in the matter of genius and public–spiritedness the people are infallible, whilst every one else is subject to mistakes,"[24] and here they are sure of their capacity. — In their own eyes they are the legitimate, competent authorities for all France, and, during three years, the sole theme their courtiers of the press, tribune, and club, vie with each other in repeating to them, is the expression of the Duc de Villeroy to Louis XIV. when a child: "Look my master, behold this great kingdom! It is all for you, it belongs to you, you are its master!" —

Undoubtedly, to swallow and digest such gross irony people must be half–fools or half–brutes; but it is exactly their capacity for self–deception which makes them different from the sensible or passive crowd and casts them into a band whose ascendancy is irresistible. Convinced that a street mob is entitled to absolute rule and that the nation expresses its sovereignty through its gatherings, they alone assemble the street mobs, they alone, by virtue of their conceit and lack of judgment, believe themselves kings .

Such is the new power which, in the early months of the year 1792, starts up alongside of the legal powers. It is not foreseen by the Constitution; nevertheless it exists and declares itself; it is visible and its recruits can be counted.[25] On the 29th of April, with the Assembly consenting, and contrary to the law, three battalions from the suburb of St. Antoine, about 1500 men,[26] march in three columns into the hall, one of which is composed of fusiliers and the other two of pikemen, "their pikes being from eight to ten feet long," of formidable aspect and of all sorts, "pikes with laurel leaves, pikes with clover leaves, pikes à carlet, pikes with turn– spits, pikes with hearts, pikes with serpents tongues, pikes with forks, pikes with daggers, pikes with three prongs, pikes with battle– axes, pikes with claws, pikes with sickles, lance–pikes covered with iron prongs." On the other side of the Seine three battalions from the suburb of St. Marcel are composed and armed in the same fashion. This constitutes a kernel of 3,000 more in other quarters of Paris. Add to these in each of the sixty battalions of the National guard the gunners, almost all of them blacksmiths, locksmiths and horse–shoers, also the majority of the gendarmes, old soldiers discharged for insubordination and naturally inclined to rioting, in all an army of about 9,000 men, not counting the usual accompaniment of vagabonds and mere bandits; ignorant and eager, but men who do their work, well armed, formed into companies, ready to march and ready to strike. Alongside of the talking authorities we have the veritable force that acts, for it is the only one which does act. As formerly the praetorian guard of the Caesars in Rome, or the Turkish guards of the Caliphs of Baghdad, it is henceforth master of the capital, and through the capital, of the Nation.

III.

Its leaders. – Their committee. –. Methods for arousing the crowd.

As the troops are so are their leaders. Bulls must have drovers to conduct them, one degree superior to the brute but only one degree, dressed, talking and acting in accordance with his occupation, without dislikes or scruples, naturally or willfully hardened, fertile in jockeying and in the expedients of the slaughterhouse, themselves belonging to the people or pretending to belong to them. Santerre is a brewer of the Faubourg St. Antoine, commander of the battalion of " Enfants Trouvés," tall, stout and ostentatious, with stentorian lungs, shaking the hand of everybody he meets in the street, and when at home treating everybody to a drink paid for by the Duke of Orleans. Legendre is a choleric butcher, who even in the Convention maintains his butchering traits. There are three or four foreign adventurers, experienced in all kinds of deadly operations, using the saber or the bayonet without warning people to get out of the way. Rotonde, the first one, is an Italian, a teacher of English and professional rioter, who, convicted of murder and robbery, is to end his days in Piedmont on the gallows. The second, Lazowski, is a Pole, a former dandy, a conceited fop, who, with Slave facility, becomes the barest of naked sans–culottes; former enjoying a sinecure, then suddenly turned out in the street, and shouting in the clubs against his protectors who he sees put down; he is elected captain of the gunners of the battalion St. Marcel, and is to be one of the September slaughterers. His drawing–room temperament, however, is not rigorous enough for the part he plays in the streets, and at the end of a year he is to die, consumed by a fever and by brandy. The third is another chief slaughterer at the September massacres. Fournier, known as the American, a former planter, who has brought with him from St. Domingo a contempt for human life; "with his livid and sinister countenance, his mustache, his triple belt of pistols, his coarse language, his oaths, he looks like a pirate." By their side we encounter a little hump–backed lawyer named Cuirette–Verrières, an unceasing speaker, who, on the 6th of October, 1789, paraded the city on a large white horse and afterwards pleaded for Marat, which two qualifications with his Punch figure, fully establish him in the popular imagination; the rugged guys, moreover, who hold nocturnal meetings at Santerre's needed a writer and he probably met their requirements. – This secret society can count on other faithfuls. "Brière, wine–dealer, Nicolas, a sapper in the 'Enfants Trouvés' battalion, Gonor, claiming to be one of the victors of the Bastille,"[27] Rossignol, an old soldier and afterwards a journeyman–jeweler, who, after presiding at the massacres of La Force, is to become an improvised general and display his incapacity, debauchery, and thievery throughout La Vendée. "There are yet more of them," Huguenin undoubtedly, a ruined ex–lawyer, afterwards carabineer, then a deserter, next a barrier–clerk, now serving as spokesman for the Faubourg St. Honoré and finally president of the September commune; there was also, doubtless, St. Huruge alias Père Adam, the great barker of the Palais–Royal, a marquis fallen into the gutter, drinking with and dressing like a common porter, always flourishing an enormous club and followed by the riffraff.[28] — These are all the leaders. The Jacobins of the municipality and of the Assembly confine their support of the enterprise to conniving at it and to giving it their encouragement.[29] It is better for the insurrection to seem spontaneous. Through caution or shyness the Girondins, Pétion, Manual and Danton himself, keep in the background – – there is not reason for their coming forward. — The rest, affiliated with the people and lost in the crowd, are better qualified to fabricate the story which their flock will like. This tale, adapted to the crowd's intellectual limits, form and activity, is both simple and somber, such as children like, or rather a melodrama taken from an alien stage in which the good appear on one side, and the wicked on the other with an ogre or tyrant in the center, some infamous traitor who is sure to be unmasked at the end of the piece and punished according to his deserts, the whole grandiloquent terms and, as a finale, winding up with a grand chorus. In the raw brain of an over– excited workman politics find their way only in the shape of rough– hewn, highly–colored imagery, such as is furnished by the Marseillaise, the Carmagnole, and the Ça ira. The requisite motto is adapted to his use; through this misshapen magnifying glass the most gracious figure appears under a diabolical aspect. Louis XVI. is represented here "as a monster using his power and treasure to oppose the regeneration of the French. A new Charles IX., he desires to bring on France death and desolation. Be gone, cruel man, your crimes must end! Damiens was less guilty than thou art! He was punished with the most horrible torture for having tried to rid France of a monster, while you, attempting twenty–five million times more, are allowed full immunity![30] Let us trample under our feet this simulacra of royalty ! Tremble tyrants, Scœvolas are still amongst you!"

All this is pronounced, declaimed or rather shouted, publicly, in full daylight, under the King's windows, by stump–speakers mounted on chairs, while similar provocations daily flow from the committee installed in Santerre's establishment, now in the shape of displays posted in the faubourgs, now in that of petitions circulated in the clubs and sections, now through motions which are gotten up "among the groups in the Tuileries, in the Palais–Royal, in the Place de Grève and especially on the

Place de la Bastille." After the 2nd of June the leaders founded a new club in the church of the "Enfants Trouvés" that they might have their special laboratory and thus do their work on the spot.[31] Like Plato's demagogues, they understand their business. They have discovered the cries which make the popular animal take note, what offense offends him, what charm attracts him, and on what road he should be made to follow. Once drawn in and under way, he will march blindly on, borne along by his own involuntary inspiration and crushing with his mass all that he encounters on his path.

IV.

The 20th of June. — The programme. — The muster. — The procession before the Assembly. — Irruption into the Château. — The King in the presence of the people.

The bait has been carefully chosen and is well presented. It takes the form of a celebration of the anniversary of the oath of the Tennis– court. A tree of Liberty will be planted on the terrace of the Feuillants and "petitions relating to circumstances" will be presented in the Assembly and then to the King. As a precaution, and to impose on the ill–disposed, the petitioners provide themselves with arms and line the approaches.[32] — A popular procession is an attractive thing, and there are so many workers who do not know what to do with their empty day! And, again, it is so pleasant to appear in a patriotic opera while many, and especially women and children, want very much to see Monsieur and Madame Veto. The people from the surrounding suburbs are invited,[33] the homeless prowlers and beggars will certainly join the party, while the numerous body of Parisian loafers, the loungers that join every spectacle can be relied on, and the curious who, even in our time, gather by hundreds along the quays, following a dog that has chanced to tumble into the river. All this forms a body which, without thinking, will follow its head.

At five o'clock in the morning on the 20th of June groups are already formed in the faubourgs St. Antoine and St. Marcel, consisting of National Guards, pikemen, gunners with their cannon, persons armed with sabers or clubs, and women and children. — A notice, indeed, just posted on the walls, prohibits any assemblage, and the municipal officers appear in their scarves and command or entreat the crowd not to break the law.[34] But, in a working–class brain, ideas are as tenacious as they are short–lived. People count on a civic procession and get up early in the morning to attend to it; the cannon have been hitched up, the maypole tree is put on wheels and all is ready for the ceremony, everybody takes a holiday and none are disposed to return home. Besides, they have only good intentions. They know the law as well as the city officials; they are "armed solely to have it observed and respected." Finally, other armed petitioners have already filed along before the National Assembly, and, as one is as good as another, "the law being equal for all," others must be admitted as well. In any event they, too, will ask permission of the National Assembly and they go expressly. This is the last and the best argument of all, and to prove to the city officials that they have no desire to engage in a riot, they request them to join the procession and march along with them.

Meanwhile, time passes. In a crowd irritated by delay, the most impatient, the rudest, those most inclined to commit violence, always lead the rest. — At the head–quarters of the Val–de–Grâce[35] the pikemen seize the cannon and drag them along; the National Guards let things take their course; Saint–Prix and Leclerc, the officers in command, threatened with death, have nothing to do but to yield with a protest. — There is the same state of things in the Montreuil section; the resistance of four out of six of the battalion officers merely served to give full power to the instigator of the insurrection, and henceforth Santerre becomes the sole leader of the assembled crowd. About half–past eleven he leaves his brewery, and, followed by cannon, the flag, and the truck which bears the poplar tree, he places himself at the head of the procession "consisting of about fifteen hundred persons including the bystanders."[36] Like a snowball, however, the troop grows as it marches along until, on reaching the National Assembly, Santerre has behind him from seven to eight thousand persons.[37] Guadet and Vergniaud move that the petitioners be introduced; their spokesman, Huguenin, in a bombastic and threatening address, denounces the ministry, the King, the accused at Orleans, the deputies of the "Right," demands "blood," and informs the Assembly that the people "resolute" is ready to take the law in their own hands.[38] Then, with drums beating and bands playing, the crowd defiles for more than an hour through the chamber under the eyes of Santerre and Saint–Huruge: here and there a few files of the National Guard pass mingled with the throng and lost in "the moving forest of pikes"; all the rest is pure rabble, "hideous faces,"[39] says a deputy, on which poverty and loose living have left their marks, ragamuffins, men "without coats," in their shirt–sleeves, armed in all sorts of ways, with chisels and shoe–knives fastened on sticks, one with a saw on a pole ten feet long, women and children, some of them brandishing a saber.[40] In the middle of this procession, an old pair of breeches [culottes] borne on a pike with this motto: Vivent les Sans–Culottes! and, on a pitch–fork, the heart of a calf with this inscription: Cœur d'aristocrate, both significant emblems of the grim humor the imaginations of rag–dealers or butchers might come up with for a political carnival. — This, indeed, it is, they have been drinking and many are drunk.[41] A parade is not enough, they want also to amuse themselves: traversing the hall they sing ça ira and dance in the intervals. They at the same time show their civism by shouting Vive les patriotes! A bas le Veto! They fraternise, as they pass along, with the good deputies of the "Left"; they jeer those of the "Right" and shake their fists at them; one of these, known by his tall stature, is told that his business will be settled for him the first opportunity.[42] Thus do they flaunt their collaborators to the Assembly, everyone prepared and willing to act, even against the Assembly itself. — And yet, with the exception of an iron–railing pushed in by the crowd and an irruption on to the terrace of the "Feuillants," no act of violence was committed. The Paris population, except when in a rage, is rather voluble and curious than ferocious; besides, thus far, no one had offered any resistance. The crowd is now sated with shouting and parading; many of them yawn with boredom and weariness;[43] at four o'clock they have stood on their legs for ten or twelve hours. The human stream issuing from the Assembly and emptying itself into the Carrousel remains stagnant there and seems ready to return to its usual channels. — This is not what the leaders had intended. Santerre, on arriving with Saint–Huruge, cries out to his men, "Why didn't you enter the château? You must go in — that is what we came here for."[44] A lieutenant of the Val–de–Grâce gunners shouts: "We have forced open the Carrousel, we must force open the château too! This is the first time the Val–de–Grâce gunners march — they are not j.... f.... Come, follow me, my men, on to the enemy![45] – "Meanwhile, outside the gate, some of the municipal officers selected by Pétion amongst the most revolutionary members of the council, overcome resistance by their speeches and commands. 'After all," says one of them, named Mouchet, "the right of petition is sacred." — " Open the gate!" shout Sergent and Boucher–René, "nobody has a right to shut it. Every citizen has a right to go through it!"[46] A gunner raises the latch, the gate opens and the court fills in the winkling of an eye;[47] the crowd rushes under the archway and up the grand stairway with such impetuosity that a cannon borne along by hand reaches the third room on the first story before it stops. The doors crack under the blows of axes and, in the large hall of the Oeil de Bœuf, the multitude find themselves face to face with the King.

In such circumstances the representatives of public authority, the directories, the municipalities, the military chiefs, and, on the 6th of October, the King himself, have all thus far yielded; they have either yielded or perished. Santerre, certain of the issue, preferred to take no part in this affair; he prudently holds back, he shies away, and lets the crowd push him into the council chamber, where the Queen, the young Dauphin, and the ladies have taken refuge.[48] There, with his tall, corpulent figure, he formed a sort of shield to forestall useless and compromising injuries. In the mean time, in the Oeil de Bœuf, he lets things take their course; everything will be done in his absence that ought to be done, and in this he seems to have calculated justly. — On one side, in a window recess, sits the King on a bench, almost alone, while in front of him, as a guard, are four or five of the National Guards; on the other side, in the apartments, is an immense crowd, hourly increasing according as the rumor of the irruption spreads in the vicinity, fifteen or twenty thousand persons, a prodigious accumulation, a pell−mell traversed by eddies, a howling sea of bodies crushing each other, and of which the simple flux and reflux would flatten against the walls obstacles ten times as strong, an uproar sufficient to shatter the window panes, "frightful yells," curses and imprecations, "Down with M. Veto!" "Let Veto go to the devil!" "Take back the patriot ministers!" "He shall sign; we won't go away till he does!"[49] — Foremost among them all, Legendre, more resolute than Santerre, declares himself the spokesman and trustee of the powers of the sovereign people: "Sir," says he to the King, who, he sees, makes a gesture of surprise, "yes, Sir, listen to us; you are made to listen to what we say! You are a traitor! You have always deceived us; you deceive us now! But look out, the measure is full; the people are tired of being played upon ! " — " Sire, Sire," exclaims another fanatic, "I ask you in the name of the hundred thousand beings around us to recall the patriot ministers. . . I demand the sanction of the decree against the priests and the twenty thousand men. Either the sanction or you shall die!" — But little is wanting for the threat to be carried out. The first comers are on hand, "presenting pikes," among them "a brigand," with a rusty sword blade on the end of a pole, "very sharp," and who points this at the King. Afterwards the attempt at assassination is many times renewed, obstinately, by three or four madmen determined to kill, and who make signs of so doing, one, a shabby, ragged fellow, who keeps up his excitement with "the foulest propositions," the second one, "a so− called conqueror of the Bastille," formerly porte−tête for Foulon and Berthier, and since driven out of the battalion, the third, a market− porter, who, "for more than an hour," armed with a saber, makes a terrible effort to make his way to the king.[50] — Nothing is done. The king remains impassible under every threat. He takes the hand of a grenadier who wishes to encourage him, and, placing it on his breast, bids him, "See if that is the beating of a heart agitated by fear."[51] To Legendre and the zealots who call upon him to sanction, he replies without the least excitement:

"I have never departed from the Constitution. . . . I will do what the Constitution requires me to do. . . . It is you who break the law."

— And, for nearly three hours, remaining standing, blockaded on his bench,[52] he persists in this without showing a sign of weakness or of anger. This cool deportment at last produces an effect, the impression it makes on the spectators not being at all that which they anticipated. It is very clear that the personage before them is not the monster which has been depicted to them, a somber, imperious tyrant, the savage, cunning Charles IX. they had hissed on the stage. They see a man somewhat stout, with placid, benevolent features, whom they would take, without his blue sash, for an ordinary, peaceable bourgeois.[53] His ministers, near by, three or four men in black coats, gentlemen and respectable employees, are just what they seem to be. In another window recess stands his sister, Madame Elizabeth, with her sweet and innocent face. This pretended tyrant is a man like other men; he speaks gently, he says that the law is on his side, and nobody says the contrary; perhaps he is less wrong than he is thought to be. If he would only become a patriot! — A woman in the room brandishes a sword with a cockade on its point; the King makes a sign and the sword is handed to him, which he raises and, hurrahing with the crowd, cries out: Vive la Nation! That is already one good sign. A red cap is shaken in the air at the end of a pole. Some one offers it to him and he puts it on his head; applause bursts forth, and shouts of Vive la Nation! Vive la Liberte! and even vive le Roi!

From this time forth the greatest danger is over. But it is not that the besiegers abandon the siege. "He did damned well," they exclaim, "to put the cap on, and if he hadn't we would have seen what would come of it. And damn it, if he does not sanction the decree against the priests, and do it right off; we will come back every day. In this way we shall tire him out and make him afraid of us. — But the day wears on. The heat is over–powering, the fatigue extreme, the King less deserted and better protected. Five or six of the deputies, three of the municipal officers, a few officers of the National Guard, have succeeded in making their way to him. Pétion himself, mounted on a sofa, harangues the people with his accustomed flattery.[54] At the same time Santerre, aware of the opportunity being lost, assumes the attitude of a liberator, and shouts in his rough voice: "I answer for the royal family. Let me see to it." A line of National Guards forms in front of the King, when, slowly and with difficulty, urged by the mayor, the crowd melts away, and, by eight o'clock in the evening, it is gone.

_____ Notes:

[1] Moniteur, X. 39 and following pages (sessions of Oct. 5 and 6, 1791). Speeches by Chabot, Couthon, Lequinio, and Vergniaud. – Mercure de France, Oct. 15. Speech by Robespierre, May 17, 1790. "The king is not the nation's representative, but its clerk. – Cf. Ernest Hamel, "Vie de Robespierre."

[2] Moniteur, XIII. 97 (session of July 6, 1792)

[3] Buchez et Roux, XIII. 61, Jan.28, 1792. The King in his usually mild way calls the attention of the Assembly to the usurpation it is committing. "The form adopted by you is open to important observations. I shall not extend these to–day; the gravity of the situation demands that I concern myself much more with maintaining harmonious sentiments than with continually discussing my rights."

[4] Sauzay, II. 99. Letter of the deputy Vernerey to the Directory of Doubs: "The Directory of the department may always act with the greatest severity against the seditious, and, apart from the article relating to their pension, follow the track marked out in the decree. If the executive desires to impede the operations of the Directory. . . the latter has its recourse in the National Assembly, which in all probability will afford it a shelter against ministerial attacks." — Moniteur, XII. 202 (session of April 23). Report of Roland, Minister of the Interior. Already at this date forty–two departments had expelled or interned the unsworn ecclesiastics.

[5] Mercure–de–France, Feb.25.

[6] Moniteur, X. 440 (session of Nov.22, 1791). A letter to M. Southon, Director of the Mint at Paris, is read, "complaining of an arbitrary order, that of the Minister of the Interior, to report himself at Pau on the 25th of this month, under penalty of dismissal." Isnard supports the charge: "M. Southon," he says, "is here at work on a very circumstantial denunciation of the Minister of the Interior [Applause from the galleries.] If citizens who are zealous enough to make war on abuses are sent back to their departments we shall never have denunciations" [The applause is renewed.] – Ibid., X, 504 (session of Nov. 29). Speech by Isnard: "Our ministers must know that we are not fully satisfied with the conduct of each of them [repeated applause]; that henceforth they must simply choose between public gratitude and the vengeance of the law, and that our understanding of the word responsibility is death." [The applause is renewed.] — The Assembly orders this speech to be printed and sent into the departments. – Cf. XII, 73, 138, etc.

[7] Moniteur, XI. 603. (Session of March 10. Speech by Brissot, to secure a decree of accusation against M. Delessart, Minister of Foreign Affairs.) M. Delessart is a "perfidious man," for having stated in a dispatch that "the Constitution, with the great majority of the nation, has become a sort of religion which is embraced with the greatest enthusiasm." Brissot denounces these two expressions as inadequate and anti–patriotic.–Ibid., XII. 438 (session of May 20). Speech by Guadet: "Larivière, the juge–de–paix, has convicted himself of the basest and most atrocious of passions, in having desired to usurp the power which the Constitution has placed in the hands of the National Assembly." — I do not believe that Laubardemont himself could have composed anything equal to these two speeches. — Cf. XII. 462 (session of May 23). Speech by Brissot and one by Gonsonné on the Austrian committee. The feebleness and absurdity of their argument is incredible.

[8] Affairs of the Minister Duport–Dutertre and of the Ambassador to Vienna, M. de Noailles.

[9] Mercure de France, March 10, 1792.

[10] Moniteur, XI. 607 (session of March 10).

[11] Moniteur, XII .396 (session of May 15). Isnard's address is the ground–plan of Roland's famous letter. — Cf. passim, the sessions of the Assembly during the Girondist ministry, especially those of May 19 and 20, June 5, etc.

[12] Dumouriez, "Mémoires," book III. ch. VI.

[13] "Letter of a young mechanician," proposing to make a constitutional king, which, "by means of a spring, would receive from the hands of the president of the Assembly a list of ministers designated by the majority" (1791).

[14] Servan, who was Girondist minister of war, proposed to let 20 000 fédérés or provincial National guards establish themselves outside Paris. (SR).

[15] You will meet this sinister expression later on when the Government ceased killing in France but

simply sent undesirables and imaginary or real opponents overseas to death–camps. Transportation was used by Stalin and Hitler only their extermination took place in their own countries not overseas. (SR).

[16] Moniteur, XI. 426 (session of May 19). Speech by Lasource: "Could not things be so arranged as to have a considerable force near enough to the capital to terrify and keep inactive the factions, the intriguers, the traitors who are plotting perfidious plans in its bosom, simultaneously with the maneuvers of outside enemies?"

[17] 'Mallet du Pan, "Mémoires." I. 303. Letter of Malouet, June 29: "The king is calm and perfectly resigned. On the 19th he wrote to his confessor: "Come, sir; never have I had so much need of your consolations. I am done with men; I must now turn my eyes to heaven. Sad events are announced for to–morrow. I shall have courage.' " — "Lettres de Coray au Protopsalte de Smyrne" (translated by M. de Queux de Saint–Hilaire,) 145, May 1st: "The court is in peril every moment. Do not be surprised if I write you some day that his unhappy king and his wife are assassinated.".."

[18] Rétif de la Bretonne, "Nuits de Paris," VoL XVI. (analyzed by Lacroix in "Bibliothèque de Rétif de la Bretonne"). —Rétif is the man in Paris who lived the most in the streets and had the most intercourse with the low class.

[19] "Archives Nationales," F7, 3276. Letter from the Directory of Clamecy, March 27, and official report of the civil commissioners, March 31, 1792, on the riot of the raftsmen. Tracu, their captain, armed with a cudgel ten feet long, compelled peaceful people to march along with him, threatening to knock them down; he tried to get the head of Peynier, the clerk of the Paris dealers in wood. "I shall have a good supper to–night," he exclaimed "(or the head of that bastard Peynier is a fat one, and I'll stick it in my Pot!"

[20] Letters of Coray, 126. "This pillaging has lasted three days, Jan. 22, 23 and 24, and we expect from hour to hour similar riots still more terrible."

[21] Mercier (" Tableau de Paris") had already noticed before the Revolution this habit of the Parisian workman, especially among the lowest class of workmen.

[22] Mortimer–Ternaux, 1.346 (letter of June 21, 1792).

[23] Buchez et Roux, VIII. 25 (session of the National Assembly, Nov.10, 1790). Petition presented by Danton in the name of the forty– eight sections of Paris.

[24] Buchez et Roux, XIV. 268 (May. 1792). Article by Robespierre against the fête decreed in honor of Simonneau, Mayor of Etampes, assassinated in a riot: "Simonneau was guilty before he became a victim."

[25] How can one forget that great seducer of the masses Hitler? In his book "Hitler Speaks" page 208 Rauschning reports Hitler as saying: "It is true that the masses are uncritical, but not in the way these idiots of Marxists and reactionaries imagine. The masses have their critical faculties, too, but

they function differently from those of the private individual. The masses are like an animal they obeys instincts. They do not reach conclusions by reasoning. My success in initiating the greatest people's movement of all time is due to my never having done anything in violation of the vital laws and feelings of the mass. These feelings may be primitive, but they have the resistance and indestructibility of natural qualities. A once intensely felt experience in the life of the masses, like ration cards and inflation, will never again be driven out of their blood. The masses have a simple system of thinking and feeling, and anything that cannot be fitted into it disturbs them. It is only because I take their vital laws into consideration that I can rule them."

[26] Moniteur, XII. 254. – According to the royal almanac of 1792 the Paris national guard comprises 32,000 men, divided into sixty battalions, to which must be added the battalions of pikemen, spontaneously organized and composed, especially of the non–active citizens. – Cf. in "Les Révolutions de Paris," Prudhomme's Journal, the engravings which represent this sort of procession.

[27] Buchez et Roux, XV. 122. Declaration of Lareynie, a volunteer soldier in the Ile Saint–Louis battalion. — To those which he names I add Huguenin, because on the 20th of June it was his duty to read the petition of the rioters; also Saint–Huruge, because he led the mob with Santerre. — About Rossignol, Cf. Dauban, "La Demagogie à Paris," 369 (according to the manuscript memoirs of Mercier du Rocher). He reaches Fontenay Aug.21, 1793, with the representative Bourbotte, Momoro, commissary–general, three adjutants, Moulins, Hasard, the ex– priest, Grammont, an ex–actor and several prostitutes. "The prettiest shared her bed with Bourbotte and Rossignol." They lodge in a mansion to which seals are affixed. "The seals were broken, and jewelry, dresses, and female apparel were confiscated for the benefit of the general and his followers. There was nothing, even down to the crockery, which did not become the booty of these self–styled republicans"

[28] Mathon de la Varenne, "Histoire particulière des événements qui ont eu lieu en juin, juillet, août, et septembre, 1792," p. 23. (He knew Saint–Huruge personally.) Saint–Huruge had married an actress at Lyons in 1778. On returning to Paris he learned through the police that his wife was a trollop, and he treated her accordingly. Enraged, she looked up Saint–Huruge's past career, and found two charges against him, one for the robbery and assassination of an alien merchant, and the other for infanticide; she obtained his incarceration by a lettre–de–cachet. He was shut in Charenton from Jan. 14, 1781, to December, 1784, when he was transferred to another prison and afterwards exiled to his estates, from which he fled to England. He returned to France on the outbreak of the Revolution.

[29] With respect to connivance, Cf. Mortimer–Ternaux, I. 132 and the following pages. – Mallet du Pan, "Mémoires," I. 300. Letter of the Abbé de Pradt, June 21, 1795. "The insurrection had been announced for several days. . . The evening before, 150 deputies so many Jacobins, had dined at their great table in the Champs–Elysées, and distributed presents of wine and food."

[30] Moniteur, XII. 642 (session of June 12, 1792, narrative of M. Delfaux, deputy). – The execution of Damiens was witnessed by Parisians still living, while "Charles IX.,," by Marie Chénier, was at this time the most popular tragedy. — The French people," says M. Ferières (I. 35), "went away from its representation eager for vengeance and tormented with a thirst for blood. At the end of the fourth act a lugubrious bell announces the moment of the massacre, and the audience, drawing in its breath sighing and groaning, furiously exclaims silence! silence! as if fearing that the sound of this death–

knell had not stirred the heart to its very depths." — " Révolutions de Paris," number for June 23, 1792. "The speakers, under full sail, distributed their parts amongst themselves," one against the staffs, another against priests, another against judges, department, and the ministers, and especially the king. "Some there are, and we agree in this with the sieur Delfaux, who pass the measure and advise murder through gestures, eyes, and speech."

[31] Mortimer–Ternaux, I. 133. — There is the same calculation and the same work–shop in the faubourg Saints–Marcel (report of Saint– Prix, commandant of the Val–de–Grâce battalion). "Minds remained tranquil until a club was opened at the Porte Saint–Marcel; now they are all excited and divided. This dub, which is in contact with that of Santerre, urges citizens to go armed to–morrow (June 20) to the National Assembly and to the king's Palace, notwithstanding the acts of the constituted authorities."

[32] Mortimer–Ternaux, I. 136. This program is first presented to the council–general of the commune by Lazowski and nine others (June 16). The council–general rejects it and refers to the law. "The petitioners, on learning this decision, loudly declare that it shall not prevent them from assembling in arms" (Buchez et Roux, XV. 120, official report by M. Borie). — The bibliography of documents relating to the 20th of June is given by Mortimer–Ternaux, I. 397 and following pages. The principal documents are found in Mortimer– Ternaux, in "L'Histoire Parlementaire" of Buchez et Roux, and in the Revue Rétrospective.

[33] "Correspondance de Mirabeau et M. de la Marck," III. 319. Letter of the Count de Montmorin, June 21, 1792. "The Paris bandits not being sufficient, they have invited in these of the neighboring villages."

[34] Reports of the municipal officers Perron (7 o'clock in the morning), Sergent (8 o'clock), Mouchet, Gujard, and Thomas (9 o'clock).

[35] Report of Saint Prix, commandant of the Val–de–Grâce battalion (10 o'clock In the morning). — Report of Alexandre, commanding the Saint–Marcel battalion. "The whole battalion was by no means ready to march." — Official report of the Montreuil section. Bonneau, the commander concludes to march only under protest and to avoid spilling blood.

[36] Deposition of Lareyrnie, a volunteer soldier of the Ile Saint– Louis battalion.

[37] Deposition of M. Witinghof, lieutenant–general. — "Correspondence of Mirabeau and M. de la Marck." Letter of M. de Montmorin, June 21. "At two o'clock the gathering amounted to 8,000 or 10,000 persons."

[38] Moniteur, XII. 717. "What a misfortune for the freemen who have transferred their powers to you, to find themselves reduced to the cruel necessity of dipping their hands in the blood of conspirators!" etc. — The character of the leaders is apparent in their style. The incompetent copyist who drew up the address did not even know the meaning of words. "The people so wills it, and its head is of more account than that of crowned despots. That head is the genealogical tree of the nation, and before that robust head the feeble reed must bend!" He has already recited the fable of "The Oak

and the Bulrush," and he knows the names of Demosthenes, Cicero, and Catiline. It seems to be the composition of a school master turned public letter writer, at a penny a page.

[39] Hua, "Mémoires," 134.

[40] Moniteur, XII. 718.

[41] "Chronique des cinquante jours," by Rœderer, syndic–attorney of the department.

[42] Hua, 134. — Bourrienne, "Mémoires," I. 49. (He was with Bonaparte in a restaurant, rue Saint–Honoré, near the Palais–Royal.) "On going out we saw a troop coming from the direction of the market, which Bonaparte estimated at from 5,000 to 6,000 men, all in rags and armed in the oddest manner, yelling and shouting the grossest provocations, and turning towards the Tuileries. It was certainly the vilest and most abject lot that could be found in the faubourgs. 'Let us follow that rabble,' said Bonaparte to me." They ascend the terrace on the river bank. "I could not easily describe the surprise and indignation which these scenes excited in him. He did not like so much weakness and forbearance. 'Che coglione! he exclaimed in a loud tone. 'How could they let those rascals in? Four or five hundred of them ought to have been swept off with cannon, and the rest would still be running!'"

[43] "Chronique des cinquante jours," by Rœderer. – Deposition of Lareynie.

[44] Deposition of Lareynie.

[45] Report of Saint–Prix.

[46] Report by Mouchet. — Deposition of Lareynie. (The interference of Sergent and Boucher–Réne is contested, but Raederer thinks it very probable.)

[47] M. Pinon, in command of the 5th legion, and M. Vannot, commanding a battalion, tried to shut the iron gate of the archway, but are driven back and told: "You want thousands to perish, do you, to save one man?" This significant expression is heard over and over again during the Revolution, and it explains the success of the insurrections. — Alexandre, in command of the Saint–Marcel battalion, says in his report: "Why make a resistance which can be of no usefulness to the public, one which may even compromise it a great deal more?..."

[48] Deposition of Lareynie. The attitude of Santerre is here clearly defined. At the foot of the staircase in the court he is stopped by a group of citizens, who threaten "to make him responsible for any harm done," and tell him: "You alone are the author of this unconstitutional assemblage; it is you alone who have led away these worthy people. You are a rascal!" – "The tone of these honest citizens in addressing the sieur Santerre made him turn pale. But, encouraged by a glance from the sieur Legendre, he resorted to a hypocritical subterfuge, and addressing the troop, he said: 'Gentlemen, draw up a report, officially stating that I refuse to enter the king's apartments.' The only answer the crowd made, accustomed to divining what Santerre meant, was to hustle the group of honest citizens out of the way.

[49] Depositions of four of the national guard, Lecrosnier, Gossé, Bidault, and Guiboult. — Reports of Acloque and de Lachesnaye, commanding officers of the legion. — "Chronique des cinquante jours," by Rœderer. – Ibid. p.65: "I have to state that, during the Convention, the butcher Legendre declared to Boissy d'Anglas, from whom I had it, that the plan was to kill the king." — Prudhomme, "Crimes de la Révolution," III.43. "The king was to be assassinated. We heard citizens all in rags say that it was a pity; he looks like a good sort of a bastard."

[50] Madame Campan, "Mémoires," II. 212. "M. Vannot, commander of the battalion, had turned aside a weapon aimed at the king. One of the grenadiers of the Filles–Saint–Thomas warded off a blow with a sword, aimed in the same direction with the same intention."

[51] Declaration of Lachesnaye, in command of the legion. – Moniteur, XII. 719 (evening session of June 20). Speech of M. Alos, an eye– witness. (The king does this twice, using about the same words, the first time immediately on the irruption of the crowd, and the second time probably after Vergniaud's harangue.) Declaration of Lachesnaye, in command of the legion. – Moniteur, XII. 719 (evening session of June 20). Speech of M. Alos, an eye–witness. (The king does this twice, using about the same words, the first time immediately on the irruption of the crowd, and the second time probably after Vergniaud's harangue.)

[52] The engraving in the "Révolutions de Paris" represents him seated, and separated from the crowd by an empty space; that is a falsehood of the party..

[53] The queen produces the same impression. Prudhomme, in his journal, calls her "the Austrian panther," which word well expresses the idea of her in the faubourgs. A prostitute stops before her and bestows on her a volley of curses. The reply of the queen is: "Have I ever done you any wrong?" "No; but it is you who do so much harm to the nation." You have been deceived," replies the queen. "I married the King of France. I am the mother of the dauphin. I am a French woman. I shall never again see my own country. I shall never be either happy or miserable anywhere but in France. When you loved me I was happy then." The prostitute burst into tears. "Ah. Madame, forgive me! I did not know you. I see that you have been very good." Santerre, however, wishing to put an end to this emotion, cries out: "The girl is drunk " –(Madame Campan, II. 214. – Report by Mandat, an officer of the legion.)

[54] Mortimer–Ternaux, I. 213. "Citizens, you have just legally made known your will to the hereditary representative of the nation; you have done this with the dignity, with the majesty of a free people! There is no doubt that your demands will be reiterated by the eighty– three departments, while the king cannot refrain from acquiescing in the manifest will of the people. . . Retire now, . . . and if you remain any longer, do not give occasion to anything which may incriminate your worthy intentions."

CHAPTER VI. THE BIRTH OF THE TERRIBLE PARIS COMMUNE.

I.

Indignation of the Constitutionalists. — Cause of their weakness. – The Girondins renew the attack. — Their double plan.

As the blow has missed the target, it must be repeated. This is the more urgent, inasmuch as the faction has thrown off the mask and "honest people"[1] on all sides become indignant at seeing the Constitution subject to the arbitrariness of the lowest class. Nearly all the higher administrative bodies, seventy–five of the department directories,[2] give in their adhesion to Lafayette's letter, or respond by supporting the proclamation, so noble and so moderate, in which the King, recounting the violence done to him, maintains his legal rights with mournful, inflexible gentleness. Many of the towns, large and small, thank him for his firmness, the addresses being signed by "the notables of the place,"[3] chevaliers of St. Louis, former officials, judges and district–administrators, physicians, notaries, lawyers, recorders, post–masters, manufacturers, merchants, people who are settled down, in short the most prominent and the most respected men. At Paris, a similar petition, drawn up by two former Constituents, contains 247 pages of signatures attested by 99 notaries.[4] Even in the council–general of the commune a majority is in favor of publicly censuring the mayor Pétion, the syndic–attorney Manuel, and the police administrators Panis, Sergent, Viguer, and Perron.[5] On the evening of June 20th, the department council orders an investigation; it follows this up; it urges it on; it proves by authentic documents the willful inaction, the hypocritical connivance, the double–dealing of the syndic–attorney and the mayor;[6] it suspends both from their functions, and cites them before the courts as well as Santerre and his accomplices. Lafayette, finally, adding to the weight of his opinion the influence of his presence, appears at the bar of the National Assembly and demands "effectual" measures against the usurpations of the Jacobin sect, insisting that the instigators of the riot of the 20th of June be punished "as guilty of lése–nation." As a last and still more significant symptom, his proceedings are approved of in the Assembly by a majority of more than one hundred votes.[7]

All this must and will be crushed out. For on the side of the Constitutionalists, whatever they may be, whether King, deputies, ministers, generals, administrators, notables or national–guards, the will to act evaporates in words; and the reason is, they are civilized beings, long accustomed to the ways of a regular community, interested from father to son in keeping the law, disconcerted at the thought of consequences, upset by multifaceted ideas, unable to comprehend that, in the state of nature to which France has reverted, but one idea is of any account, that of the man who, in accepting a declared war, meets the offensive with the offensive, loads his gun, descends into the street and contends with the savage destroyers of human society. – – Nobody comes to the support of Lafayette, who alone has the courage to take the lead; about one hundred men muster at the rendezvous named by him in the Champs–Élysées. They agree to march to the Jacobin club the following day and close it, provided the number is increased to three hundred; but the next day only thirty turn up. Lafayette can do no more than leave Paris and write a letter containing another protest. — Protestations, appeals to the Constitution, to the law, to public interest, to common sense, well–reasoned arguments; this side will never resort to anything else than speeches and paperwork; and, in the coming conflict words will be of no use. — Imagine a quarrel between two men, one ably presenting his case and the other indulging in little more than invective; the latter, having encountered an enormous mastiff on his road, has caressed him, enticed him, and led him along with him as an auxiliary. To the mastiff, clever argumentation is only so much unmeaning sound; with his eager eyes fixed on his temporary master he awaits only his signal to spring on the adversaries he points out. On the 20th of June he has almost strangled one of them, and covered him with his slaver. On the 21st,[8] he is ready to spring again. He continues to growl for fifty days, at first sullenly and then with terrific energy. On the 25th of June, July 14 and 27, August 3 and 5, he again makes a spring and is kept back only with great difficulty.[9] Already on one occasion, July 29th, his fangs are wet with human gore.[10] — At each turn of the parliamentary debate the defenseless Constitutionalists beholds those open jaws before him; it is not surprising that he throws to this dog, or allows to be thrown to him, all the decrees demanded by the Girondists as a bone for him to gnaw on. — Sure of their strength the Girondists renew the attack, and the plan of their campaign seems to be skillfully prepared. They are quite willing to retain the King on his throne, but on the condition that he shall be a mere puppet; that he shall recall the patriot ministers, allow them to appoint the Dauphin's tutor, and that Lafayette shall be removed;[11] otherwise the Assembly will pass the act of de–thronement and seize the executive power. Such is the defile with two issues in which they have placed the Assembly and the King. If the King balks at leaving by the first door, the Assembly, equally nonplused, will leave through the second; in either case, as the all–powerful ministers of the submissive King or as executive delegates of the submissive Assembly, the Girondists will become the masters of France.

II.

Pressure on the King. — Pétion and Manual brought to the Hôtel–de– ville. — The Ministry obliged to resign. — Jacobin agitation against the King. — Pressure on the Assembly. – – Petition of the Paris Commune. — Threats of the petitioners and of the galleries. — Session of August 8th. – Girondist strategy foiled in two ways.

With this in mind they begin by attacking the King, and try to make him yield through fear. — They remove the suspension pronounced against Pétion and Manuel, and restore them both to their places in the Hôtel–de–ville. They will from now on rule Paris without restriction or supervision; for the Directory of the department has resigned, and no superior authority exists to prevent them from calling upon or giving orders as they please to the armed forces; they are exempt from all subordination, as well as from all control. Behold the King of France in good hands, in those of the men who, on the 20th of June, refused to nuzzle the popular brute, declaring that it had done well, that it had right on its side, and that it may begin again. According to them, the palace of the monarch belongs to the public; people may enter it as they would a coffee–house; in any event, as the municipality is occupied with other matters, it cannot be expected to keep people out. "Is there nothing else to guard in Paris but the Tuileries and the King?"[12] — Another maneuver consists in rendering the King's instruments powerless. Honorable and inoffensive as the new ministers may be, they never appear in the Assembly without being hooted at in the tribunes. Isnard, pointing with his finger to the principal one, exclaims: "That is a traitor!"[13] Every popular outburst is imputed to them as a crime, while Guadet declares that, "as royal counselors, they are answerable for any disturbances" that the double veto might produce.[14] Not only does the faction declare them guilty of the violence provoked by itself, but, again, it demands their lives for the murders which it commits. "France must know," says Vergniaud, "that hereafter ministers are to answer with their heads for any disorders of which religion is the pretext." — "The blood just spilt at Bordeaux," says Ducos, "may be laid at the door of the executive power. "[15] La Source proposes to "punish with death," not alone the minister who is not prompt in ordering the execution of a decree, but, again, the clerks who do not fulfill the minister's instructions. Always death on every occasion, and for every one who is not of the sect. Under this constant terror, the ministers resign in a body, and the King is required at once to appoint others; meanwhile, to increase the danger of their position, the Assembly decrees that hereafter they shall "be answerable for each other." It is evident that they are aiming at the King over his minister's shoulders, while the Girondists leave nothing unturned to render government to him impossible. The King, again, signs this new decree; he declines to protest; to the persecution he is forced to undergo he opposes nothing but silence, sometimes a simple, frank, good−hearted expression,[16] some kindly, touching complaining, which seems like a suppressed moan.[17] But dogmatic obstinacy and impatient ambition are willfully deaf to the most sorrowful strains! His sincerity passes for a new false−hood. Vergniaud, Brissot, Torné, Condorcet, in the tribune, charge him with treachery, demand from the Assembly the right of suspending him,[18] and give the signal to their Jacobin auxiliaries. — At the invitation of the parent club, the provincial branches bestir themselves, while all other instruments of agitation belonging to the revolutionary machine are likewise put in motion, — gatherings on the public squares, homicidal announcements on the walls, incendiary resolutions in the clubs, shouting in the tribunes, insulting addresses and seditious deputations at the bar of the National Assembly.[19] After the working of this system for a month, the Girondists regard the King as subdued, and, on the 26th of July, Guadet, and then Brissot, in the tribune, make their last advances to him, and issue the final summons.[20] A profound delusion! He refuses, the same as on the 20th of June: "Girondist ministers, Never!"

Since he bars one of the two doors, they will pass out at the other, and, if the Girondists cannot rule through him, they will rule without him. Pétion, in the name of the Commune, appears personally and proposes a new plan, demanding the dethronement. "This important measure once passed,"[21] he says, "the confidence of the nation in the actual dynasty being very doubtful, we demand that a body of ministers, jointly responsible, appointed by the National Assembly, but, as the constitutional law provides, outside of itself, elected by the open vote of freemen, be provisionally entrusted with the executive power." Through this open vote the suffrage will be easily controlled. This is but one more decree extorted, like so many others, the majority for a long time having been subject to the same pressure as the King. "If you refuse to respond to our wishes," as a placard of the 23rd of June had already informed them, "our hands are lifted, and we shall strike all traitors wherever they can be found, even amongst yourselves."[22] — "Court favorites," says a petition of August 6, "have seats in your midst. Let their inviolability perish if the national will must always tamely submit to that lethal power!" — In the Assembly the yells from the galleries are frightful; the voices of those who speak against dethronement are overpowered; so great are the hooting, the speakers are driven out of the tribune.[23] Sometimes the "Right" abandons the discussion and leaves the chamber. The insolence of the galleries goes so far that frequently almost the entire Assembly murmurs while they applaud; the majority, in short, loudly expresses anger at its bondage.[24] — Let it be careful! In the tribunes and at the approaches to the edifice, stand the Federates, men who have a tight grip. They will force it to vote the decisive measure, the accusation of Lafayette, the decree under which the armed champion of the King and the Constitution must fall. The Girondists, to make sure of it, exact a call of the house; in this way the names are announced and printed, thus designating to the populace the opponents of the measure, so that none of them are sure of getting to their homes safe and sound. — Lafayette, however, a liberal, a democrat, and a royalist, as devoted to the Revolution as to the Law, is just the man, who, through his limited mental grasp, his disconnected political conceptions, and the nobleness of his contradictory sentiments, best represents the present opinion of the Assembly, as well as that of France.[25] Moreover, his popularity, his courage, and his army are the last refuge. The majority feels that in giving him up they themselves are given up, and, by a vote of 400 to 224, it acquits him. — On this side, again, the strategy of the Girondists is found erroneous. Power slips away from them the second time. Neither the King nor the Assembly have consented to restore it to them, while they can no longer leave it suspended in the air, or defer it until a better opportunity, and keep their Jacobin acolytes waiting. The feeble leash restraining the revolutionary dog breaks in their hands; the dog is free and in the street

III.

The Girondins have worked for the benefit of the Jacobins. — The armed force sent away or disorganized. — The Federates summoned. — Brest and Marseilles send men. — Public sessions of administrative bodies. — Permanence of administrative bodies and of the sections. – – Effect of these two measures. — The central bureau of the Hôtel– de–ville. — Origin and formation of the revolutionary Commune.

Never was better work done for another. Every measure relied on by them for getting power back, serves only to place it in the hands of the mob. — On the one hand, through a series of legislative acts and municipal ordinances, they have set aside or disbanded the army, alone capable of repressing or intimidating it. On the 29th of May they dismissed the king's guard. On the 15th of July they ordered away from Paris all regular troops. On the 16th of July,[26] they select " for the formation of a body of infantry–gendarmerie, the former French– guardsmen who served in the Revolution about the epoch of the 1st day of June, 1789, the officers, under–officers, gunners, and soldiers who gathered around the flag of liberty after the 12th of July of that year," that is to say, a body of recognized insurgents and deserters. On the 6th of July, in all towns of 50,000 souls and over, they strike down the National Guard by discharging its staff, "an aristocratic corporation," says a petition,[27] "a sort of modern feudality composed of traitors, who seem to have formed a plan for directing public opinion as they please." Early in August,[28] they strike into the heart of the National Guard by suppressing special companies, grenadiers, and chasseurs, recruited amongst well–to–do–people, the genuine elite, stripped of its uniform, reduced to equality, lost in the mass, and now, moreover, finding its 'ranks degraded by a mixture of interlopers, federates, and men armed with pikes. Finally, to complete the pell–mell, they order that the palace guard be hereafter composed daily of citizens taken from the sixty battalions,[29] so that the chiefs may no longer know their men nor the men their chiefs; so that no one may place confidence in his chief, in his subordinate, in his neighbor, or in himself; so that all the stones of the human dike may be loosened beforehand, and the barrier crumble at the first onslaught. — On the other hand, they have taken care to provide the insurrection with a fighting army and an advanced guard. By another series of legislative acts and municipal ordinances, they authorize the assemblage of the Federates at Paris; they allow them pay and military lodgings;[30] they allow them to organize under a central committee sitting at the Jacobin club, and to take their instructions from that club. Of these new–comers, two–thirds, genuine soldiers and true patriots, set out for the camp at Soissons and for the frontier; one–third of them, however, remain at Paris,[31] perhaps 2,000, the rioters and politicians, who, feasted, entertained, indoctrinated, and each lodged with a Jacobin, become more Jacobin than their hosts, and incorporate themselves with the revolutionary battalions, so as to serve the good cause with their guns.[32] — Two squads, late comers, remain separate, and are only the more formidable; both are dispatched by the towns on the sea–cost in which, four months before this, "twenty–one capital acts of insurrection had occurred, all unpunished, and several under sentence of the maritime jury."[33] The first, numbering 300 men, comes from Brest,

* where the municipality, as infatuated as those of Marseilles and Avignon, engages in armed expeditions against its neighbors; where popular murder is tolerated;

* where M. de la Jaille is nearly killed ;

* where the head of M. de la Patry is borne on a pike;

* where veteran rioters compose the crews of the fleet,

* where "workers paid by the State, clerks, masters, non−commission officers, converted into agitators, political stump−speakers, movers, and critics of the administration," ask only to be given roles to perform on a more conspicuous stage.

The second troop, summoned from Marseilles by the Girondins, Rebecqui, and Barbaroux,[34] comprises 516 men, intrepid, ferocious adventurers, from everywhere, either Marseilles or abroad, Savoyards, Italians, Spaniards, driven out of their country, almost all of the vilest class, or gaining a livelihood by infamous pursuits, "hit−men and their henchmen of evil haunts," used to blood, quick to strike, good cut−throats, picked men out of the bands that had marched on Aix, Arles, and Avignon, the froth of that froth which, for three years, in the Comtat and in the Bouches−du−Rhône, boiled over the useless barriers of the law. — The very day they reach Paris they show what they can do.[35] Welcomed with great pomp by the Jacobins and by Santerre, they are conducted, for a purpose, to the Champs−Elysées, into a tavern, near the restaurant in which the grenadiers of the Filles St. Thomas, bankers, brokers, leading men, well−known for their attachment to a monarchical constitution, were dining in a body, as announced several days in advance. The mob which had formed a convoy for the Marseilles battalion, gathers before the restaurant, shouts, throws mud, and then lets fly a volley of stones ; the grenadiers draw their sabers. Forthwith a shout is heard just in front of them, à nous les Marseillais! upon which the gang jump out of the windows with true southern agility, clamber across the ditches, fall upon the grenadiers with their swords, kill one and wound fifteen. — No début could be more brilliant. The party at last possesses men of action;[36] and they must be kept within reach! Men who do such good work, and so expeditiously, must be well posted near the Tuileries. The mayor, consequently, on the night of the 8th of August, without informing the commanding general, solely on his own authority, orders them to leave their barracks in the Rue Blanche and take up their quarters, with their arms and cannon, in the barracks belonging to the Cordeliers.[37]

Such is the military force in the hands of the Jacobin masses; nothing remains but to place the civil power in their hands also, and, as the first gift of this kind was made to them by the Girondins, they will not fail to make them the second one. — On the 1st of July, they decree that the sessions of administrative bodies should thenceforth be public; this is submitting municipalities, district, and department councils, as well as the National Assembly itself, to the clamor, the outrages, the menaces, the rule of their audiences, which in these bodies as in the National Assembly, will always be Jacobin.[38] On the 11th of July, on declaring the country in danger,[39] they render the sessions permanent, first of the administrative bodies, and next of the forty−eight sections of Paris, which is a surrender of the administrative bodies and the forty–eight sections of Paris to the Jacobin minority, which minority, through its zeal and being ever present, knows how to convert itself into a majority. — Let us trace the consequences of this, and see the selection which is thus effected by the double decree. Those who attend these meetings, day and night, are not the steady, busy people. In the first place, they are too busy in their own counting–rooms, shops and factories to lose so much time. In the next place, they are too sensible, to docile, and too honest to go and lord it over their magistrates in the Hôtel–de– ville, or regard themselves in their various sections as the sovereign people. Moreover, they are disgusted with all this bawling. Lastly, the streets of Paris, especially at night, are not safe; owing to so much outdoor politics, there is a great increase of caning and of knocking down. Accordingly, for a long time, they do not attend at the clubs, nor are they seen in the galleries of the National Assembly; nor will they be seen again at the sessions of the municipality, nor at the meetings of the sections. — Nothing, on the other hand, is more attractive to the idle tipplers of the cafés, to bar–room oracles, loungers, and talkers, living in furnished rooms,[40] to the parasites and refractory of the social army, to all who have left the social structures and unable to get back again, who want to tear things to pieces, and, for lack of a private career, establish one for themselves in public. Permanent sessions, even at night, are not too long either for them, or for lazy Federates, for disordered intellects, and for the small troop of genuine fanatics. Here they are either performers or claqueurs, an uproar not being offensive to them, because they create it. They relieve each other, so as to be always on hand in sufficient number, or compensate for a deficiency by usurpations and brutality. The section of the Théâtre–Français, for instance, in contempt of the law, removes the distinction between active and passive citizens, by granting to all residents in its circumscription the right to be present at its meetings and the right to vote. Other sections[41] admit to their sittings all well–disposed spectators, all women, children, and the nomads, all agitators, and the agitated, who, as at the National Assembly, applaud or hoot at the word of command. In the sections not disposed to be at the mercy of an anonymous public, the same herd of frantic characters make a racket at the doors, and insult the electors who pass through them. — Thanks to this itinerant throng of co–operating intruders, the Jacobin extremists rule the sections the same as the Assembly; in the sections as in the Assembly, they drive away or silence the moderates, and when the hall becomes half empty or dumb, their motion is passed. Hawked about in the vicinity, the motion is even carried off; in a few days it makes the tour of Paris, and returns to the Assembly as an authentic and unanimous expression of popular will.[42]

At present, to ensure the execution of this counterfeit will, it requires a central committee, and through a masterpiece of delusion, Pétion, the Girondist mayor, is the one who undertakes to lodge, sanction, and organize the committee. On the 17th day of July,[43] he establishes in the offices belonging to the Commune, "a central bureau of correspondence between the sections." To this a duly elected commissioner is to bring the acts passed by his section each day, and carry away the corresponding acts of the remaining forty–seven sections. Naturally, these elected commissioners will hold meetings of their own, appointing a president and secretary, and making official reports of their proceedings in the same form as a veritable municipal council. As they are elected to–day, and with a special mandate, it is natural that they should consider themselves more legitimate than a municipal council elected four or five months before them, and with a very uncertain mandate. Installed in the town hall of Paris (Hôtel–de– ville), only two steps from the municipal council, it is natural for them to attempt to take its place; to substitute themselves for it, they have only to cross over to the other side of a corridor.

IV.

Vain attempts of the Girondins to put it down. — Jacobin alarm, their enthusiasm, and their program.

Thus, hatched by the Girondins, does the terrible Commune of Paris come into being, that of August 10th, September 2nd 1792 and May 31st. 1793. The viper has hardly left its nest before it begins to hiss. A fortnight before the 10th of August[44] it begins to uncoil, and the wise statesmen who have so diligently sheltered and fed it, stand aghast at its hideous, flattened head. Accordingly, they back away from it up to the last hour, and strive to prevent it from biting them. Pétion himself visits Robespierre on the 7th of August, in order to represent to him the perils of an insurrection, and to allow the Assembly time enough to discuss the question of dethronement. The same day Verginaud and Guadet propose to the King, through the medium of Thierry, his valet–de–chambre, that, until peace is assured, the government be carried on under a regency. Pétion, on the night of August 9–10, issues a pressing circular to the sections, urging them to remain tranquil.[45]

But it is too late. Fifty days of excitement and alarm have worked up the aberrations of morbid imaginations into a delirium. — On the second of August, a crowd of men and women rush to the bar of the Assembly, exclaiming, "Vengeance! Vengeance! our brethren are being poisoned!"[46] The fact as ascertained is this: at Soissons, where the bread of the soldiery was prepared in a church, some fragments of broken glass were found in the oven, on the strength of which a rumor was started that 170 volunteers had died, and that 700 were lying in the hospital. A ferocious instinct makes men see their adversaries in their own image and thus justify them to take those measures which they imagine their enemies would have taken in their place.[47] — The committee of Jacobin leaders states positively that the Court is about to attack, and, accordingly, has devised "not merely signs of this, but of the most unmistakable proof."[48] — "It is the Trojan horse," exclaimed Panis; "We are lost if we do not succeed in disemboweling it. . . . The bomb explodes on the night of August 9– 10. . . Fifteen thousand aristocrats stand ready to slaughter all patriots." Patriots, consequently, attribute to themselves the right to slaughter aristocrats. — Late in June, in the Minimes section, "a French guardsman had already determined to kill the King," if the King persisted in his veto. When the president of the section wanted to expulse the regicide, it was the latter who was retained and the president was expelled.[49] On the 14th of July, the day of the Federation festival, another predecessor of Louvel and Fieschi, provided with a cutlass, had introduced himself into the battalion on duty at the palace, for the same purpose; during the ceremony the crowd warmed up, and, for a moment, the King owed his life to the firmness of his escort. On the 27th of July, in the garden of the Tuileries, d'Espréménil, the old Constituent[50], beaten, slashed, and his clothes torn, pursued like a stag across the Palais Royal, falls bleedings on a mattress at the gates of the Treasury.[51] On the 29th of July, whilst one of Lafayette's aides, M. Bureau de Pusy, is at the bar of the house, "they try to have a motion passed in the Palais Royal to parade his head on the end of a pike."[52] — At this level of rage and fear, the brutal and the excited can wait no longer. On the 4th of August,[53] the Mauconseil section declares "to the Assembly, to the municipality, and to all the citizens of Paris, that it no longer recognizes Louis XVI. as King of the French". Its president, the foreman of a tailor's shop, and its secretary, employed in the leather market, support their manifesto with three lines of a tragedy floating vaguely in their minds,[54] and name the Boulevard Madeleine St. Honoré as a rendezvous on the following Sunday for all well–disposed persons. On the 6th of August, Varlet, a post–office clerk, makes known to the Assembly, in the name of the petitioners of the Champ de

Mars, the program of the faction:

1. the dethronement of the King,

2. the indictment, arrest, and speedy condemnation of Lafayette,

3. the immediate convoking of the primary assemblies,

4. universal suffrage,

5. the discharge of all staff officers,

6. the renewal of the departmental directories,

7. the recall of all ambassadors,

8. the suppression of diplomacy,

9. and a return to the state of nature.

The Girondins may now delay, negotiate, beat about and argue as much as they please; their hesitation has no other effect that to consign them into the background, as being lukewarm and timid. Thanks to them, the (Jacobin) faction now has its deliberative assemblies, its executive powers, its central seat of government, its enlarged, tried, and ready army, and, forcibly or otherwise, its program will be carried out.

V.

Evening of August 8. — Session of August 9. — Morning of August 10.– Assembly purged. —

The Assembly must first of all be made to depose the King. Several times already,[55] on the 26th of July and August 4, clandestine meetings had been held where strangers decided the fate of France, and gave the signal for insurrection. — Restrained with great difficulty, they consented "to have patience until August 9, at 11 o'clock in the evening."[56] On that day the discussion of the dethronement is to take place in the Assembly, and calculations are made on a favorable vote under such a positive threat; its reluctance must yield to the certainty of a military occupation — On the 8th of August, however, the Assembly refuses, by a majority of two–thirds, to indict the great enemy, Lafayette. The double amputation essential for State security, must therefore begin with the destruction of this majority.

The moment Lafayette's acquittal is announced, the galleries, usually so vociferous, maintain "gloomy silence."[57] The word of command for them is to keep themselves in reserve for the streets. One by one the deputies who voted for Lafayette are pointed out to the mob at the doors, and a shout is raised, "the rascals, the knaves, the traitors living on the civil list! Hang them! Kill them! Put an end to them! Mud, mortar, plaster, stones are thrown at them, and they are severely pummeled. M.

Mézières, in the Rue du Dauphin, is seized by the throat, and a woman strikes at him, which he parries. In the Rue St. Honoré, a number of men in red caps surround M. Regnault–Beauceron, and decide to "string him up at the lantern"; a man in his jacket had already grabbed him from behind and raised him up, when the grenadiers of Sainte–Opportune arrive in time to set him free. In the Rue St. Louis, M. Deuzy, repeatedly struck on the back with stones, has a saber twice raised over his head. In the Passage des Feuillants, M. Desbois is pummeled, and a "snuff–box, his pocket–book, and cane" are stolen from him. In the lobbies of the Assembly, M. Girardin is on the point of being assassinated.[58] Eight deputies besides these are pursued, and take refuge in the guard–room of the Palais Royal. A Federate enters along with them, and "there, his eyes sparkling with rage and thumping on the table like a madman," he exclaims to M. Dumolard, who is the best known:" "If you are unlucky enough to put your feet in the Assembly again, I'll cut off your head with my sword!" As to the principal defender of Lafayette, M. Vaublanc, he is assailed three times, but he is wary enough not to return home; a number of infuriates, however, invest his house, yelling out that "eighty citizens are to perish by their hands, and he is one of the first"; a dozen of the gang ascend to his apartments, rummage them in every corner, make another effort to find him in the adjoining houses, and, not being able to secure him, try to find his family; he is notified that, if he returns to his house, he will be massacred. — In the evening, on the Feuillants terrace, other deputies are subjected to the same outrages; the gendarmerie tries in vain to protect them, while the 'commandant of the National Guard, on leaving his post, is attacked and cut down."[59] — Meanwhile, some of the Jacobins in the lobbies "doom the majority of the Assembly to destruction"; one orator declares that "the people have a right to form lists of proscription," and the club accordingly decides on printing and publishing the names of all the deputies who acquitted Lafayette. — Never was physical constraint displayed and applied with such open shamelessness.[60]

On the following day, August 9, armed men gather around the approaches to the Assembly, and sabers are seen even in the corridors.[61] The galleries, more imperious than ever, cheer, and break out in ironic shouts of triumph and approval every time the attacks of the previous evening are denounced in the tribune. The president calls the offenders to order more than twenty times, but his voice and his bell are drowned in the uproar. It is impossible to express an opinion. Most of the representatives who were maltreated the evening before, write that they will not return, while others, who are present, declare that they will not vote again "if they cannot be secure of freedom of conscience in their deliberations." At this utterance, which expresses the secret sentiment of "nearly the whole of the Assembly,"[62] "all the members of the 'Right', and many of the 'Left' arise simultaneously and exclaim: 'Yes, yes; we will debate no longer unless we are free!'" — As usual, however, the majority gives away the moment effective measures are to be adopted; its heart sinks, as it always has done, on being called upon to act in self–defense, while these official declarations, one on top of the other, in hiding from it the gravity of the danger, sink it deeper in its own timidity. At this same session the syndic–attorney of the department reports that the mob is ready, that 900 armed men had just entered Paris, that the tocsin would be rung at midnight, and that the municipality tolerates or favors the insurrection. At this same session, the Minister of Justice gives notice that "the laws are powerless," and that the government is no longer responsible. At this same session, Pétion, the mayor, almost avowing his complicity, appears at the bar of the house, and declares positively that he will have nothing to do with the public forces, because "it would be arming one body of citizens against another."[63] — Every support is evidently knocked away. Feeling that it is abandoned, the National Assembly gives up, and, as a last expedient, and with a degree of weakness or simplicity which admirably depicts the legislators of the epoch, it adopts a philosophic address to the people, "instructing it what to do in the exercise of its sovereignty."

How this is done, it may see the next morning. At 7 o'clock, a Jacobin deputy stops in a cab before the door of the Feuillants club; a crowd gathers around him, and he gives his name, Delmas. The crowd understood it as Dumas, a well–known Constitutionalist, and, in a rage, drag him out of the vehicle and knock him down; had not other deputies run up and given assurances that he was the patriot Delmas, of Toulouse, instead of "the traitor, Mathieu Dumas," he was a lost man.[64] Dumas makes no effort to enter. He finds on the Place Vendôme a second and not less instructive warning. Some wretches, followed by the usual rabble, carry about a number of heads on pikes, those probably of the journalist Suleau, and three others, massacred a quarter of an hour before; "boys quite young, mere children, play with these heads by tossing them in the air, and catching them on the ends of their sticks." — There is no doubt but that the deputies of the "Right" and even the "Center," would do well to go home and stay there. In fact, they are no longer seen in the Assembly.[65] In the afternoon, out of the 630 members still present the evening before, 346 do not answer the call, while about thirty others, had either withdrawn before this or sent in their resignations.[66] The purging is complete, like that to which Cromwell, in 1648, subjected the Long Parliament. Henceforth the Legislative body, reduced to 224 Jacobins or Girondins, with 60 frightened or tractable neutrals, will obey the orders of the street without any difficulty. A change has come over the spirit of the body as well as over its composition; it is nothing more now than a servile instrument in the hands of the seditious, who have mutilated it, and who, masters of it through a first misdeed, are going to use it to legalize other crimes.

VI.

Nights of August 9 and 10. — The sections. — Commissioners of the sections at the Hôtel–de–ville. — The revolutionary Commune is substituted for the legal Commune.

During the night of the 9th and 10th of August their government forms itself for action, it has been set up as it will behave, with violence and fraud. i — In vain have they annoyed and worked on the sections for the past fortnight; they are not yet submissive, only six out of forty–eight at the present hour, eleven o'clock at night, being found sufficiently excited or purged to send their commissioners forthwith, with full power, to the Hôtel–de–ville. The others will follow, but the majority rests inert or recalcitrant.[67] — It is necessary, therefore, to deceive or force this majority, and, to this end, darkness, the late hour, disorder, dread of the coming day, and the uncertainty of what to do, are precious auxiliaries. In many of the sections,[68] the meetings are already adjourned or deserted; only a few members of the permanent bureau in the room, with a few men, perhaps asleep, on the nearly empty benches. An emissary arrives from the insurgent sections, along with a company of trusty fellows belonging to the quarter, and cries out, Save the country! The sleepers open their eyes, stretch themselves, raise their hands, and elect whoever is designated, sometimes strangers and other unknown individuals, who will be disowned the coming day at a full meeting of the section. There is no official report drawn up, no balloting, the course pursued being the most prompt. At the Arsenal section, six electors present choose three among their own number to represent 1,400 active citizens. Elsewhere, a throng of shrews, night–brawlers and dishonorable persons, invade the premises, chase out the believers in law and order, and win all the desired appointments.[69] Other sections consent to elect, but without consenting to give power of attorney. Several make express reservations, stipulating that their delegates shall act in concert with the legal municipality, distrusting the future committee, and declaring in advance that they will not obey it. A few elect their commissioners only to obtain information, and, at the same time, to show that they intend earnestly to stop all rioting.[70] Finally, at least twenty sections abstain from or disapprove of the proceedings and send no delegates. — Never mind, they can be dispensed with. At three o'clock in the morning, 19 sections, and, at seven o'clock, 24 or 25,[71] are represented one way or another at the Town–hall (Hôtel–de–ville), and this representation forms a central committee. Anyhow, there is nothing to prevent seventy or eighty subordinate intriguers and desperadoes, who have slipped in or pushed through, from calling themselves authorized delegates and ministers plenipotentiary of the entire Paris population,[72] and to operate accordingly. — Scarcely are they installed under the presidency of Huguenin, with Tallien as secretary, when they issue a summons for "twenty–five armed men from each section," five hundred strapping lads, to act as guards and serve as an executive force. — Against a band of this description the municipal council, in session in the opposite chamber, is feeble enough. Moreover, the most moderate and firmest of its members, sent away on purpose, are on missions to the Assembly, at the palace, and in different quarters of Paris, while its galleries are crammed with villainous looking men, posted there to create an uproar, its deliberations being carried on under menaces of death. — That's why, as the night passes, the equilibrium between the two assemblages, one legal the other illegal, facing each other like the two sides of a scale, disappears. Lassitude, fear, discouragement, desertion, increase on one side, while numbers, audacity, force and usurpation increase on the other. At length, the latter wrests from the former all the acts it needs to start the insurrection and render defense impossible. About six o'clock in the morning the intruding committee, in the name of the people, ends the matter by suspending the legitimate council, which it then expels, and takes possession of its chairs.

The first act of the new sovereign rulers indicates at once what they mean to do. M. de Mandat, in command of the National guard, summoned to the Hôtel–de–ville, had come to explain to the council what disposition he had made of his troops, and what orders he had issued. They seize him, interrogate him in their turn,[73] depose him, appoint Santerre in his place, and, to derive all the benefit they can from his capture, they order him to withdraw one–half of his men stationed around the palace. Fully aware of what he was exposed to in this den of thieves, he nobly refuses; forthwith they consign him to prison, and send him to the Abbaye "for his greater safety." At these significant words from Danton,[74] he is murdered at the door as he leaves by Rossignol, one of Danton's acolytes, with a pistol–shot at arm's length. — After tragedy comes comedy. At the repeated entreaties of Pétion, who does not want to be requisitioned against the rioters,[75] they send him a guard of 400 men, thus confining him in his own house, and, apparently in spite of himself.

On one side, sheltered by treachery and, on the other side, by assassination, the insurrection may now go on in full security in front of the terrible hypocrite who solemnly complains of his voluntary captivity, and before the corpse, with shattered brow, lying on the steps of the Hôtel–de–ville. On the right bank of the river, the battalions of the Faubourg Saint–Antoine, and, on the left, those of the Faubourg Saint–Marcel, the Bretons, and the Marseilles band, march forth as freely as if going to parade. Measures of defense are frustrated by the murder of the commanding general, and by the mayor's duplicity; there is not resistance on guarded spots, at the arcade Saint–Jean, the passages of the bridges, along the quays, and in the court of the Louvre. An advance guard of the mob, women, children, and men, armed with cutters, cudgels, and pikes, spread over the abandoned Carrousel, and, towards eight o'clock, the advance column, led by Westerman, appears in front of the palace.

VII.

August 10. — The King's forces. — Resistance abandoned. – –The King in the National Assembly. — Conflict at the palace and discharge of the Swiss Guard. — The palace evacuated by the King's order. — The massacres. — The enslaved Assembly and its decrees.

If the King had wanted to fight, he might still have defended himself, saved himself, and even been victorious.[76] — In the Tuileries, 950 of the Swiss Guard and 200 gentlemen stood ready to die for him to the last man. Around the Tuileries, two or three thousand National Guard, the élite of the Parisian population, had just cheered him as he passed.[77] "Hurrah for the King! Hurrah for Louis XVI.! He is our King and we want no other; we want him only! Down with the rioters! Down with the Jacobins! We will defend him unto death! Let him put himself at our head! Hurrah for the Nation, the Law, the Constitution, and the King, which are all one! If the gunners were silent, and seemed ill–disposed,[78] it was simply necessary to disarm them suddenly, and hand over their pieces to loyal men. Four thousand rifles and eleven pieces of artillery, protected by the walls of the courts and by the thick masonry of the palace, were certainly sufficient against the nine or ten thousand Jacobins in Paris, most of them pikemen, badly led by improvised or rebellious battalion officers,[79] and, still worse, commanded by their new general, Santerre, who, always cautious, kept himself aloof in the Hôtel–de– ville, out of harm's way. The only staunch men in the Carrousel were the eight hundred men from Brest and Marseilles; the rest consisted of a rabble like that of July 14, October 5, and June 20;[80] the palace, says Napoleon Bonaparte, was attacked by the vilest canaille, professional rioters, Maillard's band, and the bands of Lazowski, Fournier, and Théroigne, by all the assassins, indeed of the previous night and day, and of the following day, which species of combatants, as was proved by the event, would have scattered at the first discharge of a cannon. — But, with the governing as with the governed, all notion of the State was lost, the former through humanity become a duty, and the latter through insubordination erected into a right. At the close of the eighteenth century, in the upper as well as in the middle class, there was a horror of blood;[81] refined social ways, coupled with an idyllic imagination, had softened the militant disposition. Everywhere the magistrates had forgotten that the maintenance of society and of civilization is a benefit of infinitely greater importance than the lives of a parcel of maniacs and malefactors; that the prime object of government, as well as of a police, is the preservation of order by force; that a gendarme is not a philanthropist; that, if attacked on his post, he must use his sword, and that, in sheathing it for fear of wounding his aggressors, he fails to do his duty.

This time again, in the court of the Carrousel, the magistrates on the spot, finding that "their responsibility is insupportable," concern themselves only with how to "avoid the effusion of blood;" it is with regret, and this they state to the troops, "in faltering tones," that they proclaim martial law.[82] They "forbid them to attack," merely "authorizing them to repel force with force;" in other words, they order them to stand up to the first fire; "you are not to fire until you are fired upon." — Still better, they go from company to company, "openly declaring that opposition to such a large and well–armed assemblage would be folly, and that it would be a very great misfortune to attempt it." — "I repeat to you," said Leroux, "that a defense seems to me madness." — Such is the way in which, for more than an hour, they encourage the National Guard. "All I ask," says Leroux again, "is that you wait a little longer. I hope that we shall induce the King to yield to the National Assembly." — Always the same tactics: hand the fortress and the general over rather than fire on the mob. To this end they return to the King, with Rœderer at their head, and renew their efforts: "Sire," says Rœderer, "time presses, and we ask you to consent to accompany us." — For a few moments, the last and most solemn of the monarchy, the King hesitates.[83] His good sense, probably, enabled him to see that a retreat was abdication; but his phlegmatic understanding is at first unable to clearly define its consequences; moreover, his optimism had never explored the vastness of the stupidity of the people, nor sounded the depths of human malice and spite; he cannot imagine that slander may transform his determination not to shed blood into a desire to shed blood.[84] Besides, he is bound by his past, by his habit of always yielding; by his determination, declared and maintained for the past three years, never to cause civil war; by his obstinate humanitarianism, and especially by his religious goodwill. He has systematically extinguished in himself the animal instinct of resistance, the flash of anger in all of us which starts up under unjust and brutal aggressions; the Christian has supplanted the King; he is no longer aware that duty obliges him to be a man of the sword that, in his surrender, he surrenders the State, and that to yield like a lamb is to lead all honest people, along with himself, to the slaughterhouse. "Let us go," said he, raising his right hand; "we will give, since it is necessary, one more proof of our self- sacrifice."[85] Accompanied by his family and Ministers, he sets out between two lines of National Guards and the Swiss Guard,[86] and reaches the Assembly, which sends a deputation to meet him; entering the chamber he says: "I come here to prevent a great crime. " — No pretext, indeed, for a conflict now exists. An assault on the insurgent side is useless, since the monarch, with all belonging to him and his government, have left the palace. On the other side, the garrison will not begin the fight; diminished by 150 Swiss and nearly all the grenadiers of the Filles–Saint–Thomas, who served as the King's escort to the Assembly, it is reduced to a few gentlemen, 750 Swiss, and about a hundred National Guards; the others, on learning that the King is going, consider their services at an end and disperse.[87] — All seems to be over in the sacrifice of royalty. Louis XVI. imagines that the Assembly, at the worst, will suspend him from his functions, and that he will return to the Tuileries as a private individual. On leaving the palace, indeed, he orders his valet to keep up the service until he himself returns from the National Assembly.[88]

He did not count on the exigencies, blindness and disorders of the riot. Threatened by the Jacobin gunners remaining with their artillery in the inside courts, the gatekeepers open the gates. The insurgents rush in, fraternise with the gunners, reach the vestibule, ascend the grand staircase, and summon the Swiss to surrender.[89] — These show no hostile spirit; many of them, as a mark of good humor, throw packets of cartridges out of the windows; some even go so far as to let themselves be embraced and led away. The regiment, however, faithful to its orders, will not yield to force.[90] "We are Swiss," replies the sergeant, Blaser; "the Swiss do not part with their arms but with their lives. We think that we do not merit such an insult. If the regiment is no longer wanted, let it be legally discharged. But we will not leave our post, nor will we let our arms be taken from us." The two bodies of troops remain facing each other on the staircase for three–quarters of an hour, almost intermingled, one silent and the other excited, turbulent, and active, with all the ardor and lack of discipline peculiar to a popular gathering, each insurgent striving apart, and in his own way, to corrupt, intimidate, or constrain the Swiss Guards. Granier, of Marseilles, at the head of the staircase, holds two of them at arms' length, trying in a friendly manner to draw them down.[91] At the foot of the staircase the crowd is shouting and threatening; lighter men, armed with boat–hooks, harpoon the sentinels by their shoulder–straps, and pull down four or five, like so many fishes, amid shouts of laughter. — Just at this moment a pistol goes off; nobody being able to tell which party fired it.[92] The Swiss, firing from above, clean out the vestibule and the courts, rush down into the square and seize the cannon; the insurgents scatter and fly out of range. The bravest, nevertheless, rally behind the entrances of the houses on the Carrousel, throw cartridges into the courts of the small buildings and set them on fire. During another half–hour, under the dense smoke of the first discharge and of the burning buildings, both sides fire haphazard, while the Swiss, far from giving way, have scarcely lost a few men, when a messenger from the King arrives, M. d'Hervilly, who orders in his name the firing to cease, and the men to return to their barracks.

Slowly and regularly they form in line and retire along the broad alley of the garden. At the sight of these foreigners, however, in red coats, who had just fired on Frenchmen, the guns of the battalion stationed on the terraces go off of their own accord, and the Swiss column divides in two. One body of 250 men turns to the right, reaches the Assembly, lays down its arms at the King's order, and allows itself to be shut up in the Feuillants church. The others are annihilated on crossing the garden, or cut down on the Place Louis XV. by the mounted gendarmerie. No quarter is given. The warfare is that of a mob, not civilized war, but primitive war, that of barbarians. In the abandoned palace into which the insurgents entered five minutes after the departure of the garrison,[93] they kill the wounded, the two Swiss surgeons attending to them,[94] the Swiss who had not fired a gun, and who, in the balcony on the side of the garden, "cast off their cartridge–boxes, sabers, coats, and hats, and shout: 'Friends, we are with you, we are Frenchmen, we belong to the nation!'"[95] They kill the Swiss, armed or unarmed, who remain at their posts in the apartments. They kill the Swiss gate–keepers in their boxes. They kill everybody in the kitchens, from the head cook down to the pot boys.[96] The women barely escape. Madame Campan, on her knees, seized by the back, sees an uplifted saber about to fall on her, when a voice from the foot of the staircase calls out: "What are you doing there? The women are not to be killed!" "Get up, you hussy, the nation forgives you! " — To make up for this the nation helps itself and indulges itself to its heart's content in the palace which now belongs to it. Some honest persons do, indeed, carry money and valuables to the National Assembly, but others pillage and destroy all that they can.[97] They shatter mirrors, break furniture to pieces, and throw clocks out of the window; they shout the Marseilles hymn, which one of the National Guards accompanies on a harpsichord,[98] and descend to the cellars, where they gorge themselves. "For more than a fortnight," says an eye witness,[99] "one walked on fragments of bottles." In the garden, especially, "it might be said that they had tried to pave the walks with broken glass." — Porters are seen seated on the throne in the coronation robes; a trollop occupies the Queen's bed; it is a carnival in which unbridled base and cruel instincts find plenty of good forage and abundant litter. Runaways come back after the victory and stab the dead with their pikes. Nicely dressed prostitutes fooling around with naked corpses.[100] And, as the destroyers enjoy their work, they are not disposed to be disturbed in it. In the courts of the Carrousel, where 1800 feet of building are burning, the firemen try four times to extinguish the fire; "they are shot at, and threatened with being pitched into the flames,"[101] while petitioners appear at the bar of the Assembly, and announce in a threatening tone that the Tuileries are blazing, and shall blaze until the dethronement becomes a law.

The poor Assembly, become Girondist through its late mutilation, strives in vain to arrest the downhill course of things, and maintain, as it has just sworn to do, "the constituted authorities";[102]

it strives, at least, to put Louis XVI. in the Luxembourg palace, to appoint a tutor for the Dauphin, to keep the ministers temporarily in office, and to save all prisoners, and those who walk the streets. Equally captive, and nearly as prostrate as the King himself; the Assembly merely serves as a recording office for the popular will, that very morning furnishing evidence of the value which the armed commonalty attaches to its decrees. That morning murders were committed at its door, in contempt of its safe conduct; at eight o'clock Suleau and three others, wrested from their guards, are cut down under its windows. In the afternoon, from sixty to eighty of the unarmed Swiss still remaining in the church of the Feuillants are taken out to be sent to the Hôtel-de-ville, and massacred on the way at the Place de Grève. Another detachment, conducted to the section of the Roule, is likewise disposed of in the same way.[103] Carle, at the head of the gendarmerie, is called out of the Assembly and assassinated on the Place Vendôme, and his head is carried about on a pike. The founder of the old monarchical club, M. de Clermont- Tonnerre, withdrawn from public life for two years past, and quietly passing along the streets, is recognized, dragged through the gutter and cut to pieces. — After such warnings (murder and pillage) the Assembly can only obey, and, as usual, conceal its submission beneath sonorous words. If the dictatorial committee, self-imposed at the Hôtel-de-ville, still condescends to keep it alive, it is owing to a new investiture,[104] and by declaring to it that it must not meddle with its doings now or in the future. Let it confine itself to its function, that of rendering decrees made by the faction. Accordingly, like fruit falling from a tree vigorously shaken, these decrees rattle down, one after another, into the hands that await them,[105]

1. the suspension of the King,

2. the convoking of a national convention,

3. electors and the eligible exempted from all property qualifications,

4. an indemnity for displaced electors,

5. the term of Assemblies left to the decision of the electors,[106]

6. the removal and arrest of the late ministers,

7. the re-appointment of Servan, Clavières and Roland,

8. Danton as Minister of Justice,

9. the recognition of the usurping Commune,

10. Santerre confirmed in his new rank,

11. the municipalities empowered to look after general safety,

12. the arrest of suspicious persons confided to all well-disposed citizens,[107]

13. domiciliary visits prescribed for the discovery of arms and ammunition,[108]

14. all the justices of Paris to be re-elected by those within their jurisdiction,

15. all officers of the gendarmerie subject to re-election by their soldiers,[109]

16. thirty sous per diem for the Marseilles troops from the day of their arrival,

17. a court-martial against the Swiss,

18. a tribunal for the dispatch of justice against the vanquished of August 10, and a quantity of other decrees of a still more important bearing:

19. the suspension of the commissioners appointed to enforce the execution of the law in civil and criminal courts,[110]

20. the release of all persons accused or condemned for military insubordination, for press offenses and pillaging of grain,[111]

21. the partition of communal possessions,[112]

22. the confiscation and sale of property belonging to émigrés,[113]

23. the relegation of their fathers, mothers, wives and children into the interior,

24. the banishment or transportation of unsworn ecclesiastics,[114]

25. the establishment of easy divorce at two months' notice and on demand of one of the parties,[115]

in short, every measure is taken which tend to disturb property, break up the family, persecute conscience, suspend the law, pervert justice, and rehabilitate crime. laws are promulgated to deliver:

* the judicial system,

* the full control of the nation,

* the selection of the members of the future omnipotent Assembly,

* in short, the entire government,

to an autocratic, violent minority, which, having risked all to grab the dictatorship, dares all to keep it.[116]

VIII.

State of Paris in the Interregnum. — The mass of the population. — Subaltern Jacobins. — The Jacobin leaders.

Let us stop a moment to contemplate this great city and its new rulers. — From afar, Paris seems a club of 700,000 fanatics, vociferating and deliberating on the public squares; near by, it is nothing of the sort. The slime, on rising from the bottom, has become the surface, and given its color to the stream; but the human stream flows in its ordinary channel, and, under this turbid exterior, remains about the same as it was before. It is a city of people like ourselves, governed, busy, and fond of amusement. To the great majority, even in revolutionary times, private life, too complex and absorbing, leaves but an insignificant corner for public affairs. Through routine and through necessity, manufacturing, display of wares, selling, purchasing, keeping accounts, trades, and professions, continue as usual. The clerk goes to his office, the workman to his shop, the artisan to his loft, the merchant to his warehouse, the professional to his cabinet, and the official to his duty;[117] they are devoted, first of all, to their pursuits, to their daily bread, to the discharge of their obligations, to their own advancement, to their families, and to their pleasures; to provide for these things the day is not too long. Politics only briefly distract them, and then rather out of curiosity, like a play one applauds or hisses in his seat without stepping upon the stage. — "The declaration that the country is in danger," says many eye witnesses,[118] "has made no change in the physiognomy of Paris. There are the same amusements, the same gossip. . . . The theaters are full as usual. The wine–shops and places of diversion overflow with the people, National Guards, and soldiers. . . . The fashionable world enjoys its pleasure–parties," – "The day after the decree, the effect of the ceremony, so skillfully managed, is very slight. "The National Guard in the procession, writes a patriotic journalist,[119] "first shows indifference and even boredom"; it is exasperated with night watches and patrol duty; they probably tell each others that in parading for the nation, one finds no time to work for one's self. — A few days after this the manifesto of the Duke of Brunswick "produces no sensation whatever. People laugh at it. Only the newspapers and their readers are familiar with it. . . . The mass know nothing about it. Nobody fears the coalition nor foreign troops."[120] — On the 10th of August, outside the theater of the combat, all is quiet in Paris. People walk about and chat in the streets as usual."[121] — On the 19th of August, Moore, the Englishman,[122] sees, with astonishment, the heedless crowd filling the Champs Elysées, the various diversions, the air of a fête, the countless small shops in which refreshments are sold accompanied with songs and music, and the quantities of pantomimes and marionettes. "Are these people as happy as they seem to be?" he asks of a Frenchman along with him. — "They are as jolly as gods!" — "Do you think the Duke of Brunswick is ever in their heads?" — "Monsieur, you may be sure of this, that the Duke of Brunswick is the last man they think of."

Such is the unconcern or light–heartedness of the gross, egoistic mass, otherwise busy, and always passive under any government whatever it may be, a veritable flock of sheep, allowing government to do as it pleases, provided it does not hinder it from browsing and capering as it chooses. — As to the men of sensibility who love their country, they are still less troublesome, for they are gone or going (to the army), often at the rate of a thousand and even two thousand a day, ten thousand in the last week of July,[123] fifteen thousand in the first two weeks of September,[124] in all perhaps 40,000 volunteers furnished by the capital alone and who, with their fellows proportionate in number supplied by the departments, are to be the salvation of France. — Through this departure of the worthy, and this passivity of the flock, Paris belongs to the fanatics among the population. "These are the sans–culottes," wrote the patriotic Palloy, "the scum and riffraff of Paris, and I glory in belonging to that class which has put down the so–called honest folks."[125] — "Three thousand workmen," says the Girondist Soulavie, later, "made the Revolution of the 10th of August, against the kingdom of the Feuillants, the majority of the capital and against the Legislative Assembly."[126] Workmen, day laborers, and petty shop–keepers, not counting women, common vagabonds and regular bandits, form, indeed, one–twentieth of the adult male population of the city, about 9,000 spread over all sections of Paris, the only ones to vote and act in the midst of universal stupor and indifference. — We find in the Rue de Seine, for example, seven of them, Lacaille, keeper of a roasting– shop; Philippe, "a cattle–breeder, who leads around she–asses for consumptives," now president of the section, and soon to become one of the Abbaye butchers; Guérard, "a Rouen river–man who has abandoned the navigation of the Seine on a large scale and keeps a skiff, in which he ferries people over the river from the Pont du Louvre to the Quai Mazarin," and four characters of the same stamp. Their energy, however, replaces their lack of education and numerical inferiority. One day, Guérard, on passing M. Hua, the deputy, tells him in the way of a warning, "You big rascal, you were lucky to have other people with you. If you had been alone, I would have capsized my boat, and had the pleasure of drowning a blasted aristocrat!" These are the "matadors of the quarter".[127] — Their ignorance does not trouble them; on the contrary, they take pride in coarseness and vulgarity. One of the ordinary speechmakers of the Faubourg Saint–Antoine, Gouchon, a designer for calicos, comes to the bar of the Assembly, "in the name of the men of July 14 and Augusts 10," to glorify the political reign of brutal incapacity; according to him, it is more enlightened than that of the cultivated:[128]"those great geniuses graced with the fine title of Constitutionalists are forced to do justice to men who never studied the art of governing elsewhere than in the book of experience. . . . Consulting customs and not principles, these clever people have for a long period been busy with the political balance of things; we have found it without looking for it in the heart of man: Form a government which will place the poor above their feeble resources and the rich below their means, and the balance will be perfect." [129]

This is more than clear, their declared purpose is a complete leveling, not alone of political rights, but, again, and especially, of conditions and fortunes; they promise themselves "absolute equality, real equality," and, still better, "the magistracy and all government powers."[130] France belongs to them, if they are bold enough to seize hold of it. — And, on the other hand, should they miss their prey, they feel themselves lost, for the Brunswick manifesto,[131] which had made no impression on the public, remains deeply impressed in their minds. They apply its threats to themselves, while their imagination, as usual, translates it into a specific legend:[132] all the inhabitants of Paris are to be led out on the plain of Saint–Denis, and there decimated; previous to this, the most notorious patriots will be singled out together with forty or fifty market–women and broken on the wheel. Already, on the 11th of August, a rumor is current that 800 men of the late royal guards are ready to make a descent on Paris;[133] that very day the dwelling of Beaumarchais is ransacked for seven hours;[134] the walls are pierced, the privies sounded, and the garden dug down to the rock. The same search is repeated in the adjoining house. The women are especially "enraged at not finding anything," and wish to renew the attempt, swearing that they will discover where things are hidden in ten minutes. The nightmare is evidently too much for these unballasted minds. They break down under the weight of their accidental kingship, their inflamed pride, extravagant desires, and intense and silent fears which form in them that morbid and evil concoction which, in democracy as well as in a monarchy, fashions a Nero.[135]

Their leaders, who are even more upset, conceited, and despotic, have no scruples holding them back, for the most noteworthy are corrupt, acting alone or as leaders. Of the three chiefs of the old municipality, Pétion, the mayor, actually in semi−retirement, but verbally respected, is set aside and considered as an old decoration. The other two remain active and in office, Manuel,[136] the syndic−attorney, son of a porter, a loud−talking, untalented bohemian, stole the private correspondence of Mirabeau from a public depository, falsified it, and sold it for his own benefit. Danton,[137] Manuel's deputy, faithless in two ways, receives the King's money to prevent the riot, and makes use of it to urge it on. — Varlet, "that extraordinary speech−maker, led such a foul and prodigal life as to bring his mother in sorrow to the grave; afterwards he spent what was left, and soon had nothing."[138] — Others not only lacked honor but even common honesty. Carra, with a seat in the secret Directory of the Federates, and who drew up the plan of the insurrection, had been condemned by the Mâcon tribunals to two years' imprisonment for theft and burglary.[139] Westermann, who led the attacking column, had stolen a silver dish, with a coat of arms on it, from Jean Creux, keeper of a restaurant, rue des Poules, and was twice sent away from Paris for swindling.[140] Panis, chief of the Committee of Supervision,[141] was turned out of the Treasury Department, where his uncle was a sub cashier, in 1774, for robbery. His colleague, Sergent, appropriates to himself "three gold watches, an agate ring, and other jewels," left with him on deposit.[142] "Breaking seals, false charges, breaches of trust," embezzlements, are familiar transactions. In their hands piles of silver plate and 1,100,000 francs in gold are to disappear.[143] Among the members of the new Commune, Huguenin, the president, a clerk at the barriers, is a brazen embezzler.[144] Rossignol, a journeyman jeweller, implicated in an assassination, is at this moment subject to judicial prosecution.[145] Hébert, a journalistic garbage bag, formerly check−taker in a theatre, is turned away from the Variétés for larceny.[146] Among men of action, Fournier, the American, Lazowski, and Maillard are not only murderers, but likewise robbers,[147] while, by their side, arises the future general of the Paris National Guard, Henriot, at first a domestic in the family of an attorney who turned him out for theft, then a tax−clerk, again turned adrift for theft, and, finally, a police spy, and still incarcerated in the Bicêtre prison for another theft, and, at last, a battalion officer, and one of the September executioners.[148] – Simultaneously with the bandits and rascals, monstrous maniacs come out of their holes. De Sades,[149] who lived the life of "Justine" before he wrote it, and whom the Revolution delivered from the Bastille, is secretary of the section of the Place Vendôme. Marat, the homicidal monomaniac, constitutes himself, after the 23rd of August, official journalist at the Hôtel−de−ville, political advisor and consciousness of the new Commune, and the obsessive plan, which he preaches for three years, is merely an instant and direct wholesale butchery.

"Give me," said he to Barbaroux,[150] "two hundred Neapolitans armed with daggers, and with only a hand−kerchief on their left arms for a buckler, and I will overrun France and build the Revolution."

According to him it is necessary to do away with 260,000 men "on humane grounds," for, unless this is done, there is no safety for the rest.

"The National Assembly may still save France; let it decree that all aristocrats shall wear a blue ribbon, and the moment that three of them are seen in company, let them be hung."

Another way would be

"to lay in wait in dark streets and at corners for the royalists and Feuillants, and cut their throats. Should ten patriots happen to be killed among a hundred men, what does it matter? It is only ninety for ten, which prevents mistakes. Fall upon those who own carriages, employ valets, wear silk coats, or go to the theatres. You may be sure that they are aristocrats."

The Jacobin proletariat has obviously found the leadership that suits them. They will get on with each other without difficulty. In order that this spontaneous massacre may become an administrative measure, the Neros of the gutter have but to await the word of command from the Neros of the H ô t e l – d e – v i l l e .

Notes:

[1]An expression of Lafayette's in his address to the Assembly.

[2]Lafayette, "Mémoires," I. 452. — Malouet (II. 213) states that there were seventy.

[3]Cf., for example, "Archives Nationales," A.F. II.116. Petition of 228 notables of Montargis.

[4] Petition of the 20,000, so–called, presented by Messrs. Guillaume and Dupont de Nemours. – Cf.. Mortimer–Ternaux, I. 278. — According to Buchez et Roux, the petition containing only 7,411 names.

[5] Mortimer–Ternaux, I.277.

[6] Moniteur, XIII. 89. The act (July 7) is drawn up with admirable precision and force. On comparing it with the vague, turgid exaggerations of their adversaries, it seems to measure the intellectual distance between the two parties.

[7] 339 against 224 — Rœderer ("Chronique des cinquante jours," p.79). "A strong current of opinion by a majority of the inhabitants of Paris sets in favor of the King." – C. Desmoulins; "That class of petty traders and shopkeepers, who are more afraid of the revolutionaries than of so many Uhlans. . . "

[8] Mortimer–Ternaux, I. 236. Letter of Rœderer to the president of the National Assembly, June 25. "Mr. President, I have the honor to inform the Assembly that an armed mob is marching towards the Château."

[9] Mortimer–Ternaux, I. 245, 246. – II. 81, 131, 148, 170.

[10] The murder of M. Duhamel, sub–lieutenant of the national guard.

[11] Letter of Vergniaud and Guadet to the painter Boze (in the "Mémoires de Dumouriez"). — Rœderer, "Chronique des cinquante jours," 295. — Bertrand de Molleville, "Mémoires," III. 29.

[12] Moniteur, XIII. 155 (session of July 16). — Mortimer–Ternaux, II. 69. "Favored by you," says Manuel, "all citizens are entitled to visit the first functionary of the nation. . . The prince's dwelling should be open, like a church. Fear of the people is an insult to the people. If Louis XVI. possessed

the soul of a Marcus Aurelius, he would have descended into his gardens and tried to console a hundred thousand beings, on account of the slowness of the Revolution. . . Never had there been fewer thieves in the Tuileries than on that day; for the courtiers had fled. . .The red cap was an honor to Louis XVI.s head, and ought to be his crown." At this solemn moment the fraternization of the king with the people took place, and "the next day the same king betrayed, calumniated, and disgraced the people!" Manuel's rigmarole surpasses all that can be imagined. "After this there arises in the panelings of the Louvre, at the confluence of the civil list, another channel, which leads through the shades below to Pétion's dungeon. . . The department, in dealing a blow at the municipality, explains how, at the banquet of the Law, it represents the Law in the form of a crocodile, etc."

[13] Moniteur, XIII. 93 (session of July 9); — 27 (session of July 2).

[14] Moniteur, XII. 751 (session of June 24); XIII.33 (session of July 3).

[15] Moniteur, XIII. 224 (session of July 23). Two unsworn priests had just been massacred at Bordeaux and their heads carried through the streets on pikes. Ducos adds: "Since the executive power has put its veto on laws repressing fanaticism, popular executions begin to be repeated. If the courts do not render justice, etc." — Ibid., XIII. 301 (session of July 31).

[16] Moniteur, XIII. 72 (session of July 7). The king's speech to the Assembly after the Lamourette kiss. "I confess to you, M. President, that I was very anxious for the deputation to arrive, that I might hasten to the Assembly."

[17] Moniteur, XIII. 313 (session of Aug. 3). The declaration read in the king's name must be weighed sentence by sentence; it sums up his conduct with perfect exactness and thus ends: "What are personal dangers to a king, from whom they would take the love of his people? This is what affects me most. The day will come, perhaps, when the people will know how much I prize its welfare, how much this has always been my concern and my first need. What sorrows would disappear at the slightest sign of its return!"

[18] Moniteur, XIII. 33, 56 bis 85, 97 (sessions of July 3, 5, 6 and 9).

[19] Moniteur, XIII. 26, 170, 273 (sessions of July 12, 17, 28). – Mortimer–Ternaux, II. 122 (session of July 23): Addresses of the municipal council of Marseilles, of the federates, of the Angers petitioners, of the Charente volunteers, etc. "A hereditary monarchy is opposed to the Rights of Man. Pass the act of dethronement and France is saved. . . Be brave, let the sword of the law fall on a perjured functionary and conspirator! Lafayette is the most contemptible, the guiltiest, . . . the most infamous of the assassins of the people," etc.

[20] Mortimer–Ternaux, II. 126. — Bertrand de Molleville, III. 294.

[21] Moniteur, XIII. 325 (session of Aug. 3).

[22] Moniteur, XII. 738; XII. 340.

[23] Moniteur, XIII. 170, 171, 187, 208, 335 (sessions of July 17, 18, and 23, and Aug. 5).

[24] Moniteur, XIII. 187 (session of July 18). "The galleries applaud. The Assembly murmurs." — 208 (July 21). "Murmuring, shouts, and cries of Down with the speaker! from the galleries. The president calls the house to order five times, but always fruitlessly." — 224 (July 23). "The galleries applaud; long continued murmurs are heard in the Assembly."

[25] Buzot, "Mémoires" (Ed. Dauban, 83 and 84). "The majority of the French people yearned for royalty and the constitution of 1790. . . It was at Paris particularly that this desire governed the general plan, the discussion of it being the least feared in special conversations and in private society. There were only a few noble–minded, superior men that were worthy of being republicans. . . The rest desired the constitution of 1791, and spoke of the republicans only as one speaks of very honest maniacs."

[26] Duvergier, "Collection des lois et décrets," May 29, 1792; July 15, 16, and 18; July 6–20.

[27] Moniteur, XIII. 25 (session of July 1). Petition of 150 active citizens of the Bonne–Nouvelle section.

[28] Mortimer–Ternaux, II. 194. Buchez et Roux, XVI. 253. The decree of dismissal was not passed until the 12th of August, but after the 31St of July the municipality demanded it and during the following days several Jacobin grenadiers go to the National Assembly, trample on their bearskin hats and put on the red cap of liberty.

[29] Mortimer–Ternaux, II. 192 (municipal action of Aug. 5).

[30] Decree of July 2.

[31] Mortimer–Ternaux, II. 129. — Buchez et Roux, XV. 458. According to the report of the Minister of War, read the 30th of July, at the evening session, 5,314 department federates left Paris between July 14 and 30. Pétion wrote that the levy of federates then in Paris amounted to 2,960, "of which 2,032 were getting ready to go to the camp at Soissons." — A comparison of these figures leads to the approximate number that I have adopted

[32] Buchez et Roux, XVI. 120, 133 (session of the Jacobins, Aug. 6). The federates "resolved to watch the Château, each taking a place in the battalions respectively of the sections in which they lodge, and many incorporated themselves with the battalions of the faubourg St Antoine."

[33] Mercure de France, April 14, 1793.— " The Revolution," I. p. 332.

[34] Barbaroux, "Mémoires," 37–40. — Lauront–Lautard, "Marseilles depuis 1789 jusqu'à 1815," I. 134. "The mayor, Mourdeille," who had recruited them, "was perhaps very glad to get rid of them." — On the composition of this group and on the previous rôle of Rebecqui, see chapter VI.

[35] Buchez et Roux, XVI. 197 and following pages. — Mortimer– Ternaux, II. 148 (the grenadiers

numbered only 166). — Moniteur, XIII. 310 (session of Aug. 1). Address of the grenadiers: "They swore on their honor that they did not draw their swords until after being threatened for a quarter of an hour, then insulted and humiliated, until forced to defend their lives against a troop of brigands armed with pistols, and some of them with carbines." — " The reading of this memorandum is often interrupted by hooting from the galleries, in spite of the president's orders." — Hooting again, when they file out of the chamber.

[36] The lack of men of action greatly embarrassed the Jacobin party. ("Correspondance de Mirabeau et du Comte de la Marck,2 II. 326.) Letter of M. de Montmorin, July 13, 1792. On the disposition of the people of Paris, wearied and worn out "to excess." "They will take no side, either for or against the king. . . They no longer stir for any purpose; riots are wholly factitious. This is so right that they are obliged to bring men from the South to get them up. Nearly all of those who forced the gates of the Tuileries, or rather, who got inside of them on the 20th of June, were outsiders or onlookers, got together at the sight of such a lot of pikes and red caps, etc. The cowards ran at the slightest indication of presenting arms, which was done by a portion of the national guard on the arrival of a deputation from the National Assembly, their leaders being obliged to encourage them by telling them that they were not to be fired at."

[37] Buchez et Roux, XVI. 447. "Chronique des cinquante jours," by Rœderer.

[38] Mortimer–Ternaux, II. 378.–127 Jacobins of Arras, led by Geoffroy and young Robespierre, declare to the Directory that they mean to come to its meetings and follow its deliberations. "It is time that the master should keep his eye on his agents." The Directory, therefore, resigns (July 4, 1792). – Ibid., 462 (report of Leroux, municipal officer). The Paris municipal council, on the night of August 9–10 deliberates under threats of death and the furious shouts of the galleries.

[39] Duvergier's "Collection of Laws and Decrees," July 4, 5–8, 11–12, 25–28. — Buchez et Roux, XVI. 250. The section of the Theatre Français (of which Danton is president and Chaumette and Momoro secretaries) thus interpret the declaration of the country being in danger. "After a declaration of the country being in danger by the representatives of the people, it is natural that the people itself should take back its sovereign supervision."

[40] Schmidt, "Tableaux de la Révolution," I. 99–100. Report to Roland, Oct. 29, 1792.

[41] Mortimer–Ternaux, II. 199. – Buchez et Roux, XVI. 320. – Moniteur, XIII. 336 (session of Aug. 5). Speech by Collot d'Herbois.

[42] Moniteur, XI. 20, session of Feb. 4. At this meeting Gorguereau, reporter of the committee on legislation, had already stated that "The authors of these multiplied addresses seem to command rather than demand. . . It is ever the same sections or the same individuals who deceive you in bringing to you their own false testimony for that of the capital." – "Down with the reporter! From the galleries." – Ibid., XIII. 93, session of July 11. M. Gastelier: "Addresses in the name of the people are constantly read to you, which are not even the voice of one section. We have seen the same individual coming three times a week to demand something in the name of sovereignty." (Shouts of down! down! in the galleries. Ibid., 208, session of July 21. M. Dumolard: "You must distinguish between

the people of Paris and these subaltern intriguers . . . these habitual oracles of the cafés and public squares, whose equivocal existence has for a long time occupied the attention and claimed the supervision of the police." (Down with the speaker! murmurs and hooting in the galleries).–Mortimer–Ternaux, II. 398. Protests of the arsenal section, read by Lavoisier (the chemist): "The caprice of a knot of citizens (thus) becomes the desire of an immense population."

[43] Buchez et Roux, XVI. 251. – Mortimer–Ternaux, II. 239 and 243. The central bureau is first opened in "the building of the Saint– Esprit, in the second story, near the passage communicating with the common dwelling." Afterwards the commissioners of the section occupy another room in the Hôtel–de–ville, nearly joining the throne–room, where the municipal council is holding its sessions. During the night of August 9–10 both councils sit four hours simultaneously within a few steps of each other.

[44] Robespierre, "Seventh letter to his constituents," says: "The sections. . . have been busy for more than a fortnight getting ready for the last Revolution."

[45] Robespierre, "Seventh letter to his constituents" — Malouet, II. 233, 234. — Rœderer, "Chronique des cinquante jours."

[46] Moniteur, XIII. 318, 319. The petition is drawn up apparently by people who are beside themselves. "If we did not rely on you, I would not answer for the excesses to which our despair would carry us! We would bring on ourselves all the horrors of civil war, provided we could, on dying, drag along with us some of our cowardly assassins!" – – The representatives, it must be noted, talk in the same vein. La Source exclaims: "The members here, like yourselves, call for vengeance!" – Thuriot: "The crime is atrocious!"

[47] Taine is describing a basic trait of human nature, something we see again and again whether our ancestors attacked small, harmless neighboring nations, witches, renegades, Jews, or religious people of another faith .(SR).

[48] Buchez et Roux, XIX 93, session of Sept. 23, 1792. Speech by Panis: "Many worthy citizens would like to have judicial proof; but political proofs satisfy us" — Towards the end of July the Minister of the Interior had invited Pétion to send two municipal officers to examine the Tuileries; but this the council refused to do, so as to keep up the excitement.

[49] Mallet du Pan, "Mémoires," 303. Letter of Malouet, June 29. — Bertrand de Molleville, "Mémoires," II. 301. — Hua, 148. — Weber, II. 208. — Madame Campan, "Mémoires," II. 188. Already, at the end of 1791, the king was told that he was liable to be poisoned by the pastry–cook of the palace, a Jacobin. For three or four months the bread and pastry he ate were secretly purchased in other places. On the 14th of July, 1792, his attendants, on account of the threats against his life, put a breastplate on him under his coat.

[50] member of the 1789 Constituent Assembly. (SR).

[51] Moniteur, VIII. 271, 278. A deputy, excusing his assailants, pretends that d'Ésprémesnil urged

the people to enter the Tuileries garden. It is scarcely necessary to state that during the Constituent Assembly d'Esprém, nil was one of the most conspicuous members of the extreme "Right." – Duc de Gaëte, "Mémoires," I. 18.

[52] Lafayette, "Mémoires," I. 465.

[53] Moniteur, XIII. 327, — Mortimer–Ternaux, II. 176.

[54] Moniteur, XIII. 340. — The style of these petitions is highly instructive. We see in them the state of mind and degree of education of the petitioners: sometimes a half–educated writer attempting to reason in the vein of the Contrat Social; sometimes, a schoolboy spouting the tirades of Raynal; and sometimes, the corner letter– writer putting together the expressions forming his stock in trade.

[55] Carra, "Précis historique sur l'origine et les véritables auteurs de l'insurrection du 10 Août." — Barbaroux, "Mémoires, 49. The executive directory, appointed by the central committee of the confederates, held its first meeting in a wine–shop, the Soleil d'or, on the square of the Bastille; the second at the Cadran bleu, on the boulevard; the third in Antoine's room, who then lodged in the same house with Robespierre. Camille Desmoulins was present at this latter meeting. Santerre, Westermann, Fournier the American, and Lazowski were the principal members of this Directory. Another insurrectionary plan was drawn up on the 30th of July in a wine–shop at Charenton by Barbaroux, Rebecqui, Pierre Bayle, Heron, and Fournier the American. – Cf. J. Claretie, "Camille Desmoulins," p. 192. Desmoulins wrote, a little before the 10th of August: "If the National Assembly thinks that it cannot save the country, let it declare then, that, according to the Constitution, and like the Romans, it hands this over to each citizen. Let the tocsin be rung forthwith, the whole nation assembled, and every man, as at Rome, be invested with the power of putting to death all well–known conspirators!"

[56] Mortimer–Ternaux, II. 182. Decision of the Quinze–Vingt Section, Aug. 4. – Buchez et Roux, XVI. 402–410. History of Quinze–Vingt Section.

[57] Moniteur. XIII. 367, session of Aug. 8. – Ibid., 369 and following pages. Session of Aug. 9. Letters and speeches of maltreated deputies.

[58] Moniteur, 371. Speech of M. Girardin: "I am convinced that most of those who insulted me were foreigners." — Ibid., 370. Letter of M. Frouvières: "Many of the citizens, coming out of their shops, exclaimed: How can they insult the deputies in this way? Run away! run off!" — M. Jolivet, that evening attending a meeting of the Jacobin Club, states "that the Jacobin tribunes were far from sharing in this frenzy." He heard "one individual in these tribunes exclaim, on the proposal to put the dwellings of the deputies on the list, that it was outrageous." — Countless other details show the small number and character of the factions. – Ibid., 374. Speech of Aubert–Dubacet: "I saw men dressed in the coats of the national guard, with countenances betraying everything that is most vile in wickedness." There are "a great many evil–disposed persons among the federates."

[59] Moniteur, XIII. 170 (letter of M. de Joly, Minister of Justice). – Ibid., 371, declaration of M. Jolivet. – Buchez et Roux, XVI. 370 (session of the Jacobin Club, Aug. 8, at evening). Speech by

Goupilleau.

[60] One may imagine with what satisfaction Lenin, must have read this description agreeing: "Yes, open voting by a named and identified count, that is how a leader best can control any assembly." (SR).

[61] Moniteur, XIII. 37o. – Cf. Ibid., the letter of M. Chapron. — Ibid., 372. Speech by M. A. Vaublanc. — Moore, "Journal during a Residence in France," I. 25 (Aug. 10). The impudence of the people in the galleries was intolerable. There was "a loud and universal peal of laughter from all the galleries" on the reading of a letter, in which a deputy wrote that he was threatened with decapitation. — " Fifty members were shouting at the same time; the most boisterous night I ever was witness to in the House of Commons was calmness itself alongside of this."

[62] Moniteur, Ibid., p. 371. – Lafayette, I. 467. "On the 9th of August, as can be seen in the unmutilated editions of the Logographe, the Assembly, almost to a man, arose and declared that it was not free." Ibid., 478. "On the 9th of August the Assembly had passed a decree declaring that it was not free. This decree was torn up on the 10th. But it is no that it was passed."

[63] Moniteur, XIII. 370, 374, 375. Speech by Rœderer, letter of M. de Joly, and speech by Pétion.

[64] Mathieu Dumas, "Mémoires," II. 461.

[65] "Chronique des cinquante jours," by Rœderer. – Mortimer–Ternaux, II. 260. – Buchez et Roux, XVI. 458. – Towards half–past seven in the morning there were only from sixty to eighty members present. (Testimony of two of the Ministers who leave the Assembly.)

[66] Mortimer–Ternaux, II. 205. At the ballot of July 12, not counting members on leave of absence or delegated elsewhere, and the dead not replaced, there were already twenty–seven not answering the call, while after that date three others resigned. — Buchez et Roux, XVIL 340 (session of Sept. 2, 1792). Hérault de Séchelles is elected president by 248 out of 257 voters. — Hua, 164 (after Aug. 10). "We attended the meetings of the House simply to show that we had not given them up. We took no part in the discussions, and on the vote being taken, standing or sitting, we remained in our seats. This was the only protest we could make."

[67] Mortimer–Ternaux, II. 229, 233, 417 and following pages. M. Mortimer–Ternaux is the first to expose, with documents to support him and critical discussion, the formation of the revolutionary commune. – The six sections referred to are the Lombards, Gravilliers, Mauconseil, Gobelins, Théatre–Français, and Faubourg Poissonnière.

[68] For instance, the Enfants Rouges, Louvre, Observatoire, Fontaine–Grenelle, Faubourg Saint–Denis, and Thermes de Julien..

[69] For example, at the sections of Montreuil, Popincourt, and Roi de Sicile..

[70] For example, Ponceau, Invalides, Sainte–Geneviève.

[71] Mortimer–Ternaux, II. 240.

[72] Mortimer–Ternaux, 446 (list of the commissioners who took their seats before 9 o'clock in the morning). "Le Tableau général des Commisaires des 48 sections qui ont composé le conseil général de la Commune de Paris, le 10 Août, 1792," it must be noted, was not published until three or four months later, with all the essential falsifications. It may be found in Buchez et Roux, XVI. 450. — "Relation de l'abbé Sicard." "At that time a lot of scoundrels, after the general meeting of the sections was over, passed acts in the name of the whole assemblage and had them executed, utterly unknown to those who had done this, or by those who were the unfortunate victims of these proceedings " (supported by documents).

[73] Mortimer–Ternaux, II. 270, 273. (The official report of Mandat's examination contains five false statements, either through omission or substitution.)

[74] Claretie, "Camille Desmoulins," p.467 (notes of Topino–Lebrun on Danton's trial). Danton, in the pleadings, says: "I left at 1 o'clock in the morning. I was at the revolutionary commune and pronounced sentence of death on Mandet, who had orders to fire op the people." Danton in the same place says: "I had planned the 10th of August." It is very certain that from 1 to 7 o'clock in the morning (when Mandat was killed) he was the principal leader of the insurrectional commune. Nobody was so potent, so overbearing, so well endowed physically for the control of such a conventicle as Danton. Besides, among the new– comers he was the best known and with the most influence through his position as deputy of the syndic–attorney. Hence his prestige after the victory and appointment as Minister of Justice. His hierarchical superior, the syndic–attorney Manuel, who was there also and signed his name, showed himself undoubtedly the pitiful fellow he was, an affected, crazy, ridiculous loud–talker. For this reason he was allowed to remain syndic–attorney as a tool and servant. — Beaulieu, "Essais sur la Révolution Française," III. 454. "Rossignal boasted of having committed this assassination himself."

[75] "Pièces intéressantes pour l'histoire," by Pétion, 1793. "I desired the insurrection, but I trembled for fear that it might not succeed. My position was a critical one. I had to do my duty as a citizen without sacrificing that of a magistrate; externals had to be preserved without derogating from forms. The plan was to confine me in my own house; but they forgot or delayed to carry this out. Who do you think repeatedly sent to urge the execution of this measure? Myself; yes, myself!"

[76] In "Histoire de la Révolution Française" by Ferrand Lamarque, Cavaillés, Paris 1851, vol. II. Page 225 we may read the following footnote: "This very evening, a young artillery lieutenant observed, from a window of a house in the rue de l'Echelle, the preparations which were being undertaken in the château des Tuileries: that was Napoleon Bonaparte. "–Well, right, asked the deputy Pozze di Borgo, his compatriot, what do you think of what is going on? This evening they will attack the château. Do you think the people will succeed? – I don't know, answered the future emperor, but what I can assure you is that if they gave me the command of two Swiss battalions and one hundred good horsemen, I should repel the insurgents in a manner which would for ever rid them of any desire to return." (SR)

[77] Napoleon, at this moment, was at the Carrousel, in the house of Bourrienne's brother. "I could

see conveniently," he says, "all that took place during the day. . . The king had at least as many troops in his defense as the Convention since had on the 13th Vendémaire, while the enemies of the latter were much more formidable and better disciplined. The greater part of the national guard showed that they favored the king; this justice must be done to it." (It might be helpful to some readers to know that when Napoleon refers to the 13th Vendémaire, (5th Oct. 1795) that was when he, as a young officer was given the task to defend the Convention against a royalist uprising. He was quick–witted and got hold of some guns in time, loaded them with grape–shot, placed them in front of the Parisian church of Saint– Roch and completely eliminated the superior royalist force. SR.)

[78] Official report of Leroux. On the side of the garden, along the terrace by the river, and then on the return were "a few shouts of Vive le roi! many for Vive la nation! Vivent les sans–culottes! Down with the king! Down with the veto! Down with the old porker! etc. — But I can certify that these insults were all uttered between the Pont–Turnant and the parterre, and by about a dozen men, among which were five or six gunners following the king, the same as flies follow an animal they are bent on tormenting."

[79] Mortimer–Ternaux, III. 223, 273 — Letter of Bonnaud, chief of the Sainte–Marguerite battalion: "I cannot avoid marching at their head under any pretext . . . Never will I violate the Constitution unless I am forced to." — The Gravilliers section and that of the Faubourg Poissonnière cashiered their officers and elected others.

[80] Mortimer–Ternaux, IV. 342. Speech of Fabre d'Eglantine at the Jacobin Club, Nov. 5, 1792. "Let it be loudly proclaimed that these are the same men who captured the Tuileries, broke into the prisons of the Abbaye, of Orleans and of Versailles."

[81] In this respect the riot of the Champ–de–Mars (July 17, 1791), the only one that was suppressed, is very instructive: "As the militia would not as usual ground their arms on receiving the word of command from the mob, this last began, according to custom, to pelt them with stones. To be deprived of their Sunday recreational activities, to be marching through the streets under a scorching sun, and then be remain standing like fools on a public holiday, to be knocked out with bricks, was a little more than they had patience to bear so that, without waiting for an order, they fired and killed a dozen or two of the raggamuffins. The rest of the brave chaps bolted. If the militia had waited for orders they might, I fancy, have been all knocked down before they received any. . . Lafayette was very near being killed in the morning; but the pistol failed to go off at his breast. The assassin was immediately secured, but he arranged to be let free" (Gouverneur Morris, letter of July 20, 1791). Likewise, on the 29th of August, 1792, at Rouen, the national guard, defending the Hôtel–de– ville, is pelted with stones more than an hour while many are wounded. The magistrates make every concession and try every expedient, the mayor reading the riot act five or six times. Finally the national guard, forced into it, exclaim: "If you do not allow us to repel force with force we shall leave." They fire and four persons are killed and two wounded, and the crowd breaks up. ("Archives Nationales," F7, 2265, official report of the Rouen municipality, Aug. 29; addresses of the municipality, Aug. 28; letter of the lieutenant–colonel of the gendarmerie, Aug. 30, etc.).

[82] Official report of Leroux. — "Chronique des cinquante jours," by Rœderer. — "Détails particuliers sur la journée du 10 Aout," by a bourgeois of Paris, an eye–witness (1822).

[83] Barbaroux, "Mémoires," 69. "Everything betokened victory for the court if the king had never left his post . . . If he had shown himself, if he had mounted on horseback the battalions of Paris would have declared for him."

[84] "Révolution de Paris," number for Aug. 11, 1792. "The 10th of August, 1792, is still more horrible than the 24th of August, 1572, and Louis XVI. a greater monster than Charles IX. " — "Thousands of torches were found in cellars, apparently placed there to burn down Paris at a signal from this modern Nero." In the number for Aug.18: "The place for Louis Nero and for Medicis Antoinette is not in the towers of the Temple; their heads should have fallen from the guillotine on the night of the 10th of August." (Special details of a plan of the king to massacre all patriot deputies, and intimidate Paris with a grand pillaging and by keeping the guillotine constantly at work.) "That crowned ogre and his Austrian panther."

[85] Narrative of the Minister Joly (written four days after the event). The king departs about half–past eight. — Cf. Madame Campan, "Mémoires," and Moniteur, XIII. 378.

[86] Révolution de Paris," number for Aug. 18. On his way a sans– culotte steps out in front of the rows and tries to prevent the king from proceeding. The officer of the guard argues with him, upon which he extends his hand to the king, exclaiming: "Touch that hand, bastard, and you have shaken the hand of an honest man! But I have no intention that your bitch of a wife goes with you to the Assembly; we don't want that whore." — "Louis XVI," says Prudhomme, "kept on his way without being upset by the with this noble impulse." — I regard this as a masterpiece of Jacobin interpretation.

[87] Mortimer–Ternaux, II. 311, 325. The king, at the foot of the staircase, had asked Rœderer: "what will become of the persons remaining above? "Sire," he replies, "they seem to be in plain dress. Those who have swords have merely to take them off, follow you and leave by the garden." A certain number of gentlemen, indeed, do so, and thus depart while others escape by the opposite side through the gallery of the Louvre.

[88] Mathon de la Varenne, "Histoire particulière," etc., 108. (Testimony of the valet–de–chambre Lorimier de Chamilly, with whom Mathon was imprisoned in the prison of La Force.

[89] De Lavalette, "Mémoires," I. 81. "We there found the grand staircase barred by a sort of beam placed across it, and defended by several Swiss officers, who were civilly disputing its passage with about fifty mad fellows, whose odd dress very much resembled that of the brigands in our melodramas. They were intoxicated, while their coarse language and queer imprecations indicated the town of Marseilles, which had belched them forth."

[90] Mortimer–Ternaux, II. 314, 317 (questioning of M. de Diesbach). "Their orders were not to fire until the word was given, and not before the national guard had set the example."

[91] Buchez et Roux, XVI, 443. Narration by Pétion. – Peltier, "Histoire du 10 août.

[92] M. de Nicolay wrote the following day, the 11th of August: "The federates fired first, which was

followed by a sharp volley from the château windows." (Le Comte de Fersen et la cour de France. II. 347.)

[93] Mortimer-Ternaux, II. 491. The abandonment of the Tuileries is proved by the small loss of the assailants. (List of the wounded belonging to the Marseilles corps and of the killed and wounded of the Brest corps, drawn up Oct. 16, 1792. — Statement of the aid granted to wounded Parisians, to widows, to orphans, and to the aged, October, 1792, and then 1794.) — The total amounts to 74 dead and 54 severely wounded The two corps in the hottest of the fight were the Marseilles band, which lost 22 dead and 14 wounded, and the Bretons, who lost 2 dead and 5 wounded. The sections that suffered the most were the Quinze-Vingts (4 dead and 4 wounded), the Faubourg-Montmartre (3 dead), the Lombards (4 wounded), and the Gravilliers (3 wounded). — Out of twenty-one sections reported, seven declare that they did not lose a man. — The Swiss regiment, on the contrary, lost 760 men and 26 officers.

[94] Napoleon's narrative.

[95] Pétion's account.

[96] Prudhomme's "Révolution de Paris," XIII. 236 and 237. – Barbaroux, 73. – Madame Campan, II. 250.

[97] Mortimer-Ternaux, II. 258. — Moore, I. 59. Some of the robbers are killed. Moore saw one of them thrown down the grand staircase.

[98] Michelet, III. 289.

[99] Mercier, "Le Nouveau Paris," II. 108. — "The Comte de Fersen et la Cour de France," II. 348. (Letter of Sainte-Foix, Aug. 11). "The cellars were broken open and more than 10,000 bottles of wine of which I saw the fragments in the court, so intoxicated the people that I made haste to put an end to an investigation imprudently begun amidst 2,000 sots with naked swords, handled by them very carelessly."

[100] Napoleon's narrative. — Memoirs of Barbaroux.

[101] Moniteur, XIII. 387. — Mortimer-Ternaux, II. 340.

[102] Mortimer-Ternaux, II. 303. Words of the president Vergniaud on receiving Louis XVI. – Ibid. 340, 342, 350.

[103] Mortimer-Ternaux, 356, 357.

[104] Mortimer-Ternaux, 337. Speech of Huguenin, president of the Commune, at the bar of the National Assembly: "The people by whom we are sent to you have instructed us to declare to you that they invest you anew with its confidence; but they at the same time instruct us to declare to you that, as judge of the extraordinary measures to which they have been driven by necessity and resistance to

oppression, they k now no other authority than the French people, your sovereign and ours, assembled in its primary meetings."

[105] Duvergier, "Collection des lois et décrets," (between Aug. 10 and Sept. 20).

[106] Duvergier, "Collection des lois et décrets," Aug. 11–12. "The natgional Assembly considering that it has not the right to subject sovereignty in the formation of a national Convention to imperative regulations, . . . invites citizens to conform to the following rules."

[107] August 11 (article 8)

[108] Aug. 10–12 and Aug. 28.

[109] Ibid., Aug. 10, Aug. 13. – Cf. Moniteur, XIII. 399 (session of Aug. 12).

[110] Ibid., Aug. 18.

[111] Aug. 23 and Sep. 3. After the 11th of August the Assembly passes a decree releasing Saint–Huruge and annulling the warrant against Antoine.

[112] Ibid., Aug. 14.

[113] Ibid., Aug. 14. Decree for dividing the property of the émigrés into lots of from two to four arpents, in order to "multiply small proprietors." — Ibid., Sept. 2. Other decrees against the émigrés and their relations, Aug. 14, 23, 30, and Sept. 5 and 9.

[114] Ibid., Aug. 26. Other decrees against the ecclesiastics or the property of the church, Aug. 17, 18, 19, and Sept. 9 and 19.

[115] Ibid., Sept. 20.

[116] Imagine the impression these last lines may have upon any ardent, ambitious and arrogant young man who, like Lenin in 1907, would have read this between 1893 and 1962, date of the last English reprinting of Taine's once widely know work. They summed up both what had to be done and who would be the primary beneficiaries of the revolution. Lenin, Hitler, Mussolini and countless other young hopeful political men. Read it once more and ask yourself if much of this program has not been more or less surreptitiously carried out in most western countries after the second world war? (SR).

[117] Malouet, II. 241.

[118] Mercure de France, July 21, 1792.

[119] "Révolutions de Paris," XIII. 137.

[120] Mallet du Pan. "Mémoires," I. 322. Letters to Mallet du Pan. Aug. 4 and following days.

[121] Buchez et Roux, XVI. 446. Pétion's narrative. — Arnault, "Souvenirs d'un sexagénaire," I. 342. (An eye-witness on the 10th of August.) "The massacre extended but little beyond the Carrousel, and did not cross the Seine. Everywhere else I found a population as quiet as if nothing had happened. Inside the city the people scarcely manifested any surprise; dancing went on in the public gardens. In the Marais, where I lived then, there was only a suspicion of the occurrence, the same as at Saint-Germain; it was said that something was going on in Paris, and the evening newspaper was impatiently looked for to know what it was."

[122] Moore, I. 122. — The same thing is observable at other crises in the Revolution. On the 6th of October, 1789 (Sainte-Beuve, "Causeries du Lundi," XII. 461), Sénac de Meilhan at an evening reception hears the following conversations: "'Did you see the king pass?' asks one. 'No, I was at the theater.' 'Did Molé play?' — 'As for myself; I was obliged to stay in the Tuileries; there was no way of getting out before 9 o'clock.' 'You saw the king pass then?' 'I could not see very well; it was dark.' — Another says: 'It must have taken six hours for him to come from Versailles.' — Others coolly add a few details. — To continue: 'Will you take a hand at whist?' 'I will play after supper, which is just ready.' Cannon are heard, and then a few whisperings, and a transient moment of depression,. 'The king is leaving the Hôtel-de-ville. They must be very tired.' Supper is taken and there are snatches of conversation. They play trente et quarante and while walking about watching the game and their cards they do some talking: 'What a horrid affair!' while some speak together briefly and in a low tone of voice. The clock strikes two and they all leave or go to bed. — These people seem to you insensible. Very well; there is not one of them who would not accept death at the king's feet." — On the 23d of June, 1791, at the news of the king's arrest at Varennes, "the Bois de Boulogne and the Champs Elysées were filled with people talking in a frivolous way about the most serious matters, while young men are seen, pronouncing sentences of death in their frolics with courtesans." (Mercure de France, July 9, 1791. It begins with a little piece entitled Dépit d'un Amant.) – See ch. XI. for the sentiment of the population in May and June, 1793.

[123] Moniteur, XIII. 290 (July 29) and 278 (July 30).

[124] "Archives Nationales," F7, 145. Letter of Santerre to the Minister of the Interior, Sept. 16, 1792, with the daily list of all the men that have left Paris between the3rd and 15th of September, the total amounting to 18,635, of which 15,504 are volunteers. Other letters from the same, indicating subsequent departures: Sept. 17, 1,071 men; none the following days until Sept. 21, 243; 22nd 150; up to the 26th, 813; on Oct. 1st, 113; 2nd and 3rd, 1,088 ; 4th, 1620; 16th, 196, etc. — I believe that amongst those who leave, some are passing through Paris coming from the provinces; this prevents an exact calculation of the number of Parisian volunteers. M. de Lavalette, himself a volunteer, says 60,000; but he furnishes not proofs of this.

[125] Mortimer-Ternaux, II. 362.

[126] Soulavie, "Vie privée du Maréchal duc de Richelieu," IX. 384. – – "One can scarcely comprehend," says Lafayette, (Mémoires," I. 454), "how the Jacobin minority and a gang of pretended Marseilles men could render themselves masters of Paris, while almost the whole of the

40,000 citizens forming the national guard desired the Constitution."

[127] Hua, 169.

[128] Moniteur, XIII. 437. (session of Aug. 16, the applause reiterated and the speech ordered to be printed).

[129] These words should cause society to change resulting in a leveling of incomes through proportional taxation and aids of all kinds throughout the industrialized world. Nobody could ever imagine the immense wealth which was to be produced by the efficient industry of the 20th century. (SR).

[130] Rœderer, "Œuvres Complètes." VIII 477. "The club orators displayed France to the proletariat as a sure prey if they would seize hold of it."

[131] This manifesto, was drafted for the Duke of Brunswick– Lunebourg, the general commanding the combined Prussian and Austrian forces, by the French émigré Marquis de Limon. It threatened the French and especially the Paris population with unspecified "rigors of war" should it have the temerity to resist or to harm the King and his family. It was signed in Koblenz, Germany on 25 August 1792 and published in royalist newspapers 3 days later in Paris.(SR).

[132] Moore's Journal," I. 303–309.

[133] "Archives Nationales," 474, 426. Section of Gravilliers, letter of Charles Chemin, commissary, to Santerre, and deposition of Ilingray, cavalryman of the national gendarmerie, Aug. 11.

[134] Beaumarchais, "Œuvres complètes," letter of Aug. 12, 1792. — This very interesting letter shows how mobs are composed at this epoch. A small gang of regular brigands and thieves plot together some enterprise, to which is added a frightened, infatuated crowd, which may become ferocious, but which remains honest.

[135] The words of Hobbes applied by Rœderer to the democracy of 1792: "In democratia tot possent esse Nerones quot sunt oratores qui populo adulantur; simul et plures sunt in democratia, et quotidie novi suboriuntur."

[136] Lucas de Montigny, "Mémoires de Mirabeau," II. 231 and following pages. — The preface affixed by Manuel to his edition (of Mirabeau's letters) is a masterpiece of nonsense and impertinence. — Peltier, "Histoire du 10 Aout," II. 205. — Manuel "came out of a little shop at Montargis and hawked about obscene tracts in the upper stories of Paris. He got hold of Mirabeau's letters in the drawers of the public department and sold them for 2,000 crowns." (testimony of Boquillon, juge–de–paix).

[137] Lafayette, "Mémoires," I. 467, 471. "The queen had 50,000 crowns put into Danton's hands a short time before these terrible days." — " The court had Danton under pay for two years, employing him as a spy on the Jacobins." — " Correspondance de Mirabeau et du Comte de la Marck," III. 82.

Letter from Mirabeau, March 10, 1791: "Danton received yesterday 30,000 livres". — Other testimony, Bertrand de Molleville, I. 354, II. 288. — Brissot, IV. 193 — . Miot de Melito, "Mémoires," I. 40, 42. Miot was present at the conversations which took place between Danton, Legendre, etc., at the table of Desforges, Minister of Foreign Affairs. "Danton made no concealment of his love of pleasure and money, and laughed at all conscientious and delicate scruples." — " Legendre could not say enough in praise of Danton in speaking of his talents as a public man; but he loudly censured his habits and expensive tastes, and never joined him in any of his odious speculations." — The opposite thesis has been maintained by Robinet and Bougeart in their articles on Danton. The discussion would require too much space. The important points are as follows:

Danton, a barrister in the royal council in March, 1787, loses about 10,000 francs on the refund of his charge. In his marriage–contract dated June, 1787, he admits 12,000 francs patrimony in lands and houses, while his wife brings him only 20,000 francs dowry. From 1787 to 1791 he could not earn much, being in constant attendance at the Cordeliers club and devoted to politics; Lacretelle saw him in the riots of 1788. He left at his death about 85,000 francs in national property bought in 1791. Besides, he probably held property and valuables under third parties, who kept them after his death. (De Martel, "Types Révolutionnaires," 2d part, p.139. Investigations of Blache at Choisy–sur–Seine, where a certain Fauvel seems to have been Danton's assumed name.) — See on this question, "Avocats aux conseils du Roi," by Emil Bos, pp.513–520. According to accounts proved by M. Bos, it follows that Danton, at the end of 1791, was in debt to the amount of 53,000 francs; this is the hole stopped by the court. On the other side, Danton before the Revolution signs himself Danton even in authentic writing, which is an usurpation of nobility and at that time subject to the penalty of the galleys. — The double–faced infidelity in question must have been frequent, for their leaders were anything else but sensitive. On the 7th of August Madame Elizabeth tells M. de Montmorin that the insurrection would not take place; that Pétion and Santerre were concerned in it, and that they had received 750,000 francs to prevent it and bring over the Marseilles troop to the king's side (Malouet, II. 223). — There is no doubt that Santerre, in using the king's money against the king, thought he was acting patriotically. Money is at the bottom of every riot, to pay for drink and to stimulate subordinate agents.

[138] Buchez et Roux, XXVIII. 92. Letter of Gadolle to Roland, October, 1792, according to a narrative by one of the teachers in the college d'Harcourt, in which Varlet was placed.

[139] Buchez et Roux, XIII. 254.

[140] "C. Desmoulins," by Claretie, 238 (in 1786 and in 1775). "The inquest still exists, unfortunately it is convincing." — Westermann was accused of these acts in December, 1792, by the section of the Lombards, "proofs in hand." — Gouverneur Morris, so well informed, writes to Washington, Jan. 10, 1793: The retreat of the King of Prussia "was worth to Westermann about 10,000 pounds. . . The council . . . exerted against him a prosecution for old affairs of no higher rank than petty larceny."

[141] "Archives Nationales," F7, 4434 (papers of the committee of general safety). Note on Panis, with full details and references to the occurrence.

[142] "Révolutions de Paris," No.177 (session of the council–general at the Hotel–de–ville, Nov. 8,

1792, report of the committee of surveillance). Sergent admits, except as to one of the watches, that he intended to pay for the said object the price they would have brought. It was noticed, as he said this, that he had on his finger the agate ring that was claimed."

[143] Mortimer–Ternaux, II. 638; III. 500 and following pages; IV. 132. — Cf. II. 451.

[144] Mortimer–Ternaux, II. 456.

[145] Buchez et Roux, XVI. 138, 140 (testimony of Mathon de la Varenne, who was engaged in the case).

[146] "Dictionnaire biographique," by Eymery (Leipsic, 1807), article HÉBERT.

[147] Mortimer–Ternaux, III. 484, 601. Cf. letter of the representative Cavaignac, Ibid., 399.

[148] "Dictionnaire biographique," article HENRIOT.–The lives of many of these subordinate leaders are well done. Cf. "Stanislas Maillard," by AL Sorel; "Le Patriote Palloy," by V Fournel.

[149] Granier de Cassagnac, "Histoire des Girondins," 409. – "Archives Nationales," F7 3196. Letters of de Sades on the sacking of his house near Apt, with supporting document and proofs of his civism; among others a petition drawn up by him in the name of the Pique section and read at the Convention year II. brumaire 25. "Legislators, the reign of philosophy has at last annihilated that of imposture. . . The worship of a Jewish slave of the Romans is not adapted to the descendants of Scœvola. The general prosperity which is certain to proceed from individual happiness will spread to the farthest regions of the universe and everywhere the dreaded hydra of ultramontane superstition, chased by the combined lights of reason and virtue, no longer finding a refuge in the hateful haunts of a dying aristocracy, will perish at her side in despair at finally beholding on this earth the triumph of philosophy!"

[150] Barbaroux, "Mémoires," 57, 59. The latter months of the legislative assembly.

BOOK THIRD. THE SECOND STAGE OF THE CONQUEST.

CHAPTER I. MOB RULE IN TIMES OF ANARCHY

I.

Government by gangs in times of anarchy. – Case where anarchy is recent and suddenly brought on. — The band that succeeds the fallen government and its administrative tools.

The worst feature of anarchy is not so much the absence of the overthrown government as the rise of new governments of an inferior grade. In every state which breaks up, new groups will form to conquer and become sovereign: it was so in Gaul on the fall of the Roman empire, also under the latest of Charlemagne's successors; the same state of things exists now (1875) in Rumania and in Mexico. Adventurers, gangsters, corrupted or downgraded men, social outcasts, men overwhelmed with debts and lost to honor, vagabonds, deserters, dissolute troopers, born enemies of work, of subordination, and of the law, unite to break the worm–eaten barriers which still surround the sheep–like masses; and as they are unscrupulous, they slaughter on all occasions. On this foundation their authority rests; each in turn reigns in its own area, and their government, in keeping with its brutal masters, consists in robbery and murder; nothing else can be looked for from barbarians and brigands.

But never are they so dangerous as when, in a great State recently fallen, a sudden revolution places the central power in their hands; for they then regard themselves as the legitimate inheritors of the shattered government, and, under this title, they undertake to manage the commonwealth. Now in times of anarchy the ruling power does not proceed from above, but from below; and the chiefs, therefore, who would remain such, are obliged to follow the blind impulsion of their flock.[1] Hence the important and dominant personage, the one whose ideas prevail, the veritable successor of Richelieu and of Louis XIV. is here the subordinate Jacobin, the pillar of the club, the maker of motions, the street rioter, Panis Sergent, Hébert, Varlet, Henriot, Maillard, Fournier, Lazowski, or, still lower in the scale, the Marseilles "rough," the Faubourg gunner, the drinking market–porter who elaborates his political conceptions in the interval between his hiccups.[2] — For information he has the rumors circulating in the streets which tell of a traitor to each house, and for confirmed knowledge the club slogans inciting him to rule over the vast machine. A machinery so vast and complicated, a whole assembly of entangled services ramifying in innumerable offices, with so much apparatus of special import, so delicate as to require constant adaptation to changing circumstances, diplomacy, finances, justice, army administration — all this surpasses his limited comprehension; a bottle cannot be made to contain the bulk of a hogshead.[3] In his narrow brain, perverted and turned topsy–turvy by the disproportionate notions put into it, only one idea suited to his gross instincts and aptitudes finds a place there, and that is the desire to kill his enemies; and these are also the State's enemies, however open or concealed, present or future, probable or even possible. He carries this savagery and bewilderment into politics, and hence the evil arising from his government. Simply a brigand, he would have murdered only to rob, and his murders would have been restricted. As representing the State, he undertakes wholesale massacres, of which he has the means ready at hand. — For he has not yet had time enough to take apart the old administrative implements; at all events the minor wheels, gendarmes, jailers, employees, book–keepers, and accountants, are always in their places and under control. There can be no resistance on the part of those arrested; accustomed to the protection of the laws and to peaceable ways and times, they have never relied on defending themselves nor ever could imagine that any one could be so summarily slain. As to the mass, rendered incapable of any effort of its own by ancient centralization, it remains inert and passive and lets things go their own way. — Hence, during many long, successive days, without being hurried or impeded, with official papers quite correct and accounts in perfect order, a massacre can be carried out with the same impunity and as methodically as cleaning the streets or clubbing stray dogs.[4]

II.

The development of the ideas of killings in the mass of the party. — The morning after August 10. — The tribunal of August 17. — The funereal fête of August 27. — The prison plot.

Let us trace the progress of the homicidal idea in the mass of the party. It lies at the very bottom of the revolutionary creed. Collot d'Herbois, two months after this, aptly says in the Jacobin tribune: "The second of September is the great article in the credo of our freedom."[5] It is peculiar to the Jacobin to consider himself as a legitimate sovereign, and to treat his adversaries not as belligerents, but as criminals. They are guilty of lèse– nation; they are outlaws, fit to be killed at all times and places, and deserve extinction, even when no longer able or in a condition do any harm. — Consequently, on the 10th of August the Swiss Guards, who do not fire a gun and who surrender, the wounded lying on the ground, their surgeons, the palace domestics, are killed; and worse still, persons like M. de Clermont–Tonnerre who pass quietly along the street. All this is now called in official phraseology the justice of the people. — On the 11th the Swiss Guards, collected in the Feuillants building, come near being massacred; the mob on the outside of it demand their heads;[6] "it conceives the project of visiting all the prisons in Paris to take out the prisoners and administer prompt justice on them." – On the 12th in the markets "diverse groups of the low class call Pétion a scoundrel," because "he saved the Swiss in the Palais Bourbon"; accordingly, "he and the Swiss must be hung to–day."–In these minds turned topsy–turvy the actual, palpable truth gives way to its opposite; "the attack was not begun by them; the order to sound the tocsin came from the palace; it is the palace which was besieging the nation, and not the nation which was besieging the palace."[7] The vanquished "are the assassins of the people," caught in the act; and on the 14th of August the Federates demand a court–martial "to avenge the death of their comrades."[8] And even a court–martial will not answer. "It is not sufficient to mete out punishment for crimes committed on the 10th of August, but the vengeance of the people must be extended to all conspirators;" to that "Lafayette, who probably was not in Paris, but who may have been there;" to all the ministers, generals, judges, and other officials guilty of maintaining legal order wherever it had been maintained, and of not having recognized the Jacobin government before it came into being. Let them be brought before, not the ordinary courts, which are not to be trusted because they belong to the defunct régime, but before a specially organized tribunal, a sort of "chambre ardente,"[9] elected by the sections, that is to say, by a Jacobin minority. These improvised judges must give judgment on conviction, without appeal; there must be no preliminary examinations, no interval of time between arrest and execution, no dilatory and protective formalities. And above all, the Assembly must be expeditious in passing the decree; "otherwise," it is informed by a delegate from the Commune,[10] "the tocsin will be rung at midnight and the general alarm sounded; for the people are tired of waiting to be avenged. Look out lest they do themselves justice! — A moment later, new threats and with an advanced deadline. "If the juries are not ready to act in two or three hours great misfortunes will overtake Paris."

Even if the new tribunal, set up on the spot, is quick, guillotining three innocent persons in five days; it does not move fast enough. On the 23rd of August one of the sections declares to the Commune in furious language that the people themselves, "wearied and indignant" with so many delays, mean to force open the prisons and massacre the inmates.[11] — Not only do the sections harass the judges, but they force the accused into their presence: a deputation from the Commune and the Federates summons the Assembly " to transfer the criminals at Orleans to Paris to undergo the penalty of their heinous crimes". "Otherwise," says the speaker, "we will not answer for the vengeance of the people."[12] And in a still more imperative manner:

"You have heard and you know that insurrection is a sacred duty," a sacred duty towards and against

159

all: towards the Assembly if it refuses, and towards the tribunal if it acquits. They dash at their prey contrary to all legislative and judicial formalities, like a kite across the web of a spider, while nothing detach them from their fixed ideas. On the acquittal of M. Luce de Montmorin[13] the gross audience, mistaking him for his cousin the former minister of Louis XVI., break out in murmurs. The president tries to enforce silence, which increases the uproar, and M. de Montmorin is in danger. On this the president, discovering a side issue, announces that one of the jurors is related to the accused, and that in such a case a new jury must be impaneled and a new trial take place; that the matter will be inquired into, and meanwhile the prisoner will be returned to the Conciergerie prison. Thereupon he takes M. de Montmorin by the arm and leads him out of the court–room, amidst the yells of the audience and not without risks to himself; in the outside court a soldier of the National Guard strikes at him with a saber, and the following day the court is obliged to authorize eight delegates from the audience to go and see with their own eyes that M. de Montmorin is really in prison.

At the moment of his acquittal a tragic remark is heard:

"You discharge him to–day and in two weeks he will cut our throats!"

Fear is evidently an adjunct of hatred. The Jacobin rabble is vaguely conscious of their inferior numbers, of their usurpation, of their danger, which increases in proportion as Brunswick draws near. They feel that they live above a mine, and if the mine should explode! — Since they think that their adversaries are scoundrels they feel they are capable of a dirty trick, of a plot, of a massacre. As they themselves have never behaved in any other way, they cannot conceive anything else. Through an inevitable inversion of thought, they impute to others the murderous intentions obscurely wrought out in the dark recesses of their own disturbed brains. — On the 27th of August, after the funeral procession gotten up by Sergent expressly to excite popular resentment, their suspicions, at once specific and guided, begin to take the form of certainty. Ten "commemorative" banners,[14] each borne by a volunteer on horseback, have paraded before all eyes the long list of massacres "by the court and its agents":

1. the massacre at Nancy,

2. the massacre at Nîmes,

3. the massacre at Montauban,

4. the massacre at Avignon,

5. the massacre at La Chapelle,

6. the massacre at Carpentras,

7. the massacre of the Champ de Mars, etc.

Faced with such displays, doubts and misgivings are out of the question. To the women in the galleries, to the frequenters of the clubs, and to pikemen in the suburbs it is from now beyond any doubt proved that the aristocrats are habitual killers.

And on the other side there is another sign equally alarming "This lugubrious ceremony, which ought to inspire by turns both reflection and indignation, . . . did not generally produce that effect." The National Guard in uniform, who came "apparently to make up for not appearing on the day of action," did not behave themselves with civic propriety, but, on the contrary, put on "an air of inattention and even of noisy gaiety"; they come out of curiosity, like so many Parisian onlookers, and are much more numerous than the sans–culottes with their pikes.[15] The latter could count themselves and plainly see that they are just a minority, and a very small one, and that their rage finds no echo. The organizers and their stooges are the only ones to call for speedy sentencing and for death–penalties. A foreigner, a good observer, who questions the shop–keepers of whom he makes purchases, the tradesmen he knows, and the company he finds in the coffee–houses, writes that he never had "seen any symptom of a sanguinary disposition except in the galleries of the National Assembly and at the Jacobin Club," but then the galleries are full of paid "applauders,'1 especially "females, who are more noisy and to be had cheaper than males." At the Jacobin Club are "the leaders, who dread a turnaround or who have resentments to gratify[16]": thus the only enragés are the leaders and the populace of the suburbs. — Lost in the crowd of this vast city, in the face of a National Guard still armed and three times their own number, confronting an indifferent or discontented bourgeoisie, the patriots are alarmed. In this state of anxiety a feverish imagination, exasperated by the waiting, involuntarily gives birth to imaginings passionately accepted as truths. All that is now required is an incident in order to put the final touch to complete the legend, the germ of which has unwittingly grown in their minds.

On the 1st of September a poor wagoner, Jean Julien,[17] condemned to twelve years in irons, has been exposed in the pillory. After two hours he becomes furious, probably on account of the jeers of the bystanders. With the coarseness of people of his kind he has vented his impotent rage by abuse, he has unbuttoned and exposed himself to the public, and has naturally chosen expressions which would appear most offensive to the people looking at him:

"Hurrah for the King! Hurrah for the Queen! Hurra for Lafayette! To hell with the nation!"

It is also natural that he missed being torn to pieces. He was at once led away to the Conciergerie prison, and sentenced on the spot to be guillotined as soon as possible, for being a promoter of sedition in connection with the conspiracy of August the 10th. — The conspiracy, accordingly, is still in existence. It is so declared by the tribunal, which makes no declaration without evidence. Jean Julien has certainly confessed; now what has he revealed? — On the following day, like a crop of poisonous mushrooms, the growth of a single night, the story obtains general credence. "Jean Julien has declared that all the prisons in Paris thought as he did, that there would soon be fine times, that the prisoners were armed, and that as soon as the volunteers cleared out they would be let loose on all Paris."[18] The streets are full of anxious faces. "One says that Verdun had been betrayed like Longwy. Others shook their heads and said it was the traitors within Paris and not the declared enemies on the frontier that were to be feared."[19] On the following day the story grows: "There are royalist officers and soldiers hidden away in Paris and in the outskirts. They are going to open the prisons, arm the prisoners, set the King and his family free, put the patriots in Paris to death, also the wives and children of those in the army. . . Isn't it natural for men to look after the safety of their wives and children, and to use the only efficient means to arrest the assassin's dagger."[20] — The working–class inferno has been stirred up, now it's up to the contractors of public revolt to fan and direct the flames.

III. Terror is their Salvation.

Rise of the homicidal idea among the leaders. — Their situation. — The powers they seize. — Their pillage. — The risks they run — Terror is their rescue.

They have been fanning the flames for a long time. Already, on the 11th of August, the new Commune had announced, in a proclamation,[21] that "the guilty should perish on the scaffold," while its threatening deputations force the national Assembly into the immediate institution of a bloody tribunal. Carried into power by brutal force, it must perish if it does not maintain itself, and this can be done only through terror. – Let us pause and consider this unusual situation. Installed in the Hôtel–de–ville by a nightly surprise attack, about one hundred strangers, delegated by a party which thinks or asserts itself to be the peoples' delegates, have overthrown one of the two great powers of the State, mangled and enslaved the other, and now rule in a capital of 700,000 souls, by the grace of eight or ten thousand fanatics and cut–throats. Never did a radical change promote men from so low a point and raise so high! The basest of newspaper scribblers, penny–a–liners out of the gutters, bar–room oracles, unfrocked monks and priests, the refuse of the literary guild, of the bar, and of the clergy, carpenters, turners, grocers, locksmiths, shoemakers, common laborers, many with no profession at all, strolling politicians and [22]public brawlers, who, like the sellers of counterfeit wares, have speculated for the past three years on popular credulity. There were among them a number of men in bad repute, of doubtful honesty or of proven dishonesty, who, in their youth led shiftless lives. They are still besmirched with old slime, they were put outside the pale of useful labor by their vices, driven out of inferior stations even into prohibited occupations, bruised by the perilous leap, with consciences distorted like the muscles of a tight– rope dancer. Were it not for the Revolution, they would still grovel in their native filth, awaiting prison or forced labor to which they were destined. Can one imagine their growing intoxication as they drink deep draughts from the bottomless cup of absolute power? — For it is absolute power which they demand and which they exercise.[23] Raised by a special delegation above the regular authorities, they put up with these only as subordinates, and tolerate none among them who may become their rivals. Consequently, they reduce the Legislative body simply to the function of editor and herald of their decrees; they have forced the new department electors to "abjure their title," to confine themselves to tax assessments, while they lay their ignorant hands daily on every other service, on the finances, the army, supplies, the administration, justice, at the risk of breaking the administrative wheels or of interrupting their action.

One day they summon the Minister of War before them, or, for lack of one, his chief clerk; another day they keep the whole body of officials in his department in arrest for two hours, under the pretext of finding a suspected printer.[24] At one time they affix seals on the funds devoted to extraordinary expenses; at another time they do away with the commission on supplies; at another they meddle with the course of justice, either to aggravate proceedings or to impede the execution of sentences rendered.[25] There is no principle, no law, no regulation, no verdict, no public man or establishment that is not subject to the risk of their arbitrariness. — And, as they have laid hands on power, they do the same with money. Not only do they extort from the Assembly 850,000 francs a months, with arrears from the 1st of January, 1792, more than six millions in all, to defray the expenses of their military police, which means to pay their bands,[26] but again, "invested with the municipal scarf," they seize, "in the public establishment belonging to the nation, all furniture, and whatever is of most value." "In one building alone, they carry off the value of 100,000 crowns."[27] Elsewhere, in the hands of the treasurer of the civil list, they appropriate to themselves, a box of jewels, other precious objects, and 340, 000 francs.[28] Their commissioners bring in from Chantilly three wagons each drawn by three horses "loaded with the spoils of M. de Condé," and they undertake "removing the contents of the houses of the émigrés."[29] They confiscate in the churches of Paris "the crucifixes, music–stands, bells, railings, and every object in bronze or of iron, chandeliers, cups, vases, reliquaries, statues, every article of plate," as well "on the altars as in the sacristies,"[30] and we can imagine the enormous booty obtained; to cart away the silver plate belonging to the single church of Madeleine–de–la–ville required a vehicle drawn by four horses. — Now they use all this money, so freely seized, as freely as they do power itself. One fills his pockets in the Tuileries without the slightest concern; another, in the Garde–Meuble, rummages secretaries, and carries off a wardrobe with its contents.[31] We have already seen that in the depositories of the Commune "most of the seals are broken," that enormous sums in plate, in jewels, in gold and silver coin have disappeared. Future inquests and accounts will charge on the Committee of Supervision, "abstractions, dilapidations, and embezzlements," in short, "a mass of violations and breaches of trust."— When one is king, one easily mistakes the money–drawer of the State for the drawer in which one keeps one's own money.

Unfortunately, this full possession of public power and the public funds holds only by a slender thread. Let the evicted and outraged majority dare, as subsequently at Lyons, Marseilles, and Toulon, to Return to the section assemblies and revoke the false mandate which they have arrogated to themselves through fraud and force, and, on the instance, they again become, through the sovereign will of the people, and by virtue of their own deed, what they really are, usurpers, extortioners, and robbers, there is no middle course for them between a dictatorship and the galleys. — The mind, before such an alternative, unless extraordinarily well–balanced, loses its equilibrium; they have no difficulty in deluding themselves with the idea that the State is menaced in their persons, and, in postulating the rule, that all is allowable for them, even massacre. Has not Bazire stated in the tribune that, against the enemies of the nation, "all means are fair justifiable? Has not another deputy, Jean Debry, proposed the formation of a body of 1,200 volunteers, who "will sacrifice themselves," as formerly the assassins of the Old Man of the Mountain, in "attacking tyrants, hand to hand, individually," as well as generals?[32] Have we not seen Merlin de Thionville insisting that "the wives and children of the émigrés should be kept as hostages," and declared responsible, or, in other words, ready for slaughter if their relatives continue their attacks?[33]

That is all that is left to do, since all the other measures have proved insufficient. — In vain has the Commune decreed the arrest of journalists belonging to the opposite party, and distributed their printing machinery amongst patriotic printers.[34] In vain has it declared the members of the Sainte–Chapelle club, the National Guards who have sworn allegiance to Lafayette, the signers of the petition of 8,000, and of that of 20,000, disqualified for any service whatever.[35] In vain has it multiplied domiciliary visits, even to the residence and carriages of the Venetian ambassador. In vain, through insulting and repeated examinations, does it keep at its bar, under the hootings and death–cries of its tribunes, the most honorable and most illustrious men, Lavoisier, Dupont de Nemours, the eminent surgeon Desault, the most harmless and most refined ladies, Madame de Tourzel, Mademoiselle de Tourzel, and the Princesse de Lamballe.[36] In vain, after a profusion of arrests during twenty days, it envelopes all Paris inside one cast of its net for a nocturnal search[37]during which,

1. the barriers are closed and doubly guarded,

2. sentinels are on the quays and boats stationed on the Seine to prevent escape by water,

3. the city is divided beforehand into circumscriptions, and for each section, a list of suspected persons,

4. the circulation of vehicles is stopped,

5. every citizen is ordered to stay at home,

6. the silence of death reigns after six o'clock in the evening, and then,

7. in each street, a patrol of sixty pikemen, seven hundred squads of sans–culottes, all working at the same time, and with their usual brutality,

8. doors are burst in with pile drivers,

9. wardrobes are picked by locksmiths,

10. walls are sounded by masons,

11. cellars are searched even to digging in the ground,

12. papers are seized,

13. arms are confiscated,

14. three thousand persons are arrested and led off;[38] priests, old men, the infirm, the sick.

The action lasts from ten in the evening to five o'clock in the morning, the same as in a city taken by assault, the screams of women rudely treated, the cries of prisoners compelled to march, the oaths of the guards, cursing and drinking at each grog–shop; never was there such an universal, methodical execution, so well calculated to suppress all inclination for resistance in the silence of general stupefaction.

And yet, at this very moment, there are those who act in good faith in the sections and in the Assembly, and who rebel at being under such masters. A deputation from the Lombards section, and another from the Corn–market, come to the Assembly and protest against the Commune's usurpations.[39] Choudieu, the Montagnard, denounces its blatant corrupt practices. Cambon, a stern financier, will no longer consent to have his accounts tampered with by thieving tricksters.[40] The Assembly at last seems to have recovered itself. It extends its protection to Géray, the journalist, against whom the new pashas had issued a warrant; it summons to its own bar the signers of the warrant, and orders them to confine themselves in future to the exact limits of the law which they transgress. Better still, it dissolves the interloping Council, and substitutes for it ninety–six delegates, to be elected by the sections in twenty–four hours. And, even still better, it orders an account to be rendered within two days of the objects it has seized, and the return of all gold or silver articles to the Treasury. Quashed, and summoned to disgorge their booty, the autocrats of the Hôtel–de–ville come in vain to the Assembly in force on the following day[41] to extort from it a repeal of its decrees; the Assembly, in spite of their threats and those of their satellites, stands its ground. — So much the worse for the stubborn; if they are not disposed to regard the flash of the saber, they will feel its sharp edge and point. The Commune, on the motion of Manuel, decides that, so long as public danger continues, they will stay where they are; it adopts an address by Robespierre to "restore sovereign power to the people," which means to fill the streets with armed bands;[42] it collects together its brigands by giving them the ownership of all that they stole on the 10th of August.[43] The session, prolonged into the night, does not terminate until one o'clock in the morning. Sunday has come and there is no time to lose, for, in a few hours, the sections, by virtue of the decree of the National Assembly, and following the example of the Temple section the evening before, may revoke the pretended representatives at the Hôtel–de–ville. To remain at the Hôtel–de–ville, and to be elected to the convention, demands on the part of the leaders some striking action, and this they require that very day. — That day is the second of September.

IV.

Date of the determination of this. — The actors and their parts. – Marat. — Danton. – The Commune. — Its co–operators. — Harmony of dispositions and readiness of operation.

Since the 23rd of August their resolution is taken.[44] They have arranged in their minds a plan of the massacre, and each one, little by little, spontaneously, according to his aptitudes, takes the part that suits him or is assigned to him.

Marat, foremost among them all, is the proposer and preacher of the operation, which, for him, is a perfectly natural one. It is the epitome of his political system: a dictator or tribune, with full power to slay, and with no other power but that; a good master executioner, responsible, and "tied hand and foot"; this is his program for a government since July the 14th, 1789, and he does not blush at it: "so much the worse for those who are not on a level with it!"[45] He appreciated the character of the Revolution from the first, not through genius, but sympathetically, he himself being equally as one–sided and monstrous; crazy with suspicion and beset with a homicidal mania for the past three years, reduced to one idea through mental impoverishment, that of murder, having lost the faculty for even the lowest order of reasoning, the poorest of journalists, save for pikemen and Billingsgate market–women, so monotonous in his constant paroxysms that the regular reading of his journal is like listening to hoarse cries from the cells of a madhouse.[46] From the 19th of August he excites people to attack the prisons. "The wisest and best course to pursue," he says, "is to go armed to the Abbaye, drag out the traitors, especially the Swiss officers and their accomplices, and put them to the sword. What folly it is to give them a trial! That is already done. You have massacred the soldiers, why should you spare the officers, ten times guiltier?" — Also, two days later, his brain teeming with an executioner's fancies, insisting that "the soldiers deserved a thousand deaths. As to the officers, they should be drawn and quartered, like Louis Capet and his tools of the Manège."[47] — On the strength of this the Commune adopts him as its official editor, assigns him a tribune in its assembly room, entrusts him to report its acts, and soon puts him on its supervisory or executive committee.

A fanatic of this stamp, however, is good for nothing but as a mouthpiece or instigator; he may, at best, figure in the end among the subordinate managers. — The chief of the enterprise,[48] Danton, is of another species, and of another stature, a veritable leader of men: Through his past career and actual position, through his popular cynicism, ways and language, through his capacity for taking the initiative and for command, through his excessive corporeal and intellectual vigor, through his physical ascendancy due to his ardent, absorbing will, he is well calculated for his terrible office. — He alone of the Commune has become Minister, and there is no one but him to shelter the violations of the Commune under the protection or under the passivity of the central authority. — He alone of the Commune and of the ministry is able to push things through and harmonize action in the pell–mell of the revolutionary chaos; both in the councils of the ministry which he governs, as he formerly governed at the Hôtel–de ville. In the constant uproar of incoherent discussions,[49] athwart "propositions ex abrupto, among shouts, swearing, and the going and coming of questioning petitioners," he is seen mastering his new colleagues with his "stentorian voice, his gestures of an athlete, his fearful threats," taking upon himself their duties, dictating to them what and whom he chooses, "fetching in commissions already drawn up," taking charge of everything, "making propositions, arrests, and proclamations, issuing brevets," and drawing millions out of the public treasury, casting a sop to his dogs in the Cordeliers and the Commune, "to one 20,000 francs, and to another 10,000," "for the Revolution, and on account of their patriotism," — such is a summary report of his doings. Thus gorged, the pack of hungry "brawlers" and grasping intriguers, the whole serviceable force of the sections and of the clubs, is in his hands. One is strong in times of anarchy at the head of such a herd. Indeed, during the months of August and September, Danton was king, and, later on, he may well say of the 2d of September, as he did of the 10th of August, "I did it!"[50]

Not that he is naturally vindictive or sanguinary: on the contrary, with a butcher's temperament, he has a man's heart, and, at the risk of compromising himself, against the wills of Marat and Robespierre, he will, by–and–by, save his political adversaries, Duport, Brissot, and the Girondists, the old party of the " Right."[51] Not that he is blinded by fear, enmities, or the theory; furious as a clubbist, he has the clear–sightedness of the politician; he is not the dupe of the sonorous phrases he utters, he knows the value of the rogues he employs;[52] he has no illusions about men or things, about other people or about himself; if he slays, it is with a full consciousness of what he is doing, of his party, of the situation, of the revolution, while the crude expressions which, in the tones of his bull's voice, he flings out as he passes along, are but a vivid statement of the precise truth "We are the rabble! We spring from the gutters!" With the normal principles of mankind, "we should soon get back into them. We can only rule through fear!"[53] "The Parisians are so many j . . . f . . . ; a river of blood must flow between them and the émigrés."[54] The tocsin about to be rung is not a signal of alarm, but a charge on the enemies of the country. . . What is necessary to overcome them? Boldness, boldness, always boldness![55] I have brought my mother here, seventy years of age; I have sent for my children, and they came last night. Before the Prussians enter Paris, I want my family to die with me. Let twenty thousand torches be applied, and Paris instantly reduced to ashes!"[56] "We must maintain ourselves in Paris at all hazards. Republicans are in an extreme minority, and, for fighting, we can rely only on them. The rest of France is devoted to royalty. The royalists must be terrified!"[57] — It is he who, on the 28th of August, obtains from the Assembly the great domiciliary visit, by which the Commune fills the prisons. It is he who, on the 2d of September, to paralyze the resistance of honest people, causes the penalty of death to be decreed against whoever, "directly or indirectly shall, in any manner whatsoever, refuse to execute, or who shall interfere with the orders issued, or with the measures of the executive power." It is he who, on that day, informs the journalist Prudhomme of the pretended prison plot, and who, the second day after, sends his secretary, Camille Desmoulins, to falsify the report of the massacres,[58] It is he who, on the 3rd of September, at the office of the Minister of Justice, before the battalion officers and the heads of the service, before Lacroix, president of the Assembly, and Pétion, mayor of Paris, before Clavières, Servan, Monge, Lebrun, and the entire Executive Council, except Roland, reduces at one stroke the head men of the government to the position of passive accomplices, replying to a man of feeling, who rises to stay the slaughter, "Sit down — it was necessary!"[59] It is he who, the same day, dispatches the circular, countersigned by him, by which the Committee of Supervision announces the massacre, and invites "their brethren of the departments" to follow the example of Paris.[60] It is he who, on the 10th of September, "not as Minister of Justice, but as Minister of the People," is to congratulate and thank the slaughterers of Versailles.[61] — After the 10th of August, through Billaud–Varennes, his former secretary, through Fabre d'Eglantine, his Keeper of the Seals, through Tallien, secretary of the Commune and his most trusty henchman, he is present at all deliberations in the Hôtel–de–ville, and, at the last hour, is careful to put on the Committee of Supervision one of his own men, the head clerk, Desforges.[62] — Not only was the reaping–machine constructed under his own eye, and with his assent, but, again, when it is put in motion, he holds the handle, so as to guide the scythe.

He is right; if he did not sometimes put on the brake, it would go to pieces through its own action. Introduced into the Committee as professor of political blood–letting, Marat, stubbornly following out a fixed idea, cuts down deep, much below the designated line; warrants of arrest were already out against thirty deputies, Brissot's papers were rummaged, Roland's house was surrounded, while Duport, seized in a neighboring department, is deposed in the slaughterhouse. The latter is saved with the utmost difficulty; many a blow is necessary before he can be wrested from the maniac who had seized him. With a surgeon like Marat, and medics like the four or five hundred leaders of the Commune and of the sections, it is not essential to guide the knife; it is a foregone conclusion that the amputation will be extensive. Their names speak for themselves: in the Commune, Manuel, the syndic–attorney; and his two deputies Hébert and Billaud– Varennes, Huguenin, Lhuillier, M.–J. Chénier, Audoin, Léonard Bourdon, Boula and Truchon, presidents in succession. In the Commune and the sections, Panis, Sergent, Tallien, Rossignol, Chaumette, Fabre d'Eglantine, Pache, Hassenfratz, the cobbler Simon, and the printer Momoro. From the National Guard, the commanding–general, Santerre, and the battalion commander Henriot, and, lower down, the common herd of district demagogues, Danton's, Hébert's, or Robespierre's side kicks, guillotined later on with their file–leaders, in brief, the flower of the future terrorists.[63] – Today they are taking their first steps in blood, each with their own attitude and motives:

* Chénier denounced as a member of the Sainte–Chapelle club, in danger because he is among the suspected;[64]

* Manuel, poor, excitable, bewildered, carried away, and afterwards shuddering at the sight of his own work;

* Santerre, a fine circumspect figure-head, who, on the 2nd of September, under pretense of watching the baggage, climbs on the seat of a landau standing on the street, where he remains a couple of hours, to avoid doing his duty as commanding-general;[65]

* Panis, president of the Committee of Supervision, a good subordinate, his born disciple and bootlicker, an admirer of Robespierre's whom he proposes for the dictatorship, as well as of Marat, whom he extols as a prophet;[66]

* Henriot, Hébert, and Rossignol, simple evil-doers in uniform or in their scarves;

* Collot d'Herbois, a stage poetaster, whose theatrical imagination delights in a combination of melodramatic horrors;[67]

* Billaud-Varennes, a former oratorian monk, irascible and gloomy, as cool before a murder as an inquisitor at an auto-da-fé;

finally, the wily Robespierre, pushing others without committing himself, never signing his name, giving no orders, haranguing a great deal, always advising, showing himself everywhere, getting ready to reign, and suddenly, at the last moment, pouncing like a cat on his prey, and trying to slaughter his rivals, the Girondists.[68]

Up to this time, in slaughtering or having it done, it was always as insurrectionists in the street; now, it is in places of imprisonment, as magistrates and functionaries, according to the registers of a lock-up, after proofs of identity and on snap judgments, by paid executioners, in the name of public security, methodically, and in cool blood, almost with the same regularity as subsequently under "the revolutionary government." September, indeed, is the beginning of it, a summary and a model; they will not do it differently or better than during the best days of the guillotine. Only, as they are as yet poorly supplied with tools, they are obliged to use pikes instead of the guillotine, and, as decency has not entirely disappeared, the chiefs conceal themselves behind maneuvers. Nevertheless, we can track them, take them in the act, and we have their signatures; they planned commanded, and conducted the operation. On the 30th of August, the Commune decided that the sections should try accused persons, and, on the 2nd of September, five trusted sections reply to it by resolving that the accused shall be murdered.69 The same day, September 2, Marat takes his place on the Committee of Supervision. The same day, September 2, Panis and Sergent sign the commissions of "their comrades," Maillard and associates, for the Abbaye, and "order them to judge," that is to say, kill the prisoners.[70] The same and the following days, at La Force, three members of the Commune, Hébert, Monneuse, and Rossignol, preside in turn over the assassin court.[71] The same day, a commissar of the Committee of Supervision comes and demands a dozen men of the Sans-Culottes section to help massacre the priests of Saint Firmin.[72] The same day, a commissar of the Commune visits the different prisons during the slaughter, and finds that "things are going on well in all of them."[73] The same day, at five o'clock in the afternoon, BillaudVarennes, deputy-attorney for the Commune, "in his well-known puce-colored coat and black perruque," walking over the corpses, says to the Abbaye butchers: "Fellow– citizens, you are immolating your enemies, you are performing your duty." He returns during the night, highly commends them, and confirms the promise of the "agreed wages." On the following any at noon, he again returns, congratulates them more warmly, allows each one twenty francs, and urges them to keep on.[74] — In the mean time, Santerre, summoned to the general staff headquarters by Roland, hypocritically deplores his voluntary inability, and persists in not giving the orders, without which the National Guard cannot move.[75] At the sections, the presidents, Chénier, Ceyrat, Boula, Momoro, Collot d'Herbois, dispatch or take their victims back under pikes. At the Commune, the council–general votes 12,000 francs, to be taken from the dead, to defray the expenses of the operation.[76] In the Committee of Supervision, Marat sends off dispatches to spread murder through the departments. — It is evident that the leaders and their subordinates are unanimous, each at his post and in the service he performs; through the spontaneous co–operation of the whole party, the command from above meets the impulse from below;[77] both unite in a common murderous disposition, the work being done with the more precision in proportion to its being easily done. — Jailers have received orders to open the prison doors, and give themselves no concern. Through an excess of precaution, the knives and forks of the prisoners have been taken away from them.[78] One by one, on their names being called, they will march out like oxen in a slaughter– house, while about twenty butchers to each prison, from to two to three hundred in all,[79] will suffice to do the work.

V. Abasement and Stupor.

Common workers. — Their numbers. — Their condition. — Their sentiments.— Effect of murder on the murderers. — Their degradation. — Their insensibility.

Two kinds of men make up the recruits, and it is especially on their crude brains that we have to admire the effect of the revolutionary dogma.

First, there are the Federates of the South, lusty fellows, former soldiers or old bandits, deserters, bohemians, and scoundrels of all lands and from every source, who, after finishing their work at Marseilles and Avignon, have come to Paris to begin over again. "Triple nom de Dieu!" exclaims one of them, "I didn't come a hundred and eighty leagues to restrain myself from sticking a hundred and eighty heads on the end of my pike!"[80] Accordingly, they form in themselves a special, permanent, resident body, allowing no one to divert them from their adopted occupation. "They turn a deaf ear to the excitements of spurious patriotism";[81] they are not going to be sent off to the frontier. Their post is at the capital; they have sworn "to defend liberty"; neither before nor after September make them deviate from this end. When, after having drawn money on every treasury and under every pretext, they at last consent to leave Paris, it is only on the condition that they return to Marseilles. Their operations are limited to the interior of France, and only against political adversaries. But their zeal in this field is only the greater; it is their band which, first of all, takes the twenty–four priests from the town hall, and, on the way, begins the massacre with their own hands.[82]

Then there are the "enragés" of the Paris proletariat, a few of them clerks or shopkeepers, most of them artisans of all the trades; locksmiths, masons, butchers, wheelwrights, tailors, shoemakers, waggoners, especially dockers working in the harbor, market–porters, and, above all, journeymen and apprentices of all kinds, in short, manual workers on the bottom of the social ladder.[83] Among these we find beasts of prey, murderers by instinct, or simple robbers.[84] Others who, like one of the disciples of Abbé Sicard, whom he loves and venerates, confess that they never stirred except under constraint.[85] Others are simple machines, who let themselves be driven: for instance the local forwarding agent, a good sort of man, but who, dragged along, plied with liquor, and then made crazy, kills twenty priests for his share, and dies at the end of the month, still drinking, unable to sleep, frothing at the mouth and trembling in every limb.[86] And finally the few, who, with good intentions, are carried away by the bloody whirlwind, and, struck by the grace of Revolution, become converted to the religion of murder. One of them a certain Grapin, deputized by his section to save two prisoners, seats himself alongside of Maillard, sits in judgment at his side during sixty–three hours, and demands a certificate from him.[87] The majority, however, entertain the same opinions as the cook, who, after taking the Bastille, finding himself on the spot and having cut off M. de Launay's head, regards it as a "patriotic" action, and deems himself worthy of a "medal for having destroyed a monster." These people are not common criminals, but well–disposed persons living in the vicinity, who, seeing a public service established in their neighborhood,[88] issue from their homes to give a hand; their degree of probity is about the same as we find nowadays among people of the same condition in life.

At the outset, especially, no one considers filling his pockets. At the Abbaye prison, they come honorably and place on the table in the room of the civil committee the purses and jewels of the dead.[89] If they appropriate anything to themselves, it is shoes to cover their naked feet, and then only after asking permission. As to pay, all rough work deserves it, and, moreover, between them and their recruiters, the answer is obvious. With nothing but their own hands to rely on, they cannot work for nothing,[90] and, as the work is hard, they ought to be paid double time. They require six francs a day, besides their meals and as much wine as they want. One caterer alone furnished the men at the Abbaye with 346 pints:[91] when working incessantly day and night with a task like that of sewer–cleaners and miners, nothing else will keep their courage up. — Food and wages must be paid for by the nation; the work is done for the nation, and, naturally, on interposing formalities, they get out of temper and betake themselves to Roland, to the City treasurer, to the section committees, to the Committee of Supervision,[92] murmuring, threatening, and showing their bloody pikes. That is the evidence of having done their work well. They boast of it to Pétion, impress upon him how "just and attentive" they were,[93] their discernment, the time given to the work, so many days and so many hours; they ask only for what is "due to them"; when the treasurer, on paying them, demands their names, they give them without the slightest hesitation. Those who escort a dismissed prisoner; masons, hairdressers, federates, require no recompense but "something to drink"; "we do not carry on this business for money," they say; "here is your friend; he promised us a glass of brandy, which we will take and then go back to our work."[94] — Outside of their business they possess the expansive cordiality and ready sensitivity of the Parisian workman. At the Abbaye, a federate,[95] on learning that the prisoners had been kept without water for twenty–six hours, wanted to "exterminate" the turnkey for his negligence, and would have done it if "the prisoners themselves had not pleaded for him." On the acquittal of a prisoner, the guards and the butchers, everybody, embraces him with enthusiasm; Weber is greeted again and again for more than a hundred yards; they cheer to excess. Each wants to escort the prisoner; the cab of Mathon de la Varenne is invaded; "they perch themselves on the driver's seat, at the doors, on top, and behind."[96] – A few even display strange fits of tact. Two of the butchers, still covered with blood, who lead the chevalier de Bertrand home, insist on going up stairs with him to witness the joy of his family; after their terrible task they need the relaxation of tender emotion. On entering, they wait discreetly in the drawing–room until the ladies have been prepared; the happiness of which they are witnesses melts them; they remain some time, refuse money, expressing their gratitude and depart.[97] — Still more extraordinary are the vestiges of innate politeness. A market–porter desirous of embracing a discharged prisoner, first asks his permission. Old "hags," who had just clapped their hands at the slaughtering, stop the guards "violently" as they hurry Weber along, in white silk stockings, across pools of blood: "Hey, guard, look out, you are making Monsieur walk in the gutter!"[98] In short, they display the permanent qualities of their race and class; they seem to be neither above nor below the average of their brethren, Most of them, probably, would never have done anything very monstrous had a rigid police, like that which maintains order in ordinary times, kept them in their shops or at home in their lodgings or in their tap– rooms.

But, in their own eyes, they are so many kings; "sovereignty is committed to their hands,"[99] their powers are unlimited; whoever doubts this is a traitor, and is properly punished; he must be put out of the way; while, for royal councillors, they take maniacs and rascals, who, through monomania or calculation, have preach all that to them: just like a Negro king surrounded by white slave–dealers, who urge him into raids, and by black sorcerers, who prompt him to massacre. How could such a man with such guides, and in such an office, be retarded by the formalities of justice, or by the distinctions of equity? Equity and justice are the elaborate products of civilization, while he is merely a political savage. In vain are the innocent recommended to his mercy!

"Look here, citizen,[100] do you, too, want to put us to sleep? Suppose that those cursed Prussian and Austrian beggars were in Paris, would they pick out the guilty? Wouldn't they strike right and left, the same as the Swiss did on the 10th of August? Very well, I can't make speeches, but I don't put anybody to sleep. I say, I am the father of a family — I have a wife and five children that I mean to leave here for the section to look after, while I go and fight the enemy. But I have no intention that while I am gone these villains here in prison, and other villains who would come and let them out, should cut the throats of my wife and children. I have three boys who I hope will some day be more useful to their country than those rascals you want to save. Anyhow, all that can be done is to let 'em out and give them arms, and we will fight 'em on an equal footing. Whether I die here or on the frontiers, scoundrels would kill me all the same, and I will sell my life dearly. But, whether it is done by me or by someone else, the prison shall be cleaned out of those cursed beggars, there, now!" At this a general cry is heard: "He's right! No mercy! Let us go in!"

All that the crowd assent to is an improvised tribunal, the reading of the jailer's register, and prompt judgment; condemnation and slaughter must follow, according to the famous Commune, which simplifies things — There is another simplification still more formidable, which is the condemnation and slaughter by categories. Any title suffices, Swiss, priest, officer, or servant of the King, "the 'worms' on the civil list"; wherever a lot of priests or Swiss are found, it is not worth while to have a trial, the throats of the lot can be slit. — Reduced to this, the operation is adapted to the operators; the arms of the new sovereign are as strong as his mind is weak, and, through an inevitable adaptation, he degrades his work to the level of his faculties.

His work, in its turn, degrades and perverts him. No man, and especially a man of the people, rendered pacific by an old civilization, can, with impunity, become at one stroke both sovereign and executioner. In vain does he work himself up against the condemned and heap insults on them to augment his fury;[101] I he is dimly conscious of committing a great crime, and his soul, like that of Macbeth, "is full of scorpions." Through a terrible tightening up, he hardens himself against the inborn, hereditary impulses of humanity; these resist while he becomes exasperated, and, to stifle them, there is no other way but to "gorge himself on horrors,"[102] by adding murder to murder. For murder, especially as he practices it, that is to say, with a naked sword on defense−less people, introduces into his animal and moral machine two extraordinary and disproportionate emotions which unsettle it, on the one hand, a sensation of omnipotence exercised uncontrolled, unimpeded, without danger, on human life, on throbbing flesh[103] and, on the other hand, an interest in bloody and diversified death, accompanied with an ever new series of contortions and exclamations;[104] formerly, in the Roman circus, one could not tear one's self away from it; the spectacle once seen, the spectator always returned to see it again. Just at this time each prison court is a circus, and what makes it worse is that the spectators are likewise actors.— Thus, for them, two fiery liquids mingle together in one draught. To moral intoxication is added physical intoxication, wine in profusion, bumpers at every pause, revelry over corpses; and we see rising out of this unnatural creature the demon of Dante, at once brutal and refined, not merely a destroyer, but, again, an executioner, instigator and calculator of suffering, and radiant and joyous over the evil it accomplishes.

They are merry; they dance around each new corpse, and sing the carmagnole;[105] they arouse the people of the quarter "to amuse them," and that they may have their share of "the fine fête."[106] Benches are arranged for "gentlemen" and others for "ladies": the latter, with greater curiosity, are additionally anxious to contemplate at their ease "the aristocrats" already slain; consequently, lights are required, and one is placed on the breast of each corpse. — Meanwhile, the slaughter continues, and is carried to perfection. A butcher at the Abbaye[107] complains that "the aristocrats die too quick, and that those only who strike first have the pleasure of it"; henceforth they are to be struck with the backs of the swords only, and made to run between two rows of their butchers, like soldiers formerly running a gauntlet. If there happens to be well−known person, it is agreed to take more care in prolonging the torment. At La Force, the Federates who come for M. de Rulhières swear "with frightful imprecations that they will cut the head of anyone daring to end his sufferings with a thrust of his pike"; the first thing is to strip him naked, and then, for half an hour, with the flat of their sabers, they cut and slash him until he drips with blood and is "skinned to his entrails." — All the monstrous instincts who grovels chained up in the dregs of the human heart, not only cruelty with its bared fangs,[108] but also the slimier desires, unite in fury against women whose noble or infamous repute makes them conspicuous; against Madame de Lamballe, the Queen's friend; against Madame Desrues, widow of the famous poisoner; against the flower−girl of the Palais−Royal, who, two years before, had mutilated her lover, a French guardsman, in a fit of jealousy. Ferocity here is associated with lewdness to add debasement to torture, while life is violated through outrages on modesty. In Madame de Lamballe, killed too quickly, the libidinous butchers could outrage only a corpse, but for the widow,[109] and especially the flower−girl, they revive, like so many Neros, the fire−circle of the Iroquois.[110] — From the Iroquois to the cannibal, the gulf is small, and some of them jump across it. At the Abbaye, an old soldier named Damiens, buries his saber in the side of the adjutant−general la Leu, thrusts his hand into the opening, tears out the heart "and puts it to his mouth as if to eat it"; "the blood," says an eye−witness, "trickled from his mouth and formed a sort of mustache for him."[111] At La Force, Madame de Lamballe is carved up. What Charlot, the wig−maker, who carried her head did, I to it, should not be described. I merely state that another wretch, in the Rue Saint−Antoine, bore off her heart and "ate it."[112]

They kill and they drink, and drink and kill again. Weariness comes and stupor begins. One of them, a wheelwright's apprentice, has dispatched sixteen for his share; another "has labored so hard at this merchandise as to leave the blade of his saber sticking in it"; "I was more tired," says a Federate, "with two hours pulling limbs to pieces, right and left, than any mason who for two days has been plastering a wall."[113] The first excitement is gone, and now they strike automatically.[114] Some of them fall asleep stretched out on benches. Others, huddled together, sleep off the fumes of their wine, removed on one side. The exhalation from the carnage is so strong that the president of the civil committee faints in his chair,[115] the fumes of the tavern blending with those from the charnel–house. A heavy, dull state of torpor gradually overcomes their clouded brains, the last glimmerings of reason dying out one by one, like the smoky lights on the already cold breasts of the corpses lying around them. Through the stupor spreading over the faces of butchers and cannibals, we see appearing that of the idiot. It is the revolutionary idiot, in which all conceptions, save two, have vanished, two fixed, rudimentary, and mechanical ideas, one destruction and the other that of public safety. With no others in his empty head, these blend together through an irresistible attraction, and the effect proceeding from their contact may be imagined. "Is there anything else to do? "asks one of these butchers in the deserted court. — "If there is no more to do," reply a couple of women at the gate, "you will have to think of something,"[116] and, naturally, this is done.

As the prisons are to be cleaned out, it is as well to clean them all out, and do it at once. After the Swiss, priests, the aristocrats, and the "white–skinned gentlemen," there remain convicts and those confined through the ordinary channels of justice, robbers, assassins, and those sentenced to the galleys in the Conciergerie, in the Châtelet, and in the Tour St. Bernard, with branded women, vagabonds, old beggars, and boys confined in Bicêtre and the Salpétrière. They are good for nothing, cost something to feed,[117] and, probably, cherish evil designs. At the Salpétrière, for example, the wife of Desrues, the poisoner, is, assuredly, like himself, "cunning, wicked, and capable of anything"; she must be furious at being in prison; if she could, she would set fire to Paris; she must have said so; she did say it[118] — one more sweep of the broom.— This time, as the job is more foul, the broom is wielded by fouler hands; among those who seize the handle are the frequenters of jails. The butchers at the Abbaye prison, especially towards the close, had already committed thefts;[119] here, at the Châtelet and the Conciergerie prisons, they carry away "everything which seems to them suitable," even to the clothes of the dead, prison sheets and coverlids, even the small savings of the jailers, and, besides this, they enlist their cronies. "Out of 36 prisoners set free, many were assassins and robbers, the killers attached them to their group. There were also 75 women, confined in part for larceny, who promised to faithfully serve their liberators." Later on, indeed, these are to become, at the Jacobin and Cordeliers clubs, the tricoteuses (knitters) who fill their tribunes.[120] — At the Salpétrière prison, "all the pimps of Paris, former spies, . . . libertines, the rascals of France and all Europe, prepare beforehand for the operation," and rape alternates with massacre.[121] — Thus far, at least, slaughter has been seasoned with robbery, and the grossness of eating and drinking; at Bicétre, however, it is crude butchery, the carnivorous instinct alone satisfying itself. Among other prisoners are 43 youths of the lowest class, from 17 to 19 years of age, placed there for correction by their parents, or by those to whom they are bound;[122] one need only look at them to see that they are genuine Parisian scamps, the apprentices of vice and misery, the future recruits for the reigning band, and these the band falls on, beating them to death with clubs. At this age life is tenacious, and, no life being harder to take, it requires extra efforts to dispatch them. "In that corner," said a jailer, "they made a mountain of their bodies. The next day, when they were to be buried, the sight was enough to break one's heart. One of them looked as if he were sleeping like one of God's angels, but the rest were horribly mutilated."[123] — Here, man has sunk below himself, down into the lowest strata of the animal kingdom, lower that the wolf; for wolves do not strangle their young.

VI. Jacobin Massacre.

Effect of the massacre on the public. — General dejection and the dissolution of society. — The ascendancy of the Jacobins assured in Paris. — The men of September upheld in the Commune and elected to the Convention.

There are six days and five nights of uninterrupted butchery,[124] 171 murders at the Abbaye, 169 at La Force, 223 at the Châtelet, 328 at the Consciergerie, 73 at the Tour–Saint–Bernard, 120 at the Carmelites, 79 at Saint Firmin, 170 at Bicêtre, 35 at the Salpétrière; among the dead,[125] 250 priests, 3 bishops or archbishops, general officers, magistrates, one former minister, one royal princess, belonging to the best names in France, and, on the other side, one Negro, several working class women, kids, convicts, and poor old men: What man now, little or big, does not feel himself threatened? — And all the more because the band has grown larger. Fournier, Lazowski, and Bécard, the chiefs of robbers and assassins, return from Orleans with fifteen hundred cut–throats.[126] One the way they kill M. de Brissac, M. de Lessart, and 42 others accused of lése–nation, whom they wrested from their judges' hands, and then, by the way of surplus, "following the example of Paris," twenty–one prisoners taken from the Versailles prisons. At Paris the Minister of Justice thanks them, the Commune congratulates them, and the sections feast them and embrace them.[127] — Can anybody doubt that they were ready to begin again? Can a step be taken in or out of Paris without being subject to their oppression or encountering their despotism? Should one leave the city, sentinels of their species are posted at the barriers and on the section committees in continuous session. Malouet, led before that of Roule,[128] sees before him a pandemonium of fanatics, at least a hundred individuals in the same room, the suspected, those denouncing them, collaborators, attendants, a long, green table in the center, covered with swords and daggers, with the committee around it, "twenty patriots with their shirt sleeves rolled up, some holding pistols and others pens," signing warrants of arrest, "quarreling with and threatening each other, all talking at once, and shouting: Traitor! — Conspirator! — Off to prison with him! — Guillotine him! — and behind these, a crowd of spectators, pell–mell , yelling, and gesticulating" like wild beasts pressed against each other in the same cage, showing their teeth and trying to spring at each other. "One of the most excited, brandishing his saber in order to strike an antagonist, stopped on seeing me, and exclaimed, 'There's Malouet!' — The other, however, less occupied with me than with his enemy, took advantage of the opportunity, and with a blow of his club, knocked him down." Malouet had a close shave, in Paris escapes take place by such accidents. — If one remains in the city, one is beset with lugubrious fears by,

1. the hurrying step of squads of men in each street, leading the suspected to prison or before the committee;

2. around each prison the crowds that have come "to see the disasters";

3. in the court of the Abaye the cry of the auctioneer selling the clothes of the dead;

4. the rumbling of carts on the pavement bearing away 1,300 corpses;

5. the songs of the women mounted aloft on the carts, beating time on the naked bodies.[129]

Is there a man who, after one of these encounters, does not see himself in imagination before the green table of the section committee, after this, in prison with sabers over his head, and then in the cart in the midst of the bloody pile?

Courage falters before a vision like this. All the journals approve, palliate, or keep silent; nobody dares offer resistance.[130] Property as well as lives belong to whoever wants to take them. At the barriers, at the markets, on the boulevard of the Temple, thieves, decked with the tricolor ribbon, stop people as they pass along, seize whatever they carry, and, under the pretext that jewels should be deposited on the altars of Patriotism, take purses, watches, rings, and other articles, so rudely that women who are not quick enough, have the lobes of their ears torn in unhooking their earrings[131]. Others, installed in the cellars of the Tuileries, sell the nation's wine and oil for their own profit. Others, again, given their liberty eight days before by the people, scent out a bigger job by finding their way into the Garde—meuble and stealing diamonds to the value of thirty millions.[132]

Like a man struck on the head with a mallet, Paris, felled to the ground, lets things go; the authors of the massacre have fully attained their ends. The faction has fast hold of power, and will maintain its hold. Neither in the Legislative Assembly nor in the Convention will the aims of the Girondins be successful against its tenacious usurpation. It has proved by a striking example that it is capable of anything, and boasts of it; it is still armed, it stands there ever prepared and anonymous on its murderous basis, with its speedy modes of operation, its own group of fanatical agents and bravos, with Maillard and Fournier, with its cannon and its pikes. All that does not live within it lives only through its favor from day to day, through its good will. Everybody knows that. The Assembly no longer thinks of dislodging people who meet decrees of expulsion with massacre; it is no longer a question of auditing their accounts, or of keeping them within the confines of the law. Their dictatorship is not to be disputed, and their purification continue. From four to five hundred new prisoners, arrested within eleven days, by order of the municipality, by the sections, and by this or that individual Jacobin, are crowded into cells still dripping with blood, and the report is spread that, on the 20th of September, the prisons will be emptied by a second massacre.[133] — Let the Convention, if it pleases, pompously install itself as sovereign, and grind out decrees — it makes no difference; regular or irregular, the government still marches on in the hands of those who hold the sword.[134] The Jacobins, through sudden terror, have maintained their illegal authority; through a prolongation of terror they are going to establish their legal authority. A forced suffrage is going to put them in office at the Hôtel—de—ville, in the tribunals, in the National Guard, in the sections, and in the various administrations, while they have already elected to the Convention, Marat, Danton, Fabre d'Eglantine, Camille Desmoulins, Manuel, Billaud—Varennes, Panis, Sergent, Collot d'Herbois, Robespierre, Legendre, Osselin, Fréron, David, Robert, Lavicourterie, in short, the instigators, leaders and accomplices of the massacre.[135] Nothing that could force or falsify voting is omitted.[136] In the first place the presence of the people is imposed on the electoral assembly, and, to this end, it is transferred to the large hall of the Jacobin club, under the pressure of the Jacobin galleries. As a second precaution, every opponent is excluded from voting, every Constitutionalist, every former member of the monarchical club, of the Feuillants, and of the Sainte—Chapelle club, of the Feuillants, and of the Sainte−Chapelle club, every signer of the petition of the 20,000 , or of that of the 8,000, and, on the sections protesting against this, their protest is thrown out on the ground of its being the fruit of "an intrigue." Finally, at each balloting, each elector's vote is called out, which ensures the right vote beforehand, the warnings he has received being very explicit.[137] On the 2nd of September, during the first meeting of the electoral body, held at the bishop's palace, the Marseilles troop, 500 yards away, came and took the twenty−four priests from the town−hall, and, on the way, hacked them to pieces on the Pont−Neuf. Throughout the evening and all night the agents of the municipality carried on their work at the Abbaye, at the Carmelites, and at La Force, and, on the 3rd of September, on the electoral assembly transferring itself to the Jacobin club, it passed over the Pont−au− Change between two rows of corpses, which the slaughterers had brought there from the C h â t e l e t   a n d   t h e   C o n c i e r g e r i e   p r i s o n s .

Notes:

[1] 'Thierry, son of Clovis, unwilling to take part in an expedition of his brothers into Burgundy, was told by his men: "If thou art unwilling to march into Burgundy with thy brothers, we will leave thee and follow them in thy place."— Clotaire, another of his sons, disposed to make peace with the Saxons, "the angry Francs rush upon him, revile him, and threaten to kill him if he declines to accompany them. Upon which he puts himself at their head."

[2] Social condition and degree of culture are often indicated orthographically. — Granier de Cassagnac, II. .480. Bécard, commanding the expedition which brought back the prisoners from Orleans, signs himself: "Bécard, commandant congointement aveque M. Fournier generalle. " — "Archives Nationales," F7, 4426. Letter of Chemin, commissioner of the Gravilliers section, to Santerre, Aug.11, 1792. "Mois Charles Chemin commissaire . . . fait part à Monsieur Santaire générale de la troupe parisiene que le nommé Hingray cavaliers de la gendarmeris nationale . . me délarés qu'ille sestes trouvés aux jourduis 11 aoux avec une home attachés à la cours aux Equris; quille lui aves dis quiere 800 home a peupres des sidevant garde du roy étes tous près a fondre sure Paris pour donaire du sécour a naux rébelle et a signer avec moi la presante."

[3] On the 19th of March, 1871, I met in the Rue de Varennes a man with two guns on his shoulder who had taken part in the pillage of the Ecole d'Etat−major and was on his way home. I said to him: "But this is civil war, and you will let the Prussians in Paris."− "I'd rather have the Prussians than Thiers. Thiers is Prussian on the inside!"

[4] Today, 115 years after these words were written, we have seen others, Lenin, Stalin, Hitler, Pol Pot, Mao Tse Tung, etc following in the Jacobin's footsteps. Nobles, Bourgeois, Jews and other undesirables have been methodically put away. The sheeplike majority did not read Taine or did not profit from his warnings while most of the great tyrants learned from him or from the events he described (SR.)

[5] Moniteur, Nov. 14, 1792.

[6] "Archives Nationales," F7, 4426. Letter of the police administrators, Aug. 11. Declaration of

Delaunay, Aug. 12.

[7] Buchez et Roux, XVII. 59 (session of Aug. 12) Speech by Leprieur at the bar of the house.

[8] Buchez et Roux, XVII. 47. – Mortimer–Ternaux, III. 31. Speech by Robespierre at the bar of the Assembly in the name of the commune, Aug. 15.

[9] Brissot, in his report on Robespierre's petition. – The names of the principal judges elected show its character: Fouquier–Tinville, Osselin, Coffinhal.

[10] Buchez et Roux, XVII.91 (Aug. 17).

[11] Stated by Pétion in his speech (Moniteur, Nov. 10, 1792).

[12] Buchez et Roux, XVII. 116 (session of Aug. 23).

[13] Mortimer–Ternaux, III. 461. – Moore, I. 273 (Aug. 31).

[14] Buchez et Roux, XVII. 267 (article by Prudhomme in the "Révolutions de Paris").

[15] "Les Révolutions de Paris," Ibid., "A number of sans–culottes were there with their pikes; but these were largely outnumbered by the multitude of uniforms of the various battalions." — Moore, Aug, 31: "At present the inhabitants of the faubourgs Saint–Antoine and Saint– Marceau are all that is felt of the sovereign people in Paris."

[16] More, Aug. 26.

[17] Mortimer–Ternaux, III. 471. Indictment against Jean–Julien. — In referring to M. Mortimer–Ternaux we do so because, like a true critic, he cites authentic and frequently unedited documents.

[18] Rétif de la Bretonne, "les Nuits de Paris," 11th night, p. 372.

[19] Moore, Sept. 2.

[20] Moore, Sept. 3. — Buchez et Roux, XVI. 159 (narrative by Tallien).— Official report of the Paris commune, Sept. 4 (in the collection of Barrière and Berville, the volume entitled "Mémoires sur les journées de Septembre"). The commune adopts and expands the fable, probably invented by it. Prudhomme well says that the story of the prison plot, so scandalously circulated during the Reign of Terror, appears for the first time on the 2d of September. The same report was spread through the rural districts. At Gennevilliers, a peasant while lamenting the massacres, said to Malouet: "It is, too, a terrible thing for the aristocrats to want to kill all the people by blowing up the city" (Malouet, II. 244).

[21] Official reports of the commune, Aug. 11.

[22] Mortimer–Ternaux, II. 446. List of the section commissioners sitting at the Hôtel–de–ville, Aug. 10, before 9 o'clock in the morning.

[23] Official reports of the commune, Aug. 21. "Considering that, to ensure public safety and liberty, the council–general of the commune required all the power delegated to it by the people, at the time it was compelled to resume the exercise of its rights," sends a deputation to the National Assembly to insist that "the new department be converted, pure and simple, into a tax–commissioners' office." — Mortimer–Ternaux, III. 25. Speech of Robespierre in the name of the commune: "After the people have saved the country, after decreeing a National Convention to replace you, what remains for you to do but to gratify their wishes? . . . The people, forced to see to its own salvation, has provided for this through its delegates. . . It is essential that those chosen by itself for its magistrates should enjoy the plenary powers befitting the sovereign."

[24] Official reports of the commune, Aug. 10. – Mortimer–Ternaux, III. 155. Letter of the Minister Servan, Aug. 30.–Ibid., 149.— Ibid., 148. The commission on supplies having been broken up by the commune, Roland, the Minister of the Interior, begs the Assembly to act promptly, for "he will no longer be responsible for the supplies of Paris."

[25] Official reports of the commune, Aug. 21. A resolution requiring that, on trials for lésé–nation, those who appear for the defendants should be provided with a certificate of their integrity, issued by their assembled section, and that the interviews between them and the accused be public. – Ibid., Aug.17, a resolution to suspend the execution of the two assassins of mayor Simonneau, condemned to death by the tribunal of Seine–et–Oise.

[26] Mortimer–Ternaux, III. 11. Decree of Aug.11.

[27] Prudhomme, "Révolutions de Paris" (number for Sep. 22).. Report by Roland to the National Assembly (Sept. 16, at 9 o'clock in the morning).

[28] Madame Roland, "Mémoires," II. 414 (Ed. Barrière et Berville). Report by Roland Oct. 29. The seizure in question tool place Aug.27.

[29] Mémoirs sur les journées de Septembre" (Ed. Barrière et Berville, pp. 307–322). List of sums paid by the treasurer of the commune. — See, on the prolongation of this plundering, Roland's report, Oct. 29, of money, plate, and assignats taken from the Senlis Hospital (Sept. 13), the Hotel de Coigny emptied, and sale of furniture in the Hotel d'Egmont, etc.

[30] Official reports of the commune, Aug. 17 and 20. — List of sums paid by the treasurer of the commune, p. 321. — On the 28th of August a "Saint–Roch in silver is brought to the bar of the National Assembly.

[31] Mortimer–Ternaux, III. 150, 161, 511. — Report by Roland, Oct. 29. P. 414.

[32] Moniteur.514, 542 (sessions of Aug. 23 and 26).

[33] Mortimer–Ternaux, III. 99 (sessions of Aug.15 and 23). "Procès- verbaux de la Commune," Aug. 18, a resolution to obtain a law authorizing the commune "to collect together with wives and children of the émigrés in places of security, and to make use of the former convents for this purpose."

[34] Procès–verbaux de la Commune," Aug. 12. – Ibid., Aug. 18. Not being able to find M. Geoffrey, the journalist, the commune "passes a resolution that seals be affixed to Madame Geoffroy's domicile and that she be placed in arrest until her husband appears to release her."

[35] Procès–verbaux de la Commune." Aug.17 and 18. Another resolution, again demanding of the National Assembly a list of the signers for publication.

[36] Procès–verbaux de la Commune," Aug. 18, 19, 20. — On the 20th of August the commune summons before it and examines the Venetian Ambassador. "A citizen claims to be heard against the ambassador, and states that several carriages went out of Paris in his name. The name of this citizen is Chevalier, a horse–shoer's assistant . . . The Council decrees that honorable mention be made of the affidavits brought forward in the accusation." On the tone of these examinations read Weber ("Mémoires," II. 245), who narrates his own.

[37] Buchez et Roux, XVII. 215. Narration by Peltier. — In spite of the orders of the National Assembly the affair is repeated on the following day, and it lasts from the 19th to the 31st of August, in the evening. — Moore, Aug.31. The stupid, sheep–like vanity of the bourgeois enlisted as a gendarme for the sans–culottes is here well depicted. The keeper of the Hôtel Meurice, where Moore and Lord Lauderdale put up, was on guard and on the chase the night before: "He talked a good deal of the fatigue he had undergone, and hinted a little of the dangers to which he had been exposed in the course of this severe duty. Being asked if he had been successful in his search after suspected persons —'Yes my lord, infinitely; our battalion arrested four priests.' He could not have looked more lofty if he had taken the Duke of Brunswick,"

[38] According to Rœderer, the number arrested amounted to from 5,000 to 6,000 persons.

[39] Mortimer–Ternaux, III.147, 148, Aug.28 and 29. – Ibid., 176. Other sections complain of the Commune with some bitterness. — Buchez et Roux, XVII. 358. — "Procès–verbaux de la Commune," Sept. 1. "The section of the Temple sends a deputation which declares that by virtue of a decree of the National Assembly it withdraws its powers entrusted to the commissioners elected by it to the council-general."

[40] Mortimer–Ternaux, III. 154 (session of Aug. 30).

[41] Mortimer–Ternaux, III. 171 (session of Aug. 31). — Ibid., 208. – – On the following day, Sept. 1, at the instigation of Danton, Thuriot obtains from the National Assembly an ambiguous decree which seems to allow the members of the commune to keep their places, provisionally at least, at the Hotel–de–ville.

[42] "Procès–verbaux de la Commune," Sept. 1.

[43] "Procès–verbaux de la Commune," Sept. 1. "It is resolved that whatever effects fell into the hands of the citizens who fought for liberty and equality on the 10th of August shall remain in their possession; M. Tallien, secretary–general, is therefore authorized to return a gold watch to M. Lecomte, a gendarme."

[44] Four circumstances, simultaneous and in full agreement with each other, indicate this date: 1. On the 23d of August the council–general resolves "that a tribune shall be arranged in the chamber for a journalist (M. Marat), whose duty it shall be to conduct a journal giving the acts passed and what goes on in the commune" ("Procès–verbaux de la Commune," Aug.23) 2. On the same day, "on the motion of a member with a view to separate the prisoners of lése–nation from those of the nurse's hospital and others of the same stamp in the different prisons, the council has adopted this measure" (Granier de Cassagnac, II. 100). 3. The same day the commune applauds the deputies of a section, which "in warm terms" denounce before it the tardiness of justice and declare to it that the people will "immolate" the prisoners in their prisons (Moniteur, Nov. 10, 1793, Narrative of Pétion). The same day it sends a deputation to the Assembly to order a transfer of the Orleans prisoners to Paris (Buchez et Roux, XVII. 116). The next day, in spite of the prohibitions of the Assembly, It sends Fournier and his band to Orleans (Mortimer–Ternaux, III. 364), and each knows beforehand that Fournier is commissioned to kill them on the way. (Balleydier, "Histoire politique et militaire du people de Lyon," I.79. Letter of Laussel, dated at Paris, Aug.28): "Our volunteers are at Orleans for the past two or three days to bring the anti–revolutionary prisoners here, who are treated too well there." On the day of Fournier's departure (Aug. 24) Moore observes in the Palais Royal and at the Tuileries "a greater number than usual of stump– speakers of the populace, hired for the purpose of inspiring the people with a horror of monarchy."

[45] Moniteur, Sept. 25,1792, speech by Marat in the Convention.

[46] See his two journals, "L'Ami du people" and the "Journal de la Républic Française," especially for July and October 1792. — The number for August 16 is headed: "Development of the vile plot of the court to destroy all patriots with fire and sword." — That of August 19: "The infamous conscript Fathers of the Circus, betraying the people and trying to delay the conviction of traitors until Mottié arrives, is marching with his army on Paris to destroy all patriots!" — That of Aug. 21: "The rotters of the Assembly, the perfidious accomplices of Mottié arranging for flight . . . The conscript Fathers, the assassins of patriots at Nancy, the Champ de Mars and in the Tuileries, etc." — All this was yelled out daily every morning by those who hawked these journals through the streets.

[47] Ami du Peuple, Aug.19 and 21.

[48] "Lettres autographs de Madame Roland," published by Madame Bancal des Issarts, Sept. 9. "Danton leads all; Robespierre is his puppet; Marat holds his torch and dagger."

[49] Madame Roland "Mémoires," II. 19 (note by Roland). – Ibid., 21, 23, 24. Monge says: "Danton wants to have it so; if I refuse he will denounce me to the Commune and at the Cordeliers, and have me hung." Fournier's commission to Orleans was all in order, Roland probably having signed it unawares, like those of the commissioners sent into the departments by the executive council (Cf. Mortimer–Ternaux, III. 368.)

[50] The person who gives me the following had it from the king, Louis Philippe, then an officer in Kellerman's corps:

On the evening of the battle of Valmy the young officer is sent to Paris to carry the news. On his arrival (Sept. 22 or 23. 1792) he learns that he is removed from his post and appointed governor of Strasbourg. He goes to Servan's house, Minister of War, and at first they refuse to let him in. Servan is unwell and in bed, with the ministers in his room. The young man states that he comes from the army and is the bearer of dispatches. He is admitted, and finds, indeed, Servan in bed with various personages around him, and he announces the victory. — They question him and he gives the details. — He then complains of having been displaced, and, stating that he is too young to command with any authority at Strasbourg, requests to he reinstated with the army in the field. "Impossible," replies Servan; "your place is given to another." Thereupon one of the personages present, with a peculiar visage and a rough voice, takes him aside and says to him: "Servan is a fool! Come and see me to–morrow and I will arrange the matter." "Who are you?" "I am Danton, the Minister of Justice." — The next day he calls on Danton, who tells him: "It is all right; you shall have your post back — not under Kellerman, however, but under Dumouriez; are you content?" The young man, delighted, thanks him. Danton resumes: "Let me give you one piece of advice before you go: You have talent and will succeed. But get rid of one fault . You talk too much. You have been in Paris twenty–four hours, and already you have repeatedly criticized the affair of September. I know this; I have been informed of it" "But that was a massacre; how can one help calling it horrible?" "I did it," replies Danton, "The Parisians are all so many j—— f——. A river of blood had to flow between them and the émigrés.. You are too young to understand these matters. Return to the army; it is the only place nowadays for a young man like you and of your rank. You have a future before you; but mind this — keep your mouth shut!"

[51] Hua, 167.. Narrative by his guest, the physician Lambry, an intimate friend of Danton ultra–fanatical and member of a committee in which the question came up whether the members of the "Right" should likewise be put out of the way. "Danton had energetically repelled this sanguinary proposal. 'Everybody knows,' he said, 'that I do not shrink from a criminal act when necessary; but I disdain to commit a useless one.'"

[52] Mortimer–Ternaux, Iv. 437. Danton exclaims, in relation to the hot–headed commissioners sent by him into the department: "Eh! damn it, do you suppose that we would send you young ladies?"

[53] Philippe de Ségur, "Mémoires,"I.12. Danton, in a conversation with his father, a few weeks after the 2nd of September.

[54] See above, narrative of the king, louis Philippe.

[55] Buchez et Roux, xvii. 347. The words of Danton in the National Assembly, Sept. 2nd a little before two o'clock, just as the tocsin and cannon gave the signal of alarm agreed upon. Already on the 31st of August, Tailien, his faithful ally, had told the National Assembly: "We have arrested the priests who make so much trouble. They are in confinement in a certain domicile, and in a few days the soil of liberty will be purged of their presence."

[56] Meillan, "Mémoires," 325 (Ed. Barrière et Berville). Speech by Fabre d'Eglantine at the Jacobin Club, sent around among the affiliated clubs, May 1, 1793.

[57] Robinet, "Procès des Dantonistes," 39, 45 (words of Danton in the committee on general defense). – Madame Roland, 2Mémoires," II. 30. On the 2nd of September Grandpré ordered to report to the Minister of the Interior on the state of the prisons, waits for Danton as he leaves the council and tells him his fears. "Danton, irritated by the description, exclaims in his bellowing way, suiting his word to the action. 'I don't give a damn about the prisoners! Let them take care of themselves! And he proceeded on in an angry mood. This took place in the second ante–room, in the presence of twenty persons." – Arnault, II. 101. About the time of the September massacres "Danton, in the presence of one of my friends, replied to someone that urged him to use his authority in stopping the spilling of blood: 'Isn't it time for the people to take their revenge?' "

[58] Prudhomme, "Crimes de la Révolution," iv. 90. On the 2nd of September, at the alarm given by the tocsin and cannon, Prudhomme calls on Danton at his house for information. Danton gives him the agreed story and adds: "The people, who are now aroused and know what to do, want to administer justice themselves on the nasty imprisoned persons. — Camille Desmoulins enters: "Look here," says Danton, "Prudhomme has come to ask what is going to be done?" — "Didn't you tell him that the innocent would not be confounded with the guilty? All those that are demanded by their Sections will be given up." — On the 4th, Desmoulins calls at the office of the journal and says to the editors: "Well, everything has gone off in the most perfect order. The people even set free a good many aristocrats against whom there was no direct proof. I trust that you will state all this exactly, because the Journal des Révolutions is the compass of public opinion."

[59] Prudhomme, "Crimes de la Révolution," IV. 123. According to the statements of Théophile Mandar, vice–president of a section, witness and actor in the scene; he authorizes Prudhomme to mention his name. – – Afterwards, in the next room, Mandar proposes to Pétion and Robespierre to attend the Assembly the next day and protest against the massacre; if necessary, the Assembly may appoint a director for one day. "Take care not to do that," replied Robespierre; "Brissot would be the dictator." — Pétion says nothing. "The ministers were in perfect agreement to let the massacres continue."

[60] Madame Roland, II. 37. — "Angers et le départment de Maine–et– Loire de 1787 à 1830," by Blordier Langlois. Appended to the circular was a printed address bearing the title of Compte rendu au peuple souverain, "countersigned by the Minister of Justice and with the Minister's seal on the package," and addressed to the Jacobin Clubs of the departments, that they, too, might preach massacre.

[61] Mortimer–Ternaux, III. 391, 398. — Warned by Alquier, president of the criminal court of Versailles, of the danger to which the Orleans prisoners were exposed, Danton replied: "What is that to you? That affair does not concern you. Mind your own business, and do not meddle with things outside of it!" — "But, Monsieur, the law says that prisoners must be protected."— "What do you care? Some among them are great criminals, and nobody knows yet how the people will regard them and how far their indignation will carry them." Alquier wished to pursue the matter, but Danton turned his back on him

[62] Mortimer–Ternaux, III. 217

[63] Madame Roland, "Lettres autographes, etc.," Sept. 5, 1792. "We are here under the knives of Marat and Robespierre. These fellows are striving to excite the people and turn them against the National Assembly and the council. They have organized a Star Chamber and they have a small army under pay, aided by what they found or stole in the palace and elsewhere, or by supplies purchased by Danton, who is underhandedly the chieftain of this horde." — Dusaulx, "Mémoires," 441. "On the following day (Sept. 3) I went to see one of the most estimated personalities at this epoch. 'You know,' said I to him, 'what is going on?' — 'Very well; but keep quiet; it will soon be over. A little more blood is still necessary.' — I saw others who explained themselves much more definitely. " — Mortimer–Ternaux, II. 445.

[64] Madame Roland, "Lettres autographes, etc.," Sept. 5, 1792. "We are here under the knives of Marat and Robespierre. These fellows are striving to excite the people and turn them against the National Assembly and the council. They have organized a Star Chamber and they have a small army under pay, aided by what they found or stole in the palace and elsewhere, or by supplies purchased by Danton, who is underhandedly the chieftain of this horde." — Dusaulx, "Mémoires," 441. "On the following day (Sept. 3) I went to see one of the most estimated personalities at this epoch. 'You know,' said I to him, 'what is going on?' — 'Very well; but keep quiet; it will soon be over. A little more blood is still necessary.' — I saw others who explained themselves much more definitely. " — Mortimer–Ternaux, II. 445.

[65] Madame de Staël, "Considérations sur la Révolution Française," 3rd part, ch. X.

[66] Prudhomme, "Les Révolutions de Paris" (number for Sept. 22). At one of the last sessions of the commune "M. Panis spoke of Marat as of a prophet, another Siméon Stylite. 'Marat,' said he, 'remained six weeks sitting on one thigh in a dungeon.' " – Barbaroux, 64.

[67] Weber, II. 348. Collot dwells at length, "in cool–blooded gaiety," on the murder of Madame de Lamballe and on the abominations to which her corpse was subjected. "He added, with a sigh of regret, that if he had been consulted he would have had the head of Madame de Lamballe served in a covered dish for the queen's supper."

[68] On the part played by Robespierre and his presence constantly at the Commune see Granier de Cassagnac, II. 55. — Mortimer–Ternaux, III. 205. Speech by Robespierre at the commune, Sept. 1: "No one dares name the traitors. Well, I give their names for the safety of the people: I denounce the libertycide Brissot, the Girondist factionists, the rascally commission of the Twenty–One in the National Assembly; I denounce them for having sold France to Brunswick, and for having taken in advance the reward for their dastardly act." On the 2nd of September he repeats his denunciation, and consequently on that day warrants are issued by the committee of supervision against thirty deputies and against Brissot and Roland (Mortimer–Ternaux, III. 216, 247).

[69] "Procès–verbaux de la Commune," Aug. 30. – Mortimer–Ternaux, III. 217 (resolutions of the sections Poissonnière and Luxembourg). — Granier de Cassagnac, II. 104 (adhesion of the sections Mauconseil, Louvre, and Quinze–Vingt).

[70] Granier de Cassagnac, II. 156.

[71] Mortimer–Ternaux, III. 265. — Granier de Cassagnac, XII. 402. (The other five judges were also members of the commune.)

[72] Granier de Cassagnac, II. 313. Register of the General Assembly of the sans–culottes, section, Sept. 2. — "Mémoires sur les journées de Septembre," 151 (declaration of Jourdan).

[73] "Mémoires sur les journées de Septembre," narrative of Abbé Sicard, 111.

[74] Buchez et Roux, XVIII. 109, 178. ("La vérite tout entière," by Méhée, Jr.) – Narrative of Abbé Sicard, 132, 134.

[75] Granier de Cassagnac, II. 92, 93. – On the presence and complicity of Santerre. Ibid, 89–99.

[76] Mortimer–Ternaux, III. 277 and 299 (Sept. 3). – Granier de Cassagnac, II. 257. A commissary of the section of the Quatre–Nations states in his report that "the section authorized them to pay expenses out of the affair." – Declaration of Jourdan, 151. – Lavalette, "Mémoires," I. 91. The initiative of the commune is further proved by the following detail: "Towards five o'clock (Sept. 2) city officials on horseback, carrying a flag, rode through the streets crying: 'To arms! To arms!' They added: 'The enemy is coming; you are all lost; the city will be burnt and given up to pillage. Have no fear of the traitors or conspirators behind your backs. They are in the hands of the patriots, and before you leave the thunderbolt of national justice will fall on them!" – Buchez et Roux, XXVIII. 105. Letter of Chevalier Saint–Dizier, member of the first committee of supervision, Sept. 10. "Marat, Duplain, Fréron, etc., generally do no more in their supervision of things than wreak private vengeance. . . Marat states openly that 40,000 heads must still be knocked off to ensure the success of the revolution."

[77] Buchez et Roux, XVIII. 146. "Ma Résurrection," by Mathon de la Varenne. "The evening before half–intoxicated women said publicly on the Feuillants terrace: 'To–morrow is the day when their souls will be turned inside out in the prisons."

[78] "Mémoires sur les journées de Septembre. Mon agonie," by Journiac de Saint–Méard. — Madame de la Fausse–Landry, 72. The 29th of August she obtained permission to join her uncle in prison: "M. Sergent and others told me that I was acting imprudently; that the prisons were not safe."

[79] Granier de Cassagnac, — II. 27. According to Roch Marcandier their number "did not exceed 300." According to Louvet there were "200, and perhaps not that number." According to Brissot, the massacres were committed by about "a hundred unknown brigands." — Pétion, at La Force (Ibid., 75), on September 6, finds only about a dozen executioners. According to Madame Roland (II. 35), "there were not fifteen at the Abbaye." Lavalette the first day finds only about fifty killers at the La Force prison.

[80] Mathon de la Varenne, ibid., 137.

[81] Buchez et Roux, XVII. 183 (session of the Jacobin Club, Aug. 27). Speech by a federate from Tarn. – Mortimer–Ternaux, III. 126.

[82] Sicard, 80. — Méhée, 187. — Weber, II. 279. — Cf., in Journiac de Saint–Méard, his conversation with a Provençal. — Rétif de la Bretonne, "Les Nuits de Paris," 375. "About 2 o'clock in the morning (Sept. 3) I heard a troop of cannibals passing under my window, none of whom appeared to have the Parisian accent; they were all strangers."

[83] Granier de Cassagnac, II. 164, 502. — Mortimer–Ternaux, III. 530. — Maillard's assessors at the Abbaye were a watchmaker living in the Rue Childebert, a fruit–dealer in the Rue Mazarine, a keeper of a public house in the Rue du Four–Saint–Germain, a journeyman hatter in the Rue Sainte–Marguerite, and two others whose occupation is not mentioned. — On the composition of the tribunal at La Force, Cf. Journiac de Saint–Méard, 120, and Weber, II. 261.

[84] Granier de Cassagnac, II. 507 (on Damiens), 513 (on L'empereur). — Meillan, 388 (on Laforet and his wife, old–clothes dealers on the Quai du Louvre, who on the 31st of May prepare for a second blow, and calculate this time on having for their share the pillaging of fifty houses).

[85] Sicard, 98

[86] De Ferrières (Ed. Berville et Barrière), III. 486. — Rétif de la Bretonne, 381. At the end of the Rue des Ballets a prisoner had just been killed, while the next one slipped through the railing and escaped. "A man not belonging to the butchers, but one of those thoughtless machines of which there are so many, interposed his pike and stopped him. . . The poor fellow was arrested by his pursuers and massacred. The pikeman coolly said to us: 'I couldn't know they wanted to kill him.'"

[87] Granier de Cassagnac, II. 511.

[88] The judges and slaughterers at the Abbaye, discovered in the trial of the year IV., almost all lived in the neighborhood, in the rues Dauphine, de Nevers, Guégénaud, de Bussy, Childebert, Taranne, de l'Egoût, du Vieux Colombier, de l'Echaudé–Saint–Benoit, du Four–Saint– Germain, etc.

[89] Sicard, 86, 87, 101. — Jourdan, 123. "The president of the committee of supervision replied to me that these were very honest persons; that on the previous evening or the evening before that, one of them, in a shirt and wooden shoes, presented himself before their committee all covered with blood, bringing with him in his hat twenty– five louis in gold, which he had found on the person of a man he had killed." — Another instance of probity may be found in the "Procès– verbaux du conseil–général de la Commune de Versailles," 367, 371. — On the following day, Sept. 3, robberies commence and go on increasing.

[90] Méhée, 179. "'Would you believe that I have earned only twenty– four francs?' said a baker's boy armed with a club. 'I killed more than forty for my share.'"

[91] Granier de Cassagnac. II. 153. — Cf. Ibid., 202–209, details on the meals of the workmen and on the more delicate repast of Maillard and his assistants.

[92] Mortimer–Ternaux, III. 175–176. – Granier de Cassagnac. II. 84. – – Jourdan, 222. — Méhée, 179. "At midnight they came back swearing, cursing, and foaming with rage, threatening to cut the throats of the committee in a body if they were not instantly paid."

[93] Mortimer–Ternaux, III. 320. Speech by Pétion on the charges preferred against Robespierre.

[94] Mathon de la Varenne, 156. — Journiac de Saint–Méard, 129. – Moore, 267.

[95] Journiac de Saint–Méard, 115.

[96] Weber, II. 265. — Journiac de Saint–Méard, 129. — Mathon de la Varenne, 155.

[97] Moore, 267. — Cf. Malouet, II. 240. Malouet, on the evening of Sept. 1, was at his sister–in–law's; there is a domiciliary visit at midnight; she faints on hearing the patrol mount the stairs. "I begged them not to enter the drawing–room, so as not to disturb the poor sufferer. The sight of a woman in a swoon and pleasing in appearance affected them, and they at once withdrew, leaving me alone with her." — Beaulieu, "Essais," I. 108. (Regarding the two Abbaye butchers he meets in the house of Journiac–de–Saint–Méard, and who chat with him while issuing him with a safe–conduct): "What struck me was to detect generous sentiments through their ferocity, those of men determined to protect any one whose cause they adopted."

[98] Weber, II. 265, 348.

[99] Sicard, 101. Billaud–Varennes, addressing the slaughterers. – Ibid.75. "Greater power," replied a member of the committee of supervision, "what are you thinking of? To give you greater power would be limiting those you have already. Have you forgotten that you are sovereigns? That the sovereignty of the people is confided to you, and that you are now in full exercise of it?"

[100] Méhée, 171.

[101] Sicard, 81. At the beginning the Marseilles men themselves were averse to striking the disarmed, and exclaimed to the crowd: "Here, take our swords and pikes and kill the monsters!"

[102] Macbeth by Shakespeare: "I have supped full with horrors."

[103] Observe children drowning a dog or killing a snake. Tenacity of life irritates them, as if it were a rebellion against their despotism, the effect of which is to render them only the more violent against their victim.

[104] One may recall to mind the effect of bull–fights, also the irresistible fascination which Saint–Augustin experienced on first hearing the death–cry of a gladiator in the amphitheater.

[105] Mortimer–Ternaux, III. 131. Trial of the September actors; the judge's summing up. "The third and forty–sixth witnesses stated that they saw Monneuse (member of the commune) go to and come from la Force, express his delight at those sad events that had just occurred, acting very immorally in

relation thereto, adding that there was violin playing in his presence, and that his colleague danced." – Sicard, 88.

[106] Sicard, 87, 91. This expression by a wine–merchant, who wants the custom of the murderers. – Granier de Cassagnac, II. 197–200. The original bills for wine, straw, and lights have been found.

[107] Sicard, 91. – Maton de la Varenne, 150.

[108] Mathon de la Varenne, 154. A man from the suburbs said to him (Mathon is an advocate):

"All right, Monsieur Fine–skin; I shall treat myself to a glass of your blood

[109] Rétif de la Bretonne, "Les Nuits de Paris," 9th night, p.388. "She screamed horribly, whilst the brigands amused themselves with their disgraceful acts. Her body even after death was not exempt. These people had heard that she had been beautiful."

[110] Prudhomme, "Les Révolutions de Paris," number for Sept. 8, 1792. "The people subjected the flower–girl of the Palais–Royal to the law of retaliation." – Granier de Cassagnac, II. 329. According to the bulletin of the revolutionary tribunal, number for Sept. 3. — Mortimer–Ternaux, III. 291. Deposition of the caretaker's office of the Conciergerie prison. — Buchez et Roux, XVII.198. "Histoire des hommes de proi," by Roch Marcandier.

[111] Mortimer–Ternaux III, 257. Trial of the September murderers; deposition of Roussel. – Ib., 628.

[112] Deposition of the woman Millet, ibid., 63. — Weber, II. 350. – – Roch Marcandier, 197, 198. – Rétif de la Bretonne, 381.

[113] Deposition of the woman Millet, ibid., 63. — Weber, II. 350. – – Roch Marcandier, 197, 198. – Rétif de la Bretonne, 381.

[114] On this mechanical and murderous action Cf: Dusaulx, "Mémoires," 440. He addresses the bystanders in favor of the prisoners, and, affected by his words, they hold out their hands to him. "But before this the executioners had struck me on the cheeks with the points of their pikes, from which hung pieces of flesh. Others wanted to cut off my head, which would have been done if two gendarmes had not kept them back."

[115] Jourdan, 219.

[116] Méhée, 179.

[117] Mortimer–Ternaux, III. 558. The same idea is found among the federates and Parisians composing the company of the Egalité, which brought the Orleans prisoners to Versailles and then murdered them. They explain their conduct by saying that they "hoped to put an end to the excessive expenditure to which the French empire was subject through the prolonged detention of conspirators."

[118] Rétif de la Bretonne, 388.

[119] Méhée, 177.

[120] Prudhomme, "Les Crimes de la Révolution." III. 272.

[121] Rétif de la Bretonne, 388. There were two sorts of women at the Salpêtrière, those who were banded and young girls brought in the prison. Hence the two alternatives.

[122] Mortimer–Ternaux, III. 295. See list of names, ages, and occupations.

[123] Barthélemy Maurice, "Histoire politique and anecdotique des prisons de la Seine," 329.

[124] Mortimer–Ternaux, III. 295. See list of names, ages, and occupations.

[125] The Encyclopedia "QUID" (ROBERT LAFONT, PARIS 1998) advises us that the number of victims killed with "cold steel and clubs" etc total 1395 persons. the total number of French victims due to the Revolution is considered to be between 600 000 and 800 000 dead. (SR)

[126] Mortimer–Ternaux, III. 399, 592, 602–606. – "Procès–verbal des 8, 9, 10 Septembre, extrait des registres de la municipalité de Versailles." (In the "Mémoires sur les journées de Septembre"), p. 358 and following pages. – Granier de Cassagnac, II. 483. Bonnet's exploit at Orleans, pointed out to Fournier, Sept. I. Fournier replies: "In God's name, I am not to be ordered; when the bloody beggars have had their heads cut off the trial may be held later!"

[127] Roch Marcandier, 210. Speech by Lazowski to the section of Finistère, fauborg Saint–Marceau. Lazowski had, in addition, set free the assassins of the mayor of Etampes, and laid their manacles on the bureau table.

[128] Malouet, II. 243 (Sept. 2). – Moniteur, XIII. 48 (session of Sept. 27, 1792). We see in the speech of Panis that analogous scenes took place in the committee of supervision. "Imagine our situation. We were surrounded by citizens irritated against the treachery of the court. We were told: 'Here is an aristocrat who is going to fly; you must stop him, or your yourselves are traitors!' Pistols were pointed at us and we found ourselves obliged to sign warrants, not so much for our own safety as for that of the persons denounced."

[129] Granier de Cassagnac, II. 258. – Prudhomme, "Les Crimes de la Révolution," III. 272. – Mortimer–Ternaux, III. 631. – De Ferrière, III. 391. – (The expression quoted was recorded by Rétif de la Bretonne.)

[130] That is how to do it, must any anarchist or hopeful revolutionary have thought, upon reading Taine's livid description.– But also: "Do not let the bourgeois read this, it might scare them and make our task more difficult." (SR).

[131] Moniteur, XIII. 698, 698 (numbers for Sept. 15 and 16). Ibid., Letter of Roland, 701; of Pétion,

711. – Buchez et Roux, XVIII. 33. 34. – Prudhomme's journal contains an engraving of this subject (Sept. 14) – "An Englishman admitted to the bar of the house denounces to the National Assembly a robbery committed in a house occupied by him at Chaillot by two bailiffs and their satellites. The robbery consisted of twelve louis, five guineas, five thousand pounds in assignats, and several other objects." The courts before which he appeared did not dare take up his case (Buchez et Roux, XVII. P. 1, Sept. 18).

[132] Buchez et Roux, XVII. 461. – Prudhomme, "Les Révolutions de Paris," number for Sept. 22, 1792.

[133] Moniteur, XIII. 711 (session of Sept. 16). Letter of Roland to the National Assembly. – Buchez et Roux, XVIII. 42. — Moniteur, XIII. 731 (session of Sept. 17). Speech by Pétion: "Yesterday there was some talk of again visiting the prisons, and particularly the Conciergerie."

[134] Perhaps Mao read this and later coined his famous slogan "that all political power emanates from the barrels of guns." (SR).

[135] "Archives Nationales," II. 58 to 76. Official reports of the Paris electoral assembly. – Robespierre is elected the twelfth (Sept. 5), then Danton and Collot d'Herbois (Sept. 6) then Manuel and Billaud–Varennes (Sept. 7), next C. Desmoulins (Sept. 8), Marat (Sept. 9) etc. – Mortimer–Ternaux, IV. 35 (act passed by the commune at the instigation of Robespierre for the regulation of electoral operations). – Louvet, "Mémoires." Louvet, in the electoral assembly asks to be heard on the candidacy of Marat, but is unsuccessful. "On going out I was surrounded by those men with big clubs and sabers by whom the future dictator was always attended, Robespierre's body-guard. They threatened me and told me in very concise terms: 'Before long you shall have your turn. This is the freedom of that assembly in which one declared his vote under a dagger pointed at him.'"

[136] In reading this all socialist and communists and other potential manipulators of democracy would have taken and will continue to take note. Once the hidden combination can manage to invest all the different, in theory opponent, parties with their own men, an eternal control by a hidden mafia can now take place. (SR).

[137] Such procedures set a precedence for 200 years of 'guided democracy' in many trade unions and elsewhere. (SR).

CHAPTER II. THE DEPARTMENTS .– THE EPEDEMIC AND CONTAGIOUS CHARACTER OF THE REVOLUTIONARY DISEASE.

In the departments, it is by hundreds that we enumerate days like the 20th of June, August 10, September 2. The body has its epidemic, its contagious diseases; the mind has the same; the revolutionary malady is one of them. It appears throughout the country at the same time; each infected point infects others. In each city, in each borough, the club is a Center of inflammation which disorganizes the sound parts; and the example of each disorganized Center spreads afar like contagious fumes.[1] Everywhere the same fever, delirium, and convulsions mark the presence of the same virus. That virus is the Jacobin dogma. By virtue of the Jacobin dogma, theft, usurpation, murder, take on the guise of political philosophy, and the gravest crimes against persons, against public or private property, become legitimate; for they are the acts of the legitimate supreme power, the power that has the public welfare in its keeping.

I. The Sovereignty of the People..

Its principle is the Jacobin dogma of the sovereignty of the people. – – The new right is officially proclaimed. — Public statement of the new régime. — Its object, its opponents, its methods. — Its extension from Paris to the provinces.–

That each Jacobin band should be invested with the local dictatorship in its own canton is, according to the Jacobins, a natural right. It becomes the written law from the day that the National Assembly declares the country in danger. "From that date," says their most widely read Journal,[2] and by the mere fact of that declaration, "the people of France are assembled and insurgent. They have repossessed themselves of the sovereign power." Their magistrates, their deputies, all constituted authorities, return to nothingness, their essential state. And you, temporary and revocable representatives, "you are nothing but presiding officers for the people; you have nothing to do but to collect their votes, and to announce the result when these shall have been cast with due solemnity." — Nor is this the theory of the Jacobins only; it is also official theory. The National Assembly approves of the insurrection, recognizes the Commune, keeps in the background, abdicates as far as possible, and only remains provisionally in office in order that the place may not be left vacant. It abstains from exercising power, even to provide its own successors; it merely "invites" the French people to organize a national convention; it confesses that it has "no right to put the exercise of sovereign power under binding rules"; it does no more than "indicate to citizens" the rules for the elections "to which it invites them to conform."[3] Meanwhile it is subject to the will of the sovereign people, then so–called; it dares not resist their crimes; it interferes with assassins only by entreaties. — Much more; it authorizes them, either by ministerial signature or counter– signature, to begin their work elsewhere. Roland has signed Fournier's commission to Orleans; Danton has sent the circular of Marat over all France. To reconstruct the departments the council of ministers sends the most infuriated members of the Commune and the party, Chaumette, Fréron, Westerman, Auduoin, Huguenin, Momoro, Couthon, Billaud– Varennes,[4] and others still more tainted and brutal, who preach the purest Jacobin doctrine. "They announce openly[5] that laws no longer exist; that since the people are sovereign, every one is master; that each fraction of the nation can take such measures as suit it, in the name of the country's safety; that they have the right to tax corn, to seize it in the laborer's fields, to cut off the heads of the farmers who refuse to bring their grain to market." At Lisieux, agrarian law is preached by Fufour and Momoro. At Douai, other preachers from Paris say to the popular club, "Prepare scaffolds; let the walls of the city bristle with gallows, and hang upon them every man who does not accept our opinions." — Nothing is more logical, more in conformity with their principles. The journals, deducing their consequences, explain to the people the use they ought to make of their reconquered sovereignty.[6] "Under the present circumstances, community of property is the law; everything belongs to everybody." Besides, "an equalizing of fortunes must be brought about, a leveling, which shall abolish the vicious principle of the domination of the rich over the poor." This reform is all the more pressing because "the people, the real sovereign people, have nearly as many enemies as there are proprietors, large merchants, financiers, and wealthy men. In a time of revolution, we must regard all men who have more than enough as the enemies, secret or avowed, of popular government." Therefore, "let the people of each commune, before they quit their homes" for the army, "put all those who are suspected of not loving liberty in a secure place, and under the safe–keeping of the law; let them be kept shut up until war is over; let them be guarded with pikes," and let each one of their guardians receive thirty sous per day.

* As for the partisans of the fallen government, the members of the Paris directory, "with Roederer and Blondel at their head,"

* as for the general officers, "with Lafayette and d'Affry at their head,"

* as for "the critical deputies of the Constituent Assembly, with Barnave and Lameth at their head,"

* as for the Feuillant deputies of the Legislative Assembly, "with Ramond and Jaucourt at their head,"[7]

* as for "all those who consented to soil their hands with the profits of the civil list,"

* as for "the 40,000 hired assassins who were gathered at the palace on the night of August 9–10,

they are all (say the Jacobins)furious monsters, who ought to be strangled to the last one. People! you have risen to your feet; stand firm until not one of these conspirators remains alive. Your humanity requires you for once to show yourselves inexorable. Strike terror to the wicked. The proscriptions which we impose on you as a duty, are the sacred wrath of your country."

There is no mistaking this; it is a tocsin sounding against all the powers that be, against all social superiority, against priests and nobles, proprietors, capitalists, the leaders of business and industry; it is sounding, in short, against the whole élite of France, whether of old or recent origin. The Jacobins of Paris, by their journals, their examples, their missionaries, give the signal; and in the provinces their kindred spirits, imbued with the same principles, only wait the summons to hurl themselves forward.

II.

In several departments it establishes itself in advance. An instance of this in the Var.

In many departments[8] they have forestalled the summons. In the Var, for example, pillages and proscriptions have begun with the month of May. According to custom, they first seize upon the castles and the monasteries, although these have become national property, at one time alleging as a reason for this that the administration "is too slow in carrying out sentence against the émigrés," and again, that "the château, standing on an eminence, weighs upon the inhabitants."[9] There is scarcely a village in France that does not contain twoscore wretches who are always ready to line their pockets, which is just the number of thieves who thoroughly sacked the château of Montaroux, carrying off "furniture, produce, clothing, even the jugs and bottles in the cellar." There are the same doings by the same band at the chateau of Tournon; the château of Salerne is burned, that of Flagose is pulled down; the canal of Cabris is destroyed; then the convent of Montrieux, the châteaux of

Grasse, of Canet, of Régusse, of Brovaz, and many others, all devastated, and the devastations are made "daily." — It is impossible to suppress this country brigandage. The reigning dogma, weakening authority in the magistrates' hands, and the clubs, "which cover the department," have spread the fermentation of anarchy everywhere. "Administrators, judges, municipal officers, all who are invested with any authority, and who have the courage to use it in forcing respect for law, are one by one denounced by public opinion as enemies of the constitution and of liberty; because, people say, they talk of nothing but the law, as if they did not know that the will of the people makes the law, and that we are the people."[10] This is the real principle; here, as at Paris, it instantly begets its consequences. "In many of these clubs nothing is discussed but the plundering of estates and cutting off the heads of aristocrats. And who are designated by this infamous title? In the cities, the great traders and rich proprietors; in the country, those whom we call the bourgeois; everywhere, all peaceable citizens, the friends of order, who wish to enjoy, under the shadow of the protecting law, the blessings of the Constitution. Such was the rage of their denunciations that in one of these clubs a good and brave peasant was denounced as an aristocrat; the whole of his aristocracy consisting in his having said to those who plundered the château of their seigneur, already mentioned, that they would not enjoy in peace the fruits of their crime." — Here is the Jacobin programme of Paris in advance, namely, the division of the French into two classes, the spoliation of one, the despotism of the other; the destruction of the well-to-do, orderly and honest under the dictation of those who are not so.

Here, as in Paris, the programme is carried out step by step. At Beausset, near Toulon, a man named Vidal, captain of the National Guard, "twice set at liberty by virtue of two consecutive amnesties,"[11] punishes not resistance merely, but even murmurs, with death. Two old men, one of them a notary, the other a turner, having complained of him to the public prosecutor, the general alarm is beaten, a gathering of armed men is formed in the street, and the complainants are clubbed, riddled with balls, and their bodies thrown into a pit. Many of their friends are wounded, others take to flight; seven houses are sacked, and the municipality, "either overawed or in complicity," makes no interference until all is over. There is no way of pursuing the guilty ones; the foreman of the jury, who goes, escorted by a thousand men, to hold an inquest, can get no testimony. The municipal officers feign to have heard nothing, neither the general alarm nor the guns fired under their windows. The other witnesses say not a word; but they declare, sotto voce, the reason for their silence. If they should testify, "they would be sure of being killed as soon as the troops should have gone away." The foreman of the jury is himself menaced; after remaining three-quarters of an hour, he finds it prudent to leave the city. — After this the clubs of Beausset and of the neighborhood, gaining hardihood from the impotence of the law, break out into incendiary propositions: "It is announced that after the troops retreat, nineteen houses more will be sacked; it is proposed to behead all aristocrats, that is to say, all the land-owners in the country." Many have fled, but their flight does not satisfy the clubs. Vidal orders those of Beausset who took refuge in Toulon to return at once; otherwise their houses will be demolished, and that very day, in fact, by way of warning, several houses in Beausset, among them that of a notary, are either pulled down or pillaged from top to bottom; all the riff-raff of the town are at work, "half-drunken men and women," and, as their object is to rob and drink, they would like to begin again in the principal town of the canton. — The club, accordingly, has declared that "Toulon would soon see a new St. Bartholomew"; it has allies there, and arrangements are made; each club in the small towns of the vicinity will furnish men, while all will march under the leadership of the Toulon club. At Toulon, as at Beausset, the municipality will let things take their course, while the proceedings complained of by the public prosecutor and the district and department administrators will be applied to them. They may send reports to Paris, and denounce patriots to the National Assembly and the King, if they choose; the club will reply to their scribbling with acts. Their turn is coming. Lanterns and sabers are also found at Toulon, and the faction murders them because they have lodged complaints against the murderers.

III.

Each Jacobin band a dictator in its own neighborhood. —Saint–Afrique during the interregnum.

By what it dared to do when the government still stood on its feet we may we may imagine what it will do during the interregnum. Facts, then, as always, furnish the best picture, and, to obtain a knowledge of the new sovereign, we must first observe him on a limited stage.

On the reception of the news of the 10th of August, the Jacobins of Saint–Afrique, a small town of the Aveyron,[12] likewise undertook to save the country, and, to this end, like their fellows in other boroughs of the district, they organized themselves into an "Executive Power." This institution is of an old date, especially in the South; it had flourished for eighteen months from Lyons to Montpellier, from Agen to Nîmes; but after the interregnum, its condition is still more flourishing; it consists of a secret society, the object of which is to carry out practically the motions and instructions of the club.[13] Ordinarily, they work at night, wearing masks or slouched hats, with long hair falling over the face. A list of their names, each with a number opposite to it, is kept at the meeting–place of the society. A triangular club, decked with a red ribbon, serves them both as weapon and badge; with this club, each member "may go anywhere," and do what seems good to him. At Saint–Afrique they number about eighty, among whom must be counted the rascals forming the seventh company of Tarn, staying in the town; their enrollment in the band is effected by constantly "preaching pillage to them," and by assuring them that the contents of the châteaux in the vicinity belong to them.[14] — Not that the châteaux excite any fear; most of them are empty; neither in Saint–Afrique nor in the environs do the men of the ancient régime form a party; for many months orthodox priests and the nobles have had to fly, and now the well–to–do people are escaping. The population, however, is Catholic; many of the shop–keepers, artisans, and farmers are discontented, and the object now is to make these laggards keep step. — In the first place, they order women of every condition, work–girls and servants, to attend mass performed by the sworn curé, for, if they do not, they will be made acquainted with the cudgel. — In the second place, all the suspected are disarmed; they enter their houses during the night in force, unexpectedly, and, besides their gun, carry off their provisions and money. A certain grocer who persists in his lukewarmness is visited a second time; seven or eight men, one evening, break open his door with a stick of timber; he takes refuge on his roof, dares not descend until the following day at dawn, and finds that everything in his store has been either stolen or broken to pieces.[15] In the third place, there is "punishment of the ill–disposed." At nine o'clock in the evening a squad knocks at the door of a distrusted shoemaker; it is opened by his apprentice; six of the ruffians enter, and one of them, showing a paper, says to the poor fellow:

"I come on the part of the Executive Power, by which you are condemned to a beating."

"What for?"

"If you have not done anything wrong, you are thinking about it."[16]

And so they beat him in the presence of his family. Many others like him are seized and unmercifully beaten on their own premises. — As to the expenses of the operation, these must be defrayed by the malevolent. These, therefore, are taxed according to their occupations; this or that tanner or dealer in cattle has to pay 36 francs; another, a hatter, 72 francs; otherwise "they will be attended to that very night at nine o'clock." Nobody is exempt, if he is not one of the band. Poor old men who have nothing but a five-franc assignat are compelled to give that; they take from the wife of an unskilled laborer, whose savings consist of seven sous and a half, the whole of this, exclaiming, "that is good for three mugs of wine."[17] When money is not to be had, they take goods in kind; they make short work of cellars, bee-hives, clothes-presses, and poultry-yards. They eat, drink, and break, giving themselves up to it heartily, not only in the town, but in the neighboring villages. One detachment goes to Brusque, and proceeds so vigorously that the mayor and syndic-attorney scamper off across the fields, and dare not return for a couple of days.[18] At Versol, the dwelling of the sworn curé, and at Lapeyre, that of the sworn vicar, are both sacked; the money is stolen and the casks are emptied. In the house of the curé of Douyre, "furniture, clothes, cabinets, and window-sashes are destroyed"; they feast on his wine and the contents of his cupboard, throw away what they could not consume, then go in search of the curé and his brother, a former Carthusian, shouting that "their heads must be cut off; and sausage- meat made of the rest of their bodies!" Some of them, a little shrewder than the others, light on a prize; for example, a certain Bourguière, a trooper of the line, seized a vineyard belonging to an old lady, the widow of a physician and former mayor;[19] he gathered in its crop, "publicly in broad daylight," for his own benefit, and warns the proprietress that he will kill her if she makes a complaint against him, and, as she probably does complain of him, he obliges her, in the name of the Executive Power, to pay him fifty crowns damages. — As to the common Jacobin gangsters, their reward, besides food and drink, is perfect licentiousness. In all houses invaded at eleven o'clock in the evening. Whilst the father flies, or the husband screams under the cudgel, one of the villains stations himself at the entrance with a drawn saber in his hands, and the wife or daughter remains at the mercy of the others; they seize her by the neck and maintain their hold.[20] In vain does she scream for help. "Nobody in Saint-Afrique dares go outdoors at night"; nobody comes, and, the following day, the juge-de-paix dares not receive the complaint, because "he is afraid himself." — Accordingly, on the 23rd of September, the municipal officers and the town-clerk, who made their rounds, were nearly beaten to death with clubs and stones; on the 10th of October another municipal officer was left for dead; a fortnight before this, a lieutenant of volunteers, M. Mazières, "trying to do his duty, was assassinated in his bed by his own men." Naturally, nobody dares whisper a word, and, after two months of this order of things, it may be presumed that at the municipal elections of the 21st of October, the electors will be docile. In any event, as a precaution, their notification eight days before, according to law, is dispensed with; as extra precaution, they are informed that if they do not vote for the Executive Power, they will have to do with the triangular cudgel.[21] Consequently, most of them abstain; in a town of over 600 active citizens, 40 votes give a majority; Bourgougnon and Sarrus, the two chiefs of the Executive Power, are elected, one mayor, and the other syndic-attorney, and henceforth the authority they seized by force is conferred on them by the law.

IV.

Ordinary practices of the Jacobin dictatorship. – The stationary companies of the clubs. – Their personnel. – Their leaders.

This is roughly the type of government which spring up in every commune of France after the 10th of August; the club reigns, but the form and processes of its dictatorship are different, according to circumstances. — Sometimes it operates directly through an executive gang or by lancing an excited mob; sometimes it operates indirectly through the electoral assembly it has had elected, or through the municipality, which is its accomplice. If the administrations are Jacobin, it governs through them. If they are passive, it governs alongside of them. If they are refractory, it purges them,[22] or breaks them up,[23] and, to put them down, it resorts not only to blows, but even to murder[24] and massacre.[25] Between massacre and threats, all intermediaries meet, the revolutionary seal being everywhere impressed with inequalities of relief.

In many places, threats suffice. In regions where the temperament of the people is cool, and where there is no resistance, it is pointless to resort to assault and battery. What is the use is killing in a town like Arras, for instance, where, on the day of the civic oath, the president of the department, a prudent millionaire, stalks through the streets arm in arm with Aunty Duchesne, who sells cookies down in a cellar, where, on election days, the townspeople, through cowardice, elect the club candidates under the pretense that "rascals and beggars" must be sent off to Paris to purge the town of them![26] It would be labor lost to strike people who grovel so well.[27] The faction is content to mark them as mangy curs, to put them in pens, keep them on a leash, and to annoy them.[28] It posts at the entrance of the guard–room a list of inhabitants related to an émigré; it makes domiciliary visits; it draws up a fancied list of the suspected, on which list all that are rich are found inscribed. It insults and disarms them; it confines them to the town; it forbids them to go outside of it even on foot; it orders them to present themselves daily before its committee of public safety; it condemns them to pay their taxes for a year in twenty–four hours; it breaks the seals of their letters; it confiscates, demolishes, and sells their family tombs in the cemeteries. This is all in order, as is the religious persecution,

* with the irruption into private chapels where mass is said,

* with blows with gun–stocks and the fist bestowed on the officiating priest,

* with the obligation of orthodox parents to have their children baptized by the schismatic curé,

* with the expulsion of nuns, and

* with the pursuit, imprisonment and transportation of unsworn ecclesiastics.

But if the domination of the club is not always a bloody one, the judgments are always those of an armed man, who, putting his gun to his shoulder, aims at the wayfarers whom he has stopped on the road. Generally they kneel down, tender their purses, and the shot is not fired. But the gun is cocked, nevertheless, and, to be certain of this, we have only to look at the shriveled hand grasping the trigger. We are reminded of those swarms of banditti which infested the country under the ancient regime;[29] the double–girdle of smugglers and receivers embraced within twelve hundred leagues of internal excise– duties, the poachers abounding on the four hundred leagues of guarded captaincies, the deserters so numerous that in eight years they amounted to sixty thousand, the beggars with which the prisons overflowed, the thousands of thieves and vagabonds thronging the highways, quarry of the police which the Revolution let loose and armed, and which, in its turn, from being prey, became the hunters of game. For three years these strong–armed prowlers have served as the hard–core of local jacqueries; at the present time they form the staff of the universal jacquerie. At Nîmes,[30] the head of the Executive Power is a "dancing–master." The two leading demagogues of Toulouse are a shoemaker, and an actor who plays valets.[31] At Toulon,[32] the club, more absolute than any Asiatic despot, is recruited from among the destitute, sailors, harbor–hands, soldiers, "stray peddlers," while its president, Sylvestre, sent down from Paris, is a criminal of the lowest degree. At Rheims,[33] the principal leader is an unfrocked priest, married to a nun, aided by a baker, who, an old soldier, came near being hung. Elsewhere,[34] it is some deserter tried for robbery; here, a cook or innkeeper, and there, a former lackey The oracle of Lyons is an ex–commercial traveler, an emulator of Marat, named Châlier, whose murderous delirium is complicated with morbid mysticism. The acolytes of Châlier are a barber, a hair–dresser, an old–clothes dealer, a mustard and vinegar manufacturer, a cloth– dresser, a silk–worker, a gauze–maker, while the time is near when authority is to fall into still meaner hands, those of "the dregs of the female population," who, aided by "a few bullies," elect " female commissaries," tax food, and for three days pillage the warehouses.[35] Avignon has for its masters the Glacière bandits. Arles is under the yoke of its porters and bargemen. Marseilles belongs to "a band of wretches spawned out of houses of debauchery, who recognize neither laws nor magistrates, and ruling the city through terror."[36] — It is not surprising that such men, invested with such power, use it in conformity with their nature, and that the interregnum, which is their reign, spreads over France a circle of devastations, robberies, and murders.

V.

The companies of traveling volunteers. — Quality of the recruits.— Election of officers. –Robberies and murders.

Usually, the stationary band of club members has an auxiliary band of the same species which roves about. I mean the volunteers, who inspire more fear and do more harm, because they march in a body and are armed.[37] Like their brethren in the ordinary walks of life, many of them are town and country vagabonds; most of them, living from hand to mouth, have been attracted by the pay of fifteen sous a day; they have become soldiers for lack of work and bread.[38] Each commune, moreover, having been called upon for its army contingent, "they have picked up whatever could be found in the towns, all the scamps hanging around street–corners, men with no pursuit, and, in the country, wretches and vagabonds of every description; nearly all have been forced to march by money or drawing lots," and it is probable that the various administrations thought that "in this way they would purge France."[39] To the wretched "bought by the communes," add others of the same stamp, procured by the rich as substitutes for their sons.[40] Thus do they pick over the social dunghill and obtain at a discount the natural and predestined inmates of houses of correction, poor–houses and hospitals, with an utter disregard of quality, even physical, "the halt, the maimed and the blind," the deformed and the defective, "some too old, and others too young and too feeble to support the fatigues of war, others so small as to stand a foot lower than their guns," a large number of boys of sixteen, fourteen, and thirteen; in short, the reprobate of great cities as we now see him, stunted, puny, and naturally insolent and insurgent.[41] "One–third of them are found unfit for service" on reaching the frontier.[42] — But, before reaching the frontier, they act like "pirates" on the road. — The others, with sounder bodies and better hearts, become, under the discipline of constant danger, good soldiers at the end of a year. In the mean time, however, they make no less havoc, for, if they are less disposed to robbery, they are more fanatical. Nothing is more delicate than the military organization, owing to the fact that it represents force, and man is always tempted to abuse force; for any free company of soldiers to remain inoffensive in a civil community, it must be restrained by the strongest curbs, which curbs, either within or without, were wholly wanting with the volunteers of 1792.[43]

Artisans, peasants, the petty bourgeois class, youthful enthusiasts stimulated by the prevailing doctrine, they are still much more Jacobin than patriotic; the dogma of popular sovereignty, like a heady wine, has turned their inexperienced brains; they are fully persuaded that, "destined to contend with the enemies of the republic, is an honor which permits them to exact and to dare all things."[44] The least among them believes himself superior to the law, "as formerly a Condé,[45]" and he becomes king on a small scale, self-constituted, an autocratic justiciary and avenger of wrongs, a supporter of patriots and the scourge of aristocrats, the disposer of lives and property, and, without delay or formality, taking it upon himself to complete the Revolution on the spot in every town he passes through. — He is not to be hindered in all this by his officers. "Having created his chiefs, they are of no more account to him than any of a man's creations usually are"; far from being obeyed, the officers are not even respected, "and that comes from resorting to analogies without considering military talent or moral superiority."[46] Through the natural effects of the system of election, all grades of rank have fallen upon demagogues and blusterers.

"The intriguers, loud-talkers, and especially the great boozers, have prevailed against the capable."[47]

Besides, to retain his popularity, the new officer will go to a bar and drink with his men,[48] and he must show himself more Jacobin than they are, from which it follows that, not content with tolerating their excesses, he provokes them. — Hence, after March, 1792, and even before,[49] we see the volunteers behaving in France as in a conquered country. Sometimes they make domiciliary visits, and break everything to pieces in the house they visit. Sometimes, they force the re-baptism of infants by the conventionalist curé, and shoot at the traditional father. Here, of their own accord, they make arrests; there, they join in with mutineers and stop grain-boats; elsewhere, they force a municipality to tax bread; farther on, they burn or sack châteaux, and, if a mayor happens to inform them that the château now belongs to the nation and not to an émigré; they reply with "thrusts," and threaten to cut his throat.[50] As the 10th of August draws near, the phantom of authority, which still occasionally imposed on them, completely vanishes, and "they risk nothing in killing" whoever displeases them.[51] Exasperated by the perils they are about to encounter on the frontier, they begin war in the interior. Provisionally, and as a precaution, they slaughter probable aristocrats on the way, and treat the officers, nobles and priests they meet on the road worse than their club allies. For, on the one hand, being merely on the march, they are much safer from punishment than local murderers; in a week, lost in the army, they will not be sought for in camp, and they may slay with perfect security. On the other hand, as they are strangers and newcomers, they are not able, like local persons, to identify a person. So on account of a name, a dress, qualifications, a coffee-house rumor, or an appearance, however venerable and harmless a man may be, they kill him, not because they know him, but because they do not know him.

VI.

A tour of France in the cabinet of the Minister of the Interior. — From Carcassonne to Bordeaux.— Bordeaux to Caen. — The north and the east. — Châlons–sur–Marne to Lyons. — The Comtat and Provence. — The tone and the responses of the Jacobin administration. — The programme of the party.

Let us enter the cabinet of Roland, Minister of the Interior, a fortnight after the opening of the Convention, and suppose him contemplating, some evening, in miniature, a picture of the state of the country administered by him. His clerks have placed the correspondence of the past few weeks on his table, arranged in proper order; his replies are noted in brief on the margin; he has a map of France before him, and, placing his finger on the southern section, he moves it along the great highway across the country. At every stage he recurs to the paper file of letters, and passing innumerable reports of violence, he merely gives his attention to the great revolutionary exploits.[52] Madame Roland, I imagine, works with her husband, and the couple, sitting together alone under the lamp, ponder over the doings of the ferocious brute which they have set free in the provinces the same as in Paris.

Their eyes go first to the southern extremity of France. There,[53] on the canal of the Deux–Mers, at Carcassonne, the population has seized three boats loaded with grain, demanded provisions, then a lower prices of bread, then guns and cannon from the magazine, and, lastly, the heads of the administrators; an inspector–general has been wounded by an axe, and the syndic–attorney of the department, M. Verdie; massacred. — The Minister follows with his eye the road from Carcassonne to Bordeaux, and on the right and on the left he finds traces of blood. At Castres,[54] a report is spread that a dealer in grain was trying to raise the price, whereupon a mob gathers, and, to save the dealer, he is placed in the guard–house. The volunteers, however, force open the guard–house, and throw the man out of the first–story window; they then finish him off with "blows with clubs and weights," drag his body along the street and cast it into the river. — The evening before, at Clairac,[55] M. Lartigue–Langa, an unsworn priest, pursued through the street by a troop of men and women, who wanted to remove his cassock and set him on an ass, found refuge, with great difficulty, in his country–house. They go there for him, however, fetch him back to the public promenade, and there they kill him. A number of brave fellows who interfered were charged with incivism, and severely handled. Repression is impossible; the department writes to the Minister that "at this time it would be impolitic to follow the matter up." Roland knows that by experience. The letters in his hands show him that there, as in Paris, murder engenders murder. M. d'Alespée; a gentleman, has just been assassinated at Nérac; "all reputable citizens formed around him a rampart with their bodies," but the rabble prevailed, and the murderers, "through their obscurity," escaped. — The Minister's finger stops at Bordeaux. There the federation festivities are marked with a triple assassination.[56] In order to let this dangerous moment pass by, M. de Langoiran, vicar–general of the archbishopric, had retired half a league off; in the village of Cauderan, to the residence of an octogenarian priest, who, like himself; had never meddled with public matters. On the 15th of July the National Guards of the village, excited by the speeches of the previous night, have come to the residence to pick them up, and moreover, a third priest belonging in the neighborhood. There is nothing to lay to their charge; neither the municipal officers, nor the justices before whom they are brought, can avoid declaring them innocent. As a last recourse, they are conducted to Bordeaux, before the Directory of the department. But it is getting dark, and the riotous crowd becoming impatient, makes an attack on them. The octogenarian "receives so many blows that he cannot recover"; the abbé du Puy is knocked down and dragged along by a rope attached to his feet; M. de Langoirac's head is cut off, carried about on a pike, taken to his house and presented to the servant, who is told that "her master will not come home to supper." The torment of the priests has lasted from five o'clock in the morning to seven o'clock in the evening, and the municipal authorities were duly advised; but they cannot put themselves out of the way to give succor; they are too seriously occupied in erecting a liberty-pole.

Route from Bordeaux to Caen. — The Minister's finger turns to the north, and stops at Limoges. The day following the federation has been here celebrated the same as at Bordeaux.[57] An unsworn priest, the abbé Chabrol, assailed by a gang of men and women, is first conducted to the guard-house and then to the dwelling of the juge-de- paix; for his protection a warrant of arrest is gotten out, and he is kept under guard, in sight, by four chasseurs, in one of the rooms. But the populace are not satisfied with this. In vain do the municipal officers appeal to it, in vain do the gendarmes interpose themselves between it and the prisoner; it rushes in upon them and disperses them. Meanwhile, volleys of stones smash in the windows, and the entrance door yields to the blows of axes; about thirty of the villains scale the windows, and pass the priest down like a bale of goods. A few yards off, "struck down with clubs and other instruments," he draws his last breath, his head "crushed" by twenty mortal wounds. — Farther up, towards Orleans, Roland reads the following dispatches, taken from the file for Loiret:[58] "Anarchy is at its height," writes one of the districts to the Directory of the department; "there is no longer recognition of any authority; the administrators of the district and of the municipalities are insulted, and are powerless to enforce respect. . . . Threats of slaughter, of destroying houses and giving them up to pillage prevail; plans are made to tear down all the châteaux. The municipal authorities of Achères, along with many of the inhabitants, have gone to Oison and Chaussy, where everything is smashed, broken up and carried off On the 16th of September six armed men went to the house of M. de Vaudeuil and obliged him to return the sum of 300 francs, for penalties pretended to have been paid by them. We have been notified that M. Dedeley will be visited at Achères for the same purpose to- day. M. de Lory has been similarly threatened. . . Finally, all those people there say that they want no more local administrations or tribunals, that the law is in their own hands, and they will execute it. In this extremity we have decided on the only safe course, which is to silently accept all the outrages inflicted upon us. We have not called upon you for protection, for we are well aware of the embarrassment you labor under." — The best part of the National Guard, indeed, having been disarmed at the county-town, there is no longer an armed force to put riots down. Consequently, at this same date,[59] the populace, increased by the afflux of "strangers" and ordinary nomads, hang a corn-inspector, plant his head on the end of a pike, drag his body through the streets, sack five houses and burn the furniture of a municipal officer in front of his own door. Thereupon, the obedient municipality sets the arrested rioters free, and lowers the price of bread one-sixth. Above the Loire, the dispatches of Orne and Calvados complete the picture. "Our district," writes a lieutenant of the gendarmerie,[60] "is a prey to brigandage. . . About thirty rascals have just sacked the château of Dampierre. Calls for men are constantly made upon us," which we cannot satisfy, "because the call is general on all sides." The details are curious, and here, notwithstanding the Minister's familiarity with popular misdeeds, he cannot avoid noting one extortion of a new species. "The inhabitants of the villages[61] collect together, betake themselves to different chateaux, seize the wives and children of their proprietors, and keep them as bail for promises of reimbursement which they force the latter to sign, not merely for feudal taxes, but, again, for expenses to which this taxation may have given rise," first under the actual proprietor and then under his predecessors; in the mean time they install themselves on the premises, demand payments for their time, devastate the buildings on the place, and sell the furniture. — All this is accompanied with the usual slaughter. The Directory of the department of Orne advises the Minister[62] that "a former noble has been killed (homicide) in the canton of Sepf, an ex–curé in the town of Bellême, an unsworn priest in the canton of Putanges, an ex– capuchin in the territory of Alençon." The same day, at Caen, the syndic–attorney of Calvados, M. Bayeux, a man of sterling merit, imprisoned by the local Jacobins, has just been shot down in the street and bayoneted, while the National Assembly was passing a decree proclaiming his innocence and ordering him to be set at liberty.[63]

Route of the East. — At Rouen, in front of the Hôtel–de–ville, the National Guard, stoned for more than an hour, finally fire a volley and kill four men; throughout the department violence is committed in connection with grain, while wheat is stolen or carried off by force;[64] but Roland is obliged to restrict himself; he can note only political disturbances. Besides, he is obliged to hurry up, for murders abound everywhere. In addition to the turmoil of the army and the capital,[65] each department in the vicinity of Paris or near the frontier furnishes its quota of murders. They take place at Gisors, in the Eure, at Chantilly, and at Clermont in the Oise, at Saint–Amand in the Pas–de–Calais, at Cambray in the Nord, at Retel and Charleville in the Ardennes, at Rheims and at Chalons in the Marne, at Troyes in the Aube, at Meaux in Seine–et–Marne, and at Versailles in Seine–et– Oise.[66] — Roland, I imagine, does not open this file, and for a good reason; he knows too well how M. de Brissac and M. Delessart, and the other sixty–three persons killed at Versailles; it was he who signed Fournier's commission, the commander of the murderers. At this very moment he is forced to correspond with this villain, to send him certificates of "zeal and patriotism," and to assign him, over and above his robberies, 30,000 francs to defray the expenses of the operation.[67] — But among the dispatches there are some he cannot overlook, if he desires to know to what his authority is reduced, in what contempt all authority is held, how the civil or military rabble exercises its power, with what promptitude it disposes of the most illustrious and most useful lives, especially those who have been, or are now, in command, the Minister perhaps saying to himself that his turn will come next.

Let us look at the case of M. de la Rochefoucauld. A philanthropist since he was young, a liberal on entering the Constituent Assembly, elected president of the Paris department, one of the most persistent, most generous, and most respected patriots from first to last, — who better deserved to be spared than? Arrested at Gisors[68] by order of the Paris Commune, he left the inn, escorted by the Parisian commissary, surrounded by the municipal council, twelve gendarmes and one hundred National Guards; behind him walked his mother, eighty years of age, his wife following in a carriage; there could be no fear of an escape. But, for a suspected person, death is more certain than a prison; three hundred volunteers of the Orne and the Sarthe departments, on their way through Gisors, collect and cry out: "We must have his head — nothing shall stop us!" A stone hits M. de la Rochefoucauld on the temple; he falters, his escort is broken up, and they finish him with clubs and sabers, while the municipal council "have barely time to drive off the carriage containing the ladies." — Accordingly, national justice, in the hands of the volunteers, has its sudden outbursts, its excesses, its reactions, the effect of which it is not advisable to wait for. For example, at Cambray,[69] a division of foot–gendarmerie had just left the town, and it occurs to them that they had forgotten "to purge the prison". It returns, seizes the keeper, takes him to the Hôtel–de–ville, examines the prison register, sets at liberty those whose crimes seem to it excusable, and provides them with passports. On the other hand, it kills a former royal procureur, on whom addresses are found tainted with "aristocratic principles," an unpopular lieutenant–colonel, and a suspected captain. — However slight or ill–founded a suspicion, so much the worse for the officer on whom it falls! At Charleville,[70] two loads of arms having passed through one gate instead of another, to avoid a bad road, M. Juchereau, inspector of the manufacture of arms and commander of the place, is declared a traitor by the volunteers and the crowd, torn from the hands of the municipal officers, clubbed to the ground, stamped on, and stabbed. His head, fixed to a pike, is paraded through Charleville, then into Mézières, where it is thrown into the river running between the two towns. The body remains, and this the municipality orders to be interred; but it is not worthy of burial; the murderers get hold of it, and cast it into the water that it may join the head. In the meantime the lives of the municipal officers hang by a single thread. One is seized by the throat; another is knocked out of his chair and threatened with hanging, a gun is aimed at him and he is beaten and kicked; subsequently a plot is devised "to cut off their heads and plunder their houses."

He who disposes of lives, indeed, also disposes of property. Roland has only to flick through two or three reports to see how patriotism furnishes a cloak for brutal license and greed. At Coucy, in the department of Aisne,[71] the peasantry of seventeen parishes, assembled for the purpose of furnishing their military quota, rush with a loud clamor to two houses, the property of M. des Fossés, a former deputy to the Constituent Assembly, and the two finest in the town; one of them had been occupied by Henry IV. Some of the municipal officers who try to interfere are nearly cut to pieces, and the entire municipal body takes to flight. M. des Fossés, with his two daughters, succeed in hiding themselves in an obscure corner in the vicinity, and afterwards in a small tenement offered to them by a humane gardener, and finally, after great difficulty, they reach Soissons. Of his two houses, "nothing remains but the walls. Windows, casings, doors, and wainscoting, all are shattered"; twenty thousand francs of assignats in a portfolio are destroyed or carried off; the title–deeds of the property are not to be found, and the damage is estimated at 200,000 francs. The pillage lasted from seven o'clock in the morning to seven o'clock in the evening, and, as is always the case, ended in a fête. The plunderers, entering the cellars, drank "two hogsheads of wine and two casks of brandy; thirty or forty remained dead drunk, and were taken away with considerable difficulty." There is no prosecution, no investigation; the new mayor, who, one month after, makes up his mind to denounce the act, begs the Minister not to give his name, for, he says, "the agitators in the council–general of the Commune threaten, with fearful consequences, whoever is discovered to have written to you."[72] — Such is the ever–present menace under which the gentry live, even when veterans in the service of freedom; Roland, foremost in his files, finds heartrending letters addressed directly to him, as a last recourse. Early in 1789, M. de Gouy d'Arcy[73] was the first to put his pen to paper in behalf of popular rights. A deputy of the noblesse to the Constituent Assembly, he is the first to rally to the Third–Estate; when the liberal minority of the noblesse came and took their seats in the hall of the Communes, he had already been there eight days, and, for thirty months, he "invariably seated himself on the side of the 'Left.'" Senior major–general, and ordered by the Legislative Assembly to suppress the outbreak of the 6,000 insurgents at Noyon, "he kept his rigorous orders in his pocket for ten days"; he endured their insults; he risked his life "to save those of his misguided fellow–citizens, and he had the good fortune not to spill a drop of blood." Exhausted by so much labor and effort, almost dying, ordered into the country by his physicians, "he devoted his income to the relief of poverty"; he planted on his own domain the first liberty tree that was erected; he furnished the volunteers with clothes and arms;

"instead of a fifth, he yielded up a third of his revenue under the forced system of taxation." His children live with him on the property, which has been in the family four hundred years, and the peasantry call him "their father." No one could lead a more tranquil or, indeed, a more meritorious existence. But, being a noble, he is suspected, and a delegate from the Paris Commune denounces him at Compiègne as having in his house two cannon and five hundred and fifty muskets. There is at once a domiciliary visit. Eight hundred men, infantry and cavalry, appear before the chateau d'Arcy in battle array. He meets them at the door and tenders them the keys. After a search of six hours, they find twelve fowling pieces and thirteen rusty pistols, which he has already declared. His disappointed visitors grumble, break, eat and drink to the extent of 2,000 crowns damage.[74] Nevertheless, urged by their leaders they finally retire. But M. de Gouy has 60,000 francs in rentals which would be so much gain to the nation if he would emigrate; this must be effected, by expelling him, and, moreover during his expulsion, they may fill their pockets. For eight days this matter is discussed in the Compiègne club, in the bars, in the barracks, and, on the ninth day, 150 volunteers issue from the town, declaring that they are going to kill M. de Gouy and all who belong to him. Informed of this, he departs with his family, leaving the doors of his house wide open. There is a general pillage for five hours; the mob drink the costly wines, steal the plate, demand horses to carry their booty away, and promise to return soon and take the owner's head. — In effect, on the following morning at four o'clock, there is a new invasion, a new pillage, and, this time, the last one; the servants escape under a fire of musketry, and M. de Gouy, at the request of the villagers, whose vineyards are devastated, is obliged to quit that part of the country.[75] — There is no need to go through the whole file. At Houdainville, at the house of M. de Saint-Maurice, at Nointel, on the estate of the Duc de Bourbon, at Chantilly, on the estate of the Prince de Condé, at the house of M. de Fitz-James, and elsewhere, a certain Gauthier, "commandant of the Paris detachment of Searchers, and charged with the powers of the Committee of Supervision," makes his patriotic circuit, and Roland knows beforehand of what that consists, namely, a dragonnade[76] in regular form on the domains of all nobles, absent or present.[77]

Favorite game is still found in the clergy, more vigorously hunted than the nobles; Roland, charged with the duty of maintaining public order, asks himself how the lives of inoffensive priests, which the law recommends to him, can be protected. — At Troyes, at the house of M. Fardeau, an old non-conformist curé, an altar decked with its sacred vessels is discovered, and M. Fardeau, arrested, refuses to take the civic oath. Torn from his prison, and ordered to shout "Vive la Nation!" he again refuses. On this, a volunteer, borrowing an ax from a baker, chops off his head, and this head, washed in the river, is borne to the Hôtel-de-ville.[78] — At Meaux, a brigade of Parisian gendarmerie murders seven priests, and, as an extra, six ordinary malefactors in confinement.[79] At Rheims, the Parisian volunteers first make way with the post-master and his clerk, both under suspicion because the smell of burnt paper had issued from their chimney, and, next, M. de Montrosier, an old retired officer, which is the opening of the hunt. Afterwards they fall upon two ecclesiastics with pikes and sabers, whom their game-beaters have brought in from the country, then on the former curé of Saint-Jean, and on that of Rilly; their corpses are cut up, paraded through the streets in portions, and burnt in a bonfire; one of the wounded priests, the abbé Alexandre, is thrown in still alive.[80] — Roland recognizes the men of September, who, exposing their still bloody pikes, came to his domicile to demand their wages; wherever the band passes it announces, "in the name of the people," its "plenary power to spread the example of the capital." Now, as 40,000 unsworn priests are condemned by the decree of August 26 to leave their departments in a week and France in a fortnight, shall they be allowed to depart? Eight thousand of them at Rouen, in obedience to the decree, charter transports, which the riotous population of both sides of the Seine prevent from leaving. Roland sees in his dispatches that in Rouen, as elsewhere, they crowd the municipalities for their passports,[81] but that these are often refused. Better still, at Troyes; at Meaux, at Lyons, at Dôle, and in many other towns, the same thing is done as at Paris; they are confined in particular houses or in prisons, at least, provisionally, "for fear that they may congregate under the German eagle"; so that, made rebellious and declared traitors in spite of themselves, they may still remain in their pens subject to the knife. As the exportation of specie is prohibited, those who have procured the necessary coin are robbed of it on the frontier, while others, who fly at all hazards, tracked like wild boars, or run down like hares, escape like the bishop of Barral, athwart bayonets, or like the abbé Guillon, athwart sabers, when they are not struck down, like the abbé Pescheur, by the blows of a gun–stock.[82]

It is soon dawn. The files are too numerous and too large; Roland finds that, out of eighty–three, he can examine but fifty; he must hasten on; leaving the East, his eyes again turn to the South. — On this side, too, there are strange sights. On the 2nd of September, at Châlons–sur–Marne[83], M. Chanlaire, an octogenarian and deaf, is returning, with his prayer–book under his arm, from the Mall, to which he resorted daily to read his prayers. A number of Parisian volunteers who meet him, seeing that he looks like a devotee, order him to shout, "Vive la Liberté" Unable to understand them, he makes no reply. They then seize him by the ears, and, not marching fast enough, they drag him along; his old ears give way, and, excited by seeing blood, they cut off his ears and nose, and thus, the poor old man dripping with blood, they reach the Hôtel–de–Ville. At this sight a notary, posted there as sentinel, and who is a man of feeling, is horror–stricken and escapes, while the other National Guards hasten to shut the iron gates. The Parisians, still dragging along their captive, go to the district and then to the department bureau "to denounce aristocrats"; on the way they continue to strike the tottering old man, who falls down; they then decapitate him, place pieces of his body on pikes, and parade these about. Meanwhile, in this same town, twenty–two gentlemen; at Beaune, forty priests and nobles; at Dijon, eighty–three heads of families, locked up as suspected without evidence or examination, and confined at their own expense two months under pikes, ask themselves every morning whether the populace and the volunteers, who shout death cries through the streets, mean to release them in the same way as in Paris.[84] — A trifle is sufficient to provoke a murder. On the 19th of August, at Auxerre as the National Guard is marching along, three citizens, after having taken the civic oath, "left the ranks," and, on being called back, "to make them fall in," one, either impatient or in ill–humor, "replied with an indecent gesture". The populace, taking it as an insult, instantly rush at them, and shoving aside the municipal body and the National Guards, wound one and kill the other two.[85] A fortnight after, in the same town, several young ecclesiastics are massacred, and "the corpse of one of them remains three days on a manure heap, the relatives not being allowed to bury it." About the same date, in a village of sabot makers, five leagues from Autun, four ecclesiastics provided with passports, among them a bishop and his two grand–vicars, are arrested, then examined, robbed, and murdered by the peasantry. —Below Autun, especially in the district of Roanne, the villagers burn the rent–rolls of national property; the volunteers put property–owners to ransom; both, apart from each other or together, give themselves up "to every excess and to every sort of iniquity against those whom they suspect of incivism under pretense of religious opinions."[86] However preoccupied or upset Roland's mind may be by the philosophic generalities with which it is filled, he has long inspected manufactures in this country; the name of every place is familiar to him; objects and forms are this time clearly defined to his arid imagination, and he begins to see things through and beyond mere words.

Madame Roland rests her finger on Lyons, so familiar to her two years before; she becomes excited against "the quadruple aristocracy of the town, petty nobles, priests, heavy merchants, and limbs of the law; in short, those formerly known as honest folks, according to the insolence of the ancient régime."[87] She may now find an aristocracy of another kind there, that of the gutter. Following the example of Paris, the Lyons clubbists, led by Charlier, have arranged for a massacre on a grand scale of the evil-disposed or suspected Another ringleader, Dodieu, has drawn up a list by name of two hundred aristocrats to he hung; on the 9th of September, women with pikes, the maniacs of the suburbs, bands of "the unknown," collected by the central club,[88] undertake to clean out the prisons. If the butchery is not equal to that of Paris, it is because the National Guard, more energetic, interferes just at the moment when a Parisian emissary, Saint-Charles, reads off a list of names in the prison of Roanne already taken from the prison register. But, in other places, it arrives too late. — Eight officers of the Royal-Pologne regiment, in garrison at Auch, some of them having been in the service twenty and thirty years, had been compelled to resign owing to the insubordination of their men; but, at the express desire of the Minister of War, they had patriotically remained at their posts, and, in twenty days of laborious marching, they had led their regiment from Auch to Lyons. Three days after their arrival, seized at night in their beds, conducted to Pierre-Encize, pelted with stones on the way, kept in secret confinement, and with frequent and prolonged examinations, all this merely put their services and their innocence in stronger light. They are taken from the prison by the Jacobin mob; of the eight, seven are killed in the street, and four priests along with them, while the exhibition of their work by the murderers is still more brazen than at Paris. They parade the heads of the dead all night on the ends of their pikes; they carry them to the Place des Terreaux into the coffee-houses; they set them on the tables and derisively offer them beer; they then light torches, enter the Célestins theater, and, marching on the stage with their trophies, blending real and mock tragedy. — The epilogue is both grotesque and horrible. Roland, at the bottom of the file, finds a letter from his colleague, Danton,[89] who begs him to release the officers, murdered three months ago, "for," says Danton, "if no charge can be found against them, it would be crying injustice to keep them longer in irons." Roland's clerk makes a minute on Danton's letter: "This matter disposed of." At this I imagine the couple looking at each other in silence. Madame Roland may remember that, at the beginning of the Revolution, she herself demanded heads, especially "two illustrious heads," and hoped "that the National Assembly would formally try them, or that some generous Decius"[90] would devote himself to "striking them down."[91] Her prayers are granted. The trial is about to begin in the regular way, and the Decius she has invoked is everywhere found throughout France.

The south-east corner remains, that Provence, described to him by Barbaroux as the last retreat of philosophy and freedom. Roland follows the Rhône down with his finger, and on both banks he finds, as he passes along, the usual characteristic misdeeds. – On the right bank, in Cantal and in the Gard, "the defenders of the country" fill their pockets at the expense of taxpayers designated by themselves;[92] this forced subscription is called "a voluntary gift." "Poor laborers at Nismes were taxed 50 francs, others 200, 300, 900, 1,000, under penalty of devastation and of bad treatment." — In the country near Tarascon the volunteers, returning to the old-fashioned ways of bandits, brandish the saber over the mother's head, threaten to smother the aunt in her bed, hold the child over a deep well, and thus extort from the farmer or proprietor even as much as 4,000 or 5,000 francs. Generally the farmer keeps silent, for, in case of complaint, he is sure to have his buildings burnt and his olive trees cut down.[93] – On the left bank, in the Isère, Lieutenant–colonel Spendeler, seized by the populace of Tullins, was murdered, and then hung by his feet in a tree on the roadside;[94]— in the Drôme, the volunteers of Gard forced the prison at Montélimart and hacked an innocent person to death with a saber;[95] in Vaucluse, the pillaging is general and constant. With all public offices in their hands, and they alone admitted into the National Guard, the old brigands of Avignon, with the municipality for their accomplice, sweep the town and raid about the country; in town, 450,000 francs of "voluntary gifts" are handed over to the Glacière murderers by the friends and relatives of the dead; — in the country, ransoms of 1,000 and 10,000 francs are imposed on rich cultivators, to say nothing of the orgies of conquest and the pleasures of despots, money forcibly obtained in honor of innumerable liberty trees, banquets at a cost of five or six hundred francs, paid for by extorted funds, reveling of every sort and unrestrained havoc on the invaded farms;[96] in short, the abuse drunken force amusing itself with brutality and proud of its violence.

Following this long line of murders and robbery, the Minister reaches Marseilles, and I imagine him stopping at this city some–what dumbfounded. Not that he is in any way astonished at widespread murders; undoubtedly he has had received information of them from Aix, Aubagne, Apt, Brignolles, and Eyguières, while there are a series of them at Marseilles, one in July, two in August, and two in September;[97] but this he must be used to. What disturbs him here is to see the national bond dissolving; he sees departments breaking away, new, distinct, independent, complete governments forming on the basis of popular sovereignty;[98] publicly and officially, they keep funds raised for the central government for local uses; they institute penalties against their inhabitants seeking refuge in France; they organize tribunals, levy taxes, raise troops, and undertake military expeditions.[99] Assembled together to elect representatives to the Convention, the electors of the Bouches–du–Rhône were, additionally, disposed to establish throughout the department "the reign of liberty and equality," and to this effect they found, says one of them, "an army of 1,200 heroes to purge the districts in which the bourgeois aristocracy still raises its bold, imprudent head." Consequently, at Sonas, Noves, St. Remy, Maillane, Eyrages, Graveson, Eyguières, extended over the territory consisting of the districts of Tarascon, Arles and Salon, these twelve hundred heroes are authorized to get a living out of the inhabitants at pleasure, while the rest of the expenses of the expedition are to be borne "by suspected citizens."[100] These expeditions are prolonged six weeks and more; one of them goes outside of the department, to Monosque, in the Basses–Alpes, and Monosque, obliged to pay 104,000 francs to its "saviors and fathers," as an indemnity for traveling expenses, writes to the Minister that, henceforth, it can no longer meet his impositions.

What kind of improvised sovereigns are these who have instituted perambulating brigandage? Roland, on this point, has simply to question his friend Barbaroux, their president and the executive agent of their decrees. "Nine hundred persons," Barbaroux himself writes, "generally of slight education, impatiently listening to conservatives, and yielding all attention to the effervescent, cunning in the diffusion of calumnies, petty suspicious minds, a few men of integrity but unenlightened, a few enlightened but cowardly; many of them patriotic, but without judgment, without philosophy"; in short, a Jacobin club, and Jacobin to such an extent as to "make the hall ring with applause[101] on receiving the news of the September massacre"; in the foremost ranks, "a crowd of men eager for office and money, eternal informers, imagining trouble or exaggerating it to obtain for themselves lucrative commissions;"[102] in other words, the usual pack of hungry appetites in full chase. – To really know them, Roland has only to examine the last file, that of the neighboring departments, and consider their colleagues in Var. In this great wreck of reason and of integrity, called the Jacobin Revolution, a few stray waifs still float on the surface; many of the department administrations are composed of liberals, friends of order, intelligent men, upright and firm defenders of the law. Such was the Directory of Var.[103] To get rid of it the Toulon Jacobins contrived an ambush worthy of the Borgias and Oliverettos of the sixteenth century.[104] On the 28th of July, in the forenoon, Sylvestre, president of the club, distributed among his trusty men in the suburbs and purlieus of the town an enormous sack of red caps, while he posted his squads in convenient places. In the mean time the municipal body, his accomplices, formally present themselves at the department bureau, and invite the administrators to join them in fraternizing with the people. The administrators, suspecting nothing, accompany them, each arm in arm with a municipal officer or delegate of the club. They scarcely reach the square when there rushes upon it from every avenue a troop of red-caps lying in wait. The syndic–attorney, the vice–president of the department, and two other administrators, are seized, cut down and hung; another, M. Debaux, succeeding in making his escape, hides away, scales the ramparts during the night, breaks his thigh and lies there on the ground; he is discovered the next morning; a band, led by Jassaud, a harbor–laborer, and by Lemaille, calling him self "the town hangman," come and raise him up, carry him away in a barrow, and hang him at the first lamppost. Other bands dispatch the public prosecutor in the same fashion, a district administrator, and a merchant, and then, spreading over the country, pillage and slay among the country houses. — In vain has the commandant of the place, M. Dumerbion, entreated the municipality to proclaim martial law. Not only does it refuse, but it enjoins him to order one–half of his troops back to their barracks. By way of an offset, it sets free a number of soldiers condemned to the galleys, and all that are confined for insubordination. — Henceforth every shadow of discipline vanishes, and, in the following month, murders multiply. M. de Possel, a navy administrator, is taken from his dwelling, and a rope is passed around his neck; he is saved just in time by a bombardier, the secretary of the club. M. Senis, caught in his country–house, is hung on the Place du Vieux Palais. Desidery, a captain in the navy, the curé of La Valette, and M. de Sacqui des Thourets, are beheaded in the suburbs, and their beads are brought into town on the ends of three poles. M. de Flotte d'Argenson, vice–admiral, a man of Herculean stature, of such a grave aspect, and so austere that he is nicknamed the "Père Eternel" is treacherously enticed to the entrance of the Arsenal, where he sees the lantern already dropping; he seizes a gun, defends himself; yields to numbers, and after having been slashed with sabers, is hung. M. de Rochemaure, a major–general of marines, is likewise sabred and hung in the same manner; a main artery in the neck, severed by the blow of the saber, spouts blood from the corpse and forms a pool on the pavement; Barry, one of the executioners, washes his hands in it and sprinkles the by–standers as if bestowing a blessing on them. — Barry, Lemaille, Jassaud, Sylvestre, and other leading assassins, the new kings of Toulon, sufficiently resemble those of Paris. Add to these a certain Figon, who gives audience in his garret, straightens out social inequalities, forces the daughters of large farmers to marry poor republicans, and rich young men to marry prostitutes,[105] and, taking the lists furnished by the club or neighboring municipalities, ransoming all the well–to–do and opulent persons inscribed on them. In order that the portraiture of the band may be complete, it must be noted that, on the 23rd of August, it attempted to set free the 1800 convicts; the latter, not comprehending that they were wanted for political allies, did not dare sally forth, or, at least, the reliable portion of the National Guard arrived in time to put their chains on again. But here its efforts cease, and for more than a year public authority remains in the hands of a Jacobin faction which, as far as public order is concerned, does not even have the morals of a convict.

More than once during the course of this long review the Minister must have flushed with shame; for to the reprimands dispatched by him to these apathetic administrations, they reply by citing himself as an example:

"You desire us to denounce the arbitrary arrests to the public prosecutor; have you denounced those guilty of similar and yet greater crimes committed at the capital? "[106] –

From all quarters come the cries of the oppressed appealing to "the patriot Minister, the sworn enemy of anarchy," to "the good and incorruptible Minister of the Interior, his only reproach, the common sense of his wife," and he could only reply with empty phrases and condolences:

"To lament the events which so grievously distress the province, all administrations being truly useful when they forestall evils, it being very sad to be obliged to resort to such remedies, and recommend to them a more active supervision."[107]

"To lament and find consolation in the observations made in the letter," which announces four murders, but calls attention to the fact that "the victims immolated are counter–revolutionaries."[108]

Roland has carried on written dialogues with the village municipalities, and given lessons in constitutional law to communities of pot–breakers.[109] — But, on this territory, he is defeated by his own principles, while the pure Jacobins read him a lesson in turn; they, likewise, are able to deduce the consequences of their own creed.

"Brother and Friend, Sir," write those of Rouen, "not to be always at the feet of the municipality, we have declared ourselves permanent, deliberative sections of the Commune."[110]

Let the so–called constituted authorities, the formalists and pedants of the Executive Council and the Minister of the Interior, look twice before censuring the exercise of popular sovereignty. This sovereign raises his voice and drives his clerks back into their holes; spoliation and murder, all this is just.

"Can you have forgotten that, after the tempest, as you yourself declared in the height of the storm, it is the nation which saves itself? Well, sir, this is what we have done.[111] . . What! when all France was resounding with that long expected proclamation of the abolition of tyranny, you were willing that the traitors, who strove to reestablish it, should escape public prosecution! My God, what century is this in which we find such Ministers!"

Arbitrary taxes, penalties, confiscations, revolutionary expeditions, nomadic garrisons, pillage, what fault can be found with all that?

"We do not pretend that these are legal methods; but, drawing nearer to nature, we demand what object the oppressed have in view in invoking justice. Is it to lag behind and vainly pursue an equitable adjustment which is rendered fleeting by judicial forms? Correct these abuses or do not complain of the sovereign people suppressing them in advance. . . . You, sir, with so many reasons for it, would do well to recall your insults and redeem the wrongs you have inflicted before we happen to render them public." . . . "Citizen Minister, people flatter you; you are told too often that you are virtuous; the moment this gives you pleasure you cease to be so. . . . Discard the astute brigands who surround you, listen to the people, and remember that a citizen Minister is merely the executor of the sovereign will of the people."

However narrow Roland's outlook may be, he must finally comprehend that the innumerable robberies and murders which he has just noted over are not a thoughtless eruption, a passing crisis of delirium, but a manifesto of the victorious party, the beginning of an established system of government. Under this system, write the Marseilles Jacobins,

"to–day, in our happy region, the good rule over the bad, and constitute a party which allows no contamination; whatever is vicious has gone into hiding or has been exterminated."–

The programme is very precise, and acts form its commentary. This is the programme which the faction, throughout the interregnum, sets openly before the electors.

Notes:

[1] Guillon de Montléon, I. 122. Letter of Laussel, dated Paris, 28th of August, 1792, to the Jacobins of Lyons: "Tell me how many heads have been cut off at home. It would be infamous to let our enemies escape." 1792).

[2] "Les Révolutions de Paris," by Prudhomme, Vol. XIII. pp. 59–63 (14th of July, 3 Decrees of the 10th and 11th of August, 1792.

[4] Prudhomme, number of the 15th of September, p. 483. – Mortimer– Ternaux, IV. 430.

[5] Mortimer–Ternaux. IV. II. Fauchet's report, Nov. 6, 1792. – Ib., IV. 91, 142. Discourse of M. Fockedey, administrator of the department of the north, and of M. Bailly, deputy de Seine–et–Marne.

[6] Prudhomme, number of Sept. 1, 1792, pp. 375, 381, 385: number of Sept. 22, pp. 528–530, –Cf. Guillon de Montléon, I. 144. Here are some of the principles announced by the Jacobin leaders of Lyons, Châlier, Laussel, Cusset, Rouillot, etc. "The time has come when this prophecy must be fulfilled: The rich shall be put in the place of the poor, and the poor in the place of the rich." – If a half of their property be left them the rich will still be happy." – "If the laboring people of Lyons are destitute of work and of bread, they can profit by these calamities in helping themselves to wealth in the quarter where they find it." – "No one who is near a sack of wheat can die of hunger. Do you wish the word that will buy all that you want? Slay! – or perish!"

[7] Prudhomme, number for the 28th of August, 1792, pp. 284–287.

[8] Cf.. "The French Revolution," I.346. In ten of the departments the seventh jacquerie continues the sixth without a break. Among other examples, this letter from the administrators of Tarn, June 18, 1792, may be read ("Archives Nationales," F7, 3271). "Numerous bands overran both the city

(Castres) and the country. They forcibly entered the houses of the citizens, broke the furniture to pieces, and pillaged everything that fell into their hands. Girls and women underwent shameful treatment. Commissioners sent by the district and the municipality to advocate peace were insulted and menaced. The pillage was renewed; the home of the citizen was violated." The administrators add: "In many places the progress made by the constitution was indicated by the speedy and numerous emigrations of its enemies."

[9] "Archives Nationales," F7, 3272. Letter of the administrators of the Var, May 27, 1792. —Letter of the minister, Duranthon, May 28.— Letter of the commission composing the directory Oct. 31.

[10] "Archives Nationales," Letter of the administrators of Var, May. 27.— The saying is the summary of the revolutionary spirit; it recurs constantly. — Cf. the Duc de Montpensier, "Mémoires," p. 11. At Aix one of his guards said to the sans—culotte who were breaking into the room where he had been placed: "Citizens, by what order do you enter here? and why have you forced the guard at the door?" One of them. answered: "By order of the people. Don't you know that the people is sovereign?"

[11] "Archives Nationales," letter of the public prosecutor, May 23. – Letters of the administrators of the department, May 22, and 27 (on the events of the 13th of May at Beausset).

[12] "Archives Nationales," F7 3193 and 3194. Previous details may be found in these files. This department is one of those in which the seventh jacquerie is merely a prolongation of the sixth. –Cf. F7, 3193. Letter of the royal Commissioner at Milhau, May 5, 1791.

"The situation is getting worse; the administrative bodies continue powerless and without resources. Most of their members are still unable to enter upon their duties; while the factions, who still rule, multiply their excesses in every direction. Another house in the country, near the town, has been burnt; another broken into, with a destruction of the furniture and a part of the dinner—service, and doors and windows broken open and smashed; several houses visited, under the pretense of arms or powder being concealed in them; all that is found with private persons and dealers not of the factious party is carried off; tumultuous shouts, nocturnal assemblages, plots for pillage or burning; disturbances caused by the sale of grain, searches under this pretext in private granaries, forced prices at current reductions; forty louis taken from a lady retired into the country, found in her trunk, which was broken into, and which, they say, should have been in assignats. The police and municipal officers witnesses of these outrages, are sometimes forced to sanction them with their presence; they neither dare suppress them nor punish the well—known authors of them. Such is a brief statement of the disorders committed in less than eight days." – In relation specially to Saint—Afrique. Cf. F7, 3194, the letter, among others, of the department administrator, march 29, 1792.

[13] "Archives Nationales," F7, 3193. Extract from the registers of the clerk of the juge—de—paix of Saint—Afrique, and report by the department commissioners, Nov. 10, 1792, with the testimony of the witnesses, forming a document of 115 pages.

[14] Deposition of Alexis Bro, a volunteer, and three others.

[15] Deposition of Pons, a merchant. After this devastation he is obliged to address a petition to the executive power, asking permission to remain in the town.

[16] Deposition of Capdenet, a shoemaker.

[17] Depositions of Marguerite Galzeng, wife of Guibal a miller, Pierre Canac and others.

[18] Depositions of Martin, syndic–attorney of the commune of Brusque; Aussel, curé of Versol; Martial Aussel, vicar of Lapeyre and others.

[19] Deposition of Anne Tourtoulon.

[20] Depositions of Jeanne Tuffon, of Marianne Terral, of Marguerite Thomas, of Martin syndic–attorney of the commune of Brusque, of Virot, of Brassier, and othes. The details are too specific to allow quotation.

[21] Depositions ,of Moursol, wool–carder; Louis Grand, district– administrator, and others.

[22] For example, at Limoges, Aug. 16. – Cf. Louis Guibert, "le Parti Girondin dans la Haute–Vienne," p. 14.

[23] Paris, "Histoire de Joseph Lebon," I. 60. Restoration of the Arras municipality. Joseph Lebon is proclaimed mayor Sept. 16.

[24] For example, at Caen and at Carcassonne.

[25] For example, at Toulon.

[26] "Un séjour en France," 19, 29. ("Letters of a Wittness to the French Revolution," translated by H. Taine.1872)

[27] Ibid., p. 38: 2M. de M ——, who had served for thirty years gave up his arms to a boy who treated him with the greatest insolence."

[28] Paris, Ibid., p. 55 and the following pages. – Albert Babeau, "Histoire de Troyes," I. 503–515. – Sausay, III. ch. I.

[29] "The Ancient Régime," 381, 391, 392.

[30] "Archives Nationales," F7, 3217. Letter of Castanet, an old gendarme, Aug. 21 1792.

[31] "Archives Nationales," F7, 3219. Letter of M. Alquier to the first consul, Pluviôse 18, year VIII.

[32] Lauvergne, "Histoire du Var," p. 104.

[33] Mortimer–Ternaux, III. 325, 327.

[34] "Archives–Nationales," F7, 3271. Letter of the Minister of Justice, with official reports of the municipality of Rabastens. "The juge–de–paix of Rabastens was insulted in his place by putting an end to the proceedings commenced against an old deserter at the head of the municipality, and tried for robbery. They threatened to stab the judge if he recommenced the trial. Numerous gangs of vagabonds overrun the country, pillaging and putting to ransom all owners of property. . . The people has been led off by a municipal officer, a constitutional curé, and a brother of sieur Tournal, one of the authors of the evils which have desolated the Comtat." (March 5, 1792).

[35] Guillon de Montléon, I. 84, 109, 139, 155, 158, 464. — Ibid., p.441, details concerning Châlier by his companion Chassagnon. — "Archives Nationales," F7, 3255. Letter by Laussel, Sept. 22, 1792.

[36] Barbaroux, "Mémoires," 85. Barbaroux is an eye–witness, for he has just returned to Marseilles and is about to preside over the electoral assembly of the Bouches–du–Rhône.

[37] C. Rousset, "Les Volontaires," p. 67. — In his report of June 27, 1792, Albert Dubayet estimates the number of volunteers at 84,000.

[38] C. Rousset, "Les Volontaires," 101. Letter of Kellermann, Aug.23, 1792. — " Un séjour en France," I. 347 and following pages. — "Archives Nationales," F7, 3214. Letter of an inhabitant of Nogent–le– Rotrou (Eure). "Out of 8,000 inhabitants one–half require assistance, and two–thirds of these are in a sad state, having scarcely straw enough to sleep on.(Dec. 3, 1792). — In his report of June 27, 1792, Albert Dubayet estimates the number of volunteers at 84,000.

[39] C. Rousset, "Les Volontaires," 106 (Letter of General Biron, Aug. 23, 1792).– — 226, Letter of Vezu, major, July 24, 1793.

[40] C. Rousset, "Les Volontaires," 144 (Letter of a district administrator of Moulins to General Custines, Jan. 27, 1793).— "Un séjour en France," p.27: "I am sorry to see that most the volunteers about to join the army are old men or very young boys." — C. Rousset, Ibid., 74, 108, 226 (Letter of Biron, Nov. 7, 1792); 105 (Letter of the commander of Fort Louis, Aug. 7); 127 (Letter of Captain Motmé). One–third of the 2d battalion of Haute–Saône is composed of children 13 and 14 years old.

[41] Moniteur, XIII. 742 (Sept. 21). Marshal Lückner and his aids–de– camp just miss being killed by Parisian volunteers. — Archives Nationales," BB, 16703. Letter by Labarrière aide–de–camp of General Flers, Antwerp, March 19, 1793. On the desertion en masse of gendarmes from Dumouriez's army, who return to Paris.

[42] Cf. "L'armée et la garde nationale," by Baron Poisson, III. 475. "On hostilities being declared (April, 1792), the contingent of volunteers was fixed at 200,000 men. This second attempt resulted in nothing but confused and disorderly levies. Owing to the spinelessness of the volunteer troops it was impossible to continue the war in Belgium, which allowed the enemy to cross the frontier." — Gouverneur Morris, so well informed, had already written, under date of Dec.27, 1791: "The national

211

guards, who have turned out as volunteers, are in many instances that corrupted scum of overgrown population of which large cities purge themselves, and which, without constitutions to support the fatigues... of war, have every vice and every disease which can render them the scourge of their friends and the laughing stock of their foes." — Buchez et Roux, XXVI. 177. Plan of the administrators of Hérault, presented to the Convention April 27, 1793. "The composition of the enlistment should not be concealed. Most of those of which it is made up are not volunteers; they are not citizens all classes of society, who, submitting to draft on the ballot, have willingly made up their minds to go and defend the Republic. The larger part of the recruits are substitutes who, through the attraction of a large sum, have concluded to leave their homes."

[43] C. Rousset, 47. Letter of the directory of Somme, Feb. 26, 1792.

[44] "Archives Nationales," F 7, 3270. Deliberations of the council– general of the commune of Roye, Oct. 8, 1792 (in relation to the violence committed by two divisions of Parisian gendarmerie during their passage, Oct. 7 and 8).

[45] Moore, I. 338 (Sept. 8, 1792). – (The Condés were proud princes from a branch of the royal house of Bourbon. (SR).

[46] C Rousset, 189 (Letter of the Minister of War, dated at Dunkirk, April 29, 1793). — Archives Nationales," BB, 16, 703. (Parisian national guard staff major–general, order of the day, letter of citizen Férat, commanding at Ostend, to the Minister of War, March 19, 1793): "Since we have had the gendarmes with us at Ostend there is nothing but disturbance every day. They attack the officers and volunteers, take the liberty of pulling off epaulettes and talk only of cutting and slashing, and declare that they recognize no superior being equals with everybody, and that they will do as they please. Those who are ordered to arrest them are chased and attacked with saber cuts and pistols

[47] C. Rousset, 20 (Letter of General Wimpfen, Dec. 30, 1791). — "Souvenirs" of General Pelleport, pp.7 and 8.

[48] C. Rousset, 45 (Report of General Wimpfen, Jan. 20, I792). – Letter of General Biron, Aug. 23, 1792.

[49] C. Rousset, 47, 48. — "Archives Nationales," F7, 3249. Official report of the municipality of Saint–Maxence, Jan. 21, 1792. — F 7, 3275. Official report of the municipality of Châtellerault, Dec. 27, 1791. — F7, 3285 and 3286 — F7, 3213. Letter of Servan, Minister of War, to Roland, June 12, 1792: "I frequently receive, as well as yourself and the Minister of Justice, complaints against the national volunteers. They commit the most reprehensible offenses daily in places where they are quartered, and through which they pass on their way to their destination." – Ibid., Letter of Duranthon, Minister of Justice, May 5: "These occurrences are repeated, under more or less aggravating circumstances, in all the departments."

[50] "Archives Nationales," F7, 3193. Official report of the commissaries of the department of Aveyron, April 4, 1792. "Among the pillagers and incendiaries of the chateaux of Privesac, Vaureilles, Péchins, and other threatened mansions, were a number of recruits who had already taken

the road to Rhodez to join their respective regiments." Nothing remains of the château of Privesac but a heap of ruins. The houses in the village "are filled to over flowing with pillaged articles, and the inhabitants have divided the owners' animals amongst themselves." — Comte de Seilhac, "Scènes et portraits de la Révolution dans le bas Limousin," P.305. Pillage of the châteaux of Saint–Jéal and Seilhac, April 12, 1792, by the 3rd battalion of la Corrèze, commanded by Bellegarde, a former domestic in the château.

[51] "Archives Nationales," F7, 3270. Deliberation of the council– general of the commune of Roye, Oct. 8, 1792 (passage of two divisions of Parisian gendarmes). "The inhabitants and municipal officers were by turns the sport of their insolence and brutality, constantly threatened in case of refusal with having their heads cut off, and seeing the said gendarmes, especially the gunners, with naked sabers in their hands, always threatening. The citizen mayor especially was treated most outrageously by the said gunners . . . forcing him to dance on the Place d'armes, to which they resorted with violins and where they remained until midnight, rudely pushing and hauling him about, treating him as an aristocrat, clapping the red cap on his head, with constant threats of cutting it off and that of every aristocrat in the town, a threat they swore to carry out the next day, openly stating, especially two or three amongst them, that they had massacred the Paris prisoners on the 2nd of September, and that it cost them nothing to massacre."

[52] Summaries, in the order of their date or locality, and similar to those about to be placed before the reader, sometimes occur in these files. I pursue the same course as the clerk, in conformity with Roland's methodical habits.

[53] Aug. 17, 1792 (Moniteur, XIII, 383, report of M. Emmery).

[54] "Archives Nationales," F7, 3271. Letter of the administrators of Tarn, July 21.

[55] "Archives Nationales," F7, 3234. Report of the municipal officers of Clairac, July 20.–Letter of the syndic–attorney of Lot–et–Garonne, Sept. 16.

[56] Mercure de France, number for July 28, (letters from Bordeaux).

[57] "Archives Nationales," F7, 3275. Letter of the administrators of Haute–Vienne, July 28 (with official reports).

[58] '"Archives Nationales," F7, 3223. Letter of the directory of the district of Neuville to the department–administrators, Sept 18.

[59] "Archives Nationales," report of the administrators of the department and council–general of the commune of Orleans, Sept 16 and 17. (The disarmament had been effected through the decrees of Aug.26 and Sept. 2.)

[60] "Archives Nationales," F7, 3249. Letter of the lieutenant of the gendarmerie of Dampierre, Sept 23 (with official report dated Sept 19).

[61] "Archives Nationales," draft of a letter by Roland, Oct 4, and others of the same kind. —Letter of the municipal officers of Ray, Sept 24. — Letter of M. Desdouits, proprietor, Sept 30. — Letter of the permanent council of Aigle, Oct 1, etc.

[62] "Archives Nationales," Letter of the administrators of the Orne department, Sept 7.

[63] Mortimer–Ternaux, III. 337 (Sept. 6).

[64] "Archives Nationales," F7, 3265. Letter of the lieutenant–general of the gendarmerie, Aug. 30. — Official report of the Rouen municipality on the riot of Aug. 29. — Letters of the department–administrators, Sept 18 and Oct. 11. — Letter of the same, Oct 13, etc. — Letter of David, cultivator and department administrator Oct 11.

[65] Albert Babean, "Letters of a deputy of the municipality of Troyes to the army of Dumuriez," p. 8. — (Sainte–Menehould, Sept. 7, 1792): "Our troops burn with a desire to meet the enemy. The massacre reported to have taken place in Paris does not discourage them; on the contrary, they are glad to know that suspected persons in the interior are got rid of."

[66] Moore, I.338 (Sept. 4). At Clermont, the murder of a fish–dealer, killed for insulting the Breton volunteers. — 401 (Sept. 7), the son of the post–master at Saint–Amand is killed on suspicion of communicating with the enemy. — "Archives Nationales," F7; 3249. Letter of the district–administrators of Senlis, Oct. 31 (Aug. 15). At Chantilly, M. Pigean is assassinated in the midst of 1,200 persons. — C. Rousset, p.84 (Sept. 21), lieutenant–colonel Imonnier is assassinated at Châlons–sur–Marne. – Mortimer–Ternaux, IV. 172. Four Prussian deserters are murdered at Rethel, Oct. 5, by the Parisian volunteers

[67] Mortimer–Ternaux, III. 378, 594 and following pages.

[68] Lacretelle, "Dix années d'épreuves," p. 58. Description of Liancourt. – "Archives Nationales," F7, 3249. Letter of the department–administrators of the Eure, Sept. 11 (with official report of the Gisors municipality, Sept 4). – Mortimer–Ternaux, III. 550.

[69] Archives Nationales," F7, 4394. Letter of Roland to the convention, Oct. 31 (with a copy of the documents sent by the department of the Nord on the events of Oct. 10 and 11).

[70] "Archives Nationales," F7, 3191. Official report of the municipality of Charleville; Sept. 4, and letter, Sept. 6.— Moniteur, XIII. 742, number for Sept. 21,1792 (letter of Sept. 17, On the Parisian volunteers of Marshal Lückner's army). "The Parisian volunteers again threatened to have several heads last evening, among others those of the marshal and his aids. He had threatened to return some deserters to their regiments. At this the men exclaimed that the ancient régime no longer existed, that brothers should not be treated in that way, and that he general should be arrested. Several of them had already seized the horse's bridle."

[71] "Archives Nationales," F7, 3185. Documents relating to the case of M. de Fossés. (The pillage takes place Sept. 4.)

[72] Letter of Goulard, mayor of Coucy, Oct. 4. — Letter of Osselin, notary, Nov. 7. "Threats of setting fire to M. de Fossés' two remaining farm-houses are made." — Letter of M. de Fossés, Jan. 28, 1793. He states that he has entered no complaint, and if anybody has done so for him he is much displeased. "A suit might place me in the greatest danger, from my knowledge of the state of the public mind in Coucy, and of what the guilty have done and will do to affect the minds of the people in the seventeen communes concerned in the devastation."

[73] "Archives Nationales," F7, 3249 letter of M. de Gouy to Roland, Sept. 21. (An admirable letter, which, if copied entire, would show the character of the gentleman of 1789. Lots of heart, many illusions and much verbosity.) The first attack was made Sept. 4 and the second on the 13th.

[74] Most of the domiciliary visits end in similar damages. For example, ("Archives Nationales," F7, 3265, letter of the administrators of Seine-Inferieure, Sept. 18, 1792). Visit to the château de Catteville, Sept. 7, by the national guard of the neighborhood. "The national guard get drunk, break the furniture to pieces, and fire repeated volleys at the windows and mirrors; the château is a complete ruin." The municipal officers on attempting to interfere are nearly killed.

[75] The letter ends with the following: "No, never will I abandon the French soil!" He is guillotined at Paris, Thermidor 5, year II., as an accomplice in the pretended prison-plot.

[76] Raid on Protestants under Louis XIV. (SR).

[77] "'Archives Nationales," Letter of the Oise administrators, Sept. 12 and 15. — Letter of the syndic-attorney of the department, Sept. 23. — Letter of the administrators, Sept. 20 (on Chantilly). "The vast treasures of this domain are being plundered." In the forest of Hez and in the park belonging to M. de Fitz-James, now national property, "the finest trees are sold on the spot, cut down, and carried off." – F7, 3268, Letter of the overseer of the national domains at Rambouillet, Oct. 31. Woods devastated "at a loss of more than 100,000 crowns since August 10." — "The agitators who preach liberty to citizens in the rural districts are the very ones who excite the disorders with which the country is menaced. They provoke the demand for a partition of property, with all the accompanying threats."

[78] Albert Babeau, I.504 (Aug.20).

[79] Mortimer–Ternaux, III. 322 (Sept 4).

[80] Mortimer–Ternaux, III.325. –"Archives Nationales," F7, 3239. Official report of the municipality of Rheims, Sept 6.

[81] "Archives Nationales," F7, 4394. Correspondence of the ministers in 1792 and 1793. Lists presented by Roland to the convention, on the part of various districts and departments, containing the names of priests demanding passports to go abroad, those who have gone without passports, and of sick or aged priests in the department asylums.

[82] Albert Babeau, I. 515–517. Guillon de Montléon, I. 120. At Lyons after the 10th of August the

unsworn conceal themselves; the municipality offers them passports; many who come for them are incarcerated; others receive a passport with a mark on it which serves for their recognition on the road, and which excites against them the fury of the volunteers. "A majority of the soldiers filled the air with their cries of 'Death to kings and priests!' " — Sauzay, III. ch. IX., and especially p. 193: "M. Pescheu; while running along the road from Belfort to Porentruy, is seen by a captain of the volunteers, riding along the same road with other officers; demanding his gun, he aimed at M. Pescheur and shot him."

[83] "Histoire de Chalons–sur–Marne et de ses monuments," by L. Barbat, pp. 420, 425

[84] "Archives Nationales," F7, 3207. Letter of the directory of the Côte d'Or, Aug. 28 and Sept. 26. Address of the Beaune municipality, Sept. 2. Letter of M. Jean Sallier, Oct. 9: "Allow me to appeal to you for justice and to interest yourself in behalf of my brother, myself, and five servants, who on the 14th of September last, at the order of the municipality of La Roche–en–Bressy, where we have lived for three years, were arrested by the national guard of Saulieu, and, first imprisoned here in this town, were on the 18th transferred to Semur, no reason for our detention being given, and where we have in vain demanded a trial from the directory of the district, which body, making no examination or inquiry into our case, sent us on the 25th, at great expense, to Dijon, where the department has imprisoned us again without, as before, giving any reason therefore." — The directory of the department writes "the communes of the towns and of the country arrest persons suspected by them, and instead of caring for these themselves, send them to the district" — Such arbitrary imprisonment multiply towards the end of 1792 and early in 1793. The commissaries of the convention arrest at Sedan 55 persons in one day: at Nancy, 104 in three weeks; at Arras, more than 1,000 in two months; in the Jura, 4,000 in two months. At Lons–le–Saulnier all the nobles with their domestics, at Aix all the inhabitants of one quarter without exception are put in prison. (De Sybel, II. 305.)

[85]"Archives Nationales," F7, 3276. Letters of the administrators of the Yonne, Aug. 20 and 21 .–Ibid., F7, 3255. Letter of the commissary, Bonnemant, Sept. 22. — Mortimer–Ternaux, III. 338. — Lavalette, "Mémoires," I.100.

[86] "Archives Nationales," F7, 3,255. Letter of the district administrator of Roanne, Aug. 18. Fourteen volunteers of the canton of Néronde betake themselves to Chenevoux, a mansion belonging to M. Dulieu, a supposed émigré. They exact 200 francs from the keeper of' the funds of the house under penalty of death, which he gives them. — Letter of the same. Sept. 1. "Every day repressive means are non– existent. Juges–de–paix before whom complaints are made dare not report them, nor try citizens who cause themselves to be feared. Witnesses dare not give testimony for fear of being maltreated or pillaged by the criminals." — Letter of the same, Aug. 22. — Official report of the municipality of Charlieu, Sept. 9, on the destruction of the land registry books. "We replied that not having the force with which to oppose them, since they themselves were the force, we would abstain." — Letter of an officer of the gendarmerie, Sept.9, etc.

[87] "Lettres autographes de Madame Roland," published by Madame Bancal des Issarts, p. 5 (June 2, 1790)

[88] "Archives Nationales," F7, 3245. — Letter of the mayor and municipal officers of Lyons, Aug.

2. — Letter of the deputy procureur of the commune, Aug. 29. — Copy of a letter by Dodieu, Aug. 27. (Roland replies with consternation and says that there must be a prosecution.) — Official report of the 9th of September, and letter of the municipality, Sept. 11. — Memorandum of the officers of the Royal–Pologne regiment, Sept. 7. — Letter of M. Perigny, father–in– law of one of the officers slain, Sept. 19. — Mortimer–Ternaux, III. 342. – Guillon de Montléon, I. 124. – Balleyder, "Histoire du peuple de Lyon," 91.

[89] "Archives Nationales," Letter of Danton, Oct. 3.

[90] Decius, Roman emperor from 248 to 251 famous for having persecuted the Christians. He was unable to tolerate their refusal to join in communal corporate pagan observances. He insisted that they do so and once they had done it, a Certificate of Sacrifice (libellus), was issued. (SR).

[91] "Etude sur Madame Roland," by Dauban, 82. Letter of Madame Roland to Bosc, July 26, 1798. "You busy yourselves with a municipality and allow heads to escape which will devise new horrors. You are mere children; your enthusiasm is merely a straw bonfire! If the National Assembly does not try two illustrious heads in regular form or some generous Décius strike them down, you are all lost. — " Ibid.,, May 17, 1790: "Our rural districts are much dissatisfied with the decree on feudal privileges . . . A reform is necessary, in which more châteaux must be burnt. It would not be a serious evil were there not some danger of the enemies of the Revolution profiting by these discontents to lessen the confidence of the people in the National Assembly." — Sept. 27, 1790. "The worst party is successful; it is forgotten that insurrection is the most sacred of duties when the country is in danger." — Jan.24, 1791. "The wise man shuts his eyes to the grievances or weaknesses of the private individual; but the citizen should show no mercy, even to his father, when the public welfare is at stake."

[92] "Archives Nationales," F7, 3202. Report of the commissary, member of the Cantal directory, Oct. 24. On the 16th of October at Chaudesaigues the volunteers break open a door and then kill one of their comrades who opposes them, whom the commissary tries to save. The mayor of the place, in uniform, leads them to the dwellings of aristocrats, urging them on to pillage; they enter a number of houses by force and exact wine. The next day at Saint–Urcize they break into the house of the former curé, devastate or pillage it, and "sell his furniture to different persons in the neighborhood." The same treatment is awarded to sieur Vaissier, mayor, and to lady Lavalette; their cellars are forced open, barrels of wine are taken to the public square, and drinking takes place from the tap. After this "the volunteers go in squads into the neighboring parishes and compel the inhabitants to give them money or effects." The commissary and municipal officers of St. Urcize who tried to mediate were nearly killed and were saved only through the efforts of a detachment of regular cavalry. As to the Jacobin mayor of Chaudesaigues, it was natural that he should preach pillage; on the sale of the effects of the nuns "he kept all bidders away, and had things knocked down to him for almost nothing."

[93] "Archives Nationales," F7, 3217. Letter or Castanet, an old gendarme, Nîmes, Aug.21. — Letter of M. Griolet, syndic–attorney of the Gard, Sept. 8: "I beg, sir, that this letter may he considered as confidential; I pray you do not compromise me. " — Letter of M. Gilles, juge–de–paix at Rocquemaure, Oct.31 (with official reports).

[94] "Archives Nationales," F7, 3227. Letter of the municipal officers of Tullins, Sept. 8.

[95] "Archives Nationales," F7, 3190. Letter of Danton, Oct. 9. — Memorandum of M. Casimir Audiffret (with documents in support of it). His son had been locked up by mistake, instead of another Audiffret, belonging to the Comtat; he was slashed with a saber in prison Aug.25. Report of the surgeon, Oct. 17: "The wounded man has two gashes more on the head, one on the left cheek and the right leg is paralyzed; he has been so roughly treated in carrying him from prison to prison as to bring on an abscess on the wrist; if he is kept there he will soon die."

[96] "Archives Nationales," F7, 3195. Letter of M. Amiel, president of the bureau of conciliation, Oct. 28. — Letter of an inhabitant of Avignon, Oct. 7. — Other letters without signatures. — Letter of M. Gilles, juge–de–paix, Jan. 23, 1793.

[97] Fabre, "Histoire de Marseilles," II. 478 and following pages. — "Archives Nationales," F7, 3195. Letter of the Minister of Justice, M. de Joly (with supporting documents), Aug. 6. — Official reports of the Marseilles municipality, July 21, 22, 23. — Official report of the municipality of Aix, Aug. 24. — Letter of the syndic–attorney of the department (with a letter of the municipality of Aubagne), Sept. 22, etc., in which M. Jourdan, a ministerial officer, is accused of "aristocracy." A guard is assigned to him. About midnight the guard is overcome, he is carried off, and then killed in spite of the entreaties of his wife and son. The letter of the municipality ends with the following: "Their lamentations pierced our hearts. But, alas, who can resist the French people when aroused? We remain, gentlemen, very cordially yours, the municipal officers of Aubagne."

[98] This stage of revolution seems to be sought after by the secret communist revolutionaries arranging for the break–up of formerly powerful independent states such as Germany, Yougoslavia, India etc. (SR).

[99] Moniteur, XIII. 560. Act passed by the administrators of the Bouches–du–Rhône, Aug. 3, "forbidding special collectors from henceforth paying taxes with the national treasury." –Ibid., 744. A report by Roland. The department of Var, having called a meeting of commissaries at Avignon to provide for the defense of these regions, the Minister says: "This step, subversive of all government, nullifies the general regulations of the executive power." — "Archives Nationales," F7, 3195. Deliberation of the three administrative bodies assembled at Marseilles, Nov. 5, 1792. — Petition of Anselme, a citizen of Avignon, residing in Paris, Dec. 14. – Report of the Saint- Rémy affair, etc.

[100] "Archives Nationales," CII. I. 32. Official Report of the Electoral Assembly of Bouches–du–Rhône, Sept. 4. "To defray the expenses of this expenditure the syndic–attorney of the district of Tarascon is authorized to draw upon the funds of public registry and vendor of revenue stamps, and in addition thereto on the collector of direct taxation. The expenses of this expedition will be borne by the anti–revolutionary agitators who have made it necessary. A list, therefore, is to be drawn up and sent to the National Assembly. The commissioners will be empowered to suspend the district administrations, municipal officers, and generally all public functionaries who, through incivism or improper conduct, shall have endangered the public weal. They may even arrest them as well as suspected citizens. They will see that the law regarding the disarming of suspected citizens and the banishment of priests be faithfully executed." – Ibid., F7, 3195. Letter of Truchement,

commissary of the department, Nov. 15. — Memorandum of the community of Eyguières and letter of the municipality of Eyguières, Sept. 13. — Letter of M. Jaubert, secretary of the Salon popular club, Oct. 22: "The department of Bouches–du–Rhône has for a month past been ravaged by commissions. . . The despotism of one is abolished, and we now stagger under the much more burdensome yoke of a crowd of despots." — Situation of the department in September and October, 1792 (with supporting documents).

[101] Barbaroux, "Mémoires," 89.

[102] "Archives Nationales," F7, 3196 .— Letters and petition of citizen de Sades, Nov., 1792, Feb.17, 1793, and Ventose 8, year III.: "Towards the middle of Sept., 1792 (old style), some Marseilles brigands broke into a house of mine near Apt. Not content with carrying away six loads of furniture . . they broke the mirrors and wood–work." The damage is estimated at 80,000 francs. Report of the executive council according to the official statement of the municipality of Coste. On the 27th of September Montbrion, commissioner of the administration of the Bouche–du–Rhône, sends two messengers to fetch the furniture to Apt. On reaching Apt Montbrion and his colleague Bergier have the vehicles unloaded, putting the most valuable effects on one cart, which they appropriate to themselves, and drive away with it to some distance out of sight, paying the driver out of their own pockets: "No doubt whatever exists as to the knavery of Montbrion and Bergier; administrators and commissioners of the administration of the department." — De Sades, the author of "Justine," pleads his well–known civism and the ultra–revolutionary petitions drawn up by him in the name of the section of the Pikes.

[103] "Archives Nationales," F7, 3272. Read in this file the entire correspondence of the directory and the public prosecutor.

[104] Deliberation of the commune of Toulon. July 28 and following days. — That of the three administrative bodies, Sep. 10 — Lauvergne, "Histoire du department du Var," 104–137.

[105] "Mémoires" of Chancelier Pasquier. Vol. I. p. 106. Librarie Plon, Paris 1893 – Pasquier and his wife stopped in Picardy, brought to Paris by a member of the commune, a small, bandy–legged fellow formerly a chair–letter in his parish church, imbued with the doctrines of the day and a determined leveler. At the village of Saralles they passed the house of M. de Livry, a rich man enjoying an income of 50,000 francs, and the lover of Saunier, an opera–dancer. "He is a good fellow," exclaims Pasquier's bandy–legged guardian: "we have just made hint marry. Look here, we said to him, it is time that to put a stop to that behavior! Down with prejudice! Marquises and dancers ought to marry each other. He made her his wife, and it is well he did; otherwise he would have been done for a long time ago, or caged behind the Luxembourg walls." – Elsewhere, on passing a chateau being demolished, the former chair–letter quotes Rousseau: "For every chateau that falls, twenty cottages rise in its place." His mind was stored with similar phrases and tirades, uttered by him as the occasion warranted. This man may be considered as an excellent specimen of the average Jacobin.

[106] "Archives Nationales," F7, 3,207. Letter of the administrators of the Côte d'Or to the Minister, Oct. 6, 1792.

[107] "Archives Nationales" F7, 3195. Letter of the administrators of the Bouche–du–Rhône, Oct 29, and the Minister's answer on the margin.

[108] "Archives Nationales," F7, 3249. Letter of the administrators of the Orne, Sept. 7, and the Minister's reply noted on the margin.

[109] "Archives Nationales," F', 3,249. Correspondence with the municipality of Saint–Firmin (Oise). Letter of Roland, Dec. 3: "I have read the letter addressed to me on the 25th of the past month, and I cannot conceal from you the pain it gives me to find in it principles so destructive of all the ties of subordination existing between constituted authorities, principles so erroneous that should the communes adopt them every form of government would be impossible and all society broken up. Can the commune of Saint–Firmin, indeed, have persuaded itself that it is sovereign, as the letter states? and have the citizens composing it forgotten that the sovereign is the entire nation, and not the forty–four thousandth part of it? that Saint– Firmin is simply a fraction of it, contributing its share to endowing the deputies of the National Convention, the administrators of departments and districts with the power of acting for the greatest advantage of the commune, but which, the moment it elects its own administrators and agents, can no longer revoke the powers it has bestowed, without a total subversion of order? etc." — All the documents belonging to this affair ought to be quoted; there is nothing more instructive or ludicrous, and especially the style of the secretary–clerk of Saint–Firmin: "We conjure you to remember that the administrators of the district of Senlis strive to play the part of the sirens who sought to enchant Ulysses."

[110] Letter of the central bureau of the Rouen sections, Aug. 30.

[111] "Archives Nationales," F7, 3195. Letter of the three administrative bodies and commissaries of the sections of Marseilles, Nov. 15, 1792. Letter of the electors of Bouches–du–Rhône, Nov. 28. — (Forms of politeness are omitted at the end of these letters, and no doubt purposely.) Roland replies (Dec. 31): "While fully admiring the civism of the brave Marseilles people, . . . do not fully agree with you on the exercise of popular Sovereignty." He ends by stating that all their letters with replies have been transmitted to the deputies of the Bouches–du–Rhône, and that the latter are in accord with him and will arrange matters.

CHAPTER III. THE NEW SOVEREIGNS

I.

The second stage of the Jacobin conquest. — The importance and multitude of vacant offices.

The second stage of the Jacobin conquest will,[1] after August 10th and during the next three months, extend and multiply all vacancies from the top to the bottom of the hierarchy, for the purpose of filling them with their own men. — In the first place, the faction (the party) installs representatives on the summits of public authority which represent itself alone, seven hundred and forty–nine omnipotent deputies, in a Convention which, curbed neither by collateral powers nor by a previously established constitution, disposes at pleasure of the property, the lives and the consciences of all French people. — Then, through this barely installed convention, it decrees the complete renewal[2] of all administrative and judicial bodies, councils and directories of departments, councils and communal municipalities, civil, criminal and commercial tribunals, justices and their assistants in the lower courts, deputies of the justices, national commissaries of the civil courts, with secretaries and bailiffs belonging to the various tribunals and administrations.[3] The obligation of having practiced as a lawyer is abolished by the same stroke, so that the first comer, if he belongs to the club (party) may become a judge without knowing how to write, and even without being able to read.[4] — Just before this the staff of the National Guard, in all towns above fifty thousand souls, and afterwards in all the towns on the frontier, has again passed through the electoral sieve.[5] In like manner, the officers of the gendarmerie at Paris and throughout France once more undergo an election by their men. Finally, all post–masters and post–office comptrollers have to submit to election. — Even better, below or alongside the elected officials, this administrative purge concerns all non–elective functionaries and employees, no matter how insignificant their service, however feeble and indirect their office may be connected with political matters. This is because tax receivers and assessors, directors and other agents of rivers and forests, engineers, notaries, attorneys, clerks and scribes belonging to the administrative branch, are all subject to dismissal if they do not obtain a certificate of civism from their municipality. At Troyes, out of fifteen notaries, it is refused to four,[6] which leaves four places to be filled by their Jacobin clerks. At Paris,[7] "all honest folks, all clerks who are educated," are driven out of the navy offices; the war department is getting to be "a den where everybody on duty wears a red cap, where all thee–and–thou each other, even the Minister, where four hundred employees, among which are a number of women, show off in the dirtiest dress, affect the coolest cynicism, do nothing, and steal on all sides." — Under the denunciation of the clubs, the broom is applied even at the bottom of the hierarchical scale, even to secretaries of village councils, to messengers and call–boys in the towns, to jail–keepers and door–keepers, to beadles and sextons, to foresters, field–custodians, and others of this class.[8] All these persons must be, or appear to be, Jacobin; otherwise, their place slips away from them, for there is always some one to covet it, apply for it and take it. — Outside of employees the sweeping operation reaches the suppliers and contractors; even here there are the faithful to be provided for, and nowhere is the bait so important. The State, even in ordinary times, is always the largest of consumers, and, at this moment, it is expending monthly, merely on the war, two hundred millions extra. What fish may be caught in such disturbed waters![9] — All these lucrative orders as well as all these remunerated positions are at the disposition of the Jacobins, and they seize the opportunity; they are the lawful owner, who comes home after a long absence and gives or withdraws his custom as the pleases, while he makes a clean sweep in his own household. — The administrative and judicial services alone number 1,300,000 places, all those in the treasury department, in that of public works, in that of public education, and in the Church; all posts in the National Guard and in the army, from that of commander–in–chief down to a drummer; the whole of the central or local power, with the vast patronage flowing from this. Never had such rich spoils been made available to the general public in one go. Lots will be drawn, apparently, by vote; but it is evident that the Jacobins have no intention of surrendering their prey to the hazards of a free ballot; they mean to keep it the way they got it; by force, and will leave no stone unturned to control the elections.

II.

The elections. — The young and the poor invited to the ballot–box.— Danger of the Conservatives if candidates. – –Their chiefs absent themselves. — Proportion of absentees at the primary assemblies.

They begin by paving their way.[10] A new decree has at once suppressed the feeble and last legal requirement for impartiality, integrity and competence of the elector and the eligible candidate. No more discrimination between active and passive citizens; no longer any difference between poll tax of an elector of the first degree and that of the second degree: no electoral poll tax qualification whatever. All Frenchmen, except domestics, of whom they are distrustful, supposing them under their employer's influence, may vote at the primary assemblies, and not longer at the age of twenty–five, but at twenty–one, which brings to the polls the two most revolutionary groups, on the one hand the young, and on the other the poor, the latter in great numbers in these times of unemployment, dearth and poverty, amounting in all to two millions and a half, and, perhaps, three millions of new electors. – At Besançon the number of the registered voters is doubled.[11] — Thus are the usual clients of the Jacobins admitted within the electoral boundaries, from which they had hitherto been excluded,[12] and, to ensure their coming, their leaders decide that every elector obliged to travel "shall receive twenty sous mileage," besides "three francs per diem during his stay."[13]

While attracting their supporters they drove their adversaries away. The political banditry, through which they dominate and terrify France, has already taken care of that. Many arbitrary arrests and unpunished murders are a warning to all candidates who do not belong to their party; and I do not speak about to the nobles or friends of the ancient regime that have fled or are in prison, but the Constitutionalists and the Feuillants. Any electoral enterprise on their part would be madness, almost a suicide. Accordingly, none of them call attention to themselves. If any outrageous moderate, like Durand de Maillane, appears on a list, it is because the revolutionaries have adopted him without knowing him, and because he swears that he hates royalty.[14] The others, more honest, do not want to don the popular livery and resort to club patronage, so they carefully stay away; they know too well that to do otherwise would mark their heads for pikes and their homes for pillage. At the very moment of depositing the vote the domains of several deputies are sacked simply because, "on the comparative lists of seven calls by name," sent to the departments from Paris by the Jacobins, their names are found on the right.[15] — Through an excess of precaution the Constitutionalists of the Legislative body are kept at the capital, their passports being refused to them to prevent them from returning into the provinces and obtaining votes by publicly stating the truth in relation to the recent revolution. — In the same way, all conservative journals are suppressed, reduced to silence, or compelled to become turncoats. — Now, when one has neither the possibility to speak up nor a candidate which might become one's representative, of what use is it to vote? And especially, since the primary assemblies are places of disorder and violence,[16] patriots alone, in many places, being admitted,[17] a conservative being "insulted and overwhelmed with numbers," and, if he utters an opinion, exposed to danger, also, if he remains silent, incurring the risk of denunciations, threats, and blows. To keep in the background, remain on the sidelines, avoid being seen, and to strive to be forgotten, is the rule under a pasha, and especially when this pasha is a mob. Hence the absenteeism of the majority; around the ballot–box there is an enormous void. At Paris, in the election of mayor and municipal officers, the balloting of October, November and December collect together only 14,000 out of 160,000 registered voters, later 10,000, and, later again, only 7,000.[18] At Besançon, 7,000. registered voters result in less than 600; there is the same proportion in other towns, as for example, in Troyes. In like manner, in the rural cantons, east of Doubs and west of Loire–Inférieure, but one–tenth of the electors dare exercise their right to vote.[19] The electoral source is so exhausted, so often disturbed, and so stopped up as to be almost dry: in these primary assemblies which, directly or indirectly, delegate all public powers, and which, in the expression of the common will, should be full, there are lacking six millions three hundred thousands electors out of seven millions.[20]

III.

Composition and tone of the secondary assemblies. – Exclusion of "Feuillant" electors. – Pressure on other electors.– Persons elected by the conservatives obliged to resign. – Elections by the Catholics canceled. – Secession of the Jacobin minorities. – The election of their men made valid. – Public opinion not in accord with official selections.

Through this anticipated purge the assemblies of the first degree find themselves, for the most part, Jacobin; consequently the electors of the second degree, appointed by them, are for the most part, Jacobin; in many departments, their assembly becomes the most anarchical, the most turbulent, and the most usurping of all the clubs. Here there is only shouting, denunciations, oath–taking, incendiary motions, cheering which carry all questions, furious speeches by Parisian commissaries, by delegates from the local club, by passing Federates, and by female wretches demanding arms.[21] The Pas–de–Calais assemblage sets free and applauds a woman imprisoned for having beaten a drum in a mob. The Paris assembly fraternizes with the Versailles slaughterers and the assassins of the mayor of Etampes. The assembly of the Bouches–du–Rhône gives a certificate o virtue to Jourdan, the Glacière murderer. The assembly of Seine–et–Marne applauds the proposal to cast a cannon which might contain the head of Louis XVI. for a cannon–ball to be fired at the enemy. — It is not surprising that an electoral body without self–respect should respect nothing, and practice self–mutilation under the pretext of purification.[22] The object of the despotic majority was to reign at once, without any contest, on its own authority, and to expel all offensive electors. At Paris, in the Aisne, in Haute–Loire, in Ille–et–Vilaine, in Maine–et– Loire, it excludes as unworthy the members of old Feuillants and monarchical clubs, and the signers of Constitutionalist protests. In Hérault it cancels the elections in the canton of Servian, because the elected men, it says, are "mad aristocrats." In Orne it drives away an old Constituent, Goupil de Préfeln, because he voted for the revision, also, his son–in–law, because he is his son–in–law. In the Bouches– du–Rhône, where the canton of Seignon, by mistake or through routine, swore "to maintain the constitution of the kingdom," it sets aside these retrograde elected representatives, commences proceedings against the "crime committed," and sends troops against Noves because the Noves elector, a justice who is denounced and in peril, has escaped from the electoral den. — After the purification of persons it proceeds to the purification of sentiments. At Paris, and in at least nine departments,[23] and in contempt of the law, is suppresses the secret ballot, the last refuge of timid conservatives, and imposes on each elector a verbal public vote, loud and clear, on his name being called; that is to say, if he does not vote as he ought to, he risks the gallows.[24] Nothing could more surely convert hesitation and indecision into good sense, while, in many a place, still more powerful machinery is violently opposed to the elections. At Paris the elections are carried on in the midst of atrocities, under the pikes of the butchers, and con ducted by their instigators. At Meaux and at Rheims the electors in session were within hearing of the screeches of the murdered priests. At Rheims the butchers themselves ordered the electoral assembly to elect their candidates, Drouet, the famous post– master, and Armonville, a tipsy wool–carder, upon which one–half of the assembly withdrew, while the two candidates of the assassins are elected. At Lyons, two days after the massacre, the Jacobin commander writes to the Minister: "Yesterday's catastrophe puts the aristocrats to flight, and ensures us the majority in Lyons."[25] From universal suffrage thus subjected to so much sifting, submitted to such heavy pressure, heated and refined in the revolutionary alembic, those who control it obtain all they want, a concentrated extract, the quintessence of the Jacobin spirit.

And yet, should this extract not seem to them sufficiently strong, wherever they are sovereign, they throw it away and begin over again. At Paris,[26] by means of a purifying and surplus ballot, the new Council of the Commune undertakes the expulsion of its lukewarm members, while d'Ormesson, the mayor elect of the moderates, is assailed with so many threats that, on the verge of his installation, he resigns. At Lyons,[27] another moderate, Nivière–Chol, twice elected, and, by 9,000 out of 11,000 votes, is twice compelled to abandon his place; after him, Gilibert, the physician, who, supported by the same voters, is about to obtain the majority, is seized suddenly and cast into prison; even in prison, he is elected; the clubbists confine him there more rigidly, and do not let him out even after extorting his resignation. — Elsewhere in the rural cantons, for example, in Franche–Comté,[28] a number of elections are canceled when the person elected happens to be a Catholic. The Jacobin minority frequently secede, meet in a tavern, elect their mayor or justice of the peace, and the validity of his election is secured because he is a patriot; so much the worse for that of the majority, whose more numerous votes are null because given by "fanatics." — The response of universal suffrage thus appealed to cannot be other than that which is framed for it. Indisputable facts are to show to what extent this response is compulsive or perverted, what a distance there is between an official choice and public opinion, how the elections give a contrary meaning to popular sentiment. The departments of Deux–Sèvres, Maine–et–Loire, la Vendée, Loire–Infèrieure, Morbihan, and Finistère, send only anti–Catholic republicans to the Convention, while these same departments are to become the inexhaustible nursery of the great catholic and royalist insurrection. Three regicides out of four deputies represent Lozère, where, six months later, thirty thousand peasants are to march under the Royal white banner. Six regicides out of nine deputies represent la Vendée, which is going to rise from one end of it to the other in the name of the King.[29]

IV.

Composition of the National Convention. – Number of Montagnards at the start. – Opinions and sentiments of the deputies of the Plain. – The Gironde. – Ascendancy of the Girondins in the Convention. – Their intellectual character. – Their principles. – The plan of their Constitution. – Their fanaticism. – Their sincerity, culture and tastes. – How they differ from pure Jacobins. – How they comprehend popular sovereignty. – Their stipulations with regard to the initiative of individuals and of groups. – Weakness of philosophic thought and of parliamentary authority in times of anarchy.

However vigorous the electoral pressure may have been, the voting machine has not provided the expected results. At the opening of the session, out of 749 deputies, only about fifty[30] are found to approve of the Commune, nearly all of the elected in places where, as at Rheims and Paris, terror has the elector by the throat, "under the clubs, axes, daggers, and bludgeons of the butchers."[31] But where the physical impressions of murder have not been so tangible and impressive, some sense of decency has prevented too glaring elections. The inclination to vote for well–known names could not wholly be arrested; seventy–seven former members of the Constituent Assembly, and one hundred and eighty–six of the previous Legislative Assembly enter the Convention, and the practical knowledge which many of these have of government business has given them some insights. In short, the consciences of six hundred and fifty deputies are only in part perverted.

They are all, unquestionably, decided republicans, enemies of tradition, apostles of reason, and trained in deductive politics; only on these conditions could they be elected. Every candidate is supposed to possess the Jacobin faith, or, at least, to recite the revolutionary creed. The Convention, consequently, at its opening session votes unanimously, with cheers and enthusiasm, the abolition of royalty, and three months later it pronounces, by a large majority, Louis XVI.,

"guilty of conspiring against the liberty of the nation, and of assaults on

the general welfare of the State."[32]

Nevertheless, social habitudes still subsist under political prejudices. A man who is born in and lives for a long time in an old community, is, through this alone, marked with its imprint; the customs to which he conforms have crystallized in him in the shape of sentiments: if it is well−regulated and civilized, he has involuntarily arrived at respect for property and for human life, and, in most characters, this respect has taken very deep root. A theory, even if adopted, does not wholly succeed in destroying this respect; only in rare instances is it successful, when it encounters coarse and defective natures; to take full hold, it is necessary that it should fall on the scattered inheritors of former destructive appetites, on those hopelessly degenerate souls in which the passions of an anterior date are slumbering; then only does its malevolence fully appear, for it rouses the ferocious or plundering instincts of the barbarian, the raider, the inquisitor, and the pasha. On the contrary, with the greatest number, do what it will, integrity and humanity always remain powerful motives. Nearly all these legislators, who originate in the middle class, are at bottom, irrespective of a momentary delusion, what they always have been up to now, advocates, attorneys, merchants, priests, or physicians of the ancient regime, and what they will become later on, docile administrators or zealous functionaries of Napoleon's empire,[33] that is to say, ordinary civilized persons belonging to the eighteenth and nineteenth centuries, sufficiently honest in private life to have a desire to be equally so in public life. — Hence their horror of anarchy, of Marat,[34] and of the September butchers and robbers. Three days after their assembling together they vote, "almost unanimously," the preparation of a law "against the instigators of murder and assassination." "Almost unanimously," they desire to raise a guard, recruited in the 83 departments, against the armed bands of Paris and the Commune. Pétition is elected as their first president by "almost the totality of suffrages." Roland who has just read his report to them, is greeted with the "loudest" applause from nearly the "entire" Assembly. In short they are for the ideal republic against actual brigands. This accounts for their ranging themselves around those upright and sincere deputies, who, in the two preceding Assemblies or alongside of them, were the ablest defenders of both principles and humanity, around Buzot, Lanjuinais, Pétition, and Rabaut−Saint−Etienne; around Brissot, Vergniaud, Guadet, Gensonné, Isnard, and Condorcet; around Roland, Louvet, Barbaroux, and the five hundred deputies of the "Plain,"[35] marching in one body under the leadership of the 180 Girondists who now form the "Right."[36]

These latter, among the republicans, are the most sincere and have the most faith; for they have long been such, after much thought, study and as a matter of principle. Nearly all of them are well−read educated men, reasoners, philosophers, disciples of Diderot or of Rousseau, satisfied that absolute truth had been revealed by their masters, thoroughly imbued with the Encyclopédie[37] or the Contrat Social, the same as the Puritans formerly were with the Bible.[38] At the age when the mind is maturing, and fondly clings to general ideas,[39] they embraced the theory and aimed at a reconstruction of society according to abstract principles. They have accordingly set to work as pure logicians, rigorously applying the superficial and false system of analysis then in vogue.[40] They have formed for themselves an idea of man in general, the same in all times and ages, an extract or minimum of man; they have pondered over several thousands of or millions of these abstract mortals, erected their imaginary wills into primordial rights, and drawn up in anticipation the chimerical contract which is to regulate their impossible union. There are to be no more privileges, no more heredity, no qualifications of any kind; all are to be electors, all eligible and all of equal members of the sovereignty; all powers are to be of short date, and conferred through election; there must be but one assembly, elected and entirely renewed annually, one executive council elected and one–half renewed annually, a national treasury–board elected and one–third renewed annually; all local administrations and tribunals must be elected; a referendum to the people, the electoral body endowed with the initiative, a constant appeal to the sovereignty, which, always consulted and always active, will manifest its will not alone by the choice of its mandatories but, again, through "the censure" which it will apply to the laws — such is the Constitution they forge for themselves.[41] "The English Constitution," says Condorcet, "is made for the rich, that of America for citizens well–off; the French Constitution should be made for all men." – It is, for this reason, the only legitimate one; every institution that deviates from it is opposed to natural rights and, therefore, fit only to be put down.–This is what the Girondists have done during the Legislative sessions; we know how they, armed with the illusions[42] of their new philosophy and triumphing through a rigid, rash and hasty reason, have

* persecuted Catholic consciences,

* violated feudal property,

* encroached on the legal authority of the King,

* persecuted the remains of the ancient regime,

* tolerated crimes committed by the crowds,

* even plunged France into an European war,

* armed even the paupers,

* caused the overthrow of all government. –

As far as his Utopia is concerned, the Girondist is a sectarian, and he knows no scruples.

* Little does he care that nine out of ten electors do not vote: he regards himself as the authorized representative of all ten.

* Little does he care whether the great majority of Frenchmen favor the Constitution of 1791; it is his business to impose on them his own.

* Little does he care whether his former opponents, King, émigrés, unsworn ecclesiastics, are honorable men or at least excusable; he will launch against them every rigorous legal proceeding, transportation, confiscation, civil death and physical death.[43]

In his own eyes he is the justiciary, and his investiture is bestowed upon him by eternal right. There is no human infatuation so pernicious to man as that of absolute right; nothing is better calculated for the destruction in him of the hereditary accumulation of moral conceptions. — Within the narrow bounds of their creed, however, the Girondins are sincere and consistent. They are masters of their formulae; they know how to deduce consequences from them; they believe in them the same as a surveyor in his theorems, and a theologian in the articles of his faith; they are anxious to apply them, to devise a constitution, to establish a regular government, to emerge from a barbarous state, to put an end to fighting in the street, to pillaging, to murders, to the sway of brutal force and of naked arms.

The disorder, mover, so repugnant to them as logicians is still more repugnant to them as cultivated, polished men. They have a sense of what is proper,[44] of becoming ways, and their tastes are even refined. They are not familiar with, nor do they desire to imitate, the rude manners of Danton, his coarse language, his oaths, and his low associations with the people. They have not, like Robespierre, gone to lodge with a master joiner, to live him and eat with his family. Unlike Pache, Minister of War, no one among them "feels honored" by "going down to dine with his porter," and by sending his daughters to the club to give a fraternal kiss to drunken Jacobins.[45] At Madame Roland's house there is a salon, although it is stiff and pedantic; Barbaroux send verses to a marchioness, who, after the 2nd of June, elopes with him to Caen.[46] Condorcet has lived in high society, while his wife, a former canoness, possess the charms, the repose, the instruction, and the elegance of an accomplished woman. Men of this stamp cannot endure close alongside of them the inept and gross dictatorship of an armed rabble. In providing for the public treasury they require regular taxes and not tyrannical confiscations.[47] To repress the malevolent they propose "punishment and not banishment."[48] In all State trials they oppose irregular courts, and strive to maintain for those under indictment some of the usual safeguards.[49] On declaring the King guilty they hesitate in pronouncing the sentence of death, and try to lighten their responsibility by appealing to the people. The line "laws and not blood," was a line which, causing a stir in a play of the day, presented in a nutshell their political ideas. And, naturally, the law, especially Republican law, is the law of all; once enacted, nobody, no citizen, no city, no party, can refuse to obey it without being criminal. It is monstrous that one city should arrogate to itself the privilege of ruling the nation; Paris, like other departments, should be reduced to its on−eighty−third proportion of influence. It is monstrous that, in a capital of 700,000 souls, five or six thousand radical Jacobins should oppress the sections and alone elect their candidates; in the sections and at the polls, all citizens, at least all republicans, should enjoy an equal and free vote. It is monstrous that the principle of popular sovereignty should be used to cover up attacks against popular sovereignty, that, under the pretense of saving the State, the first that comes along may kill whom he pleases, that, on the pretext that they are resisting oppression, each mob should have the "Right" to put the government down. — Hence, this militant "Right" must be pacified, enclosed within legal boundaries, and subjected to a fixed process.[50] Should any individual desire a law, a reform or a public measure, let him state his on paper over his own signature and that of fifty other citizens of the same primary assembly; then the proposition must be submitted to his own primary assembly; then in case it obtains a majority, to the primary assemblies of his arrondissement; then, in case of a majority, to the primary assemblies of his department; then, in case of a majority, to all the primary assemblies of the nation, so that after a second verdict of the same assemblies twice consulted, the Legislative body, yielding to the majority of primary suffrages, may dissolve and a new Legislative body, in which all old members shall be declared ineligible, take its place. — This is the final expression and the master idea, of the theory. Condorcet, its able constructor, has outdone himself. Impossible to design on paper a more ingenious or complicated mechanism. The Girondists, in the closing article of this faultless constitution, believe that they have discovered a way to muzzle the beast and allow the sovereign people to fully assert their rights.

As if, with some kind of constitution and especially with this one, one could muzzle the beast! As if it was in the mood to crane the neck allowing them to put the muzzle on! Robespierre, on behalf of the Jacobins, counters with a clause radically opposed to the one drafted by Condorcet[51]:

" To submit 'the right to resist oppression' to legal formalities is the ultimate refinement of tyranny. . . When a government violates the people's rights, a general insurrection of the people, as well as portions of the people, is the most sacred of duties."

Political orthodoxy, close reasoning, and oratorical talent are, however, no weapon against this ever–muttering insurrection.

"Our philosophers," says a good observer,[52] "want to attain their ends by persuasion; which is equivalent to saying that battles may be won by eloquence, fine speeches, and plans of constitution. Very soon, according to them, ... if will suffice to carry complete copies of Macchiavelli, Rousseau and Montesquieu into battle instead of cannon, it never occurring to them that these authors, like their works, never were, and never will be, anything but fools when put up against a cut–throat provided with a good sword."

The parliamentary landscape has fallen away; things have returned to a state of nature, that is, to a state of war, and one is no longer concerned with debate but with brute force. To be in the right, to convince the convention, to obtain majorities, to pass decrees, would be appropriate in ordinary times, under a government provided with an armed force and a regular administration, by which, from the summits of public authority, the decrees of a majority descend through submissive functionaries to a sympathetic and obedient population. But, in times of anarchy, and above all, in the den of the Commune, in Paris, such as the 10th of August and the 2nd of September made it, all this is of no account.

V. The Jacobins forming alone the Sovereign People.

Opinion in Paris. — The majority of the population constitutional. — The new régime unpopular. — Scarcity and high cost of food. – Catholic customs obstructed. –Universal and increasing discontent. — Aversion or indifference to the Girondins. — Political resignation of the majority. — Modern customs incompatible with pure democracy. — Men of property and income, manufacturers and tradesmen, keep aloof. – – Dissension, timidity, and feebleness of the Conservatives. — The Jacobins alone form the sovereign people.

And it is of no account because, first of all, in this great city of Paris the Girondists are isolated, and have no group of zealous partisans to depend upon. For, if the large majority is opposed to their adversaries, that is not in their favor, it having secretly, at heart, remained "Constitutionalists."[53] "I would make myself master of Paris," says a professional observer, "in ten days without striking a blow if I had but six thousand men, and one of Lafayette's stable– boys to command them." Lafayette, indeed, since the departure or concealment of the royalists, represents the old, fixed, and innermost opinion of the capital. Paris submits to the Girondists as well as to the Montagnards as usurpers; the mass of the public regards them with ill–will, and not only the bourgeoisie, but likewise the majority of the people loathe the established government.

Work is scarce and food is dear; brandy has tripled in price; only four hundred oxen are brought in at the Poissy market instead of seven or eight thousand; the butchers declare that there will be no meat in Paris next week except for the sick.[54] To obtain a small ration of bread it is necessary to wait five or six hours in a line at the baker's shops, and,[55] as is customary, workmen and housekeepers impute all this to the government. This government, which so poorly provides for its needs, offends them yet more in their deepest feelings, in the habits most dear to them, in their faith and worship. The common people, even at Paris, is still at this time very religious, much more so than at the present day. When the priest bearing the Host passes along the street, the crowd "gathers from all sides, men, women, and children, young and old, and fall on their knees in worship."[56] The day on which the relics of saint Leu are borne in procession through the Rue St. Martin, "everybody kneels; I did not see a man," says a careful observer, "that did not take off his hat. At the guard–house of the Mauconseil section, the entire company presented arms." At the same time the "citoyennes around the markets talked with each other to know if there was any way of decking houses with tapestry."[57] The following week they compel the revolutionary committee of Saint–Eustache[58] to authorize another procession, and again each one kneels: "everybody approved of the ceremony, no one, that I heard of; making any objection. This is a striking picture. . . . I saw repentance, I saw the parallel each is forced to draw between the actual state of things and the former one. I saw what a privation the people had to endure in the loss of that which, formerly, was the most imposing of all church ceremonies. People of all ranks and ages were deeply affected and humble, and many had tears in their eyes." Now, in this respect, the Girondists, by virtue of being philosophers, are more iconoclastic, more intolerant than any one, and there is no reason for preferring them to their adversaries. At bottom, the government installed by the recent electoral comedy, for the major portion of the Parisians, has no authority but the fact of its existence; people put up with it because there is no other, fully recognizing its worthlessness;[59] it is a government of strangers, of interlopers, of bunglers, of cantankerous, weak and violent persons. The Convention has no hold either on the people or on the bourgeois class, and in proportion as it glides more rapidly down the revolutionary hill, it breaks one by one the ties with which it is still connected to the undecided.

In a reign of eight months the Convention has alienated public opinion entirely. "Almost all who have property of any kind are conservative,"[60] and all the conservatives are against it. "The gendarmes here openly speak up against the Revolution, even up to the revolutionary tribunal, whose judgments they loudly condemn. All the old soldiers detest the actual order of things."[61] — The volunteers "who come back from the army appear angry at putting the King to death, and on that account they would flay all the Jacobins."[62] — No party in the Convention escapes this universal disaffection and growing aversion. "If the question of guillotining the members of the Convention could be put to an open vote, it would be carried against them by a majority of nineteen–twentieths,"[63] which, in fact, is about the proportion of electors who, through fright or disgust, keep away from the polls. Let the "Right" or the "Left" of the Convention be victors or vanquished, that is a matter which concerns them; the public at large does not enter into the discussions of its conquerors, and no longer cares for either Gironde or "Mountain." Its old grievances always revive "against the Vergniauds, Guadets" and company;[64] it does not like them, and has no confidence in them, and will let them be crushed without helping them. The infuriates may expel the Thirty–Two, if they choose, and put them under lock and key. "There is nothing the aristocracy (meaning by this, owners of property, merchants, bankers, the rich, and the well–to–do), desire so much as to see them guillotined."[65] 'Even the inferior aristocracy (meaning petty tradesmen and head–workmen) take no more interest in their fate than if they were so many escaped wild beasts . . . again caught and put in their cages."[66] "Guadet, Pétion, Brissot, would not find thirty persons in Paris who would take their part, or even take the first step to save them."[67]

Apart from all this, it makes little difference whether the majority has any preferences; its sympathies, if it has any, will never be other than platonic. It no longer counts for anything in either camp, it has withdrawn from the battle–field, it is now simply the stakes of the conflict, the prey and the booty of the winner. For, unable or unwilling to comply with the political system imposed on it, it is self–condemned to utter powerlessness. This system is the direct government of the people by the people, with all that ensues, permanence of the section assemblies, club debates in public, uproar in the galleries, motions in the open air, mobs and manifestations in the streets; nothing is less attractive and more impracticable to civilized and busy people. In our modern communities, work, the family, and social intercourse absorb nearly all our time; hence, such a system suits only the idle and rough outcasts who feel at home there; the others refuse to enter an environment expressly set up for singles, orphans, unskilled persons, living in lodgings, foul–mouthed, lacking the sense of smell, with a gift of the gab, robust arms, tough hide, solid haunches, expert in hustling, and with whom blows replace arguments.[68] — After the September massacres, and on the opening of the barriers, a number of proprietors and persons living on their incomes, not alone the suspected but those who thought they might become so, escaped from Paris, and, during the following months, the emigration increases along with the danger. Towards December rumor has it that lists have been made up of former Feuillants; "we are assured that during the past eight days more than fourteen thousand persons have left the capital."[69] According to the report of the Minister himself;[70] "many who are independent in fortune and position abandon a city where the renewal of proscription is talked of daily." — " Grass grows in the finest streets," writes a deputy, "while the silence of the grave reigns in the Thébaïdes (isolated villas) of the faubourg Saint–Germain." — As to the conservatives who remain, they confine themselves to private life, from which it follows that, in the political balance, those present are of no more account than the absentees. At the municipal elections in October, November, and December, out of 160,000 registered voters, there are at first 144,000, then 150,000, and finally 153,000 who stay away from the polls; these, certainly, and for a much better reason, do not show themselves at the assemblies of their sections. Commonly, out of three or four thousand citizens, only fifty or sixty attend; one of these, called a general assembly, which signifies the will of the people to the Convention, is composed of twenty–five voters.[71] Accordingly, what would a sensible man, a friend of order, do in these dens of fanatics? He stays at home, as on stormy days; he lets the shower of words spend itself, not caring to be spattered in the gutter of nonsense which carries off the filth of this district.

If he leaves his house at all he goes out for a walk, the same as in old times, to indulge the tastes he had under the old régime, those of a talkative, curious on–looker and friendly stroller, of a Parisian safe in his well run town. "Yesterday evening," writes a man who feels the coming Reign of Terror, "I took my stand in the middle of the right alley of the Champs–Elysées;[72] it was thronged with — who do you think? Would you believe it, with moderates, aristocrats, owners of property, and very pretty women, elegantly dressed, seeking the caresses of the balmy spring breeze! It was a charming sight. All were gay and smiling. I was the only one that was not so. . . I withdrew hastily, and, on passing through the Tuileries garden, I saw a repetition of what I had seen before, forty thousand wealthy people scattered here and there, almost as many as Paris contains." — These are evidently the sheep ready for the slaughter–house. They no longer think of defense, they have abandoned their posts to the sans– culottes, "they refuse all civil and military functions,"[73] they avoid doing duty in the National Guard and instead pay their substitutes. In short, they withdraw from a game which, in 1789, they desired to play without understanding it, and in which, since the end of 1791, they have always burnt their fingers. The cards may be handed over to others, especially as the cards are dirty and the players fling them in each others' faces; as for themselves they are spectators, they have no other ambitions. — "Leave them their old enjoyments,[74] leave them the pleasure of going and coming throughout the kingdom; but do not force them to take part in the war. Subject them to the heaviest taxation and they will not complain; nobody will even know that they exist, while the most serious question that disturbs them in their thoughtful days is, can one amuse one's self as much under a republican form of government as under the ancient régime?" They hope, perhaps, to escape under cover of inoffensive neutrality. Is it likely that the victor, whoever he is, will regard people as enemies who are resigned to his rule before–hand? "A dandy[75] alongside of me remarked, yesterday morning, 'They will not take my arms away, for I never had any.' Alas,' I replied to him, 'don't make a boast of it, for you may find forty thousand simpletons in Paris that would say the same thing, and, indeed, it is not at all to the credit of Paris.'" — Such is the blindness or self–complacency of the city dweller who, having always lived under a good police, is unwilling to change his habits, and is not aware that the time has come for him to turn fighting man in his turn.

The manufacturers, the merchants and the man living on his income are even less disposed than the independent gentleman, to give up his private affairs for public affairs. His business will not wait for him, he being confined to his office, store or counting–room. For example, "the wine–dealers[76] are nearly all aristocrats in the sense of this word at this period," but "never were their sales so great as during the insurrections of the people and in revolutionary days." Hence the impossibility of obtaining their services in those days. "They are seen on their premises very active, with three or four of their assistants," and turn a deaf ear to every appeal. "How can we leave when custom is so good? People must have their wants supplied. Who will attend to them if I and the waiters should go away? " — There are other causes of their weakness. All grades in the National Guard and all places in the municipality having been given up to the Jacobin extremists, they have no chiefs: the Girondists are incapable of rallying them, while Garat, the Minister, is unwilling to employ them. Moreover, they are divided amongst themselves, no one having any confidence in the other, "it being necessary to chain them together to have anything accomplished."[77] Besides this, the remembrance of September weighs upon their spirits like a nightmare. — All this converts people into a timid flock, ready to scamper at the slightest alarm. "In the Contrat Social section," says an officer of the National Guard, "one–third of those who are able to defend the section are off in the country; another third are hiding away in their houses, and the other third dare not do anything."[78] "If, out of fifty thousand moderates, you can collect together three thousand, I shall be very much astonished. And if; out of these three thousand, five hundred only are found to agree, and have courage enough to express their opinion, I shall be still more astonished. The latter, for instance, must expect to be Septemberized!"[79] This they know, and hence they keep silent and bend beneath the yoke. "What, indeed, would the majority of the sections do when it is demonstrated that a dozen raving maniacs at the head of a sans–culottes section puts the other forty–seven sections of Paris to flight? " — Through this desertion of the state and themselves, they surrender in advance, and, in this great city, as formerly in ancient Athens and Rome, we see alongside of an immense population of subjects without any rights, a small despotic oligarchy in itself composing the sovereign people.[80]

VI.

Composition of the party. — Its numbers and quality decline. — The Underlings. — Idle and dissipated workmen. — The suburban rabble. — Bandits and blackguards. — Prostitutes. — The September actors.

Not that this minority has been on the increase since the 10th of August, quite the reverse. — On the 19th of November, 1792, its candidate for the office of Mayor of Paris, Lhuillier, obtains only 4,896 votes.[81] On the 18th of June, 1793, its candidate for the command of the National Guard, Henriot, will secure but 4,573 votes; to ensure his election it will be necessary to cancel the election twice, impose the open vote, and relieve voters from showing their section tickets, which will permit the trusty to vote successively in other quarters and apparently double their number by allowing each to vote two or three times.[82] Putting all together, there are not six thousand Jacobins in Paris, all of them sans–culottes and partisans of the "Mountain."[83] Ordinarily, in a section assembly, they number "ten or fifteen," at most "thirty or forty," "organized into a permanent tyrannical board." . . . "The rest listen and raise their hands mechanically." . . . "Three or four hundred Visionaries, whose devotion is as frank as it is stupid, and two or three hundred more to whom the result of the last revolution did not bring the places and honors they too evidently relied on," form the entire staff of the party; "these are the clamorers of the sections and of the groups, the only ones who have clearly declared themselves against order, the apostles of a new sedition, scathed or ruined men who need disturbance to keep alive," while under these comes the train of Marat, vile women, worthless wretches, and "paid shouters at three francs a day."[84]

To this must be added that the quality of the factious is still more reduced than their number. Plenty of honest men, small tradesmen, wine dealers, cook–shop keepers, clerks, who, on the 10th of August, were against the Court, are now against the Commune.[85] The September affair, probably, disgusted them, and they were not disposed to recommence the massacres. A workman named Gonchon, for example, the usual spokesman of the faubourg SaintAntoine, an upright man, sincere and disinterested, supports Roland, and, very soon, at Lyons, seeing how things are with his own eyes, he is to loyally endorse the revolt of the moderates against the Maratists.[86] "The respectable class of the arts, says observers, " is gradually leaving the faction to join the sane party."[87] "Now that water–carriers, porters and the like storm the loudest in the sections, it is plain to all eyes that the gangrene of disgust has reached the fruit–sellers, tailors, shoe– makers, bar owners," and others of that class.[88] — Towards the end, "butchers of both classes, high and low, are aristocratized." — In the same way, "the women in the markets, except a few who are paid and whose husbands are Jacobins, curse and swear, fume, fret and storm." "This morning," says a merchant, "four or five of them were here; they no longer insist on being called citoyennes; they declare that they "spit on the republic."[89] – The only remaining patriot females are from the lowest of the low class, the harpies who pillage shops as much through envy as through necessity, "boat–women, embittered by hard labor,[90] . . . jealous of the grocer's wife, better dressed than herself, as the latter was of the wives of the attorney and counselor, as these were of those of the financier and noble. The woman of the people thinks she cannot do too much to lower the grocer's wife to her own level."

Thus reduced to its dregs through the withdrawal of its tolerably honest recruits, the faction now comprises none but the scum of the populace, first, "subordinate workmen who look upon the downfall of their employers with a certain satisfaction," then, the small retailers, the old–clothes dealers, plasterers, "those who offer second–hand coats for sale on the fringes of the market, fourth–rate cooks who, at the cemetery of the Innocents, sell meat and beans under umbrella tops,"[91] next, domestics highly pleased with now being masters of their masters, kitchen helpers, grooms, lackeys, janitors, every species of valet, who, in contempt of the law, voted at the elections[92] and at the Jacobin club form a group of "silly people" satisfied "that they were universal geographers because they had ridden post once or twice," and that they were politicians "because they had read 'The Four Sons of Aymon.'"[93] — But, in this mud, spouting and spreading around in broad daylight, it is the ordinary scum of great cities which forms the grossest flux, the outcasts of every trade and profession, dissipated workmen of all kinds, the irregular and marauding troops of the social army, the class which, "discharged from La Pitié, run through a career of disorder and end in Bicêtre."[94] "From La Pitié to Bicêtre" is a well known popular adage. Men of this stamp are without any principle whatever. If they have fifty francs they live on fifty, and if they have only five they live on five; spending everything, they are always out of pocket and save nothing. This is the class that took the Bastille,[95] got up the 10th of August, etc. It is the same class which filled the galleries in the Assembly with all sorts of characters, filling up the groups," and, during all this time it never did a stroke of work. Consequently, "a wife who owns a watch, ear–rings, finger–rings, any jewels, first takes them to the pawnbrokers where they end up being sold. At this period many of these people owe the butcher, the baker, the wine– dealer, etc.; nobody trusts them any more. They have ceased to love their wives, and their children cry for food, while the father is at the Jacobin club or at the Tuileries. Many of them have abandoned their position and trade," while, either through "indolence" or consciousness "of their incapacity," . . . "they would with a kind of sadness see this trade come back to life." That of a political gossip, of a paid claqueur, is more agreeable, and such is the opinion of all the idlers, summoned by the bugle to work on the camps around Paris. – – Here,[96] eight thousand men are paid forty sous a day "to do nothing"; "the workmen come along at eight, nine and ten o'clock in the morning. If they remain after roll–call . . . they merely trundle about a few wheelbarrow loads of dirt. Others play cards all day, and most of them leave at three or four o'clock, after dinner. On asking the inspectors about this they reply that they are not strong enough to enforce discipline, and are not disposed to have their throats slit." Whereupon, on the Convention decreeing piece–work, the pretended workers fall back on their equality, remind it that they had risen on the 10th of August, and wish to massacre the commissioners. It is not until the 2nd of November that they are finally dismissed with an allowance of three sous per league mileage for those of the departments. Enough, however, remain in Paris to increase immeasurably the troop of drones which, accustomed to consuming the store of honey, think they have a right to be paid by the public for buzzing around the State.

As a rear-guard, they have "the rabble of the suburbs of Paris, which flocks in at every tap of the drum because it hopes to make something."[97] As advance-guard they have "brigands," while the front ranks contain "all the robbers in Paris, which the faction has enrolled in its party to use when required;" the second ranks are made up of "a number of former domestics, the bullies of gambling-houses and of houses of ill-fame, all the vilest class."[98] — Naturally, lost women form a part of the crowd "Citoyennes," Henriot says, addressing the prostitutes of the Palais-Royal, whom he has assembled in its garden, "citoyennes, are you good republicans?" "Yes, general, yes!" "Have you, by chance, any refractory priest, any Austrian, any Prussian, concealed in your apartments?" "Fie, fie! We have nobody but sans-culottes! "[99] — Along with these are the thieves and prostitutes out of the Châtelet and Conciergerie, set at liberty and then enlisted by the September slaughterers, under the command of an old hag named Rose Lacombe,[100] forming the usual audience of the Convention; on important days, seven or eight hundred of these may be counted, sometimes two thousand, stationed at the entrance and in the galleries, from nine o'clock in the morning.[101] — Male and female, "this anti-social vermin "102thus crawls around at the sessions of the Assembly, the Commune, the Jacobin club, the revolutionary tribunal, the sections and one may imagine the physiognomies it offers to view. "It would seem," says a deputy,[103] "as if every sink in Paris and other great cities had been scoured to find whatever was foul, the most hideous, and the most infected. . . . Ugly, cadaverous features, black or bronzed, surmounted with tufts of greasy hair, and with eyes sunken half-way into the head. . . . They belched forth with their nauseous breath the grossest insults amidst sharp cries like those of carnivorous animals." Among them there can be distinguished "the September murderers, whom" says an observer[104] in a position to know them, "I can compare to nothing but lazy tigers licking their paws, growling and trying to find a few more drops of blood just spilled, awaiting a fresh supply." Far from hiding away they strut about and show themselves. One of them, Petit-Mamain, son of an innkeeper at Bordeaux and a former soldier, "with a pale, wrinkled face, sharp eyes and bold air, wearing a scimitar at his side and pistols at his belt," promenades the Palais-Royal[105] "accompanied or followed at a distance by others of the same species," and "taking part in every conversation." "It was me," he says, "who ripped open La Lamballe and tore her heart out. . . . All I have to regret is that the massacre was such a short one. But we shall have it over again. Only wait a fortnight!" and, thereupon, he calls out his own name in defiance. — Another, who has no need of stating his well-known name, Maillard, president of the Abbaye massacres, has his head-quarters at the café Chrétien,[106] Rue Favart, from which, guzzling drams of brandy, "he dispatches his mustached men, sixty-eight cutthroats, the terror of the surrounding region;" we see them in coffee-houses and in the foyers of the theaters "drawing their huge sabers," and telling inoffensive people: "I am Mr. so and so; if you look at me with contempt I'll cut you down! — A few months more and, under the command of one of Henriot's aids, a squad of this band will rob and toast (chauffer) peasants in the environment of Corbeil and Meaux.[107] In the meantime, even in Paris, they toast, rob, and rape on grand occasions. On the 25th and 26th of February, 1793,[108] they pillage wholesale and retail groceries, "save those belonging to Jacobins," in the Rue des Lombards, Rue des Cinq-Diamants, Rue Beaurepaire, Rue Montmartre, in the Ile Saint-Louis, on the Port-au- Blé, before the Hôtel-de-ville, Rue Saint-Jacques, in short, twelve hundred of them, not alone articles of prime necessity, soap and candles, but again, sugar, brandy, cinnamon, vanilla, indigo and tea. "In the Rue de la Bourdonnaie, a number of persons came out with loaves of sugar they had not paid for and which they re-sold." The affair was arranged beforehand, the same as on the 5th of October, 1789; among the women are seen "several men in disguise who did not even take the precaution of shaving," and in many places, thanks to the confusion, they heartily abandon themselves to it. With his feet in the fire or a pistol at his head, the master of the house is compelled to give them "gold, money, assignats and jewels," only too glad if his wife and daughters are not raped before his eyes as in a town taken by assault.

VII. The Jacobin Chieftains.

The make up of the rulers. — The nature and scope of their intellect. — The political views of M. Saule.

Such are the politicians who, after the last months of the year 1792, rule over Paris, and, through Paris, over the whole of France, five thousand brutes and blackguards with two thousand hussies, just about the number a good police force would expel from the city, were it important to give the capital a cleaning out;[109] they too, were convinced of their rights, all the more ardent in their revolutionary faith, because the creed converts their vices into virtues, and transforms their misdeeds into public services.[110] They are the actual sovereign people, this is why we should try to unravel their innermost thoughts. If we truly are to comprehend the past events we must discern the spontaneous feelings moving them on the trial of the King, the defeat of Neerwinden, at the defection of Dumouriez, on the insurrection in La Vendée, at the accusation of Marat, the arrest of Hébert, and each of the dangers which in turn fall on their heads. For, this is not borrowed emotion; it does not descend from above; they are not a trusty army of disciplined soldiers, but a suspicious accumulation of temporary adherents. To command them requires obedience to them, their leaders always remaining their tool. However popular and firmly established a chief may seem to be, he is there only for a short time, at all times subject to their approval as the bullhorn for their passions and the purveyor to their appetites.[111] Such was Pétion in July, 1792, and such is Marat since the days of September. "One Marat more or less (which will soon be seen) would not change the course of events."[112] — "But one only would remain,[113] Chaumette, for instance; one would suffice to lead the horde," because it is the horde itself which leads. "Its attachment will always be awarded to whoever shows a disposition to follow it the closest in its outrages without in any respect caring for its former leaders. . . Its liking for Marat and Robespierre is not so great as for those who will exclaim, Let us kill, let us plunder!" Let the leader of the day stop following the current of the day, and he will be crushed as an obstacle or cast off as a piece of wreckage. — Judge if they are willing to be entangled in the spider's web which the Girondins put in their way. Instead of the metaphysical constitution with which the Girondins confront them, they have one in their own head ready made, simple to the last point, adapted to their capacity and their instincts. The reader will call to mind one of their chiefs, whom we have already met, M. Saule, "a stout, stunted little old man, drunk all his life, formerly an upholsterer, then a peddler of quackeries in the shape of four-penny boxes of hangman's grease, to cure pains in the loins,[114] afterwards chief of the claque in the galleries of the Constituent Assembly and driven out for rascality, restored under the Legislative Assembly, and, under the protection of a groom of the Court, favored with a spot near the Assembly door, to set up a patriotic coffee-shop, then awarded six hundred francs as a recompense, provided with national quarters, appointed inspector of the tribunes, a regulator of public opinion, and now "one of the madcaps of the Corn-market." Such a man is typical, an average specimen of his party, not only in education, character and conduct, but, again, in ambition, principles, logic and success. "He swore that he would make his fortune, and he did it. His constant cry was that nobles and priests should be put down, and we no longer have either. He has constantly shouted against the civil list, and the civil list has been suppressed. At last, lodged in the house belonging to Louis XVI., he told him to his face that his head ought to be struck off, and the head of Louis XVI. has fallen." — Here, in a nutshell, is the history and the portrait of all the others; it is not surprising that genuine Jacobins see the Revolution in the same way as M. Saule,[115]

* when, for them, the sole legitimate Constitution is the definitive establishment of their omnipotence;

* when they designate as order and justice the boundless despotism they exercise over property and life;

* when their instinct, as narrow and violent as that of a Turkish bey, comprises only extreme and destructive measures, arrests, deportations, confiscations, executions, all of which is done with head erect, with delight as if a patriotic duty, by right of a moral priesthood, in the name of the people, either directly and tumultuously with their own hands, or indirectly and legally by the hands of their docile representatives.

This is the sum of their political system, from which nothing will detach them; for they are anchored fast to it with the full weight and with every hold upon it that characterizes their immorality, ignorance and folly. Through the hypocritical glitter of compulsory parades, their one fixed idea imposes itself on the orator that he may utter it in tirades, on the legislator that he may put it into decrees, on the administrator that he may put it in practice, and, from their opening campaign up to their final victory, they will tolerate but one variation, and this variation is trifling. In September, 1792, they declare by their acts:

"Those whose opinions are opposed to ours will be assassinated, and their gold, jewels and pocketbooks will belong to us."

In November, 1793, they are to declare through the official inauguration of the revolutionary government:

"those whose opinions differ from ours will be guillotined and we shall be their heirs."[116]

Between this program, which is supported by the Jacobin population and the program of the Girondins which the majority in the Convention supports, between Condorcet's Constitution and the summary articles of M. Saule, it is easy to see which will prevail. "These Parisian blackguards," says a Girondist, "take us for their valets![117] Let a valet contradict his master and he is sure to lose his place. From the first day, when the Convention in a body traversed the streets to begin its sessions, certain significant expressions enabled it to see into what hands it had fallen:

"Why should so many folks come here to govern France," says a bystander, "haven't we enough in

Paris?"[118]

Notes:

[1] Any contempory Western reader take notice ! ! The proof of any Jacobin or Socialist or Communist take–over, surreptitious or open– handed, lies in their take–over of the important posts in politics, the judicial system, the media and the administration. They may be years in doing this, placing convinced or controlled men and women, first in the faculties, later in career post, so that they, 30 years later, have their people on all leading posts; or they may do it all at once, like the Jacobins in France, Lenin in Russia or Stalin in the conquered territories after the second world war. (SR).

[2] Duvergier, "Collection des lois et décrets," decrees of Sept. 22 and Oct. 19, 1792. The electoral assemblies and clubs had already proceeded in many places to renew on their own authority the decree rendering their appointments valid.

[3] The necessity of placing Jacobins everywhere is well shown in the following letter: "Please designate by a cross, on the margin of the jury–panel for your district, those Jacobins that it will do to put on the list of 200 for the next quarter. We require patriots." (Letter from the attorney–general of Doubs, Dec. 23, 1792. Sauzay, III. 220.)

[4] Pétion, "Mémoires" (Ed. Dauban), p. 118: "The justice who accompanied me was very talkative, but could not speak a word of French. He told me that he had been a stone–cutter before he became a justice, having taken this office on patriotic grounds. He wanted to draw up a statement and give me a guard of two gendarmes; he did not know how, so I dictated to him what to say; but my patience was severely taxed by his incredibly slow writing.

[5] Decrees of July 6, Aug. 15 and 20, Sept. 26, 1792.

[6] Decree of Nov. 1, 1792.— Albert Babeau, II. 14, 39, 40.

[7] Dumouriez, III. 309, 355. — Miot de Melito, "Mémoires," I.31, 33.— Gouverneur Morris, letter of Feb. 14, 1793: "The state of disorganization appears to be irremediable. The venality is such that, if there be no traitors, it is because the enemy have not common sense."

[8] "Archives Nationales," F7, 3268. Letter of the municipal officers of Rambouillet, Oct. 3, 1792. They denounce a petition of the Jacobins of the town, who strive to deprive forty foresters of their places, nearly all with families, 'on account of their once having been in the pay of a perjured king." — Arnault ("Souvenirs d'un sexagénaire"), II. 15. He resigns a small place he had in the assignate manufacture, because, he says, "the most insignificant place being sought for, he found himself exposed to every kind of denunciation."

[9] Dumouriez, III. 339. — Meillan, "Mémoires," 27. "Eight days after his installation as Minister of

War, Beurnonville confessed to me that he had been offered sums to the amount of 500,000 francs to lend himself to embezzlements." He tries to sweep out the vermin of stealing employees, and is forthwith denounced by Marat. — Barbaroux, "Mémoires" (Ed. Dauban). (Letter of Feb. 5, 1793.) "I found the Minister of the Interior in tears at the obstinacy of Vieilz, who wanted him to violate the law of Oct. 12, 1791 (on promotion)." Vieilz had been in the service only four months, instead of five years, as the law required, and the Minister did not dare to make an enemy of a man of so much influence in the clubs. Buchez et Roux, XXVIII.19 ("Publication des pièces relatives au 31 Mai," at Caen, by Bergoing, June 28, 1793): "My friend learned that the place had been given to another, who had paid 50 louis to the deputy. — The places in the bureaus, the armies, the administrations and commissions are estimated at 9,000. The deputies of the Mountain have exclusive disposal of them and set their price on them, the rates being almost publicly stated." The number greatly increases during the following year (Mallet du Pan, II.56, March, 1794). "The public employees at the capital alone amount to 35,000."

[10] Decree of Aug. 11, 12, 1792.

[11] Sauzay, III. 45. The number increases from 3,200 to 7,000.

[12] Durand–Maillane, "Mémoires," p. 30: "This proceeding converted the French proletariat, which had no property or tenacity, into the dominant party at electoral assemblages.. . . The various clubs established in France (were) then masters of the elections." In the Bouches–du–Rhône "400 electors in Marseilles, one–sixth of whom had not the income of a silver marc, despotically controlled our Electoral Assembly. Not a voice was allowed to be raised against them. . . Only those were elected whom Barbaroux designated."

[13] Decree of Aug. 11, 12, "Archives Nationales," CII. 58 to 76. Official report of the Electoral Assembly of the Rhône–et–Loire, held at Saint–Etienne. The electors of Saint–Etienne demand remuneration the same as the others, considering that they gave their time in the same way. Granted.

[14] "Archives Nationales," CII. 1 to 32. Official report of the Electoral Assembly of the Bouches–du–Rhône, speech by Durand–Maillane: "Could I in the National Convention be otherwise than I have been in relation to the former Louis XVI., who, after his flight on the 22d of June, appeared to me unworthy of the throne? Can I do otherwise than abhor royalty, after so many of our regal crimes?"

[15] Moniteur, XIII. 623, session of Sept. 8, speech by Larivière. – "Archives Nationales," CII., 1 to 83. (The official reports make frequent mention of the dispatch of this comparative lists, and the Jacobins who send it request the Electoral Assembly to have it read forthwith.)

[16] Rétif de la Bretonne, "Les Nuits de Paris," Night X. p. 301: "As soon as the primary assemblies had been set up, the plotters began to work, electors were nominated, and through the vicious system adopted in the sections, an uproar made it out for a majority of voices. — Cf. Schmidt, "Tableaux de la Révolution Française," I. 98. Letter of Damour, vice–president of the section of the Théatre–Français, Oct.29. — " Un Séjour en France," p.29: "The primary assemblies have already begun in this department (Pas–de–Calais). We happened to enter a church, where we found young

Robespierre haranguing an audience as small in point of number as it was in that of respectability. They applauded vigorously as if to make up for their other shortcomings."

[17] Albert Babeau, I. 518. At Troyes, Aug.26, the revolutionaries in most of the sections have it decided that the relations of an émigré, designated as hostages and the signers of royalist addresses, shall not be entitled to vote: "The sovereign people in their primary assembly may admit among its members only pure citizens against whom there is not the slightest reproach" (resolution of the Madeleine section). — Sauzay, III. 47, 49 and following pages. At Quinsy, Aug. 26, Lout, working the Chattily furnaces, along with a hundred of his men armed with clubs, keeps away from the ballot−box the electors of the commune of Courcelles, "suspected of incivisme. " — " Archives Nationales," F7, 3217. Letters of Gilles, justice an the canton of Roquemaure (Gard), Oct. 31, 1792, and Jan. 23, 1793, on the electoral proceedings employed in this canton: Dutour, president of the club, left his chair to support the motion for "lanterning" the grumpy and all the false patriots. . . On the 4th of November "he forced contributions by threatening to cut off heads and destroy houses." He was elected juge−de−paix. — Another, Magère, "approved of the motion for setting up a gallows, provided that it was not placed in front of his windows, and stated openly in the club that if people followed the law they would never accomplish anything to be remembered." He was elected member of the department directory. — A third, Fournier, "wrote that the gifts which citizens made to save their lives were voluntary gifts." He is made a department councilor. "Peaceable citizens are storing their furniture in safe places in order to take to flight . . . There is no security in France; the epithet of aristocrat, of Feuillant, of moderate affixed to the most honest citizen's name is enough to make him an object of spoliation and to expose him to losing his life. . . I insist on regarding the false idea which is current in relation to popular sovereignty as the principal cause of the existing anarchy."

[18] Schmidt, "Pariser Zustande," I. 50 and following pages. — Mortimer−Ternaux, V. 95. 109, 117, 129. (Ballot of Oct. 4, 14,137 voters; Oct. 22, 14,006; Nov.19, 10,223, Dec. 6, 7062.)

[19] Sauzay, III. 45, 46, 221. — Albert Babeau, I. 517. — Lallié, "Le district de Machecoul, 225. — Cf. in the above the history of the elections 'of Saint−Affrique: out of more than 600 registered electors the mayor and syndic−attorney are elected by forty votes. — The plebiscite of September, 1795, on the constitution of the year III. calls out only 958,000 voters. Repugnance to voting still exists. "Ninety times out of a hundred, on asking: 'Citizen, how did the Electoral Assembly of your canton go off?' they would reply (in patois): 'Me, citizen? why should I go there? They have a good deal of trouble in getting along together.' Or, 'What would you? Only a few will come; honest people will stay at home!'" (Meissner, "Voyage à Paris," towards the end of 1795.)

[20] Stalin easily found a remedy. He obliged all to vote and falsified the count so that 99% now voted for him and his men. (SR).

[21] " Archives Nationales," CII. 1 to 76, passim, especially the official reports of the assemblies of the Bouches−du−Rhône, Hérault and Paris. Speech by Barbaroux to the Electoral Assembly of the Bouches−du−Rhône: "Brothers and friends, liberty will perish if you do not elect men to the National Convention whose hearts are filled with hatred of royalty. . . Mine is the soul of a freeman; ever since my fourth year it has been nourished on hatred to kings. I will relieve France from this detestable race, or I will die in the attempt. Before I leave you I will sign my own death−warrant, I will

designate what I love most, I will show you all my possessions, I will lay a dagger on the table which shall pierce my heart if ever for an instant I prove false to the cause of the people!" (session of Sept. 3). – Guillon de Montléon, I, 135.

[22] Durand–Maillane, I.33. In the Electoral Assembly of the Bouches– du–Rhône "there was a desire to kill an elector suspected of aristocracy."

[23] Mortimer–Ternaux, IV. 52. "Archives Nationales," CII. I to 32. — Official report of the Electoral Assembly of Bouches–du–Rhône. Speech by Pierre Bayle, Sept. 3: "That man is not free who tries to conceal his conscience in the shadow of a vote. The Romans openly elected their tribunes. . . Who amongst us would reject so wise a measure? The galleries of the National Assembly have had as much to do with fostering the Revolution as the bayonets of patriots. " — In Seine–et–Marne the Assembly at first decided for the secret vote; at the request of the Paris commissaries, Ronsin and Lacroix, it rescinds its decision and adopts voting aloud and by call.

[24] Barbaroux, "Mémoires," 379: "One day, on proceeding to the elections, tumultuous shouts break out: 'That is an anti–revolutionary from Arles, hang him!' An Arlesian had, indeed, been arrested on the square, brought into the Assembly, and they were lowering the lantern to run him up."

[25] Mortimer–Ternaux, III. 338. — De Sybel, "Histoire de l'Europe pendant la Révolution Française" (Dosquet's translation), I. 525. (Correspondence of the army of the South, letter by Charles de Hesse, commanding the regular troops at Lyons.)

[26] Mortimer–Ternaux, V.101, 122 and following pages.

[27] Guillon de Montléon, I. 172, 196 and following pages.

[28] Sauzay, III. 220 and following pages. — Albert Babeau, II. 15. At Troyes, two mayors elected refuse in turn. At the third ballot in this town of from 32,000 to 35,000 souls, the mayor–elect obtains 400 out of 555 votes.

[29] Moniteur, XV. 184 to 233 (the roll–call of those who voted for the death of Louis XVI).—Dumouriez, II. 73 (Dumouriez reaches Paris Feb. 2, 1793, after visiting the coasts of Dunkirk and Antwerp): "All through Picardy, Artois, and maritime Flanders Dumouriez found the people in consternation at the tragic end of Louis XVI. He noticed that the very name of Jacobin excited horror as well as fear."

[30] This number, so important, is verified by the following passages: — Moniteur, session of Dec. 39, 1792. Speech by Birotteau: "Fifty members against 690. . . About twenty former nobles, fifteen or twenty priests, and a dozen September judges (want to prevail against) 700 deputies." — Ibid., 851 (Dec.26, on the motion to defer the trial of the king): "About fifty voices, with energy, No! no! " — Ibid., 865, (Dec.27, a violent speech by Lequinio, applauded by the extreme "Left" and the galleries; the president calls them to order): "The applause continues of about fifty members of the extreme 'Left.' " — Mortimer– Ternaux, VI. 557. (Address by Tallien to the Parisians, Dec.23, against the banishment of the Duke of Orleans): "To–morrow, under the vain pretext of another measure of

general safety, the 60 or 80 members who on account of their courageous and inflexible adherence to principles are offensive to the Brissotine faction, will be driven out." — Moniteur, XV. 74 (Jan. 6). Robespierre, addressing Roland, utters this expression: "the factious ministers." "Cries of Order! A vote of censure! To the Abbaye/ 'Is the honest minister whom all France esteems,' says a member, 'to be treated in this way?' — Shouts of laughter greet the exclamation from about sixty members." — Ibid., XV. 114. (Jan. 11). Denunciation of the party of anarchists by Buzot. Garnier replies to him: "You calumniate Paris; you preach civil war!" "Yes! yes! 'exclaim about sixty members. — Buchez et Roux, XXIV. 368 (Feb. 26). The question is whether Marat shall be indicted. "Murmurs from the extreme left, about a dozen members noisily demanding the order of the day."

[31] Mercier, "Le nouveau Paris," II. 200.

[32] Buchez et Roux, XIX. 17. XXVIII. 168. – The king is declared guilty by 683 votes; 37 abstain from voting, as judges; of these 37, 26, either as individuals or legislators, declare the king guilty. None of the other 11 declare him innocent.

[33] "Dictionnaire biographique," by Eymery, 1807 (4 vols). The situation of the conventionists who survive the Revolution may here be ascertained. Most of them will become civil or criminal judges, prefects, commissaries of police, heads of bureaus, post-office employees, or registry clerks, collectors, review-inspectors, etc. The following is the proportion of regicides among those thus in office: Out of 23 prefects 21 voted for the king" death; 42 out of 43 magistrates voted for it, the 43rd being ill at the time of the sentence. Of 5 senators 4 voted for his death, and 14 deputies out of 16. Out of 36 other functionaries of various kinds 35 voted for death. Among the remaining regicides we again find 2 councillors of state, 4 diplomatic agents and consuls, 2 generals, 2 receiver-generals, 1 commissary-general of the police, 1 minister in the cabinet of King Joseph, the minister of police, and the arch-chancellor of the empire.

[34] Buchez et Roux, XIX, 97, session of Sept. 25, 1792. Marat states: " 'I have many personal enemies in this assembly.' 'All! all!' exclaim the entire Assembly, indignantly rising." – Ibid., XIX. 9, 49, 63, 338.

[35] "Right" and "Left", only refers to the right and left wings of the hemicycles of the hall in which the Assembly meets. The Plain and the Mountain refer to the same Assembly but here to those on the lower or the upper benches.(SR).

[36] Meillan, "Mémoires," 20. – Buchez et Roux, XXVI. Session of April 15, 1793. Denunciation of the Twenty-two Girondists by the sections of Paris: Royer-Fonfrède regrets "that his name is not inscribed on this honorable list. 'And all of us – all! All!' exclaim three-quarters of the Assembly, rising from their seats."

[37] The Philosophe Denis Diderot (1713-84) was largely responsible for the 28 volume Encyclopédie (1751-729, which incorporated the latest knowledge and progressive ideas, and which helped spread the ideas of the Enlightenment in France and in other parts of Europe. (Guinness Encyclopedia).

[38] "Archives Nationales," A.F. 45. Letter of Thomas Paine to Danton, May 6, 1792 (in English). "I do not know better men or better patriots." This letter, compared with the speeches or publications of the day, produces a singular impression through its practical good sense. This Anglo–American, however radical he may be, relies on nothing but experience and example in his political discussions.

[39] Cf. The memoirs of Buzot, Barbaroux, Louvet, Madame Roland, etc.

[40] And for some incomprehensible reason still in fashion at the end of the 20th Century. (SR).

[41] Buchez et Roux, XXIV. 102. (Plan drawn up by Condorcet, and reported in the name of the Committee on the Constitution, April 15 and 16, 1793.) Condorcet adds to this a report of his own, of which he publishes and abstract in the Chronique de Paris.

[42] Buchez et Roux, XXIV. 102. Condorcet's abstract contains the following extraordinary sentence: "In all free countries the influence of the populace is feared with reason; but give all men the same rights and there will be no populace."

[43] Cf. Edmond Biré. "La Légende des Girondins," on the part of the Girondists in all these odious measures.

[44] These traits are well defined in the charges of the popular party against them made by Fabre d'Eglantine. Maillan, "Mémoires," 323. (Speech of Fabre d'Eglantine at the Jacobin Club in relation to the address of the commune, demanding the expulsion of the Twenty– Two.) "You have often taken the people to task; you have even sometimes tried to flatter them; but there was about this flattery that aristocratic air of coldness and dislike which could deceive nobody. Your ways of a bourgeois patrician are always perceptible in your words and acts; you never wanted to mix with the people. Here is your doctrine in few words: after the people have served in revolutions they must return to dust, be of no account, and allow themselves to be led by those who know more than they and who are willing to take the trouble to lead them. You, Brissot, and especially you, Pétion, you have received us formally, haughtily, and with reserve. You extend to us one finger, but you never grasp the whole hand. You have not even refused yourselves that keen delight of the ambitious, insolence and disdain."

[45] Buzot, "Mémoires," 78.

[46] Edmond Biré, "La légende des Girondins." (Inedited fragments of the memoirs of Pétion and Barbaroux, quoted by Vatel in "Charlotte Corday and the Girondists," III. 472, 478.)

[47] Buchez et Roux, XXVI. A financial plan offered by the department of Hérault adopted by Cambon and rejected by the Girondists.

[48] Buchez et Roux, XXV. Speech by Vergniaud (April 10), pp. 376, 377, 378. "An effort is made to accomplish the Revolution by terror. I would accomplish it through love."

[49] Maillan, 22.

[50] Buchez et Roux, XXIV. 109. Plan of a constitution presented by Condorcet. Declaration of rights, article 32. "In every free government the mode of resistance to different acts of oppression should be regulated by law." – Ibid., 136. Title VIII. Of the Constitution "De la Censure des lois."

[51] Buchez et Roux, 93. Session of the Jacobin Club, April 21, 1793.

[52] Schmidt, "Tableaux de la révolution Française," II.4 (Report of Dutard, June 6, 1793.) – The mental traits of the Jacobins form a contrast and are fully visible in the following speeches: "We desire despotically a popular constitution." (Address of the Paris Jacobin Club to the clubs in the departments, Jan. 7, 1793.) – Buchez et Roux, XXIII. 288 – Ibid., 274. (Speech by Legros in the Jacobin Club, Jan. 1.) "Patriots are not counted; they go by weight. . . One patriot in a scale weights more than 100,000 aristocrats. One Jacobin weights more than 10,000 Feuillants. One republican weights more than 100,000 monarchists. One patriot of the Mountain weights more than 100,000 Brissotins. Hence I conclude that the convention should not be stopped by the large number of votes against the death–sentence of Louis XVI., (and that) even (if there should be) but a minority of the nation desiring Capet's death." – "Applauded." (I am obliged to correct the last sentence, as it would otherwise be obscure.)

[53] Buzot, "Mémoires," 33: "The majority of French people yearned after royalty and the Constitution of 1790. This was the strongest feeling, and especially at Paris . . This people is only republican because it is threatened by the guillotine. . All its desires, all its hopes incline to the constitution of 1791."—–Schmidt, I. 232 (Dutard, May 16). Dutard, an old advocate and friend of Garat, is one of those rare men who see facts behind words; clear–sighted, energetic, active, abounding in practical counsels, and deserving of a better chief than Garat.

[54] Schmidt, ibid., I. 173, 179 (May 1, 1793).

[55] "La Démagogie à en Paris en 1793," p.152. Dauban ("Diurnal de Beaulieu," April 17). – "Archives Nationales," AF II. 45 (report by the police, May 20). "The dearness of supplies is the leading cause of agitation and complaints." — (Ib., May 24). "The calm which now appear to prevail in Paris will soon be disturbed if the prices of the prime necessities of life do not shortly diminish." — (Ibid., May 25). "Complaints against dear food increase daily end this circumstance looks as if it might become one of the motives of forthcoming events.

[56] Schmidt, I. 198 (Dutard, May 9).

[57] Schmidt, I. 350; II. 6 (Dutard, May 30, June 7 and 8).

[58] Durand–Maillane,100: "The Girondist party was yet more impious than Robespierre." — A deputy having demanded that mention should be made of the Supreme Being in the preamble of the constitution, Vergniaud replied: "We have no more to do with Numa's nymph than with Mahomet's pigeon; reason is sufficient to give France a good constitution." — Buchez et Roux, XIII. 444. Robespierre having spoken of the Emperor Leopold's death as a stroke of Providence, Guadet replies that he sees "no sense in that idea," and blames Robespierre for "endeavoring to return the people to slavery of superstition." – Ibid., XXVI. 63 (session of April 19, 1793). Speech by Vergniaud against

article IX of the Declaration of Rights, which states that "all men are free to worship as they please." This article, says Vergniaud, "is a result of the despotism and superstition under which we have so long languished." — Salle : "I ask the Convention to draw up an article by which each citizen, whatever his form of worship, shall bind himself to submit to the law " – Lanjuinais, who often ranked along with the Girondists, is a Catholic and confirmed Gallican.

[59] Schmidt, I. 347 (Dutard, May 30). "What do I now behold? A discontented people hating the Convention, all its administrators, and the actual state of things generally."

[60] Schmidt, I. 278. (Dutard, May 23).

[61] Schmidt, I. 216 (Dutard, May 13).

[62] Schmidt, I. 240 (Dutard, May 17).

[63] Schmidt, I. 217 (Dutard, May 13).

[64] Schmidt, I. 163 (Dutard, April 30).

[65] Schmidt, II. 377 (Dutard, June 13). Cf. Ibid., II. 80. (Dutard, June 21): "If the guillotining of the Thirty–Two were subject to a roll call, and the vote a secret one I declare to you no respectable man would fail to hasten in from the country to give his vote and that none of those now in Paris would fail to betake themselves to their section."

[66] Schmidt, II. 35 (Dutard, June 13). On the sense of these two words, inferior aristocracy, Cf. All of Dutard's reports and those of other observers in the employ of Garat.

[67] Schmidt, II. 37 (Dutard, June 13).

[68] Schmidt, I. 328 (Perrière, May 28): "Intelligent men and property–owners abandoned the section assemblies and handed them to others as these were places where the workman's fist prevailed against the speaker's tongue." – Moniteur. XV. 114 (session of Jan. 11, speech by Buzot). "There is not a man in this town who owns anything, that is not afraid of being insulted and struck in his section if he dares raise his voice against the ruling power. . . The permanent assemblies of Paris consist of a small number of men who have succeeded in keeping other citizens away." – Schmidt, I. 235 (Dutard, May 28): "Another plan would be to drill young men in the use of the staff. One must be a sans–culotte, must live with sans–culottes, to discover the value of expedients of this kind. There is nothing the sans–culotte fears as much as a truncheon. A number of young men lately carried them in their trousers, and everybody trembled as they passed. I wished that the fashion were general."

[69] Moniteur, XV. 95 (Letter of Charles Villette, deputy).

[70] Moniteur, XV. 179 (Letter of Roland, Jan. 11. 1793).

[71] Moniteur, XV. 66, session of Jan. 5, speech of the mayor of Paris; (Chambon) – Ib., XV 114,

session of Jan. 14, speech by Buzot; – – Ib., XV. 136, session of Jan. 13. Speech by a deputation of Federates. – Buchez et Roux, XXVIII. 91 (Letter of Gadolle to Roland, October, 1792). — XXI. 417 (Dec. 20, article by Marat): " Boredom and disgust have emptied the assemblies. — Schmidt, II, 69 (Dutard, June 18).

[72] Schmidt, I. 203. (Dutard, May 10). The engravings published during the early period of the Revolution and under the directory exhibit this scene perfectly (cabinet des estampes, Paris).

[73] Moniteur, XV. 67 (session of Jan. 5, 1793). Speech by the mayor of Paris.

[74] Schmidt, I. 378 (Blanc, June 12).

[75] Schmidt, II. 5 (Dutard, June 5).

[76] Schmidt, II. (Dutard, June 11) — Ibid., II. (Dutard, June i8): "I should like to visit with you," if it were possible, "the 3,000 or 4,000 wine–dealers, and the equally numerous places of refreshment in Paris; you would find the 15,000 clerks they employ constantly busy. If we should then go to the offices of the 114 notaries, we should again find two–thirds of these gentlemen in their caps and red slippers, also very much engaged. We might then, again, go to the 200 or 300 printing establishments, where we should find 4,000 or 5,000 editors, compositors, clerks, and porters all conservatized because they no longer earn what they did before; and some because they have made a fortune." — The incompatibility between modern life and direct democratic rule strikes one at every step, owing to modern life being carried out under other conditions than those which characterized life in ancient times. For modern life these conditions are, the magnitude of States, the division of labor, the suppression of slavery and the requirements of personal comforts and prosperity. Neither the Girondists nor the Montagnards, who aimed to revive Athenian and Spartan ways, comprehended the precisely opposite conditions on which Athens and Sparta flourished.

[77] Schmidt, I. 207 (Dutard, May 10).

[78] Schmidt, II. 79 (Dutard, June 19).

[79] Schmidt, II.70 (Dutard, June 10).

[80] Lenin must have felt encouraged by reading these lines which can only have increase his disdain for the "capitalist" and bourgeoisie. (SR).

[81] Mortimer–Ternaux, V. 101.

[82] Meillan, 54. — Raffet, Henriot's competitor and denounced as an aristocrat, had at first the most votes, 4,953 against 4,578. At the last ballot, out of about 15,000 he still has 5,900 against 9,087 for Henriot. — Mortimer–Ternaux, VIII. 31: "The electors had to vote thirty at a time. All who dared give their votes to Raffet were marked with a red cross on the roll–call, followed by the epithet of anti– revolutionary."

[83] Schmidt, II. 37 (Dutard, June 13): "Marat and others have a party of from 4,000 to 6,000 men, who would do anything to rescue them." — Meillan, 155 (depositions taken by the Commission of the Twelve): Laforet has stated that there were 6,000 sans–culottes to massacre objectionable deputies at the first signal. — Schmidt, II, 87 (Dutard, June 24): "I know that there are not in all Paris 3,000 decided revolutionaries."

[84] Moniteur, XV. 114, session of Jan. 11, speech by Buzot. — Ibid., 136, session of Jan. 13, speech of the Federates of Finisterre. – Buchez et Roux, XXVIII. 80, 81, 87, 91, 93 (Letter of Gadolle to Roland, October 1792). – Schmidt, I. 207 (Dutard, May 10, 1793).

[85] Schmidt, II. 37 (Dutard, May 10, 1793).

[86] Mortimer–Ternaux, IV. 269 (petition presented by Gonchon.) – "Archives Nationales, AF, II 43. Letters of Gonchon to the Minister Garat, May 31, June 1, June 3, 1793). These are very odd and naive. He addresses the Minister Garat: "Citizen Garra."

[87] Schmidt, I, 254 (Dutard, May 19). – Moniteur, XIV. 522 (Letter addressed to Roland number for Nov. 21, 1792): "The sections (are) composed of, or at least frequented, nineteen–twentieth of them, by the lowest class, both in manners and information."

[88] Schmidt, II. 39 (Dutard, June 13).

[89] Schmidt, II.87 (Dutard, June 14). The expression of these fish– women is still coarser.

[90] Rétif de la Bretonne ("Bibliographie de ses oeuvres, par Jacob, 287). — (On the pillage of shops, Feb.25 and 26, 1793).

[91] Schmidt, II. 61; I. 265 (Dutard, May 21 and June 17).

[92] Schmidt, I.96 (Letter of citizen Lauchou to the president of the Convention, Oct. 11, 1792). – II. 37 (Dutard, June 13). Statement of a wigmaker's wife: "They are a vile set, the servants. Some of them come here every day. They chatter away and say all sorts of horrible things about their masters. They are all just alike. Nobody is crazier than they are. I knew that some of them had received benefits from their masters, and others who were :still being kindly treated; but nothing stopped them."

[93] Schmidt, I. 246 (Dutard, May 18). — Grégoire, "Mémoires," I. 387. The mental and moral decline of the party is well shown in the new composition of the Jacobin Club after September, 1792: "I went back there," says Grégoire in September, 1792 (after a year's absence), "and found it unrecognizable; no opinions could be expressed there other than those of the Paris section . . . I did not set foot there again; (it was) a factious disreputable drinking place." — Buchez et Roux, XXVI. 214 (session of April 30,1793, speech by Buzot). "Behold that once famous club. But. thirty of its founders remain there; you find there none but men steeped in debt and crime."

[94] Schmidt, I. 189 (Dutard, May 6).

[95] Cf. Rétif de la Bretonne, "Nuits de Paris," vol. XVI. (July 12, 1789). At this date Rétif is in the Palais–Royal, where "since the 13th of June numerous meetings have been held and motions made. . . I found there none but brutal fellows with keen eyes, preparing themselves for plunder rather than for liberty."

[96] Mortimer–Ternaux, V.226 and following pages (address of the sans– culottes section, Sept. 25). — "Archives Nationales," F7, 146 (address of the Roule section, Sept. 23). In relation to the threatening tone of those at work on the camp, the petitioners add: "Such was the language of the workshops in 1789 and 1790."

[97] Schmidt, II.12 (Dutard, June 7): "During a few days past I have seen men from Neuilly, Versailles, and Saint–Germain staying here, attracted by the scent."

[98 Schmidt, I.254 (Dutard, May 19) .— At this date robbers swarm in Paris; Mayor Chambon, in his report to the Convention, himself admits it (Moniteur, XV. 67, session of Jan. 5, 1793).

[99] De Concourt, "La Société Française pendant 'a Révolution." (According to the" Courrier de l'Egalité, Jul. 1793).

[100] Buzot, 72.

[101] Moore, Nov.10, 1792 (according to an article in the Chronique de Paris). 'The day Robespierre made his "apology," "the galleries contained from seven to eight hundred women, and two hundred men at most. Robespierre is a priest who has his congregation of devotees." – – Mortimer–Ternaux, VII. 562 (letter of the deputy Michel, May 20, 1793): "Two or three thousand women, organized and drilled by the Fraternal Society in session at the Jacobin Club, began their uproar. which lasted until 6 o'clock, when the house adjourned. Most of these creatures are prostitutes."

[102] An expression of Gadol's in his letter to Roland.

[103] Buzot, 57.

[104] Buchez et Roux, XXVIII. 80 (Letter of Gadolle to Roland).

[105] Beaulieu, "Essais," I. 108 (an eye–witness). – Schmidt, II. 15. Report by Perrières, June 8.

[106] Beaulieu, "Essais," I. 100. "Maillard died, his stomach eaten away by brandy" (April 15, 1794). – Alexandre Sorel, "Stanislas Maillard," pp. 32 to 42. Report of Fabre d'Eglantine on Maillard, Dec. 17, 1793. A decree subjecting him to indictment along with Ronsin and Vincent, Maillard publishes his apology, in which we see that he was already active in the Rue Favart before the 31st of May. "I am one of the members of that meeting of true patriots and I am proud of it, for it is there that the spark of that sacred insurrection of the 31st of May was kindled."

[107] Alexandre Sorel, ibid. (denunciation of the circumstance by Lecointre, Dec.14, 1793 accompanied with official reports of the justices). — "Archives Nationales," F7, 3268 (letter of the

directory of Corbeil to the Minister, with official report, Nov. 28,1792). On the 26th of November eight or ten armed men, foot–soldiers, and others on horseback, entered the farm–house of a man named Ruelle, in the commune of Lisse. They dealt him two blows with their sabers, then put a bag over his head, kicked him in the face, tormented him, and almost smothered his wife and two women servants, to make him give up his money. A carter was shot with a pistol in the shoulder and twice struck with a saber; the hands about the premises were tied and bound like so many cattle. Finally the bandits went away, carrying with them silver plate, a watch, rings, laces, two guns, etc.

[108] Moniteur, XV. 565. — Buchez et Roux, XXIV. 335 and following pages. – Rétif de la Bretonne, "Nuits de Paris," VIII. 460. (an eye witness). The last of these details are given by him.

[109] Cf. Ed. Fleury, "Baboeuf;" pp.139 and 150. Through a striking coincidence the party staff is still of the same order in 1796. Baboeuf estimates his adherents in Paris as "4,000 revolutionaries, 1,500 members of the former authorities, and 1,000 bourgeois gunners," besides soldiers, prisoners, and a police force. He also recruited a good many prostitutes. The men who come to him are workmen who pretend to have arsouillé109 in the Revolution and who are ready to repeat the job, provided it is for the purpose of killing those rich rascals, the monopolizers, merchants, informers, and panachés at the Luxembourg." (Letter of the agent of the Bonne–Nouvelle section, April 13, 1796.)

[110] The proportion, composition and spirit of the party are everywhere the same, especially at Lyons (Guillon de Montléon, "Mémoires," and Balleydier, "Histoire du peuple de Lyon,". passim); at Toulon (Lauvergne, "Histoire du department du Var"); at Marseilles, Bordeaux, Toulouse, Strasbourg, Besançon, etc. — At Bordeaux (Riouffe, "Mémoires," 23) "it consisted wholly of vagabonds, Savoyards, Biscayans, even Germans, . .brokers, and water–carriers, who had become so powerful that they arrested the rich, and so well– off that they traveled by post" Riouffe adds: "When I read this passage in the Conciergerie men from every corner of the republic exclaimed in one voice: 'It is the same in all the communes!'" — Cf. Durand–Maillane, "Mémoires," 67: "This people, thus qualified, since the suppression of the silver marc has been the most vicious and most depraved in the community." – Dumouriez, II. 51. "The Jacobins, taken for the most part, from the most abject and most brutal of the nation, unable to furnish men of sufficient dignity for offices, have degraded offices to their own level. . . They are drunken, barbarous Helots that have taken the places of the Spartans." — The sign of their advent is the expulsion of the liberals and of the refined of 1789. ("Archives Nationales," F7, 4434, No.6. Letter of Richard to the committee on Public Safety, Ventôse 3, year II.). During the proconsulate of Baudot at Toulouse "almost all the patriots of 1789 were excluded from the popular club they had founded; an immense number were admitted whose patriotism reached only as far back as the 10th of August 1792, if it even went so far as the 31st of last May. It is an established fact that out of more than 1,000 persons who now compose the club there are not fifty whose patriotism as far back as the beginning of the Revolution."

[111] Any tribune taking command of a mob of brutes is well advised to understand Taine's analysis. One might think Hitler had read Taine pr somebody who had learned from his wisdom, somewhat like the Devil who had read the Bible. See page 208, The Secret of Ruling the Masses, in Rauschning's book, "Hitler Speaks". (SR).

[112] Rœderer, "Chronique des cinquante jours."

[113] Schmidt, I. 246 (Dutard, May 18).

[114] Schmidt, I. 215 (Dutard, May 25).

[115] Buchez et Roux, XXV. 156 (extract from the Patriote Français, March 30, 1793).Speech by Chasles at the Jacobin Club, March 27: "We have announced to our fellow–citizens in the country that by means of the war–tax the poor could be fed by the rich, and that they would find in the purses of those egoists the wherewithal to live on." Ibid., 269. Speech by Rose Lacombe: "Let us make sure of the aristocrats; let us force them to meet the enemies which Dumouriez is bringing against Paris. Let us give them to understand that if they prove treacherous their wives and children shall have their throats cut, and that we will burn their houses. . I do not want patriots to leave the city; I want them to guard Paris. And if we are beaten, the first man who hesitates to apply the torch, let him be stabbed at once. I want all the owners of property who have grabbed everything and excited the people's anger, to kill the tyrants themselves or else be killed." [Applause — April 3.] – Ibid., 302 (in the Convention, April 8): "Marat demands that 100,000 relatives and friends of the émigrés be seized as hostages for the safety of the commissioners in the hands of the enemy." — Cf. Balleydier, 117, 122. At Lyons, Jan. 26, 1793, Challier addresses the central club: "Sans–culottes, rejoice! the blood of the royal tiger has flowed in sight of his den! But full justice is not yet done to the people There are still 500 among you deserving of the tyrant's fate! " — He proposes on the 5th of February a revolutionary tribunal for trying arrested persons in a revolutionary manner. "It is the only way to force it (the Revolution) on royal and aristocratic factionists, the only rational way to avenge the sovereignty of the brave sans–culottes, who belong only to us." – – Hydens, a national commissioner adds: "Let 25,000,000 of Frenchmen perish a hundred times over rather than one single indivisible Republic!"

[116] Mallet du Pan, the last expression.

[117] Buzot, 64.

[118] Michelet, IV. 6 (according to an oral statement by Daunou). — Buchez et Roux, 101 (Letter of Louvet to Roland): "At the moment of the presentation of their petition against armed force (departmental) by the so–called commissioners of the 48 sections of Paris, I heard Santerre say in a loud tone to those around him, somewhat in these words: 'You see, now, these deputies are not up to the Revolution. . . That all comes from fifty, a hundred two hundred leagues off; they don't understand one word you say!'"

CHAPTER IV. PRECARIOUS SITUATION OF A CENTRAL GOVERNMENT LOCKED UP WITHIN A LOCAL JURISDICTION.

"Citizen Danton," wrote the deputy Thomas Paine,[1] "the danger, every day increasing, is of a rupture between Paris and departments. The departments did not send their deputies to Paris to be insulted, and every insult shown to them is an insult to the department that elected them. I see but one effective plan to prevent this rupture taking place, and that is to fix the residence of the Convention and of the future assemblies at a distance from Paris. . . . I saw, during the American Revolution, the exceeding inconvenience that arose from having the government of Congress within the limits of any municipal jurisdiction. Congress first resided in Philadelphia, and, after a residence of four years, it found it necessary to leave it. It then adjourned to the State of Jersey. It afterwards removed to New York. It again removed from New York to Philadelphia, and, after experiencing in every one of these places the great inconvenience of a government within a government, it formed the project of building a town not within the limits of any municipal jurisdiction for the future residence of Congress. In every one of the places where Congress resided, the municipal authority privately or publicly opposed itself to the authority of Congress, and the people of each of those places expected more attention from Congress than their equal share with the other States amounted to. The same thing now takes place in France, but in a greater excess."

Danton knew all this, and he is sufficiently clear–headed to comprehend the danger; but the furrow is laid out, traced, and by himself. Since the 10th of August Paris holds France down while a handful of revolutionaries tyrannize Paris.[2]

I.

Jacobin advantages. — Their sway in the section assemblies. — Maintenance, re–election and completion of the Commune.— Its new chiefs, Chaumette, Hébert and Pache. — The National Guard recast. — Jacobins elected officers and sub–officers.— The paid band of roughs. — Public and secret funds of the party.

Owing to the composition and the holding of the section assemblies, the original source of power has remained Jacobin, and has become of a darker and darker hue; accordingly, the electoral processes which, under the legislative body, had fashioned the usurping Commune of the 10th of August, are perpetuated and aggravated under the Convention.[3] "In nearly all the sections[4] it is the sans–culottes who occupy the chair, arrange things inside the chamber, place the sentinels and provide the censors and auditors. Five or six spies, familiar with the section, and paid forty sous a day, remain during the session, and ready to undertake any enterprise. These same individuals will take orders from one Committee of Surveillance to another, . . so that if the sans–culottes of one section are not strong enough they may call in those of a neighboring section." — In such assemblies the elections are decided beforehand, and we see how the faction keeps forcibly in its hands, or obtains by force, every elective position. The Council of the Commune, in spite of the hostile inclinations of the Legislative Assembly and the Convention, succeeds at first in maintaining itself four months; then, in December,[5] when it is at last compelled to break up, it reappears through the authorization of the suffrage, reinforced and completed by its own class, with three chiefs, a syndic–attorney, a deputy and a mayor, all three authors or abettors of the September massacre; with Chaumette, Anaxagoras, so–called, once a cabin–boy, then a clerk, always in debt, a windbag, and given to drink; Hébert, called "Père Duchesne," which states about all that is necessary for him; Pache, a subaltern busy– body, a bland, smooth–faced intriguer, who, with his simple air and seeming worth, pushes himself up to the head of the War Department, where he used all its resources for pillaging, and who, born in a door–keeper's lodgings, returns there, either through craft or inclination, to take his dinner. — The Jacobins, with the civil power in their hands, also grab the military power. Immediately after the 10th of August,[6] the National Guard is reorganized and distributed in as many battalions as there are sections, each battalion thus becoming "a section in arms"; by this we may judge its composition, and the kind of rabble–rousers they select as officers and non– commissioned officers. "The title of National Guard," writes a deputy, "can no longer be given to the lot of pikemen and substitutes, mixed with a few bourgeois, who, since the 10th of August, maintain the military service in Paris." There are, indeed, 110,000 names on paper; when called out on important occasions, all who are registered may respond, if not disarmed, but, in general, almost all stay at home and pay a sans–culotte to mount guard in their place. In fact, there is for the daily service only a hired reserve in each section, about one hundred men, always the same individuals. This makes in Paris a band of four or five thousand roughs, in which the squads may be distinguished which have already been seen in September: Maillard and his 68 men at the Abbaye, Gauthier and his 40 men at Chantilly, Audouin, the Sapper of the Carmelites," and his 350 men in the suburbs of Paris, Fournier, Lazowski and their 1,500 men at Orleans and Versailles.[7] As to the pay of these and that of their civil auxiliaries, the faction is not troubled about that; for, along with power, it has seized money. To say nothing of its rapine in September,[8] and without including the lucrative offices at its disposition, four hundred of these being distributed by Pache alone, and four hundred more by Chaumette,[9] the Commune has 850,000 francs per month for its military police. Other bleedings at the Treasury cause more public money to flow into the pockets of its clients. One million per month supports the idle workmen which fife and drum have collected together to form the camp around Paris. Five millions of francs protect the petty tradesmen of the capital against the depreciation in value of certificates of credit. Twelve thousand francs a day keep down the price of bread for the Paris poor.[10] To these regularly allowed subsidies add the funds which are diverted or extorted. On one side, in the War Department, Pache, its accomplice before becoming its mayor, organizes a steady stream of waste and theft; in three months he succeeds in bringing about a deficiency of 130,000,000, "without vouchers."[11] On another side, the Duke of Orleans, become Philippe–Egalité, dragged along by the men once in his pay, with a rope around his neck and almost strangled, has to pay out more than ever, even down to the very depths of his purse; to save his own life he consents to vote for the King's death, besides resigning himself to other sacrifices;[12] it is probable that a large portion of his 74,000,000 of indebtedness at his death is due to all this. — Thus in possession of civil and military offices, of arms and money, the faction, masters of Paris, has nothing to do but master the isolated Convention, and this it invests on all sides.[13]

II.

Its parliamentary recruits. — Their characters and minds. — Saint– Just. — Violence of the minority in the Convention. — Pressure of the galleries. — Menaces of the streets.

Through the elections, the Jacobin advance–guard of fifty deputies is already posted there; while, owing to the fascination it has to excitable and despotic natures, to brutal temperaments, narrow, disjointed minds, weak imaginations, doubtful honesty, and old religious or social rancor, it succeeds in doubling this number at the end of six months.[14] On the benches of the extreme "Left," around Robespierre, Danton and Marat, the original nucleus of the September faction, sit men of their stamp, first, the corrupt, like Chabot, Tallien and Barras, wretches like Fouché, Guffroy and Javogues, crazy enthusiasts like David, savage maniacs like Carrier, paltry simpletons like Joseph Lebon, common fanatics like Levasseur, Baubot, Jeanbon– Saint–André, Romme and Lebas. Add also, and especially, the future iron–handed representatives, uncouth, authoritarian, and narrow– minded, excellent troopers for a political militia, Bourbotte, Duquesnoy, Rewbell, and Bentabole, "a lot of ignorant bastards," said Danton,[15] "without any common sense, and patriotic only when drunk. Marat is nothing but a bawler. Legendre is fit for nothing but to cut up his meat. The rest are good for little else than voting by either sitting down or standing up, but they are cold blooded and have broad shoulders." From amongst these energetic nonentities we see ascending a young monster, with calm, handsome features, Saint–Just. He is a kind of precocious Sylla, 25 years old and a new–comer, who springs at once from the ranks and, by dint of atrocities, obtains a prominent position.[16] Six years before this he began life by a domestic robbery; on a visit to his mother, he left the house during the night, carrying off the plate and jewels, which he squandered while living in a lodging house in the Rue Fromenteau, in the center of Parisian prostitution;[17] on the strength of this, and at the demand of his friends, he is shut up in a house of correction for six months. On returning to his lodgings he occupied himself with writing an obscene poem in the style of La Pucelle and then, through a fit of rage resembling a spasm, he plunged headlong into the Revolution. He possessed a "blood calcified by study," a colossal pride, an unhinged conscience, a pompous, gloomy imagination haunted with the bloody recollections of Rome and Sparta, an intelligence so warped and twisted as to be comfortable only among excessive paradoxes, shameless sophistry, and devastating lies.[18] All these dangerous ingredients which, mingled in the crucible of suppressed, concentrated ambition, long and silently boiling within him, have led to a constant defiance, a determined callousness, an automatic rigidity, and to the summary politics of the Utopian dictator and exterminator. — It is plain that such a minority will not obey parliamentary rules, and, rather than yield to the majority that it will introduce into the debate boos and hisses, insults, threats, and scuffles with daggers, pistols, sabers and even the "blunder busses" of a veritable combat.

"Vile intriguers, calumniators, scoundrels, monsters, assassins, blackguards, fools and hogs," such are the usual terms in which they address each other, and these form the least of their outrages.[19] The president, at certain sessions, is obliged three times to put on his hat and, at last, breaks his bell. They insult him, force him to leave his seat and demand that "he be removed.' Bazire tries to snatch a declaration presented by him "out of his hands." Bourdon, from the department of Oise, cries out to him that if he "dares to read it he will assassinate him."[20] The chamber "has become an arena of gladiators."[21] Sometimes the entire "Mountain" darts from its benches on the left, while a similar human wave rolls down from those on the right; both clash in the center of the room amidst furious screams and shouts; in one of these hubbubs one of the "Mountain" having drawn a pistol the Girondist Duperret draws his sword.[22] After the middle of December prominent members of the "Right," constantly persecuted, threatened and outraged," reduced to "being out every night, are compelled to carry arms in self–defense,"[23] and, after the King's execution, "almost all" bring them to the sessions of the Convention. Any day, indeed, they may look for the final attack, and they are not disposed to die unavenged: during the night of March 9, finding that they are only forty–three, they agree to launch themselves in a body "at the first hostile movement, against their adversaries and kill as many as possible" before perishing.[24]

It is a desperate resource, but the only one. For, besides the madmen belonging to the Convention, they have against them the madmen in the galleries, and these likewise are September murderers. The vilest Jacobin rabble purposely takes its stand near them, at first in the old Riding–school, and then in the new hall in the Tuileries. They see above and in a circle around them drilled adversaries, eight or nine hundred heads packed "in the great gallery at the bottom, under a deep and silent vault," and, besides these, on the sides, a thousand or fifteen hundred more, two immense tribunes completely filled.[25] The galleries of the Constituent and Legislative Assemblies, compared with these, were calm. Nothing is more disgraceful to the Convention, writes a foreign spectator,[26] than the insolence of the audience. One of the regulations prohibits, indeed, any mark of approval or disapproval, "but it is violated every day, and nobody is ever punished for this delinquency." The majority in vain expresses its indignation at this "gang of hired ruffians," who beset and oppress it, while at the very time that it utters its complaints, it endures and tolerates it. "The struggle is frightful," says a deputy,[27] "screams, murmurs, stampings, shouts. . . The foulest insults were launched from the galleries." "For a long time," says another, "no one can speak here without obtaining their permission."[28] The day that Buzot obtains the floor to speak against Marat, "they break out furiously, yelling, stamping, and threatening";[29] every time that Buzot tries to begin his voice is drowned in the clamor, while he remains half an hour in the tribune without completing a sentence. On the calls of the House, especially, their cries resemble those of the excited crowd at a Spanish bull–fight, with their eager eyes and heaving breasts, watching the contest between the bull and the picadores; every time that a deputy votes against the death of the King or for an appeal to the people, there are the "vociferations of cannibals," and "interminable yells" every time that one votes for the indictment of Marat. "I declare," say deputies in the tribune, "that I am not free here; I declare that I am forced to debate under the knife."[30] Charles Villette is told at the entrance that "if he does not vote for the King's death he will be massacred." — And these are not empty threats. On the 10th of March, awaiting the promised riot, "the tribunes, duly advised, . . . had already loaded their pistols."[31] In the month of May, the tattered women hired for the purpose, under the title of "Ladies of the Fraternity," formed a club, came daily early in the morning to mount guard, with arms in their hands, in the corridors of the Convention; they tear up all tickets given to men or women not of their band; they take possession of all the seats, show pistols and daggers, and declare that "eighteen hundred heads must be knocked off to make things go on right."[32]

Behind these two first rows of assailants is a third, much more compact, the more fearful because it is undefined and obscure, namely, the vague multitude forming the anarchical set, scattered throughout Paris, and always ready to renew the 10th of August and 2nd of September against the obstinate majority. Incendiary motions and demands for riots come incessantly from the Commune, and Jacobin, Cordeliers, and l'Evêché clubs; from the assemblies of the sections and groups stationed at the Tuileries and in the streets. "Yesterday," writes the president of the Tuileries section,[33] "at the same moment, at various points about Paris, the Rue du Bac, at the Marais, in the Church of St. Eustache, at the Palace of the Revolution, on the Feuillants terrace, scoundrels were preaching pillage and assassination." — On the following day, again on the Feuillants terrace, that is to say, right under the windows of the Convention, "they urge the assassination of Louvel for having denounced Robespierre." — Minister Roland writes: "I hear of nothing but conspiracy and plans to murder." — Three weeks later, for several days, "an up–rising is announced in Paris";[34] the Minister is warned that "alarm guns would be fired," while the heads are designated beforehand on which this ever muttering insurrection will burst. In the following month, in spite of the recent precise law, "the electoral assembly prints and circulates gratis the list of members of the Feuillants and Sainte–Chapelle clubs; it likewise orders the printing and circulation of the list of the eight thousand, and of the twenty thousand, as well as of the clubs of 1789 and of Montaigu."[35] In January, "hawkers cry through the streets a list of the aristocrats and royalists who voted for an appeal to the people."[36] Some of the appelants are singled out by name through placards; Thibaut, bishop of Cantal, while reading the poster on the wall relating to him, hears some one along side of him say: "I should like to know that bishop of Cantal; I would make bread tasteless to him." Roughs point out certain deputies leaving the Assembly, and exclaim: "Those are the beggars to cut up!" — From week to week signs of insurrection increase and multiply, like flashes of lightning in a coming tempest. On the 1st of January, "it is rumored that the barriers are to be closed at night, and that domiciliary visits are going to begin again."[37] On the 7th of January, on the motion of the Gravilliers section, the Commune demands of the Minister of War 132 cannon stored at Saint Denis, to divide among the sections. On the 15th of January the same section proposes to the other forty–seven to appoint, as on the 10th of August, special commissaries to meet at the Evêché and watch over public safety. That same day, to prevent the Convention from misunderstanding the object of these proceedings, it is openly stated in the tribunes that the cannon brought to Paris "are for another 10th of August against that body." The same day, military force has to be employed to prevent bandits from going to the prisons "to renew the massacres." On the 28th of January the Palais–Royal, the resort of the pleasure–seeking, is surrounded by Santerre, at eight o'clock in the evening, and "about six thousand men, found without a certificate of civism," are arrested, subject to the decision one by one of their section. — Not only does the lightning flash, but already the bolt descends in isolated places.[38] On the 31st of December a man named Louvain, formerly denounced by Marat as Lafayette's agent, is slain in the faubourg St. Antoine, and his corpse dragged through the streets to the Morgue. On the 25th of February, the grocer shops are pillaged at the instigation of Marat, with the connivance or sanction of the Commune. On the 9th of March the printing establishment of Gorsas is sacked by two hundred men armed with sabers and pistols. The same evening and on the next morning the riot extends to the Convention itself; "the committee of the Jacobin club summons every section in Paris to arms to "get rid" of the appelant deputies and the ministers; the Cordeliers club requests the Parisian authorities "to take sovereignty into their own hands and place the treacherous deputies under arrest"; Fournier, Varlet, and Champion ask the Commune "to declare itself in insurrection and close the barriers"; all the approaches to the Convention are occupied by the "dictators of massacre," Pétion[39] and Beurnonville being recognized on their passing, pursued and in danger of death, while furious mobs gather on the Feuillants terrace "to award popular judgment," "to cut off heads" and "send them into the departments." — Luckily, it rains, which always cools down popular effervescence. Kervélegan, a deputy from Finistère, who escapes, finds means of sending to the other end of the faubourg St. Marceau for a battalion of volunteers from Brest that had arrived a few days before, and who were still loyal; these come in time and save the Convention. — Thus does the majority live under the triple pressure of the "Mountain," the galleries and the outside populace, and from month to month, especially after March 10, the pressure gets to be worse and worse.

III. Physical fear and moral cowardice.

Defection among the majority. — Effect of physical fear. — Effect of moral cowardice. — Effect of political necessity. — Internal weakness of the Girondins. — Accomplices in principle of the Montagnards.

Month by month the majority relents under this pressure. — Some are simply overcome by physical fear. On the King's trial, at the third call of the House, as the deputies on the upper benches voted one by one for his death, the deputy alongside Daunou "showed in a most energetic manner his disapproval of this." On his turn coming, "the galleries, which had undoubtedly noticed his attitude," burst out in such violent threats that for some minutes his voice could not be heard; "silence was at length restored, and he voted — death."[40] — Others, like Durand–Maillane, "warned by Robespierre that the strongest party is the safest," say to themselves "that it is prudent, and necessary not to annoy the people in their furor," make up their minds "to keep aloof shielded by their silence and insignificance."[41] Among the five hundred deputies of the Plain, many are of this stamp. They begin to be called "the Marsh Frogs." In six months they settle down of themselves into so many silent onlookers, or, rather, homicidal puppets, "whose hearts, shrunk through fear, rise in their throats"[42] every time that Robespierre looks at them. Long before the fall of the Girondists, "downcast at the present state of things, and no longer finding any inspiration in their heart," their faces already disclosing "the pallor of fear or the resignation of despair.[43] Cambacérès hedges to find shelter in his Committee on Legislation.[44] Barrère, born a valet, and a valet ready for anything, places his southern mode of doing things at the service of the probable majority, up to the time of devoting his cruel rhetoric to the service of the dominant minority. Sièyes, after casting his vote for death, maintains an obstinate silence, as much through disgust as through prudence:

"What does my glass of wine matter in this torrent of booze?"[45]

Many, even among the Girondists, use sophistry to color their concessions in their own eyes. Some among these "think that they enjoy some degree of popularity, and fear that this will be compromised.[46] Again, they put forth the pretext of the necessity of maintaining one's influence for important occasions. Occasionally, they affect to say, or say it in good faith, Let them (the extravagant) keep on, they will find each other out and use themselves up." — Frequently, the motives alleged are scandalous or grotesque. According to Barbaroux, immediate execution must be voted, because that is the best way to exculpate the Gironde and shut the mouths of their Jacobin calumniators.[47] According to Berlier, it is essential to vote death for, why vote for exile? Louis XVI. would be torn to pieces before reaching the frontier.[48] — On the eve of the verdict, Vergniaud says to M. de Ségur: "I vote Death? It is an insult to suppose me capable of such a disgraceful act!" And, "he sets forth the frightful iniquity of such a course, its uselessness, and even its danger." "I would rather stand alone in my opinion than vote Death!"[49] The next day, having voted Death, he excuses himself by saying "that he did not think he ought to put the life of one man in the scale against the public welfare."[50] Fifteen or twenty deputies, influenced by his example, voted as he did, which was enough to turn the majority.[51] The same weakness is found at other decisive moments. Charged with the denunciation of the conspiracy of the 10th of March, Vergniaud attributes it to the aristocrats, and admits to Louvet that "he did not wish to name the real conspirators for fear of embittering violent men already pushing things to excess."[52] The truth is, the Girondists, as formerly the Constitutionalists, are too civilized for their adversaries, and submit to force for lack of resolution to employ it themselves.

"To put down the faction," says one of them,[53] "can be done only by cutting its throat, which, perhaps, would not be difficult to do. All Paris is as weary as we are of its yoke, and if we had any liking for or knowledge how to deal with insurrections, we could soon throw it off. But how can we make men adopt such necessary atrocious measures when they are criticizing their adversaries for taking these? And yet they would have saved the country." Consequently, incapable of action, able only to talk, reduced to protests, to barring the way to revolutionary decrees, to making appeals to the department against Paris, they stand as an obstacle to all the practical people who are heartily engaged in the brunt of the action. — "There is no doubt that Carnot is as honest as they are, as honest as a fanatic spectator can be."[54] Cambon, undoubtedly with as much integrity as Roland, spoke as loudly up as he against the 2nd of September, the Commune, and anarchy.[55] — But, to Carnot and Cambon, who pass their nights, one in establishing his budgets, and the other in studying his military maps, they require, first of all, a government which will provide them with money and with soldiers, and, therefore, an unscrupulous and unanimous Convention ; that is to say, there being no other expedient, a Convention under compulsion, i.e. a Convention purged of troublesome some, dissentient speakers;[56] in other words, the dictatorship of the Parisian proletariat. After the 15th of December, 1792, Cambon completely accepts this, and even erects the dictatorship of the proletariat into an European system. From that time[57] he preaches universal sans–culotterie, a form of government in which the poor will rule and the rich will pay, in short, the restoration of privileges in an inverse sense. The later expression of Siéyès which has already come true: the problem is no longer how to apply the principles of the Revolution, but the salvation of its men. Faced with this more and more distressing imperative, many of undecided deputies go with the tide, letting the Montagnards have their own way and separate themselves from the Girondists.

And, what is graver still, the Girondists, apart from all these defections, are untrue to themselves. Not only are they ignorant of how to draw a line, of how to form themselves into a compact body: not only "is the very idea of a collective proceeding repulsive, each member desiring to keep himself independent. and act as he thinks best,"[58] make motions without consulting others, and vote as the occasion calls for against his party, but, through its abstract principle, they are in accord with their adversaries, and, on the fatal declivity whereon their honorable and humane instincts still retain them, this common dogma, like a concealed weight, causes them to sink lower and lower down, even into the bottomless pit, where the State, according to the formula of Jean Jacques, omnipotent, philosophic, anti–Catholic, anti–Christian, despotic, leveling, intolerant, and propagandist, seizes education, levels fortunes, persecutes the Church, oppresses consciences, crushes out the individual, and, by military foice, imposes its structures abroad.[59] Basically, apart from the Jacobin excess of brutality and of precipitation, the Girondists, setting out from the same principles as the Jacobin "Mountain," march forward to the same end along with them. Hence the effect of ideological prejudice on them in weakening their moral attitudes. Secretly, in their hearts, revolutionary desires conspire with those of their enemies, and, on many occasions, make them betray themselves. — Through these devices and multiplied weaknesses, on the one hand, the majority diminishes so as to present but 279 votes against 228.[60] And, on the other hand, through frequent failures, it surrenders to the besiegers one by one every commanding post of the public citadel. Now, at the first attack, nothing remains but to fly, or to beg for mercy.

IV. Jacobin victory over Girondin majority.

Principal decrees of the Girondist majority. — Arms and means of attack surrendered by it to its adversaries.

The Convention had voted, on principle, for the establishment of a military departmental guard, but, owing to the opposition of the Montagnards, it fails to put the principle into operation. — For six months it is protected, and, on the 10th of March, saved, through the spontaneous aid of provincial federates, but, far from organizing these passing auxiliaries into a permanent body of faithful defenders, it allows them to be dispersed or corrupted by Pache and the Jacobins. — It passes decrees frequently for the punishment of the abettors of the September crime, but, on their menacing petition, the trials are indefinitely postponed.[61] — It has summoned to its bar Fournier, Lazowski, Deffieux, and other leaders, who, on the 10th of March, were disposed to throw it out of the windows, but, on making their impudent apology, it sends them away acquitted, free, and ready to begin over again.[62] At the War Department it raises up in turn two cunning Jacobins, Pache and Bouchotte, who are to work against it unceasingly. At the Department of the Interior it allows the fall of its firmest support, Roland, and appoints Garat in his place, an ideologist, whose mind, composed of glittering generalities, with a character made up of contradictory inclinations, fritters itself away in reticences, in falsehoods and in half–way treachery, under the burden of his too onerous duties. — It votes the murder of the King, which places an insurmountable barrier of blood between it and all honest persons. — It plunges the nation into a war in behalf of principles,[63] and excites an European league against France, which league, in transferring the perils arising from the September crime to the frontier, permanently establishes the September régime in the interior. — It forges in advance the vilest instruments of the forthcoming Reign of Terror,

* through the decree which establishes the revolutionary tribune, with Fouquier–Tinville as public prosecutor, and the obligation for each juryman to utter his verdict aloud;[64]

* through the decree condemning every émigré to civil death, and the confiscation of his property "of either sex," even a simple fugitive, even returned within six months;[65]

* through the decree which "outlaws aristocrats and enemies of the Revolution";[66]

* through the decree which, in each commune, establishes a tax on the wealth of the commune in order to adapt the price of bread to wages;[67]

* through the decree which subjects every bag of grain to declaration and to the maximum (price conrol);[68]

* through the decree which awards six years in irons for any traffic in the currency;[69]

* through the decree which orders a forced loan of a billion, extorted from the rich;[70]

* through the decree which raises in each town a paid army of sans– culottes "to hold aristocrats under their pikes "[71] and at last,

* through the decree which, instituting the Committee of Public Safety,[72] fashions a central motor to set these sharp scythes agoing and mow down fortunes and lives with the utmost rapidity. –

To these engines of general destruction it adds one more, which is special and operates against itself. Not only does it furnish its rivals of the Commune with the millions they need to pay their bands; not only does it advance to the different sections,[73] in the form of a loan, the hundreds of thousands of francs which are needed to satisfy the thirst of their yelpers; but again, at the end of March, just at the moment when it happens to escape the first Jacobin invasion, it provides for the election by each section of a Committee of Supervision, authorized to make domiciliary visits and to disarm the suspected;[74] it allows this committee to make arrests and inflict special taxes; to facilitate its operations it orders a list of the inmates of each house, legibly "stating names, surnames, ages and professions," to be affixed to the entrance,[75] a copy of which must be left with the committee, and which is subject to its control.

To end the matter, it submits itself; and, "regardless of the inviolability of a representative of the French nation,"[76] it decides that, in case of political denunciation, its own members may be brought to trial.

V. Jacobin violence against the people.

Committees of Supervision after March 28, 1793. – The régime of August and September, 1792, revived. – Disarmament. – Certificates of civism. – Forced enlistment. – Forced loans. – Use made of the sums raised. – Vain resistance of the population. – Manifestations by young men repressed. – Violence and victory of the Jacobins in the assemblies of the sections.

"I seem to hear you," writes a sarcastic observer,[77] "addressing the (Jacobin) faction in these terms:

'Now, look here, we have the means, but we are not disposed to make use of them against you; it would be unfair to attack you unarmed. Public power emanates from two sources, legal authority and armed force. Now we will at once create committees of supervision, of which you shall appoint the heads, for the reason that, with a whip of this kind, you can lash every honest man in Paris, and thus regulate public opinion. We will do more than this, because our sacrifice is not yet complete; we are disposed to make you a present of our armed force, with authority to disarm anybody that you may suspect. As far as we are concerned, we are ready to surrender even our pocketknives,[78] and remain apart, content with our virtues and talents. — But mind what you are about. Should you be so ungrateful as to attack our sacred persons, we shall find avengers in the departments.'

'What good will the departments do you, let loose against each other, after you are out of the way?' " (was the imaginary Jacobin reply!)

No summary could be more exact nor any prediction more accurately based. Henceforth, and by virtue of the Convention's own decrees, not only have the Jacobins the whole of the executive power in their hands, as this is found in civilized countries, but likewise the discretionary power of the antique tyrant or modern pasha, that arbitrary, strong arm which, singling out the individual, falls upon him and takes from him his arms, his freedom, and his money. After the 28th of March, we see in Paris a resumption of the system which, instituted by the 10th of August, was completed by the 2nd of September. In the morning, drums beat to arms; at noon, the barriers are shut, the bridges and passages guarded, and sentinels stand on the corners of the streets; no one is allowed "to pass outside the limits of his section," or circulate within them without showing his certificate of civism; houses are invested, numbers of persons are arrested,[79] and, during the succeeding months, this operation is carried on under the sway of the Committee of Supervision. Now, this Committee, in almost all the sections, "is made up of sans–culottes," not fathers of families, men of judgment and experience, people living a long time in the quarter, but "strangers, or young men trying to be something,"[80] ambitious underlings, ignorant daredevils, despotic intruders, fierce, touchy and inexperienced inquisitors".

The first thing is the disarmament of the suspected. "It is enough that any citizen shall be denounced, and that the case is made known to the Committee";[81] or that his certificate of civism is less than one month old,[82] to make a delegate, accompanied by ten armed men, search his house. In the section of the Réunion alone, on the first day, 57 denounced persons are thus disarmed for "acts of incivism or expressions adverse to the Republic," not merely lawyers, notaries, architects, and other prominent men, but petty tradesmen and shop- keepers, hatters, dyers, locksmiths, mechanics, gilders, and bar- keepers. One section; in defiance of the law, adds to these in block the signers of the petition of the eight thousand and that of the twenty thousand. "Through such schemes," says an observer,[83] "all the guns in Paris, numbering more than a hundred thousand, pass into the hands of the faction. None remain for its adversaries, even in the gunshops; for, through an ordinance of the Commune, no one may purchase a gun without a certificate issued by the Committee of Supervision of the section.[84] — On the other hand, owing to the power of granting or refusing certificates of civism, each Committee, on its own authority, interposes barriers as it pleases in all directions, public or private, to every inhabitant within its bounds. It is impossible for any person who has not obtained his certificate[85] to have a passport for traveling, although a tradesman; no public employee, no clerk of the administration, advocate or notary can keep his place without it; no one can go out of Paris or return late at night. If one goes out to take a walk, there is danger of being arrested and brought back between two soldiers to the committee of the section; if one stays at home, it is with the chance of being inspected as a harbourer of priests or nobles. Any Parisian opening his windows in the morning may find his house surrounded by a company of carmagnoles, if he has not the indispensable certificate in his pocket.[86] In the eyes of a Jacobin committee, there is no civism but in Jacobinism, and we can imagine whether this patent would be willingly conferred on opponents, or even on the lukewarm; what examinations they would have to undergo; what questions they would be obliged to answer; how many goings and comings, solicitations, appearances and waitings would be imposed on them; with what persistency it would excite delay, and with what satisfaction it would be refused. Buzot presented himself four times at the Committee of Quatre-Nations to obtain a certificate for his domestic, and failed to get it.[87] There is another still more effective expedient for keeping the ill-disposed in check The committee of each section, aided by a member of the Commune,[88] designates the twelve thousand men drafted for the expedition into La Vendée, and picks them by name, one by one, as it may select them; the effect of this is to purge Paris of twelve thousand anti-Jacobins, and tranquilize the section assemblies, where opposition is often objectionable. To this end the committee selects first, and gives the preference to, the clerks of lawyers and notaries, those of banking- houses, the administration, and of merchants, the unmarried in all offices and counting-rooms, in short, all the Parisian middle class bachelors, of which there are more than twenty-five thousand.[89] The ordinance stipulates that one out of two should be taken, undoubtedly those with the poorest reputation with the Committee, this proceeding will silence the others and prevent them from speaking up in their sections.[90]

While one hand clutches the collar, the other rummages the pocket. The Committee of Supervision of each section, always aided by a member of the Commune,[91] designates all persons in easy circumstances, estimates their incomes as it pleases, or according to common report, and sends them an order to pay a particular sum in proportion to their surplus, and according to a progressive tax. The allowance which is exempt for the head of a family is 1,500 francs per annum, besides 1,000 francs for his wife and 1,000 francs for each child; if the excess is over 15,000 or 20,000 francs, they assess it 5,000 francs; if more than 40,000 or 50,000 francs, they assess it 20,000; in no case may the surplus retained exceed 30,000 francs; all above this amount goes to the State. The first third of this sudden contribution to the public funds is required in forty–eight hours, the second in a fortnight, and the remaining third in a month, under serious penalties. If the tax happens to be exaggerated, if an income is uncertain or imaginary, if receipts are yet to come in, if there is no ready money, if; like Francœur, the opera manager, a man "has nothing but debts," so much the worse. "In case of refusal," writes the section of Bon–Conseil, "his personal and real property shall be sold by the revolutionary committee, and his person declared suspected."[92] — Even this is simply an installment on account:

"There is no desire on the part of the Committee at the present moment to demand more than a portion of your surplus," that which rest will be taken later. Desfieux, the bankrupt,[93] has already, in the tribune of the Jacobin club, estimated the fortunes of one hundred of the wealthiest notaries and financiers in Paris at 640,000,000 francs; the municipality sent a list of their names to the sections to have it completed; if only one–tenth was taken from them, it would amount to 64,000,000, which "big sponges," thoroughly squeezed, would disgorge a much larger amount.

"The richest of Frenchmen," says Robespierre, "should not have more than 3,000 francs a year."[94]

The contributions of "these gentlemen" suffice to arm the sans– culottes, "remunerate artisans for their attendance in the section meetings, and support laborers without work."[95] Already through the sovereign virtue of summary requisitions, everything is spoil; carriage–horses are seized in their stables, while vehicles belonging to aged ladies, mostly widows, and the last of the berlins and elegant carriages still remaining in Paris, are taken out of the livery– stables.[96]

With such powers used in this way, the section makes the most of the old deep–seated enmity of the poor against the rich;[97] it secures the firm loyalty of the needy and of vagabonds; thanks to the vigorous arms of its active clients, it completely overcomes the feeble, transient, poorly–contrived resistance which the National Convention and the Parisian population still oppose to its rule.

On the 13th of April Marat, accused three months before and daily becoming bolder in his fractiousness, is finally indicted through a decree of the incensed majority;[98] on the 24th he appears before the revolutionary tribunal. But the revolutionary tribunal, like other newly organized institutions, is composed of pure Jacobins, and, moreover, the party has taken its precautions. Marat, for his escort to the court–room has "the municipal commissaries, envoys from the various sections, delegates from all the patriotic clubs"; besides these, "a multitude of good patriots" fill the hall beforehand; "early in the morning the other chambers of the Palais de Justice, the corridors, the courts and adjacent streets" overflow with "sans– culottes ready to avenge any outrage that may be perpetrated on their favorite defender."[99] Naturally, excessively conceited, he speaks not like an accused, but "as an apostle and martyr." He is overwhelmed with applause, unanimously acquitted, crowned with laurel, borne in triumph to the Convention, where he thunders a song of victory, while the Girondist majority is obliged to suffer his presence awaiting to be subjected to their banishments. — Equally as impotent as the moderates of the Legislative Assembly are the moderates in the street who recover themselves only again to be felled to the ground. On the 4th and 5th of May, five or six hundred young fellows, well–dressed and without arms, have assembled in the Champs–Elysées and at the Luxembourg to protest against the ordinance of the Commune, which drafts them for the expedition to La Vendée;[100] they shout, "Vive la Republique! Vive la Loi! Down with anarchists! Send Marat, Danton and Robespierre to the Devil!" Naturally, Santerre's paid guard disperses these young sparks; about a thousand are arrested, and henceforth the rest will be careful not to make any open demonstration on the public thoroughfares. — Again, for lack of something better to do, we see them frequently returning to the section assemblies, especially early in May; they find themselves in a majority, and enter on discussions against Jacobin tyranny; at the Bon–Conseil section, and at those of Marseilles and l'Unité, Lhuillier is hooted at, Marat threatened, and Chaumette denounced.[101] — But these are only flashes in the pan; to be firmly in charge in these permanent assemblies, the moderates, like the sans–culottes, would have to be in constant attendance, and use their fists every night. Unfortunately, the young men of 1793 have not yet arrived at that painful experience, that implacable hate, that athletic ruggedness which is to sustain them in 1795. "After one evening, in which the seats everywhere were broken "[102] on the backs of the contestants, they falter, and never recover themselves, the professional roughs, at the end of a fortnight, being victorious all along the line. — The better to put resistance down, the roughs form a special league amongst themselves, and go around from section to section to give each other help.[103] Under the title of a deputation, under the pretext of preventing disturbance, a troop of sturdy fellows, dispatched by the neighboring section, arrives at the meeting, and suddenly transforms the minority into a majority, or controls the vote by force of clamor. Sometimes, at a late hour, when the hall is nearly empty, they declare themselves a general meeting, and about twenty or thirty will cancel the discussions of the day. At other times, being, through the municipality, in possession of the police, they summon an armed force to their aid, and oblige the refractory to decamp. And, as examples are necessary to secure perfect silence, the fifteen or twenty who have formed themselves into a full meeting, with the five or six who form the Committee of Supervision, issue warrants of arrest against the most prominent of their opponents. The vice–president of the Bon–Conseil section, and the juge–de–paix of the Unité section, learn in prison that it is dangerous to present to the Convention an address against anarchists or sign a debate against Chaumette.[104] — Towards the end of May, in the section assemblies, nobody dares open his mouth against a Jacobin motion; often, even, there are none present but Jacobins; for example, at the Gravilliers, they have driven out all not of their band, and henceforth no "intriguer"[105] is imprudent enough to present himself there. — Having become the sovereign People assembled in Council, with full power to

* disarm,

* put on the index,

* displace,

* tax,

* send off to the army, and

* imprison whoever gives them umbrage,

they are able now, with the municipality at their back and as guides, to turn the armament which they have obtained from the Convention against it, attack the Girondists in their last refuge, and possess themselves of the only fort not yet surrendered.

VI. Jacobin tactics.

Jacobin tactics to constrain the Convention. – Petition of April 15 against the Girondins. – Means employed to obtain signatures. – The Convention declares the petition calumnious. – The commission of Twelve and the arrest of Hébert. – Plans for massacres. – Intervention of the Mountain leaders.

To conquer the last bastion of the Girondists all they have to do is simultaneously in all sections to do what they used to do separately in each section: substituting themselves, by fraud and by force, for the Veritable people, they are able to conjure up before the Convention the phantom of popular disapproval. — From the municipality, holding its sessions at the Hôtel–de–ville, and from the conventicle established at the Evêché, emissaries are sent forth who present the same formal communication in writing at the same time in every section in Paris.[106] "Here is a petition for signatures." — "Read it." — "But that is unnecessary — it is already adopted by a majority of the sections." — This lie is accepted by some and several sign in good faith without reading it. In others they read it and refuse to sign it; in others, again, it is read and they pass to the order of the day. What happens? The plotters and ringleaders remain behind until all conscientious citizens have withdrawn; then, masters of the debate, they decide that the petition must be signed, and they accordingly affix their signatures. The next day, on the arrival of citizens at the section, the petition is handed to them for their names, and the debate of the previous evening is advanced against them. If they offer any remarks, they are met with these terrifying words:

Sign, or no certificate of civism!

And, as if approving this threat, several of the sections which are mastered by those who draw up the lists of proscriptions, decide that the certificates of civism must be renewed, new ones being refused to those refusing to sign the petition. They do not rest content with these moves; men armed with pikes are posted in the streets to force the signatures of those who pass."[107] — The whole weight of municipal authority has been publicly cast into the scale. "Commissaries of the Commune, accompanied by municipal secretaries, with tables, inkstands, paper and registers, promenade about Paris preceded by drums and a body of militia." From time to time, they make "a solemn halt," and declaim against Brissot, Vergniaud, Guadet, and then "demand and obtain signatures."[108]— Thus extorted and borne to the Convention by the mayor, in the name of the council–general of the Commune and of the thirty–five sections, the imperious petition denounces twenty–two Girondists as traitors, and insolently demands their expulsion. — Another day it is found that a similar summons and similarly presented, in the name of the forty–eight sections, is authorized only by thirteen or fourteen.[109] — Sometimes the political parade is still more incautious. Pretended deputies of the Faubourg St. Antoine appear before the Convention and assert the revolutionary program. "If you do not adopt it," they say, "we will declare ourselves in a state of insurrection; there are 40,000 men at the door."[110] The truth is, "about fifty bandits, scarcely known in the Faubourg," and led by a former upholsterer, now a commissary of police, "have gathered together on their route" all they could find in the workshops "and in the stores," the multitude packed into the Place Vendôme not knowing what was demanded in their name.[111] — These dummy tumults are, however, useful; they show the Convention its master, and prepare the way for a more efficient invasion. The day Marat was acquitted, the whole of his sewer, male and female, came along with him; under pretext of parading before the Convention, they invaded the hall, scattered themselves over the benches and steps, and, supported by the galleries, installed anew in the tribune, amidst a tempest of applause and of tumult, the usual promoter of insurrection, pillage and assassination.[112] – And yet, however energetic and however persistent the pressure, the Convention, which has yielded on so many points, will not consent to mutilate itself. It pronounces the petition presented against the Twenty–two calumnious; it institutes a special commission of twelve members to search the papers of the Commune and the sections for legal proofs of the plot openly and steadily maintained by the Jacobins against the national representation; Mayor Pache is summoned to the bar of the house; warrants of arrest are issued against Hébert, Dobsen and Varlet. — Since popular manifestations have not answered the purpose, and the Convention, instead of obeying, is rebellious, nothing is left but to employ force.

"Since the 10th of March," says Vergniaud, in the tribune,[113] "murder is openly and unceasingly fomented against you." — "It is a terrible time," says an observer, "strongly resembling that preceding the 2nd of September."[114] — That same evening, at the Jacobin club, a member proposes to "exterminate the scoundrels before leaving. "I have studied the Convention," he says[115] "it is composed in part of scoundrels who ought to be punished. All the supporters of Dumouriez and the other conspirators should be put out of the way; fire the alarm gun and close the barriers!" The following forenoon, "all the walls in Paris are covered with posters," calling on the Parisians to "hurry up and slit the throats of the statesmen."[116] — " We must do something to put an end to this!" is the slogan of the sans–culottes. — The following week, at the Jacobin club, as elsewhere, "immediate insurrection is the order of the day. . . . What we formerly called the sacred enthusiasm of freedom and patriotism, is now metamorphosed into the fury of an excited populace, which can no longer be regulated or disciplined except by force. There is not one of these scoundrels who would not accept a counter–revolution, provided they could be allowed to crush and stamp on the most noted conservatives.[117] . . . The conclusion is that the day, the hour, the minute that the faction believes that it can usefully and without risk bring into play all the brigands in Paris,[118] then the insurrection will undoubtedly take place." Already the plan of the massacre is under consideration by the lowest class of fanatics at the mayoralty, the Evêché, and the Jacobin club.[119]

Some isolated house is to be selected, with a suite of three rooms on the ground floor, and a small court in the rear; the twenty–two Girondists are to be caught in the night and brought to this slaughter–house arranged beforehand; each in turn is to be passed along to the last room, where he is to be killed and his body tumbled into a hole dug in the middle of the court, and then the whole covered over with quick–lime; it will be supposed that they have emigrated, and, to establish the fact, false correspondence will be printed.[120] A member of the Committee on the Municipal Police declares that the plan is feasible:

"We will Septemberize(kill) them — not we ourselves, but men who are ready, and who will be well paid for it."

The Montagnards present Léonard Bourdon and Legendre, make no objection. The latter simply remarks that the Girondists should not be seized in the Convention; outside the Convention "they are scoundrels whose death would save the Republic," and the act is lawful; he would like to see "with them every rascal on the 'black' side perish without interfering." — Several, instead of 22 deputies, demand 30 or 32, and some 300; the suspected of each district may be added, while ten or a dozen proscription lists are already made out. Through a clean sweep, executed the same night, at the same hour, they may be conducted to the Carmelites, near the Luxembourg, and, "if there is not room enough there," to Bicêtre; here, "they will disappear from the surface of the globe."[121] Certain leaders desired to entrust the purification of Paris to the sagacity of popular instinct. "In loose and disconnected phrases" they address the people: "Rouse yourselves, and act according to your inclinations, as my indications might only startle those you should strike down and thereby allow them to escape!" Varlet proposes, on the contrary, a plan of public safety, very full and explicit, in fifteen articles:

"Sweep away the deputies of the 'Plain,' and other deputies of the Constituent and Legislative Assemblies, all nobles, priests, pettifoggers, etc.; exterminate the whole of that race, and the Bourbons, too, with entire suppression of the Ministers."

Hébert, for his part, alluding to the Girondists, writes in his gazette that "the last hour of their death is going to strike," and that, "when their foul blood shall have been spilled, aristocratic brawlers will return to their holes, the same as on the 10th of August. "Naturally, the professional slaughterers are notified. A certain Laforet, an old–clothes dealer on the Quai–du–Louvre, who, with his wife, had already distinguished themselves on the 2nd of September, reckons that "there are in Paris 6,000 sans–culottes ready to massacre at the first sign all dangerous deputies, and eight thousand petitioners," undoubtedly those who, in the several sections, signed the addresses to the Convention against the Commune. — Another "Septemberizer,"[122] commanding the battalion of the Jardin des Plantes, Henriot, on meeting a gang of men working on the wharves, exclaims in his rough voice:

"Good morning, my good fellows, we shall need you soon, and at better work. You won't have wood to carry in your carts — you'll have to carry dead bodies."

"All right," replies one of the hands, half tipsy, "we'll do it as we did the 2nd of September. We'll turn a penny by it." –

Cheynard, a locksmith and machinist at the mint, is manufacturing daggers, and the women of the tribunes are already supplied with two hundred of them." –

Finally, on the 29th of May, Hébert proposes, in the Jacobin club,[123] "to pounce down on the Commission of Twelve," and another Jacobin declares that "those who have usurped dictatorial power," meaning by that the Girondists, "are outlawed."

All this is extreme, clumsily done, useless and dangerous, or, at least, premature, and the chiefs of the "Mountain," Danton, Robespierre, and Marat himself; better informed and less shortsighted, are well aware that brutal murder would be revolting to the already half–aroused departments.[124] The legislative machinery is not to be shattered, but made use of; it must be employed against itself to effect the required injury; in this way the operation at a distance will appear legal, and, garnished with the usual high-flown speeches, impose on the provincial mind.[125] From the 3rd of April, Robespierre, in the Jacobin club, always circumspect and considerate, had limited and defined in advance the coming insurrection. "Let all good citizens," he says, "meet in their sections, and come and force us to place the disloyal deputies under arrest." Nothing can be more moderate, and, if they refer to principles, nothing can be more correct. The people always reserves the right to cooperate with its mandatories, which right it practices daily in the galleries. Through extreme precaution, which well describes the man,[126] Robespierre refuses to go any further in his interference. "I am incapable of advising the people what steps to take for its salvation. That is not given to one man alone. I, who am exhausted by four years of revolution, and by the heart-rending spectacle of the triumph of tyranny, am not thus favored. . . . I, who am wasted by a slow fever, and, above all by the fever of patriotism. As I have said, there remains for me no other duty to fulfill at the present moment." What's more, he enjoins the municipality "to unite with the people, and form a close alliance with it." — In other words, the blow must be struck by the Commune, the "Mountain" must appear to have nothing to do with it. But, "it is privy to the secret";[127] its chiefs pull the wires which set the brutal dancing-jacks in motion on the public trestles of the Hôtel-de-ville. Danton and Lacroix wrote in the bureau of the Committee of "Public Safety," the insolent summons which the procureur of the Commune is to read to the Convention on the 31st of May, and, during seven days of crisis, Danton, Robespierre and Marat are the counselors, directors and moderators of all proceedings, and lead, push on or restrain their stooges of the insurrection within the limits of this program.

VII. The central Jacobin committee in power.

The 27th day of May. – The central revolutionary committee. – The municipal body displaced and then restored. – Henriot, commanding general. –

It is a tragicomic drama in three acts, each winding up with a coup de théâtre, always the same and always foreseen. Legendre, one of the principal stage hands, has taken care to announce beforehand that,

"If this lasts any longer," said he, at the Cordeliers club,[128] "if the 'Mountain' remains quiet any longer, I shall call in the people, and tell the galleries to come down and take part with us in the deliberations."

At first, on the 27th of May, in relation to the arrest of Hébert and his companions, the "Mountain," supported by the galleries, becomes furious.[129] In vain does the majority again and again demonstrate its numerical superiority. "We shall resist," says Danton, "so long as there are a hundred true citizens to help us." — "President," exclaims Marat to Isnard, you are a tyrant! a despicable tyrant!" — "I demand," says Couthon, "that the President be impeached!" — "Off with the President to the Abbaye!" — The "Mountain" has decided that he shall not preside; it springs from the benches and rushes at him, shouts "death to him," becomes hoarse with its vociferations, and compels him to leave the chair through weariness and exhaustion. It drives out his successor, Fonfrède, in the same manner, and ends by putting Hérault-Séchelles, one of its own accomplices, in the chair. — Meanwhile, at the entrance of the Convention, "the regulations have been violated"; a crowd of armed men "have spread through the passages and obstructed the approaches"; the deputies, Meillan, Chiappe and Lydon, on attempting to leave, are arrested, Lydon being stopped "by the point of a saber at his breast,"[130] while the leaders on the inside encourage, protect and justify their trusty aids outdoors. — Marat, with his usual audacity, on learning that Raffet, the commandant, was clearing the passages, comes to him "with a pistol in his hand and puts him under arrest,"[131] on the ground that the people and its sacred rights of petition and the petitioners must be respected. There are "five or six hundred, almost all of them armed,"[132] stationed for three hours at the doors of the hall; at the last moment, two other troops, dispatched by the Gravilliers and Croix–Rouge sections, arrive and bring them their final afflux. Thus strengthened, they spring over the benches assigned to them, spread through the hall, and mingle with the deputies who still remain in their seats. It is after midnight; many of the representatives, worn out with fatigue and disgust, have left; Pétion, Lasource, and a few others, who wish to get in, "cannot penetrate the threatening crowd." To compensate themselves, and in the places of the absent, the petitioners, constituting themselves representatives of France, vote with the "Mountain," while the Jacobin president, far from turning them out, himself invites them "to set aside all obstacles prejudicial to the welfare of the people.." In this gesticulating crowd, in the half–light of smoky lamps, amidst the uproar of the galleries, it is difficult to hear well what motion is put to vote; it is not easy to see who rises or sits down, and two decrees pass, or seem to pass, one releasing Hébert and his accomplices, and the other revoking the commission of the Twelve.[133] Forthwith the messengers who await the issue run out and carry the good news to the Hôtel–de–ville, the Commune celebrating its triumph with an explosion of applause.

The next morning, however, notwithstanding the terrors of a call of the House and the fury of the "Mountain," the majority, as a defensive stroke, revokes the decree by which it is disarmed, while a new decree maintains the commission of the Twelve; the operation, accordingly, is to be done over again, but not the whole of it; for Hébert and the others imprisoned remain at liberty, while the majority, which, through a sense of propriety or the instinct of self–preservation, had again placed its sentinels on the outposts, consents, either through weakness or hopes of conciliation, to let the prisoners remain free. The result is they have had the worst of the fight. Their adversaries, accordingly, are encouraged, and at once renew the attack, their tactics, very simple, being those which have already proved so successful on the 10th of August.

The matter now in hand is to invoke against the derived and provisional rights of the government, the superior and inalienable right of the people; also, to substitute for legal authority, which, in its nature, is limited, revolutionary power, which, in its essence, is absolute. To this end the section of the City, under the vice– presidency of Maillard, the "Septemberizer," invites the other forty– seven sections each to elect two commissaries, with "unlimited powers." In thirty–three sections, purged, terrified, or deserted, the Jacobins, alone, or almost alone,[134] elect the most determined of their band, particularly strangers and rascals, in all sixty–six commissaries, who, on the evening of the 29th, meet at the Evêché, and select nine from their midst to form, under the presidency of Dobsen, a central and revolutionary executive committee. These nine persons are entirely unknown;[135] all are obscure subordinates,[136] mere puppets and manikins; eight days later, on finishing their performance, when they are no longer needed, they will be withdrawn behind the scenes. In the mean time they pass for the mandatories of the popular sovereign, with full power in all directions, because he has delegated his omnipotence to them, and the sole power, because their investiture is the most recent; under this sanction, they stalk around somewhat like supernumeraries at the Opera, dressed in purple and gold, representing a conclave of cardinals or the Diet of the Holy Empire. Never has the political drama degenerated into such an impudent farce! — On the 31st, at half–past six in the morning, Dobsen and his bullies present themselves at the council–general of the Commune, tender their credentials, and make known to it its deposition. The Council, with edifying complacency, accepts the fiat and leaves the department. With no less grateful readiness Dobsen summons it back, and reinstates it in all its functions, in the name of the people, and declares that it merits the esteem of the country.[137] At the same time another demagogue, Varlet, performs the same ceremony with the Council of the department, and both bodies, consecrated by a new baptism, join the sixty–six commissaries to share the dictatorship. — What could be more legitimate? The Convention would err in making any opposition:

"It was elected merely to condemn the tyrant and to frame a constitution; the sovereign people has invested it with no other power;[138] accordingly, the other acts, its warrants of arrest, are simply usurpations and despotism. Paris, moreover, represents France better than it does, for Paris is "the extract of all the departments, the mirror of opinion,"[139] the advance–guard of patriotism. "Remember the 10th of August;[140] previous to that time, the opinions in the Republic were divided; but, scarcely had you struck the decisive blow when all subsided into silence. Have no fear of the departments; with a little terror and a few instructions, we shall turn all minds in our favor." Grumblers persist in demanding the convocation of primary assemblies. "Was not the 10th of August necessary? Did not the departments then endorse what Paris did? They will do so this time. It is Paris which saved them."[141]

Consequently, the new government places Henriot, a reliable man, and one of the September slaughterers, in full command of the armed force; then, through a violation by law declared as a capital offense, it orders the alarm gun to be fired; then, on the other hand, it beats a general call to arms, sounds the tocsin and closes the barriers; the post office managers are put in arrest, and letters are intercepted and opened; the order is given to disarm the suspected and hand their arms over to patriots; "forty sous a day are allowed to citizens with small means while under arms."[142] Notice is given without fail the preceding evening to the trusty men of the quarter; accordingly, early in the morning, the Committee of Supervision has already selected from the Jacobin sections "the most needy companies in order to arm those the most worthy of combating for liberty," while all its guns are distributed "to the good republican workmen." [143] — From hour to hour as the day advances, we see in the refractory sections all authority passing over to the side of force; at the Finistère, Butte–des–Moulins, Lombards, Fraternité, and Marais[144] sections, the encouraged sans–culottes obtain the ascendancy, nullify the deliberations of the moderates, and, in the afternoon, their delegates go and take the oath at the Hôtel–de–ville.

Meanwhile the Commune, dragging behind it the semblance of popular unanimity, besieges the Convention with multiplied and threatening petitions. As on the 27th of May, the petitioners invade the hall, and "mix in fraternally with the members of the 'Left.'" Forthwith, on the motion of Levasseur, the "Mountain," "confident of its place being well guarded," leaves it and passes over to the "Right."[145] Invaded in its turn, the "Right" refuses to join in the deliberations; Vergniaud demands that "the Assembly join the armed force on the square, and put itself under its protection"; he and his friends leave the hall, and the decapitated majority falls back upon its usual hesitating course. All is hubbub and uproar around it. In the hall the clamors of the "Mountain," the petitioners, and the galleries, seem like the constant roar of a tempest. Outside, twenty or thirty thousand men will probably clash in the streets;[146] the battalion of Butte–des–Moulins, with detachments sent by neighboring sections, is entrenched in the Palais–Royal, and Henriot, spreading the report that the rich sections of the center have displayed the white cockade, send against it the sans–culottes of the faubourgs Saint–Antoine and Saint– Marceau; cannon are pointed on both sides. — These loaded cannon must not be discharged; the signal of civil war must not be given; it is simply necessary "to forestall the consequences of a movement which could be only disastrous to liberty,"[147] and it is important to ensure public order. The majority, accordingly, think that it is acting courageously in refusing to the Commune the arrest of the Twenty–two, and of the Ministers, Lebrun and Clavière; in exchange for this it consents to suppress its commission of Twelve; it confirms the act of the Commune which allows forty sous a day to the workmen under arms; it declares freedom of entry into its tribunes, and, thanking all the sections, those who defended as well as those who attacked it, it maintains the National Guard on permanent call, announces a general federation for the 10th of August following, and goes off to fraternize with the battalions in the PalaisRoyal, in battle array against each other through the calumnies of the Commune, and which, set right at the last moment, now embrace instead of cutting each other's throats.

This time, again, the advantage is on the side of the Commune. Not only have many of its requirements been converted into decrees, but again, its revolutionary baptism remains in full force; its executive committee is tacitly recognized, the new government performs its functions, its usurpations are endorsed, its general, Henriot, keeps command of the entire armed force, and all its dictatorial measures are carried out without let or hindrance. — There is another reason why they should be maintained and aggravated. "Your victory is only half–won," writes Hébert in his Père Duchesne, "all those bastards of intriguers still live! " — On the evening of the 31st of May the Commune issues warrants of arrest against the ministers Clavière and Lebrun, and against Roland and his wife. That same evening and throughout the following day and night, and again the day after, the Committees of Supervision of the forty–eight sections, according to instructions from the Hôtel–de–ville[148] study the lists of their quarters,[149] add new names to these, and send commissaries to disarm and arrest the suspected. Whoever has spoken against revolutionary committees, or disapproved of the assaults of the 31st of May, or not openly shown himself on the 10th of August, or voted on the wrong side in the old Legislative Assembly, might be arrested. It is a general, simultaneous raid; in all the streets we see nothing but people seized and under escort sent to prison, or put before the section committee. "Anti–patriotic" journalists are arrested first of all, the entire impression of their journals being additionally confiscated, and the journal suppressed; the printing–rooms of Gorsas are sacked, seals placed on his presses,[150] and Prudhomme himself is locked up. All resistance is overcome in the Contrat–Social, Fraternity, Marais and Marseilles sections, leaving the Commune free, as far as the street is concerned, to recommence its attack on the Convention. "Lists of sans– culottes workmen" have been drawn up in each section, and six francs a head is allowed them, payable by the Convention, as indemnity for their temporary suspension from work;[151] this is a premium offered to voters, and as nothing is more potent than cash in hand, Pache provides the funds by diverting 150,000 francs intended for the colonists in San Domingo; the whole day on the 2nd of June, trusted men go about among the ranks distributing five–franc assignats.[152] Vehicles loaded with supplies accompany each battalion, the better to keep the men under arms;[153] the stomach needs filling up, and a pint of wine is excellent for strengthening patriotic sentiment. Henriot has ordered back from Courbevoie the battalions of volunteers which a few days before had been enlisted for La Vendée,[154] crooked adventurers and looters, later known as "the heroes of the 500 francs." Besides these he has under his thumb Rosenthal's hussars, a body of

German veterans who do not understand French, and will remain deaf to any legal summons. Finally, he surrounds the Convention with a circle of picked sans–culottes, especially the artillerists, the best of Jacobins,[155] who drag along with them the most formidable park of artillery, 163 cannons, with grates and charcoal to heat the balls. The Tuileries is thus encircled by bands of roughs and fanatics; the National Guard, five or six times as many,[156] brought out "to give an appearance of a popular movement to the proceedings of five or six thousand bandits," cannot come to the aid of the Convention, it being stationed out of reach, beyond the Pont Tournant, which is raised, and behind the wooden fence separating the Carrousel from the palace. Kept in its position by its orders, merely serving as a stationary piece of scenery, employed against itself unbeknown to itself,[157] it can do no more than let the factionists act who serve as its advanced guard. — Early in the morning the vestibules, stairs and passages in the hall of the convention have been invaded by the frequenters of the galleries and the women under pay. The commandant of the post, with his officers, have been confined by "men with moustaches," armed with sabers and pistols; the legal guard has been replaced with an extraordinary guard,[158] and the deputies are prisoners. If one of them is obliged to go out for a moment, it is under the supervision of four fusiliers, "who conduct him, wait for him, and bring him back."[159] Others, in trying to look out the windows, are aimed at; the venerable Dussaulx is struck, and Boissy d'Anglas, seized by the throat, returns with his cravat and shirt all in shreds. For six hours by the clock the Convention is under arrest, and when the decree is passed, ordering the removal of the armed force bearing upon it, Henriot replies to the officer who notifies him of it: "Tell your damned president that he and his Assembly may go to hell. If he don't surrender the Twenty–two in an hour, I'll send him there!"[160]

In the hall the majority, abandoned by its recognized guides and its favorite spokesmen, grows more and more feeble from hour to hour. Brissot, Pétion, Guadet, Gensonné, Buzot, Salle, Grangeneuve, and others, two–thirds of the Twenty–two, kept away by their friends, remain at home.[161] Vergniaud, who had come, remains silent, and then leaves; the "Mountain," probably, gaining by his absence, allows him to pass out. Four other Girondists who remain in the Assembly to the end, Isnard, Dussaulx, Lauthenas, and Fauchet, consent to resign; when the generals give up their swords, the soldiers soon lay down their arms. Lanjuinais, alone, who is not a Girondist, but a Catholic and Breton, speaks like a man against this outrageous attack on the nation's representatives They rush at him and assail him in the tribune; the butcher, Legendre, simulating "the cleaver's blow," cries out to him, "Come down or I'll knock you down! A group of Montagnards spring forward to help Legendre, and one of them claps a pistol to his throat;[162] he clings fast to the tribune and strives in vain, for his party around him are losing courage. — At this moment Barrère, remarkable for expedients, proposes to the Convention to adjourn, and hold the session "amidst the armed force that will afford it protection."[163] All other things failing, the majority avails itself of this last straw. It rises in a body, in spite of the vociferations in the galleries, descends the great staircase, and proceeds to the entrance of the Carrousel. There the Montagnard president, Hérault– Séchelles, reads the decree of Henriot, which enjoins him to withdraw, and he officially and correctly summons him in the usual way. But a large number of the Montagnards have followed the majority, and are there to encourage the insurrection; Danton takes Henriot's hand and tells him, in a low voice, "Go ahead, don't be afraid; we want to show that the Assembly is free, be firm."[164] At this the tall bedizened gawky recovers his assurance, and in his husky voice, he addresses the president: "Hérault, the people have not come here to listen to big words. You are a good patriot . . . Do you promise on your head that the Twenty–two shall be given up in twenty–four hours?" — "No." — "Then, in that case, I am not responsible. To arms, cannoneers, make your guns ready!" The cannoneers take their lighted matches, "the cavalry draw their sabers, and the infantry aim at the deputies."[165] Forced back on this side, the unhappy Convention turns to the left, passes through the archway, follows the broad avenue through the garden, and advances to the Pont–Tournant to find an outlet. There is no outlet; the bridge is raised, and everywhere the barrier of pikes and bayonets remains impenetrable; shouts of "Vive la Montagne! vive Marat! To the guillotine with Brissot, Vergniaud, Guadet and Gensonné! Away with bad blood!" greet the deputies on all sides, and the Convention, similar to a flock of sheep, in vain turns round and round in its pen. At this moment, to get them back into the fold, Marat, like a barking dog, runs up as fast as his short legs will allow, followed by his troop of tatterdemalions, and exclaims: "Let all loyal deputies return to their posts!" With bowed heads, they mechanically return to the hall; it is immediately closed, and they are once more in confinement. To assist them in their deliberations a crowd of the well–disposed entered pell–mell along with them. To watch them and hurry on the matter, the sans–culottes, with fixed bayonets, gesticulate and threaten them from the galleries. Outside and inside, necessity, with its iron hand, has seized them and holds them fast. There is a dead silence. Couthon, a paralytic, tries to stand up; his friends carry him in their arms to the tribune; an intimate friend of Robespierre's, he is a grave and important personage; he sits down, and in his mild tone of voice, he speaks: "Citizens, all members of the Convention must now be satisfied of their freedom. . . . You are now aware that there is no restraint on your deliberations."[166]

The comedy is at an end. Even in Molière there is none like it. The sentimental cripple in the tribune winds up by demanding that the Twenty–two, the Twelve, and the Ministers, Clavière and Lebrun be placed in arrest. Nobody opposes the motion,[167] "because physical necessities begin to be felt, and an impression of terror pervades the Assembly." Several say to themselves, "Well, after all, those who are proscribed will be as well off at home, where they will be safe. . . . It is better to put up with a lesser evil than encounter a greater one." Another exclaims: "It is better not to vote than to betray one's trust." The salvo being found, all consciences are easy. Two–thirds of the Assembly declare that they will no longer take part in the discussions, hold aloof; and remain in their seats at each calling of the vote. With the exception of about fifty members of the "Right," who rise on the side of the Girondists, the "Mountain," whose forces are increased by the insurgents and amateurs sitting fraternally in its midst, alone votes for, and finally passes the decree. — Now that the Convention has mutilated itself; it is check–mated, and is about to become a governing machine in the service of a clique; the Jacobin conquest is completed, and in the hands of the victors, the grand operations of the guillotine are going to commence.

VIII. Right or Wrong, my Country.

Character of the new governors. – Why France accepted them.

Let us observe them at this decisive moment. I doubt if any such contrast ever presented itself in any country or in any age. – Through a series of purifications in an inverse sense, the faction has become reduced to its dregs; nothing remains of the vast surging wave of 1789 but its froth and its slime; the rest has been cast off or has withdrawn to one side; at first the highest class, the clergy, the nobles, and the parliamentarians; next the middle class of traders, manufacturers, and the bourgeois; and finally the best of the inferior class, small proprietors, farmers,[168] and master–workmen — in short, the prominent in every pursuit, profession, state, or occupation, whoever possesses capital, a revenue, an establishment, respectability, public esteem, education and mental and moral culture. The party in June, 1793, is composed of little more than unreliable workmen, town and country vagabonds, the habitués of hospices[169], sluts of the gutter, degraded and dangerous persons,[170] the déclassé, the corrupt, the perverted, the maniacs of all sorts. In Paris, from which they command the rest of France, their troop, an insignificant minority, is recruited from that refuse of humanity infesting all capitals, amongst the epileptic and scrofulous rabble which, heirs of vitiated blood and, further degrading this by its misconduct, introduces into civilization the degeneracy, imbecility, and infatuations of shattered temperaments, retrograde instincts, and deformed brains.[171] What it did with the powers of the State is narrated by three or four contemporary witnesses; we see it face to face, in itself, and in its chiefs, we contemplate the true nature of the men of action and of enterprise who have led the last attack and who represent it the best.

Since the 2nd of June "nearly one-half of the deputies in the Convention refrain from taking any part in its deliberations; more than one hundred and fifty have even fled or disappeared[172]"; the silent, the fugitives, the incarcerated, and the convicted, all this has been accomplished by the party. On the evening of June 2nd its bosom friend, its conscience, the filthy monstrosity, charlatan, monomaniac and murderer, who regularly every morning, effuses his political poison into its bosom, Marat, has at last obtained the discretionary powers craved by him for the last four years, that of Marius and Sylla, that of Octavius, Antony, and Lepidus; the power of adding or removing names from lists of proscription:

"while the reading was going on he indicated cancellations or additions, the secretary effacing or adding names as he suggested them, without any consultation whatever with the Assembly."[173]

At the Hôtel-de-ville on the 3rd of June, in the Salle de la Reine, Pétion and Guadet, under arrest, see with their own eyes this Central Committee which has just started the insurrection, and which through its singular delegation sits enthroned over all other established authorities.

"They were snoring,[174] some stretched out on the benches and others leaning on the tables with their elbows, some were barefoot others were wearing their shoes slipshod like slippers; almost all were dirty and poorly clad; their clothes were unbuttoned, their hair uncombed, and their faces frightful; they wore pistols in their belts, and sabers, with scarves turned into shoulder-straps. Bottles, bits of bread, fragments of meat and bones lay strewn around on the floor, and smell was rotten."

It looks like a tapestry of a middle age battle field. The chief of the band here is not Chaumette, who has legal qualms,[175] nor Pache, who cunningly tacks under his mask of Swiss phlegm, but Hébert, another Marat, yet more brutal and depraved, and who profits by the opportunity to "put more coal into the furnace of his Père Duchesne," striking off 600,000 copies of it, pocketing 135,000 francs for the numbers sent to the armies, and gaining seventy-five per cent on the contract.[176] — In the street the active body of supporters consists of two bands, one military and other civil, the former composed of roughs who are soon to furnish the revolutionary army. "This army,[177] considered to be a recent institution, has actually existed since 1789. The agents of the Duke of Orleans formed its first nucleus. It grew, became organized, had officers appointed to it, mustering points, orders of the day, and a peculiar slang. . . . All the revolutions were carried out by its aid; it gave impetus to popular violence wherever it did not appear en masse. On the 12th of July, 1789, it had Necker's bust carried in public and the theaters closed; on the 5th of October it started the populace off to Versailles; on the 20th of April, 1791, it caused the king's arrest in the court of the Tuileries. . . Led by Westermann and Fournier, it formed the central battalion in the attack of August 10, 1792; it carried out the September massacres; it protected the Maratists on the 31st of May, 1793, . . . its composition is in keeping with its exploits and its functions. It contains the most determined scoundrels, the brigands of Avignon, the scum of Marseilles, Brabant, Liège, Switzerland and the shores of Genoa." Through a careful sifting,[178] it is to be inspected, strengthened, aggravated, and converted into a legal body of Janissaries on triple pay; once "enlarged with idle hairdressers, unemployed lackeys, designers of mad schemes, and other scoundrels unable to earn their keep in an honest manner," it will supply the detachments needed for garrison at Bordeaux, Lyons, Dijon and Nantes, still leaving "ten thousand of these Mamelukes to keep down the capital."

The civilian body of supporters comprises, first, those who haunt the sections, and are about to receive 40 sous for attending each meeting; next; the troop of figure–heads who, in other public places, are to represent the people, about 1,000 bawlers and claqueurs, "two–thirds of which are women." "While I was free," says Beaulieu,[179] "I closely observed their movements. It was a magic–lantern constantly in operation. They traveled to and from the Convention to the Revolutionary Tribunal, and from this to the Jacobin Club, or to the Commune, which held its meetings in the evening. . . . They scarcely took time for their natural requirements; they were often seen dining and supping at their posts when some action or an important murder was in the offing. Henriot, the commander–in–chief of both hordes, was at one time a swindler, then a police–informer, then imprisoned at Bicêtre for robbery, and then one of the September murderers. His military bearing and popularity are due to parading the streets in the uniform of a general, and appearing in humbug performances; he is the type of a swaggerer, always drunk or soaked with brandy. A blockhead, with a beery voice, blinking eyes, and a face distorted by nervous twitching, he possesses all the external characteristics of his employment. In talking, he vociferates like men with the scurvy; his voice is sepulchral, and when he stops talking his features come to rest only after repeated agitations; he blinks three times, after which his face recovers its equilibrium."[180]

Marat, Hébert, and Henriot, the maniac, the thief and the brute. Were it not for the dagger of Charlotte Corday,[181] it is probable that this trio, master of the press and of the armed force, aided by Jacques Roux, Leclerc, Vincent, Ronsin, and other madmen of the slums, would have put aside Danton, suppressed Robespierre, and governed France. Such are the counselors, the favorites, and the leaders of the ruling revolutionary class; did one not know what was to occur during the next fourteen months, one might form an idea of its government from the quality of these men.

And yet, such as this government is, France accepts or submits to it. In fact, Lyons, Marseilles, Toulon, Nîmes, Bordeaux, Caen, and other cities, feeling the knife at their throats,[182] turn aside the stroke with a movement of horror. They rise against their local Jacobins; but it is nothing more than an instinctive movement. They do not think of forming States within the State, as the "Mountain" pretends that they do, nor of usurping the central authority, as the "Mountain" actually does. Lyons cries, "Long live the Republic, one and indivisible," receives with honor the commissioners of the Convention, permits convoys of arms and horses destined for the army of the Alps to pass. To excite a revolt there, requires the insane demands of Parisian despotism just as it requires the brutal persistence of religious persecution to render the province of la Vendée insurgent. Without the prolonged oppression that weighs down consciences, and the danger to life always imminent, no city or province would have attempted secession. Even under this government of inquisitors and butchers no community, save those of Lyons and La Vendée, makes any sustained effort to break up the State, withdraw from it and live by itself. The national sheaf has been too strongly bound together by secular centralization. One's country exists; and when that country is in danger, when the armed stranger attacks the frontier, one follows the flag–bearer, whoever he may be, whether usurper, adventurer, blackguard, or cut–throat, provided only that he marches in the van and holds the banner with a firm hand.[183] To tear that flag from him, to contest his pretended right, to expel him and replace him by another, would be a complete destruction of the common weal. Brave men sacrifice their own repugnance for the sake of the common good; in order to serve France, they serve her unworthy government. In the committee of war, the engineering and staff officers who give their days to the study of military maps, think of nothing else than of knowing it thoroughly; one of them, d'Arcon, "managed the raising of the siege of Dunkirk, and of the blockade of Maubeuge;[184] nobody excels him in penetration, in practical knowledge, in quick perception and in imagination; it is a spirit of flame, a brain compact of resources. I speak of him, says Mallet du Pan, "from an intimate acquaintance of ten years. He is no more a revolutionnaire than I am." Carnot[185] does even more than this: he gives up his honor when, with his colleagues on the Committee of Public Safety, Billaud–Varennes, Couthon, Saint–Just, Robespierre, he puts his name to decrees which are assassinations. A similar devotion brings recruits into the armies by hundreds of thousands, bourgeois[186] and peasants, from the volunteers of 1791 to the levies of 1793; and the latter class fight not only for France, but also, and more than all, for the Revolution. For, now that the sword is drawn, the mutual and growing exasperation leaves only the extreme parties in the field. Since the 10th of August, and more especially since the 21st of January, it has no longer been a question how to deal with the ancient regime, of cutting away its dead portions or its troublesome thorns, of accommodating it to modern requirements, of establishing civil equality, a limited monarchy, a parliamentary government. The question is how to escape conquest by armed force to avert the military executions of Brunswick,[187] the vengeance of the proscribed émigrés, the restoration and the aggravation of the old feudal and fiscal order of things. Both through their traditions and their experience, the mass of the country people hate this ancient order, and with all the accumulated hatred which an unceasing and secular spoliation has caused. Irrespective of costs, the rural masses will never again suffer the tax–collector among them, nor the excise man in the cellar, nor the fiscal agent on the frontier. For them the ancient regime is nothing more than these things; and, in fact, they have paid no taxes, or scarcely any, since the beginning of the Revolution. On this matter the people's idea is fixed, positive, unalterable; and as soon as they perceive in the distant future the possible re–establishment of the taille, the tithe, and the seignorial rights, they choose their side; they will fight to the death. — As to the artisans and lesser bourgeois, their spur is the magnificent prospect of careers, to which the doors are thrown open, of unbounded advancement, of promotion offered to merit; more than all, their illusions are still intact.

Camped out there, facing the enemy, those noble ideals, which in the hands of the Parisian demagogues had turned into sanguinary harlots, remain pure and virginal in the minds of the soldiers and their officers. Liberty, equality, the rights of man, the reign of reason — all these vague and sublime images moved before their eyes when they climbed the escarpment of Jemmapes under a storm of grapeshot, or when they wintered, with naked feet, among the snows of the Vosges. These ideas, in descending from heaven to earth, were not dishonored and distorted under their feet, they did not see them transformed in their hands to frightful caricatures. These men are not pillars of clubs, nor brawlers in the sections, nor the inquisitors of a committee, nor hired informers, nor providers for the scaffold. Apart from the sabbath revolutionaire, brought back to earth by their danger, and having understood the inequality of talents and the need for discipline, they do the work of men; they suffer, they fast, they face bullets, they are conscious of their generosity and their sacrifices; they are heroes, and they look upon themselves as liberators.[188] They are proud of this. According to an astute observer[189] who knew their survivors,

"many of them believed that the French alone were reasonable beings. . . In our eyes the people in the rest of Europe, who were fighting to keep their chains, were only pitiable imbeciles or knaves sold to the despots who were attacking us. Pitt and Cobourg seemed to us the chiefs of these knaves and the personification of all the treachery and stupidity in the world. . . In 1794 our inmost, serious sentiment was wholly contained in this idea: to be useful to our country; all other things, our clothes, our food, advancement, were poor ephemeral details. As society did not exist, there was no such thing for us as social success, that leading element in the character of our nation. Our only gatherings were national festivals, moving ceremonies which nourished in us the love of our country. In the streets our eyes filled with tears when we saw an inscription in honor of the young drummer, Barra. . . This sentiment was the only religion we had."[190]

But it was a religion. When the heart of a nation is so high it will deliver itself, in spite of its rulers, whatever their excesses may be, whatever their crimes; for the nation atones for their follies by its courage; it hides their crimes beneath its great achievements.

Notes:

[1] "Archives Nationales," AF II, 45, May 6, 1793 (in English).

[2] Moore, II. 185 (October 20). "It is evident that all the departments of France are in theory allowed to have an equal share in the government; yet in fact the single department of Paris has the whole power of the government." Through the pressure of the mob Paris makes the law for the Convention and for all France. – Ibid., II. 534 (during the king's trial). "All the departments of France, including that of Paris, are in reality often obliged to submit to the clamorous tyranny of a set of hired ruffians in the tribunes who usurp the name and functions of the sovereign people, and, secretly direct by a few demagogues, govern this unhappy nation." Cf. Ibid., II. (Nov. 13).

[3] Schmidt, I. 96. Letter of Lauchou to the president of the Convention, Oct. 11, 1792: "The section of 1792 on its own authority decreed on the 5th of this month that all persons in a menial service could be allowed to vote in our primary assemblies . . . It would be well for the National Convention to convince the inhabitants of Paris that they alone do not constitute the entire republic. However absurd this idea may be, it is gaining ground every day." – Ibid., Letter of Damour, vice–president of the Pantheon section, Oct. 29: "The citizen Paris . . . has said that when the law is in conflict with general opinion no attention must be paid to it. . . These disturbers of the public peace who desire to monopolize all places, either in the municipality or elsewhere, are themselves the cause of the greatest

tumult."

[4] Schmidt, I. 223 (report by Dutard, May 14).

[5] Mortimer–Ternaux, VI. 117; VII. 59 (balloting of Dec. 2 and 4). In most of these and the following elections the number of voters is but one–twentieth of those registered. Chaumette is elected in his section by 53 votes; Hébert by 56; Gency, a master–cooper, by 34; Lechenard, a tailor, by 39; Douce, a building–hand, by 24. — Pache is elected mayor Feb. 15, 1793, by 11,881 votes, out of 160,000 registered.

[6] Buchez et Roux, XVII. 101. (Decree of Aug. 19, 1792). – Mortimer– Ternaux, IV. 223. – Beaulieu, "Essais," III. 454. "The National Guard ceased to exist after the 10th of August." — Buzot, 454. — Schmidt, I. 533 (Dutard, May 29). "It is certain that the armed forces of Paris is nonexistent."

[7] Beaulieu, Ibid., IV. 6. — "Archives Nationales," F7, 3249 (Oise). — Letters of the Oise administrators, Aug. 24, Sept. 12 and 20, 1792. Letters of the administrators of the district of Clermont, Sept. 14, etc.

[8] Cf. above, ch. IX.–"Archives Nationales," F7, 3249. Letter of the administrators of the district of Senlis, Oct. 31, 1792. Two of the administrators of the Senlis hospital were arrested by Paris commissaries and conducted "before the pretended Committee of Public Safety in Paris, with all that they possessed in money, jewels, and assignats." The same commissaries carry off two of the hospital sisters of charity, with all the silver plate in the establishment; the sisters are released, but the plate is not returned. — Buchez et Roux, XXVI. 209 (Patriote Français). Session of April 30, 1793, the final report of the commission appointed to examine the accounts of the old Committee of Supervision: " Panis and Sergent are convicted of breaking seals." . . . "67,580 francs found in Septenil's domicile have disappeared, as well as many articles of value."

[9] Schmidt, I, 270.

[10] Mortimer–Ternaux, IV. 221 to 229, 242 to 260; VI. 43 to 52.

[11] De Sybel, "Histoire de l'Europe pendant la Révolution Française," II 76. — Madame Roland, II.152. "It was not only impossible to make out the accounts, but to imagine where 130,000,000 had gone. . . The day he was dismissed he made sixty appointments, . . . from his son– in–law, who, a vicar, was made a director at 19,000 francs salary, to his hair–dresser, a young scapegrace of nineteen, whom he makes a commissary of war" . . "It was proved that he paid in full regiments that were actually reduced to a few men. — Meillan, 20. "The faction became the master of Paris through hired brigands, aided by the millions placed at its disposition by the municipality, under the pretext of ensuring supplies."

[12] See in the "Memoirs of Mme. Elliot," the particulars of this vote. — Beaulieu, I.445. "I saw a placard signed by Marat posted on the corners of the streets, stating that he had demanded 15,000 francs of the Duke of Orleans as compensation for what he had done for him. Gouverneur Morris, I. 260 (Letter of Dec. 21, 1792). The galleries force the Convention to revoke its decree against the

expulsion of the Bourbons. — On the 22nd of December the sections present a petition in the same sense, while there is a sort of riot in the suburbs in favor of Philippe–Egalité.

[13] Schmidt, I. 246 (Dutard, May 13). "The Convention cannot count in all Paris thirty persons ready to side with them.

[14] Buchez et Roux, XXV. 463. On the call of the houses, April 13, 1793, ninety–two deputies vote for Marat.

[15] Prudhomme, "Crimes de la Révolution," V. 133. Conversation with Danton, December, 1792. — De Barante, III.123. The same conversation, probably after another verbal tradition. — I am obliged to substitute less coarse terms for those of the quotation.

[16] He is the first speaker on the part of the "Mountain" in the king's trial, and at once becomes president of the Jacobin Club. His speech against Louis XVI. is significant. " "Louis is another Catiline." He should be executed, first as traitor taken in the act, and next as king; that is to say, as a natural enemy and wild beast taken in a net.

[17] Vatel, "Charlotte Corday and the Girondists," I. preface, CXLI. (with all the documents, the letters of Madame de Saint–Just, the examination on the 6th of October, 1786, etc.) The articles stolen consisted of six pieces of plate, a fine ring, gold–mounted pistols, packets of silver lace, etc.— The youth declares that he is "about to enter the Comte d'Artois' regiment of guards until he is old enough to enter the king's guards." He also had an idea of entering the Oratoire.

[18] Cf. his upeech against the king, hishis report on Danton, on the Girondists, etc. If the reader would comprehend Saint–Just's character he has only to read his letter to d'Aubigny, July 20, 1792: "Since I came here I am consumed with a republican fury, which is wasting me away. . . It is unfortunate that I cannot remain in Paris. I feel something within me which tells me that I shall float on the waves of this century. . . You dastards, you have not appreciated me! My renown will yet blaze forth and cast yours in the shade. Wretches that you are, you call me a thief, a villain, because I can give you no money. Tear my heart out of my body and eat it, and you will become what you are not now — great!"

[19] Buchez et Roux, XXIV. 296, 363; XXV. 323; XXVII. 144, 145. — Moniteur, XIV 80 (terms employed by Danton, David, Legendre, and Marat).

[20] Moniteur, XV. 74. — Buchez et Roux, XXVII. 254, 257, sessions of Jan. 6 and May 27.

[21] Moniteur, XIV. 851. (Session of Dec.26, 1792. Speech by Julien.)

[22] Moniteur, XIV. 768 (session of Dec. 16). The president says: "I have called Calon to order three times, and three times has he resisted. " — Vergnieud declares that "The majority of the Assembly is under the yoke of a seditious minority." – Ibid, XIV. 851, 853, 865 (session of Dec. 26 and 27). — Buchez et Roux, XXV. 396 (session of April 11.)

[23] Louvet, 72

[24] Meillan, 24: "We were for some time all armed with sabres, pistols, and blunderbusses." — Moore, II. 235 (October, 1792). A number of deputies already at this date carried sword canes and pocket–pistols.

[25] Dauban, "La Demagogie en 1793," p.101. Description of the hall by Prudhomme, with illustrations. – Ibid., 199. Letter of Brissot to his constituents: "The brigands and the bacchantes have found their way into the new hall. – According to Prudhomme the galleries hold 1,400 persons in all, and according to Dulaure, 20,000 or 3,000.

[26] Moore, I.44 (Oct. 10), and II. 534.

[27] Moniteur. XIV. 795. Speech by Lanjuinais, Dec. 19, 1792.

[28] Buchez et Roux, XX. 5, 396. Speech by Duperret, session of April 11, 1793.

[29] Dauban, 143. Letter of Valazé, April 14. — Cf. Moniteur, XIV. 746, session of Dec. 14. – Ibid., 800, session of Dec. 20. – Ibid., 853, session of Dec. 26.

[30] Speech by Salles. — Lanjuinais also says: "One seems to deliberate here in a free Convention; but it is only under the dagger and cannon of the factions." – Moniteur. XV. 180, session of Jan. 16. Speech by N——, deputy, its delivery insisted on by Charles Vilette.

[31] Meillan, 24.

32 "Archives Nationales," AF, II.45. Police reports, May 16, 18, 19. "There is fear of a bloody scene the first day." — Buchez et Roux, XXVII. 125. Report of Gamon inspector of the Convention hall.

[33] Moniteur, XIV. 362 (Nov. 1, 1792).– Ibid., 387, session of Nov. 4. Speech by Royer and Gorsas.–Ibid., 382. Letter by Roland, Nov. 5.

[34] Moniteur, XIV. 699. Letter of Roland, Nov. 28.

[35] Moniteur, XIV. 697, number for Dec. 11.

[36] Moniteur, XV. 180, session of Jan. 16. Speech by Lehardy, Hugues, and Thibaut. — Meillan, 14: "A line of separation between the two sides of the Assembly was then traced. Several deputies which the faction wished to put out of the way had voted for death (of the king). Almost all of these were down on the list of those in favor of the appeal to the people, which was the basis preferred. We were then known as appellants."

[37] Moniteur, XV. 8. Speech by Rabaut–Saint–Ètienne. — Buchez et Roux, XXIII 24. Mortimer–Ternaux, V. 418. – Moniteur, XV.180, session of Jan. 16. — Buchez et Roux, XXIV. 292. — Moniteur, XV. 182. Letter of the mayor of Paris, Jan. 16. – Ibid., 179. Letter of Roland, Jan. 16.

— Buchez et Roux, XXIV. 448. Report by Santerre.

[38] Buchez et Roux, XXV. 23 to 26. — Mortimer–Ternaux, VI. 184 (Manifesto of the central committee, March 9, 2 o'clock in the morning).–Ibid. 193. Narrative of Fournier at the bar of the Convention, March 12. — Report of the mayor of Paris, March 10. — Report of the Minister of Justice, March 13. — Meillan, 24. — Louvet, 72, 74.

[39] Pétion, "Mémoires," 106 (Ed. Dauban): "How many times I heard, 'You rascal, we'll have your head!' And I have no doubt that they often planned my assassination."

[40] Taillandier, "Documents biographiques," on Daunou (Narrative by Daunou),p. 38. — Doulcet de Pontécoulant, "Mémoires," I. 139: "It was then that the 'Mountain' used all the means of intimidation it knew so well how to bring into play, filling the galleries with its satellites, who shouted out to each other the name of each deputy as he stepped up to the president's table to give his vote, and yelling savagely at every one who did not vote for immediate and unconditional death. – Carnot, "Mémoires," I.293. Carnot voted for the death of the king; yet afterward he avowed that "Louis XVI. would have been saved, if the Convention had not held its deliberations under the dagger."

[41] Durand–Maillane, 35, 38, 57.

[42] An expression by Dussaulx, in his "Fragments pour servir à l'histoire de la Convention."

[43] Madame Roland, "Mémoires," ed. Barrière et Berville, II. 52. – (Note by Roland.)

[44] Moniteur, XV, 187. Cambacérès votes: "Louis has incurred the penalties established in the penal code against conspirators. . . The execution to be postponed until hostilities cease. In case of invasion of the French territory by the enemies of the republic, the decree to be enforced." — On Barrère, see Macaulay's crushing article in "Biographical Essays."

[45] Sainte–Beuve, "Causeries du Lundi," V. 209. ("Sièyes," according to his unpublished manuscripts.)

[46] Madame Roland, II.56. Note by Roland.

[47] Mortimer–Ternaux, V. 476.

[48] Mortimer–Ternaux, V. 513.

[49] Comte de Ségur, "Mémoires." I. 13.

[50] Harmand de la Meuse (member of the Convention), "Anecdotes relative à la Révolution," 83, 85.

[51] Meissner, 148, Voyage à Paris" (last months of 1795).. Testimony of the regicide Audrein.

[52] Louvet, 775.

[53] Meillan, 16.

[54] Remark by M. Guirot ("Mémoires"), II. 73.

[55] Moniteur, XIV. 432, session of Nov. 10, 1792. Speech by Cambon: "That is the reason why I shall always detest the 2nd of September; for never will I approve of assassinations." In the same speech he justifies the Girondists against any reproach of federalism.

[56] "Le Maréchal Davoust," by Madame de Bocqueville. Letter of Davoust, battalion officer, June 2, 1793: "We are animated with the spirit of Lepelletier, which is all that need be said with respect to our opinions and what we will do in the coming crisis, in which, perhaps, a faction will try to plunge us anew into a civil war between the departments and Paris. Perfidious eloquence. . . conservative Tartufes."

[57] Moniteur, XIV. 738. Report by Cambon, Dec. 15. "On the way French generals are to act in countries occupied by the armies of the republic." This important document is a true manifesto of the Revolution. — Buchez et Roux, XXVII 140, session of May 20, and XXVI. 177, session of April 27, speech by Cambon: "The department of Hérault says to this or that individual: 'You are rich; your opinions cause us expenditure . . I mean to fix you to the Revolution in spite of yourself. You shall lend your fortune to the republic, and when liberty is established the republic will return your capital to you. – "I should like, then, following the example of the department of Hérault, that the Convention should organize a civic loan of one billion, to be supplied by egoists and the indifferent. – Decree of May 20, "passed almost unanimously. A forced loan of one billion shall be made on wealthy citizens."

[58] Meillan. 100.

[59] Speech by Ducos, March 20. "We must choose between domestic education and liberty. So long as the poor and the rich are not brought close together through a common education, in vain will your laws proclaim sacred equality! " — Rabaut–Saint–Étienne: "In every township a national temple will be erected, in which every Sunday its municipal officers will give moral instruction to the assembled citizens. This instruction will be drawn from books approved of by the legislative body, and followed by hymns also approved of by the legislative. A catechism, as simple as it is short, drawn up by the legislative body, shall be taught and every boy will know it by heart." — On the sentiments of the Girondists in relation to Christianity, see chapters V. and XI. of this volume. — On the means for equalizing the fortunes, see articles by Rabaut–Saint–Étienne (Buchez et Roux, XXIII. 467). – Ibid., XXIV. 475 (March 7–11) decree abolishing the testamentary right. — Condorcet, in his "Tableau des progrés de l'Esprit humain," assigns the leveling of conditions as the purpose of society. — On propaganda abroad, read the report by Cambon (Dec. 15). This report is nearly unanimously accepted, and Buzot exacerbates it by adding an amendment

[60] Buchez et Roux, XXVII. 287, session of May 28, vote on the maintenance of the Commission of Twelve.

[61] Moniteur. XV. 395, session of Feb. 8, 1793.

279

[62] Decrees of March 13 and 14.

[63] Moore, II. 44 (October 1792). Danton declares in the tribune that "the Convention should be a committee of instruction for kings throughout the universe." On which Moore remarks that this is equivalent to declaring war against all Europe except Switzerland. – Mallet du Pan, "Considerations sur la Revolution de France," p.37: "In a letter which chance has brought to my notice, Brissot wrote to one of his minister–generals towards the close of last year: 'The four quarters of Europe must be set on fire; that is our salvation.'"

[64] Duvergier, "Collection des lois et décrets." Decree of March 10– 12. Title I. articles 4, 12, 13; title II. articles 2, 3. Add to this the decree of March 29–31, establishing the penalty of death against whoever composes or prints documents favoring the re–establishment of royalty.

[65] Ib., Decree of March 28 – April 5 (article 6). – Cf. the decrees of March 18–22, and April 23–24.

[66] Decree of March 27–30.

[67] Decree of April 5–7.

[68] Decree of May 4. (A law fixing the highest price at which grain shall be sold. TR.)

[69] Decree of April 11–16 (bearing on the reduction in value of the legal currency. –TR).

[70] Decree of May 20–25.

[71] Decree of April 5–7. Words used by Danton in the course of the debate.

[72] Decree of April 5–11.

[73] Decrees of May 13, 16, 22, 23, 24, 25, 26, and 29, June 1.

[74] Decrees of March 21–23 and March 26–30.

[75] Decrees of March 29–31.

[76] Decree of April 1–5.

[77] Schmidt, I. 232. Report by Dutard, May 10.

[78] "Archives Nationales," F7, 2401 to 2505. Records of the section debates in Paris. — Many of these begin March 28, 1793, and contain the deliberations of revolutionary committees; for example, F7, 2475, the section of the Pikes or of the Place Vendôme. We see by the official reports dated March 28 and the following days that the suspected were deprived all weapons, even the smallest, every species of swordcane, including dress–swords with steel or silver handles.

[79] Buchez et Roux, XXV. 157. — "Archives Nationales," F7, 2494, section of the Réunion, official report, March 28.

[80] Schmidt, I. 223 (Dutard, May 14). — Ibid., 224. "If the Convention allows committees of supervision to exercise its authority, I will not give it eight days." – Meillan, 111: "Almost all the section agitators were strangers" —"Archives Nationales," F7, 3294 and 3297, records of debate in the committees of supervision belonging to the sections of the Réunion and Droits de l'Homme. Quality of mind and education are both indicated by orthography. For instance: "Le dit jour et an que déçus." – "Orloger." – "Lecture d'une lettre du comité de surté général de la convention qui invite le comité à se transporter de suites chez le citoyen Louis Féline rue Baubourg, à leffets de faire perquisition chez lui et dans tout ces papiers, et que ceux qui paraîtrons suspect lon y metes les selés."

[81] "Archives Nationales," F7, 3294. Section of the Réunion, official report. March 28.

[82] Buchez et Roux, XXV. 168. An ordinance of the commune, March 27.

[83] Schmidt, I.223. Report by Dutard, May 14.

[84] Buchez et Roux, XXV. 167. Ordinance of May 27. XXXVII. 151. Ordinance of May 20.

[85] "Archives Nationales," F7, 3294. See in particular, the official reports of the month of April. — Buchez et Roux, XXV. 149, and XXVI. 342. (ordinances of the Commune, March 27 and May 2).

[86] Buchez et Roux, XXVI. 402 (article from the Patriote Français, May 8). "Arrests are nultiplied lately to a frightful extent. The mayoralty overflows with prisoners. Nobody has any idea of the insolence and harshness with which citizens are treated. Slaughter and a Saint–Bartholomew are all that are talked of. " — Meillan, 55. "Let anybody in any assemblage or club express any opinion not in unison with municipal views, and he is sure to be arrested the following night. " — Gouverneur Morris, March 29, 1793. "Yesterday I was arrested in the street and conducted to the section of Butte–des– Moulins. . . Armed men came to my house yesterday. " — Reply of the minister Lebrun, April 3. "Domiciliary visits were a general measure from which no house in Paris was exempt."

[87] Buchez et Roux, XXVI. 384. Speech by Buzot, session of May 8.

[88] Buchez et Roux, XXVI. 332. Ordinance of the commune, May 1.

[89] Schmidt, I. 216. Report by Dutard, May 13.

[90] Schmidt, I.301. "In our sections the best class of citizens are still afraid of imprisonment or of being disarmed. Nobody talks freely." — The Lyons revolutionaries make the same calculation ("Archives Nationales," AF, II. 43). Letter addressed to the representatives of the people by the administrators of the department of the Rhône, June 4, 1793. The revolutionary committee "designated for La Vendée those citizens who were most comfortably off or those it hated, whilst conditional enlistment with the privilege of remaining in the department were granted only to those in favor of disorganization."— Cf. Guillon de Montléon, I. 235.

[91] Buchez et Roux, XXVI. 399. Ordinance of the commune, May 3, on a forced loan of twelve millions, article 6. "The revolutionary committees will regard the apportionment 'lists simply as guides, without regarding them as a basis of action." — Article 14. "The personal and real property of those who have not conformed to the patriotic draft will be seized and sold at the suit of the revolutionary committees, and their persons declared suspected."

[92] Buchez et Roux, XXVII. 17 (Patriote Français, number for May 14). Francœur is taxed at 3,600 francs. — The same process at Lyons (Balleydier, 174, and Guillon de Montléon, I. 238). The authorized tax by the commissaries of the convention amounted to six millions. The revolutionary committee levied thirty and forty millions, payable in twenty–four hours on warrants without delay (May 13 and 14). Many persons are taxed from 80,000 to 100,000 francs, the text of the requisitions conveying ironically a hostile spirit.

[93] Buchez et Roux, XXVI. 463, session of the Jacobin Club, May 11.

[94] Meillan, 17.

[95] Buchez et Roux, XXVI. 463, session of the Jacobin club, May11. Speech by Hassenfratz. – Ibid., 455, session of the Jacobin club, May 10, speech by Robespierre. "The rich are all anti–revolutionaries; only beggars and the people can save the country." – Ibid. N——: "Revolutionary battalions should be maintained in the department at the expense of the rich, who are cowards." –Ibid., XXVII. 317. Petition of the Faubourg Saint–Antoine, May 11. — Schmidt, I. 315 (Report by Dutard, May 13). "There is no recruiting in the faubourgs, because people there know that they are more wanted here than in La Vendée. They let the rich go and fight. They watch things here, and trust nobody but themselves to guard Paris."

[96] "Archives Nationales," F7, 2494. Section of the Réunion, official reports of May 15 and 16. — Buchez et Roux, XXV. 167, ordance of the commune, March 27.

[97] Schmidt, I.327. Report of Perriére, May 28. "Our group itself seemed to governed by nothing but hatred of the rich by the poor. One must be a dull observer not to see by a thousand symptoms that these two natural enemies stand in battle array, only awaiting the signal or the opportunity."

[98] Buchez et Roux, XXV. 460. The papers examined by the accusers are the numbers of Marat's journal of the 5th of January and of the 25th of February. The article which provoked the decree is his "Address to the National Convention," pp. 446 and 450.

[99] Buchez et Roux, XXVI. 149; Narrative by Marat,114. Bulletin of the revolutionary tribunal, session of the Convention.

[100] Buchez et Roux, XXVI. 358, article in the Chronique de Paris; 358, article by Marat. – Schmidt, I. 184. Report by Dutard, May 5. — Paris, Histoire de Joseph Lebon," I. 81. Letter by Robespierre, Jr., May 7.

[101] Buchez et Roux, XXV. 240 and 246. Protest of the Mail section, of the electoral body of the

Arsenal, Marais, Gravelliers, and Arcis sections. (The Convention, session of April 2; the commune, session of April 2.) — XXVI. 358 Protests of the sections of Bon–Conseil and the Unité, (May 5). — XXVII. 71. Defeat of the anarchists in the section of Butté–des–Moulins. "A great many sections openly show a determination to put anarchy down." (Patriote Français, May 15). – Ibid., 137. Protests of the Panthéon Français, Piques, Mail, and several other sections (Patriote Français, May 19). – Ibid., 175. Protest of the Fraternité section (session of the Convention, May 23).

[102] Schmidt, I. 189. Dutard, May 6.

[103] Mortimer–Ternaux, VII. 218. Official report of the reunion of the two sections of the Lombards and Bon–Conseil (April 12), "by which the two said sections promise and swear union, aid, fraternity, and mutual help, in case the aristocracy are disposed to destroy liberty." — "Consequently," says the Bon–Conseil section, "many of the citizens of the Lombards section, justly alarmed at the disturbances occasioned by the evil–disposed, came and proffered their assistance." — Adhesion of the section of Les Amis de la Patrie. — Buchez et Roux, XXVII. 138. (Article of the Patriote Français, May 19): "This brigandage is called assembly of combined sections." — Ibid., 236, May 26, session of the commune. "Deputations of the Montreuil, Quinze– Vingts and Droits de l'Homme sections came to the assistance of the Arsenal patriots; the aristocrats took to flight, leaving their hats behind them." — Schmidt, I. 213, 313 (Dutard, May 13 and 27). Violent treatment of the moderates in the Bon–Conseil and Arsenal sections; "struck with chairs, several persons wounded, one captain carried off on a bench; the gutter–jumpers and dumpy shopkeepers cleared out, leaving the sans–culottes masters of the field." — Meillan, 111. — Buchez et Roux, XXVII. 237, session of the Jacobin club, May 26. "In the section of Butte–des–Moulins the patriots, finding they were not in force, seized the chairs and drove the aristocrats out."

[104] Buchez et Roux, 78, XXVII. On the juge–de–paix Roux, carried off at night and imprisoned. April 16. – Mortimer–Ternaux, III. 220, on the vice–president Sagnier, May 10. – Buchez et Roux, XXVII. 231, May 26, on the five citizens of the Unité section arrested by the revolutionary committee of the section "for having spoken against Robespierre and Marat."

[105] Buchez et Roux, XXVII. 154. Speech of Léonard Bourdon to the Jacobins, May 20.

[106] Buchez et Roux, XXVI. 3. Address drawn up by the commissaries of the 48 sections approved of by 35 sections, also by the commune, and presented to the Convention April 15. – Others have preceded it, like pilot ballons. – Ibid., XXV. 319. Petition of the Bon–Conseil, Alpril 8. – XXV. 320. Petition of the section of the Halleau–Blé, April 10.

[107] Buchez et Roux, XXVL. 83. Speech by Vergniaud to the convention, session of April 20. "These facts are accepted. Nobody can contradict them. More than 10,000 witnesses would confirm them." — There are the same proceedings at Lyons Jan.13, 1792, against the petition far an appeal to the people (Guillon de Montléon, I.145, 155). The official report of the Jacobins claims that the petition obtained 40,215 signatures. "The petition was first signed by about 200 clubbists, who pretended to be the people. . . They spread the report among the people that all who would not sign the address would be blacklisted or proscribed. That's why they had desks set up in all the public squares, and seized by the arm all who came, and forced them to sign. As this approach did not prove

fruitful they made children ten years of age, women, and ignorant rustics put down their name." They were told that the object was to put down the price of bread. "I swear to you that this address is the work a hundred persons at most; the great majority of the citizens of Lyons desire to avail themselves of their own sovereignty in the judgment of Louis." (Letter of David of Lyons to the president of the convention, Jan. 16.)

[108] "Fragment," by Lanjuinais (in the memoirs of Durand–Maillane, p. 297).

[109] Meillan, 113.

[110] Buchez et Roux, XXVI. 3!9 (May 12). – Meillan, 113.

[111] Buchez et Roux, XVI. 327. On being informed of this the crowd sent new deputies, the latter stating in relation to the others: "We do not recognise them."

[112] Buchez et Roux, XXVI. 143.

[113] Buchez et Roux, XXVII. 175, May 23.

[114] Schmidt, I. 212. Report of Dutard, May 13. – I. 218. "A plot is really under way, and many heads are singled out." (Terrasson, May 13.)

[115] Buchez et Roux, XXVII 9. Speech of Guadet to the Convention, May 14.

[116] Buchez et Roux, XXVII. 2. Patriote Français, May 13.

[117] Schmidt, I 242. Report of Dutard, May 18. – Also 245.

[118] Schmidt, I 254. Report of Dutard, May 19.

[119] Bergoeing, Chatry, Dubosq, "Pièces recueillies par la Commission des Douze et publiées à Caen." June 28, 1793 (in the "Mémoires" of Meillan, pp. 176–198). Attempts at murder had already occurred. "Lanjuinais came near being killed. Many of the deputies were insulted and threatened. The armed force joins with the malefactors; we have accordingly no means of repression." (Mortimer–Ternaux, VII.562, letter of the deputy Michel to his constituents, May 20.)

[120] Bergoeing, "Pièces, etc." — Meillan, pp. 39 and 40. — The depositions are all made by eye witnesses. The propositions for the massacre were made in the meetings at the town–hall, May 19, 20 and 21, and at the Cordeliers club May 22 and 23.

[121] The Jacobins at Lyons plot the same thing (Guilion de Montléon, 248). Chalier says to the club: "We shall not fail to have 300 noted heads. Get hold of the members of the department, the presidents and secretaries of the sections, and let us make a bundle of them for the guillotine; we will wash our hands in their blood." Thereupon, on the night of May 28 the revolutionary municipality seize the arsenal and plant cannon on the Hôtel–de–ville. The Lyons sections, however, more energetic than

those of Paris, take, up arms and after a terrible fight they get possession of the Hôtel–de–ville. The moral difference between the two parties is very marked in Gonchon's letters. ("Archives Nationales," AF, II. 43. letters of Gonchon to Garat, May 31, June 1 and 3.) "Keep up the courage of the Convention. It need not be afraid. The citizens of Lyons have covered themselves with glory. They displayed the greatest courage in every fight that took place in various quarters of the town, and the greatest magnanimity to their enemies, who behaved most villainously." The municipal body had sent a flag of truce, pretending to negotiate, and then treacherously opened fire with its cannon on the columns of the sections, and cast the wounded into the river. The citizens of Lyons, so often slandered, will be the first to have set an example of true republican character. Find me a similar instance, if you can, in the history of revolutions: being victorious and yet not then to have shed a drop of blood!" They cared for the wounded, and raised a subscription for the widows and orphans of the dead, without distinction of party. Cf. Lauvergne, "Histoire du Var," 175. The same occurs at Toulon (insurrection of the moderates, July 12 and 13, 1793). — At Toulon, as at Lyons, there was no murder after the victory; only regular trials and the execution of two or three assassins whose crimes were legally proved.

[122] Schmidt, I. 335. Report of Perrière, May 29.

[123] Bergoeing, "Pièces, etc.", p. 195. – Buchez et Roux, XXVII 296.

[124] The insurrection at Lyons took place on May 29. On the 2nd of June it is announced in the Convention that the insurgent army of Lozère, more than 30,000 strong, has taken Marvejols, and is about to take Mende (Buchez et Roux XXVII. 387).— A threatening address from Bordeaux (May 14) and from thirty–two sections in Marseilles (May 25) against the Jacobins (Buchez et Roux, XXVII. 3. 214). – Cf. Robinet in "Le procès des Dantonistes, 303, 305.

[125] Mortimer–Ternaux, VII 38.

[126] Buchez et Roux, XXVII. 297, session of the Jacobins, May 29.

[127] Barrère, "Mémoires," II. 91, 94. As untruthful as Barrère is, here his testimony may be accepted. I see no reason why he should state what is not true; he was well informed, as he belonged to the Committee of Public Safety. His statements, besides, on the complicity d the Mountain and on the rôle of Danton are confirmed by the whole mass of facts. – Buchez et Roux, XXVIII. 200 (speech by Danton in the Convention, June 13). "Without the canon of the 31st of May, without the insurrection the conspirators would have triumphed; they would have given us the law. Let the crime of that insurrection be on our heads! That insurrection – I myself demanded it! . . . I demand a declaration by the Convention, that without the insurrection of May 31, liberty would be no more! "— Ibid., 220. Speech by Leclerc at the Cordeliers club, June 27: "Was it not Legendre who rendered abortive our wise measures, so often taken, to exterminate our enemies? He and Danton it was, who, through their culpable resistance, reduced us to the moderation of the 31st of May, Legendre and Danton are the men who opposed the revolutionary steps which we had taken on those great days to crush out all the aristocrats in Paris!"

[128] Schmidt, I. 244. Report by Dutard, May 18.

[129] Buchez et Roux, XXVII. 253 and following pages, session of May 27. – Mortimer–Ternaux, VII. 294. — Buchez et Roux, XXVIII. 9 ("Précis rapide" by Gorsas).

[130] Buchez et Roux, XXVII. 258. Meillan, 43.

[131] Buchez et Roux, XXVII. 259 (words of Raffet).

[132] Meillan, 44. — Buchez et Roux, XXVII. 267, 280.

[133] Meillan, 44. Placed opposite the president, within ten paces of him, with my eyes constantly fixed on him, because in the horrible din which disgraced the Assembly we could have no other compass to steer by, I can testify that I neither saw nor heard the decree put to vote."— Buchez et Roux, XXVII. 278. Speech by Osselin, session of May 28: "I presented the decree as drawn up to the secretaries for their signatures this morning. One of them, after reading it, observed to me that the last article had not been decreed, but that the preceding articles had been." – Mortimer–Ternaux, VII. 562. Letter of the deputy Michel. May 29. "The guards were forced, and the sanctuary of the law invested from about four to ten hours, so that nobody could leave the hall even for the most urgent purposes.

[134] Mortimer–Ternaux, VII. 308. Extract from the official reports of the patriotic club of Butte–des–Moulins, May 30. "Considering that the majority of the section, known for incivism and its antirevolutionary spirit, would decline this election or would elect commissaries not enjoying the confidence of patriots," . . the patriotic club takes upon itself the duty of electing the two commissaries demanded.

[135] Durand–Maillan, 297. "Fragment," by Lanjuinais. "Seven strangers, seven outside agents, Desfieux, Proly, Pereyra, Dubuisson, Gusman, the two brothers Frey, etc., were set up by the commune as an insurrectionary committee." Most of them are vile fellows, as is the case with Varlet, Dobsen, Hassenfratz, Rousselin, Desfieux, Gusman, etc.

[136] Buchez et Roux, XXVIII. 156. "We, members of the revolutionary commission, citizens Clémence, of the Bon–Conseil section; Dunouy, of the Sans–culottes section; Bonin, of the section of Les Marchés, Auvray of the section of Mont–Blanc; Séguy, of the section of Butte– des–Moulins; Moissard, of Grenelle; Berot, canton d'Issy; Rousselin, section of the Unité; Marchand, section of Mont–Blanc; Grespin, section of Gravilliers." They resign on the 6th of June. — The commission, at first composed of nine members, ends in comprising eleven (Buchez et Roux, XXVII. 316, official reports of the commune. May 31.) then 25 (Speech by Pache to the Committee of Public Safety, June 1.)

[137] Buchez et Roux XXVII. 306. Official reports of the commune, May 31. – Ibid., 316. Mortimer–Ternaux, VII. 319.

[138] Buchez et Roux, XXVII. 274 Speech by Hassenfratz to the Jacobin Club, May 27.

[139] Buchez et Roux, XXVII. 346 (speech by Lhuillier in the Convention, May 31).

[140] Buchez et Roux, XXVII. 302, session of the Convention, May 30. Words uttered by Hassenfratz, Varlet, and Chabot, and denounced by Lanjuinais.

[141] Madame Roland, "Appel à l'impartiale postérité." Conversation of Madam Roland on the evening of May 31on the Place du Carrusel with an artillerist.

[142] Buchez et Roux, 307–323. Official reports of the commune, May 31.

[143] "Archives Nationales," F7, 2494, register of the revolutionary committee of the Réunion section, official report of May 31, 6 o'clock in the morning.

[144] Buchez et Roux, XXVII. 335, session of the Convention, May 31. Petition presented by the commissaries in the name of forty–eight sections; their credentials show that they are not at first authorized by more than twenty–six sections.

[145] Buchez et Roux, 347, 348. Mortimer–Ternaux, VII. 350 (third dispatch of the Hôtel–de–ville delegates, present at the session): "The National Assembly was not able to accept the above important measures. . . until the perturbators of the Assembly, known under the title of the 'Right,' did themselves the justice to perceive that they were not worthy of taking part in them; they evacuated the Assembly, after the great gesticulations and imprecations, to which you know they are liable."

[146] Dauban, "La Demagogie en 1793." Diary of Beaulieu, May 31. – Declaration of Henriot, Germinal 4, year III. – Buchez et Roux, XXVIII. 351

[147] Mortimer–Ternaux, VII. 565. Letter of the deputy Loiseau, June 5.

[148] Buchez et Roux, XXVII. 352 to 360, 368 to 377. Official reports of the commune, June 1 and 2. Proclamation of the revolutionary committee, June 1. "Your delegates have ordered the arrest of all suspected persons concealing themselves in the sections of Paris. This arrest is in progress in all quarters."

[149] "Archives Nationales," F7, 2494. Section of the Réunion, official report, June 1.— Ibid., June 2. Citizen Robin is arrested on the 2nd of June, "for having manifested opinions contrary to the sovereignty of the people in the National Assembly." The same day a proclamation is made on the territory of the section by a deputation of the commune, accompanied by one member and two drummers, "tending (tendantes) to make known to the people that the country will be saved by awaiting (en atendans) with courage the decree which is to be rendered to prevent traitors (les traitre) from longer sitting in the senate house." — Ibid., June 4. The committee decides that it will add new members to its number, but they will be taken only from all "good sans–culote; no notary, no notary's clerk, no lawyers nor their clerks, no banker nor rich landlord" being admissible, unless he gives evidence of unmistakable civism since 1789. —Cf. F7, 2497 (section of the Droits de l'Homme), F7, 2484 (section of the Halle–au–blé), the resemblance in orthography and in their acts; the registry of the Piques section (F7, 2475) is one of the most interesting; here may be found the details of the appearance of the ministers before it; the committee that examines them does not even spell their names correctly, "Clavier" being often written for Clavière, and "Goyer" for Gohier.

[150] Buchez et Roux, XXVIII. 19.

[151] Buchez et Roux, XXVII.357. Official reports of the commune, June 1.

[152] Meillan, 307. — "Fragment," by Lanuinais. – "Diurnal," of Beaulieu, June 2. – Buchez et Roux, XXVII. 399 (speech by Barère).

[153] Buchez et Roux, XXVII. 357. Official reports of the commune, June 1.

[154] Meillan, 53, 58, 307. Buchez et Roux, XXVIII. 14 (Précis, by Gordas).

[155] Buchez et Roux, XXVII 359. Official reports of the commune, June 1. "One member of the Council stated that on going to the Beaurepaire section he was not well received; that the president of this section spoke uncivilly to him and took him for an imaginary municipalist; that he was threatened with the lock–up, and that his liberty was solely due to the brave citizens of the Sans–culottes section and the gunners of the Beaurepaire section who went with him." — Preparations for the investment began on the 1st of June. ("Archives Nationales," F7, 2497, official reports of the Droits de l'Homme section, June 1.) Orders of Henriot to the commandant of the section to send "400 homme et la compagnie de canonier avec le 2 pièces de canon au Carouzel le long des Thuilerie plasse de la Révolution."

[156] "Lanjuinais states 100,000 men, Meillan 50,000; the deputies of the Somme say 60,000, but without any evidence. Judging by various indications I should put the number much lower, on account of the disarmament and absentees: say 30,000 men, the same as May 31.

[157] Mortimer–Ternaux, VII. 566. Letter of the deputy Loiseau: "I passed through the whole of one battalion; the men all said that they did not know why the movement was made, that only their officers knew." (June 1.)

[158] Buchez et Roux, XXVII. 400. Session of the Convention, June 2. – – XXVIII. 43 (report by Saladin).

[159] Mortimer–Ternaux, VII. 392. Official report of the Jacobin Club, June 2 "The deputies were so surrounded as not to be able to go out even for special purposes." — Ibid., 568 Letter of the deputy Loiseau.

[160] Buchez et Roux, XXVIII. 44. Report by Saladin. — Meillan, 237. — Mortimer–Ternaux VII. 547. Declaration of the deputies of the Somme.

[161] Meillan, 52. — Pétion, "Mémoires," 109 (Edition Dauban). — Lanjuinais ("Fragment") — "Nearly all those called Girondists thought it best to stay away." — Letter of Vergniaud June 3 (in the Republican Français, June 5, 1793). "I left the Assembly yesterday between 1 and 2 o'clock."

[162] Lanjuinais, "Fragment," 299.

[163] Buchez et Roux, XXVII. 400.

[164] Robinet, "Le Procès de Danton," 169. Words of Danton (according to the notes of a juryman, Topino–Lebrun).

[165] Buchez et Roux, XXVII. 44. Report by Saladin. – Meillan, 59. – Lanjuinais, 308, 310.

[166] Buchez et Roux, XXVII. 401

[167] Mortimer–Ternaux, VII. 569. Letter of the deputy Loiseau. – Meillan, 62.

[168] Buchez et Roux, XXVI. 341. Speech by Chasles in the Convention, May 2: "The farmers . . . are nearly all aristocrats."

[169] Or workhouses, see Taine: "Notes on England" page 214: "It is an English principle that the indigent, by giving up their freedom, have a right to be supported. Society pays the cost, but shuts them up and sets them to work. As this condition is repugnant to them, they avoid the workhouse as much as possible." Similar institutions existed in France before the revolution. (SR).

[170] Sieyès (quoted by Barante, "Histoire de la Convention," III. 169) thus describes it: "The fake people, the deadliest enemy which the French people ever had, blocked incessantly the approaches to the Convention . . . At the entrance or exit of the Convention the astonished spectator thought that a new invasion of barbarian hordes had suddenly occurred, a new irruption of voracious, sanguinary harpies, flocking there to seize hold of the revolution as if it were the natural prey of their species."

[171] Gouverneur Morris, II. 241. Letter of Oct. 23, 1792. "The populace – something, thank God, that is unknown in America"" — He often insists on this essential characteristic of the French Revolution. – On this ever–present class, see the accurate and complete work well supported by facts, of Dr. Lombrose, "L'Uomo delinquente."

[172] Mortimer–Ternaux, VII. Letter of the deputy Laplaigne, July 6.

[173] Meillan, 51. – Buchez et Roux, XXVII. 356. Official report of the commune, session of June 1. In the afternoon Marat comes to the commune, harrangues the council, and gives the insurrection the last impetus. It is plain that he was chief actor on both these days (June 1 and 2).

[174] Pétion, 116.

[175] Schmidt, I. 370. – Mortimer–Ternaux, VII. 391. Letter of Marchand, member of the Central Committee. "I saw Chaumette do everything he could to hinder this glorious revolution, . . . exclaim, shed tears, and tear his hair." – Buchez et Roux, XXVIII. 46. According to Saladin, Chaumette went so far as to demand Hébert's arrest.

[176] Mortimer–Ternaux, VII. 300. – Cf. "Le vieux Cordelier," by C. Desmoulins, No. 5.

[177] Mallet du Pan, II. 52. (March 8, 1794). – The titular general of the revolutionary army was Ronsin. "Previous to the Revolution he was a seedy author earning his living and reputation by working for the boulevard stalls. . . One day a person informed him that his staff 'was behaving very badly, acting tyrannically in the most outrageous manner at the theaters and everywhere else, striking women and tearing their bonnets to pieces. Your men commit rape, pillage, and massacre." To which he replied; 'Well, what shall I do? I know that they are a lot of ruffians as well as you do; but those are the follows I need for my revolutionary army. Find me honest people, if you can, that will do that business.'" (Prudhomme, "Crimes de la Révolution," V. 130.)

[178] Buchez et Roux, XXIX. 152.

[179] Beaulieu, "Essais sur la Révolution," V. 200.

[180] Schmidt, II. 85. Report of Dutard, June 24 (on the review of the previous evening) 2A sort of low–class artisan who seemed to me to have been a soldier. . . Apparently he had associated only with disorderly men; I am sure that he would be found fond of gaming, wine, women, and everything that denotes a bad character."

[181] Charlotte de Corday d'Armont, 1768 to 1793. Young French girl who knifed Marat in his bath. Adherent of the Revolution, she considered Marat as being responsible for the elimination of the Girondists and the establishment of the terror. She was guillotined. (SR.)

[182] Lauvergne, "Histoire de la Révolution dans le département du Var," 176. At Toulon "the spirit of counter–revolution was nothing else than the sentiment of self–preservation." It was the same thing at Lyons. (Nolhac, "Souvenir de trois année de la Révolution à Lyon," p. 14.)

[183] Gouverneur Morris, II. 395. Letter of Jan. 21, 1794. "Admitting what has been asserted by persons in a situation to know the truth and deeply interested to prove the contrary, it is an undoubted truth that ninety–nine–hundredths are opposed to all ideas of a dismemberment, and will fight to prevent it.

[184] Mallet du Pan, II. 44.

[185] Carnot, Lazare, Nicolas, 1753–1823, military engineer and mathematician, member of the committee of public safety, organized the armies of the republic and their offensive tactics. (SR).

[186] Among other documents, the following letter will show the quality of these recruits, especially of the recruits of 1791, who were much the best men. (Letter from the municipal officers of Dorat, December 28, 1792, "Archives Nationales," F7, 3275.) "The commune of Dorat is made up of three classes of citizens: The richest class, composed of persons confirmed in the prejudices of the ancient régime, has been disarmed. The second, composed of well–to–do people, fills the administrative positions. It is against them that the fury of the turbulent is aimed; but those of this class who could make resistance have gone to fight the enemy abroad. The third class, and the most numerous, is made up in part of the seditious and in part of laborers, who, not daring to mix in the revolt, content themselves with coveting the tax on grain." – Toulongeon, "Histoire de France depuis la Révolution,"

IV. 94. "Do not degrade a nation by ascribing base motives to it and a servile fear. Every one, on the contrary, felt himself infused by an exalted instinct for the public welfare." – Gouvion Saint–Cyr, "Mémoires," I. 56: A young man would have blushed to remain at home when the independence of the nation was threatened. Each one quitted his studies or his profession.

[187] Gouvion–Saint–Cyr, 26. "The manifesto of Brunswick assigns to France more than a hundred battalions, which, within three weeks, were raised, armed, and put in the field."

[188] In respect of these sentiments, cf. Gouvion Saint–Cyr, "Mémoires, and Fervel, "Campagnes de la Révolution Française dans les Pyrénées orientales."

[189] Stendhal, Memoires sur Napoléon.

[190] Gouvion–Saint–Cyr, "Memoires," p.43. "Patriotism made up for everything; it alone gave us victory; it supplied our most pressing needs."

Printed in the United States
82838LV00005B/65/A